Healthcare Security

Healthcare Security

Solutions for Management, Operations, and Administration

Bernard J. Scaglione, CPP, CHPA, CHSP and
Anthony Luizzo, PhD, CFE, CST

A PRODUCTIVITY PRESS BOOK

First published 2022
by Routledge
605 Third Avenue, New York, NY 10158

and by Routledge
2 Park Square, Milton Park, Abingdon, Oxon, OX14 4RN

Routledge is an imprint of the Taylor & Francis Group, an informa business

© 2022 Bernard J. Scaglione & Anthony Luizzo

The right of Bernard J. Scaglione & Anthony Luizzo to be identified as author[/s] of this work has been asserted by him/her/them in accordance with sections 77 and 78 of the Copyright, Designs and Patents Act 1988.

All rights reserved. No part of this book may be reprinted or reproduced or utilised in any form or by any electronic, mechanical, or other means, now known or hereafter invented, including photocopying and recording, or in any information storage or retrieval system, without permission in writing from the publishers.

Trademark notice: Product or corporate names may be trademarks or registered trademarks, and are used only for identification and explanation without intent to infringe.

Library of Congress Cataloging-in-Publication Data
A catalog record for this book has been requested

ISBN: 978-1-032-10549-9 (hbk)
ISBN: 978-1-032-10547-5 (pbk)
ISBN: 978-1-003-21585-1 (ebk)

DOI: 10.4324/9781003215851

Typeset in Garamond
by Apex CoVantage, LLC

Contents

Preface ix

Acknowledgements xi

About the Authors xiii

Introduction xv

1. The Changing Face of Healthcare Security 1
How has Hospital Security Changed Since 9/11? 1
Aspects of Hospital Security: How is Hospital Security Changing in the
New Century? 4
Hospital Security in the 21ˢᵗ Century: What Should We Expect 7
The Changing Face of the Hospital Security: Re-tooling for the Future 11
The Changing Face of Hospital Security 16

2. Security Management 23
The Hidden Cost of Downsizing: Where Loyalty Dies, Fraud Grows 23
Stretching the Security Dollar 29
Investigating in a New Environment 31
Shoplifter Profiles and Tips on How They Steal 35
Asking the Right Questions About Fire Prevention 38
Putting the Spotlight on Security 40
Improving the Dependability of an ID Program 44

3. Disaster Preparedness 47
Training Security Officers to Recognize the Perils of Weapons of Mass
Destruction and Pandemic Flu Contaminates – Part I 47
Training Security Operatives to Recognize the Perils of Weapons of Mass
Exposure Contaminates – Part II 53
Disaster Planning: Training for the Perils of Weapons of Mass Exposure 2020 59

4. The Security Survey 67
Beyond "Target Hardening" – Approaches in Applying Crime Risk Management
Principles and Techniques in Community Surveys 67
The Access Control Security Survey 72
The Security Survey: A Prescription for Enhancing Security 76
Aspects of the Security Survey: Distinctions Between: Single-Client, Multi-Client,
Access Control, & Community–Wide Security Surveys 79
The Security Survey: An Investigative Tool – Part I 82
The Security Survey: An Investigative Tool – Part II 87

v

vi ■ *Contents*

Revising the Security Survey 91
The Many Faces of the Security Survey 96

5. Practical Crime Prevention **101**
An Alternate Perspective on Healthcare Crime Prevention 101
A Clinical Approach to Crime Detection 103
A Clinical Approach to Hospital Security 107
The Art and Science of Proactive Security Programming 111
The Varied Roles of the Crime Prevention Expert 115
How is Crime Risk Measured and Managed? 120
Using Access and ID Control to Prevent Workplace Violence 123
Workplace Violence Prevention: A Guide to Active Shooter and Workplace
Violence Resources 125
Aspects of Crime and Violence Avoidance 131
Squeezing the Most from Your Security Dollar 137

6. Metrics and Data Application **141**
An Alternative View in the Development of Healthcare Security Metrics 141
Resources Available for Applying Metrics in Security and Safety Programming 146
Applying Metrics to 21st Century Healthcare Security 150

7. Physical Security Applications **155**
The Man Behind the Security Camera 155
Shell Hardening 159
Digital Security Technology Simplified 161
Determining and Implementing Successful Access Control Solutions 168

8. Customer Service Initiatives **171**
The Patient Wish List: Getting Customer Service Right 171
Creating a Customer Service Program for Healthcare Security 173

9. Auditing and Forensics **175**
Auditing Proactive Security Programs 175
Auditing Investigative Techniques 178
Auditing Hospital Security 182
Auditing Crime Analysis Programs 185
Auditing Warehouse and Loading Dock Security 187
Auditing Access Control Procedures 192
Auditing Loss Prevention Programs 195
The Environmental School of Criminology: Proactive vs. Reactive Security 198
Auditing Hospital Security: Is Your Security Program In Compliance 201
Security Auditing: A Prescription for Keeping Protection Programs Healthy 205
Aspects of Preparing for a "No Prior Notice" Regulatory Audit 209
Forensic Accounting and the Criminal Justice Process 213
How Have the Terrorist Attacks of 9/11/01 Affected the Corporate
Hiring Process? 217
Background Checks: A Diagnostic Tool to Decipher Deception 221
A New Approach to Handling Incoming Verifications 227
Forensics Role in the Investigative Process 231

Contents ■ vii

10. Fraud Detection and Prevention 235

Play it Safe: A Guide to Preventing Shoplifting, Fraud and Employee Theft 235
A Team Approach to Fraud Prevention 243
Delving Deeper to Decipher Fraud 246
The Fraud Prevention Jackpot 249
Safeguarding Assets Against Fraud 255
Objections to Active Fraud Prevention 257
Steps in a Fraud Audit 259
Investigating Money Laundering Schemes 262
Fraud Audit Checklist 264
The Fraud Equation 266
Ten Questions an Entrepreneur Should Ask About Fraud 268
What is Business Espionage and How Can it be Effectively Controlled? 272
Auditing for Identity Fraud 274
Aspects of Fraud Prevention: Where Loyalty Dies, Fraud Grows 278
Aspects of Controlling Fraud in Healthcare Facilities: Taking the Threat Seriously 282

11. Interview and Interrogation 287

Interview vs. Interrogation 287
Demystifying the Investigative Process 290
Decrypting the Interrogation Process 296
The Art of Non-Target Interviewing 301
Effective Interview Techniques 305

12. VIP Protection 311

Aspects of Hospital Security: Protecting the VIP 311
Aspects of Hospital Security: Protecting the VIP – Part II 316

Index 321

Preface

The authors have a long history of working in the healthcare sector. As managers of hospital security and safety, we were often asked to address a host of serious protection threats embracing security-related technological and procedural breakdowns, homicides, VIP security threats, terrorism, disasters, and pandemics. Two important lessons we've learned over the many years in healthcare security: There is no silver bullet to deal with every issue that comes galloping into the security executive's office and never be afraid to leave the land of the familiar for the land of the unfamiliar to find solutions to pressing problems.

Security fixes can come in many forms – so security administrators need to be thermostats not thermometers to effectively get the job done. Today's security executive instinctively knows that a danger foreseen is half avoided, simply being comfortable is the greatest hinderance to continued growth, and when security sneezes the institution catches a cold. Realizing that enlightened security executives know how to pick a plum from the security tree of knowledge, it is in this vein that we gathered several of our previously published articles for this desk reference book that we thought would be helpful in finding solutions to pressing protection problems. The articles we've chosen to include in our book cover a galaxy of security and safety issues embodying access control breeches, ID card preferences, fire prevention, security survey design, CCTV monitoring, security auditing and forensics, fraud prevention and detection, background screening and due diligence, VIP protection, interview and interrogation techniques, internal thievery, customer service strategies, metric and data applications, disaster preparedness, WMD and pandemic flu contaminate handling, and security design strategies for handling tomorrow's pandemic catastrophes.

It is our hope that this book serves as a marketplace of ideas to help find solutions to pressing problems. As the world-famous crooner "Perry Como" said in a song "catch a falling star and put it in your pocket and save it for a rainy day" - we hope that you will put this book on your desk and save it for that rain-soaked day when you are looking for that light at the end of the tunnel to help guide you!

Acknowledgements

As legacy healthcare security professionals we have had the privilege of publishing our experiences, expertise and thoughts in the printed media. For more than three decades, security executives from around the world have accessed and read our articles and publications. We have been very fortunate that organizations showed interest in our articles and were willing to publish them for all to see.

We want to thank those organizations and publications that have recognized us as industry experts and have allowed us to expose our thoughts to the security industry. We feel it is important to recognize those organizations and thank them for their support over the last three decades. They include:

- International Association for Healthcare Security and Safety and their publications, The Journal of Healthcare Protection Management
- Security Magazine
- Internal Auditing Report: Warren Gorham and Lamont: RIA Group
- PI Magazine
- International Society of Crime Prevention Practitioners
- The Campus Law Enforcement Journal
- Security ENewsletter
- Security Management Magazine
- Association of Certified Fraud Examiners - Fraud Magazine
- NYC Mayor's Office of Business Services

Thank you for your continued support and recognition. We are grateful for the opportunities you have provided us over the years which have led to the publishing of this book.

About the Authors

Bernard J. (Ben) Scaglione, CPP, CHPA, CHSP, is principal of The Secure Hospital a blogging and resource management site. The site is dedicated to dialog related to healthcare and specifically healthcare security. Ben is author of the book, "Security Management for Healthcare: Proactive Event Prevention and Effective Resolution." He has served as a security director for more than 25 years directing programs for some of the most prestigious healthcare institutions within the New York City area, including New York Presbyterian, Bellevue Hospital, and Atlantic Health System. Ben ventured into the contract guard business working as the healthcare subject matter expert for G4S Secure Solutions. Providing expertise to clients, training to security staff and sales team members. He worked as the Director of Healthcare Services at Lowers and Associates where he provided risk assessment services to key healthcare clients. He worked designing security systems and conducting security risk assessments in the healthcare sector for Ross & Baruzzini.

Ben has served in multiple capacities for International Association for Healthcare Security and Safety (IAHSS) over the past 10 years, including several councils, committees, and the IAHSS Board of Directors. He is past Chairman of the ASIS International Healthcare Council and past President of the New York City Metropolitan Healthcare Safety and Security Directors Association.

Throughout his career Ben has been an outspoken advocate for security, healthcare security and healthcare in general. Demonstrating his passion through writing, speaking and teaching. Ben has presented in front of many organizations over the past 25 years. He has served as an adjunct faculty member at Pratt Institute, Interboro Institute, New Jersey City University, and while working at Bellevue Hospital taught ethics and basic security practices at the John Jay College Peace Officer Academy.

Ben continues today to be an advocate for healthcare security presenting at various venues on healthcare security, active shooter and workplace violence prevention, and talking about the future of healthcare and healthcare security. Cntinuing his quest to advance the field of hospital security and the healthcare security industry as a whole.

Anthony Luizzo, CFE, CST, PI (RET. NYPD), is certified fraud examiner, certified security trainer, licensed private investigator, and a licensed locksmith. He is a court qualified security expert (cited in the New York Jury Reporter: Bronx Supreme Court (October 1998). As a member of the NYPD's Crime Prevention Division, he was responsible for writing security surveys for industrial, commercial, and institutional businesses and administering a four-million-dollar federal block grant program to help small and large businesses in NYC obtain matching funds for security enhancement. He was a member of a six-person team of specialists selected to write security surveys of all 31 NYC public healthcare facilities (hospitals, long-term care facilities and neighborhood family care clinics). Post his retirement from the NYPD, he was Director xiv ■ *About the Authors*

of Security Programs for the NYC Office of Economic Development / Business Services, and Corporate Director of Loss Prevention for the NYC Health and Hospitals Corporation (largest public healthcare system in the U.S.). He authored dozens of articles for professional journals and magazines and was a contributing author/editor for (Reuters) RIA Group – Thomson Publications. He held adjunct faculty positions at Long Island University, New York University, College of Staten Island, and John Jay College of Criminal Justice Studies. He was the 1st elected Eastern Region Governor of the Association of Certified Fraud Examiners, founding member / president emeritus: New York Chapter Association of Certified Fraud Examiners, and past president of the Society of Professional Investigators.

Citations:

- Resolution: New York State Legislature (Senate # 613 – Assembly # 599) - 1983
- Citation: 98th U.S. Congress, Hon. Joseph P. Addabbo: - Congressional Record - 1984
- Citation: Brooklyn Borough President: - 1990
- Distinguished Achievement Award: Association of Certified Fraud Examiners - 1996

Introduction

Over the past three decades healthcare has been at a crossroads. Reimbursement restrictions, increased regulation and societal changes have all impacted the healthcare industry. Inclusive to these changes are the dramatic changes occurring within healthcare security. Over the past three decades healthcare security has survived 9/11, three biological incidents, increased workplace violence, major weather events, a pandemic, continual changes in the reimbursement process and key advances in security technology.

The shifting healthcare environment has placed increased stress on the healthcare security professional. Security departments can no longer be reactive. Today, security executives must be proactive, quickly adjusting to a continually changing healthcare environment. Security executives know that a well-structured protection program helps to deepen and strengthen security response planning strategies. Utilizing lessons learned from actual and planned events, along with best practices, and current trends, helps to make the plan more efficient and effective.

Current issues effecting healthcare security include an increasingly violent environment. Violence continues to challenge the healthcare sector. Domestic violence, child abuse, behavioral health, drug and alcohol abuse all continue to create increased demands on hospital security staff.

The Affordable Care Act (ACA) is currently up in the air, so reimbursement rates are questionable. This fluctuation will undoubtedly influence future budgetary allocations for healthcare security technological improvements and staffing advancements.

As the Covid pandemic subsides, criminality will once again raise its ugly head and healthcare security professionals need to be ready. Seeing that the camera of security will be watching, they must make sure that response protocols never shy away from all challenges, and always able to anticipate unintended consequences.

The potential for terrorist attack is real. The recent pandemic has shown that terrorist threats have been committed on a small number of hospitals in the US. Hospital security executives must keep their eyes on the prize and be prepared and ready to meet any and all terrorist episodes that come knocking on their institution's door.

Severe weather has the potential to impact all healthcare systems across the globe. A comprehensive emergency management plan is needed so weather related disaster scenarios are adequately addressed. The keys to success in countering weather-related catastrophe is targeted training and repetition.

The issues described above are but a few of the pressing challenges that healthcare security professionals face each day. To help in the never-ending war on criminality, healthcare security executives need to have as many reference resources as possible at their fingertips. We hope Healthcare Security: Solutions for Management, Operations, and Administration becomes one of those cherished resources you turn to for answers to pressing problems. This book combines wisdom across decades of the authors' experiences, expertise, and knowledge which we hope will serve as a beacon

xvi ■ *Introduction*

to help find answers to pressing crime problems involving fraud, violence, disasters, pandemics, terrorism, and more. One important lesson we did learn over these many years laboring in health-care security and safety quoting former President Harry S. Truman is that *"not every reader needs to be a leader, but every leader needs to be a reader"*. We hope our book finds a place on your bookshelf and that it does not gather too much dust.

Chapter 1

The Changing Face of Healthcare Security

How has Hospital Security Changed Since 9/11?

Anthony Luizzo and Bernard J. Scaglione

The tragic events of September 11, 2001 brought about the myriad of security-related changes in hospital security. Gone are the days of unrestricted access into hospitals, municipal buildings, bridges, tunnels, and mercantile establishments. In today's security-conscious atmosphere, hospitals must now screen all persons entering their facilities. Beyond stricter guidelines in controlling ingress and egress and enhancing infrastructure security, the horrific threat of terrorism has put taxing demands on all hospitals across America to be better prepared to medically treat massive amounts of people rapidly. In a 2003 Office of Homeland Security (OHS) publication entitled *The National Strategy for the Physical Protection of Critical Infrastructures and Key Assets*, hospitals are identified as a key link in the defensive chain against terrorism. The report goes on to mention that hospitals serve as the primary caretaker of emergency services personnel, injured attack victims, as well as serving as a community-wide haven for area residents. Moreover, the report highlights the need for formulating protective strategies to thwart contamination, theft of toxic agents, and sabotage.

Hospital Security Prior to 9/11

Historically, hospitals offered free unobstructed access to inpatients areas. As a matter of course, prior to 9/11 this trend was on the rise, due in large measure to increased competition between hospitals. In fact, many healthcare institutions had or were contemplating establishing a totally free unrestricted access control program.

From *The Journal of Healthcare Protection Management* International Assoc. of Hospital Security & Safety Rusting Publications. (20):2, pp. 44–48. 2004.

DOI: 10.4324/9781003215851-1

Hospital Security Post 9/11

Changing times require changing strategies. At the urgency of OHS, healthcare institutions are being asked to begin screening all incoming persons, consider extensive upgrades of electronic technologies (i.e., security television, card access and manual and/or electronic locking systems), and commence purchasing access capturing systems such as turnstiles, magnetometers, and video pass systems. To better protect against sabotage and theft, healthcare institutions are being asked to conduct security surveys of high-risk locations including but not necessarily limited to pharmaceutical storage rooms, parking garages and research facilities that hose critical biological, chemical, and radiological agents.

In addition, other equally critical areas including utility distribution rooms, emergency generators, medical supply areas, gas and oil tanks and oxygen and medical gases distribution points and storage areas should also be surveyed. All storage areas which house pharmaceuticals used to treat victims exposed to radiological, chemical, biological agents must be kept secured and access adequately restricted. Environs that house radiological, biological, and chemical waste must be secured to terrorists *cannot* gain access to potentially harmful substances.

Finally, teaching and research facilities that utilize radiological, chemical, and biological agents need to be added to the periodical survey list.

Dealing with Identified Threats

The Office of Homeland Security recommends that hospital's utilize physical security measures such as dead bolt locksets, door alarm contacts, card access technologies, a closed-circuit television (CCTV) to secure and restrict access into these high-risk areas. In addition, OHS suggests periodical monitoring to ensure that these areas are not compromised.

Response to Catastrophic Occurrences

Since 9/11, hospitals have changed their emergency response procedures. Today, when a catastrophic disaster occurs, hospitals restrict access to everyone to adequately screen incoming persons for contaminated agents. From a disaster preparedness perspective, access portals that have historically never been closed are now being shut down, entry doors that have never been locked are now being shunted from the access grid. In emergencies, hospital security operatives are being asked to refuse entrance and/or at the very least screen all persons wishing to gain entry so that they can screen for contaminates, the screening process outside the facility re their whereabouts at the time of the disaster to determine whether the person might have been exposed and possibly infected.

Hospital personnel and security operatives are receiving state-of-the-art training to identify and handle toxic exposures. This training often includes:

- How to effectively screen persons from outside of the hospital?
- How to spot exposed persons?
- How to properly wear "Tyvek" body suits, masks, and knee-high latex gloves?

Furthermore, OHS is requiring all hospitals in the US with emergency room services for injured persons to provide decontamination services for injured persons. This means hospitals must be able to identify certain basic toxic agents and provide decontamination services to patients and emergency service workers before they enter the emergency room for treatment. Hospitals are now required to stockpile certain immunizations for emergency distribution. Drugs needed for chemical and biological exposure are now stored in hospital pharmacies for emergency distribution. Certain hospitals located in strategic geographical sections of the country are being asked to stockpile certain immunizations in environmentally secure housings for rapid distribution to area hospitals.

Disaster Management Training

Since the early 80's, hospitals have been required to conduct disaster drills annually to test internal procedures in the treatment of injuries sustained during a flood, tornado, or plane crash. Since 2000, hospitals have been asked to drill for mass casualty incidents related to bombs and exposure to chemical, biological, and radiological agents. Handling mass casualty incidents has been on the minds of the federal government since Y2K. Since 9/11, hospitals are required to not only drill on handling mass casualties, but they must also coordinate these drills with area hospitals, local governments, and private corporate entities. Hospitals must have a plan to evacuate their respective facilities and transfer patients to other area hospitals. Further, hospitals must have written legal agreements with area vendors and local police agencies to ensure the delivery of goods and services in the event of a major disaster.

Ten Questions to Ask when Evaluating Security Compliance

1. Is the healthcare institution in compliance with Homeland Security mandates?
2. Does the hospital have a written disaster preparedness plan?
3. Does the plan meet local law enforcement and fire department mandates?
4. Are disaster drills held to test the plan?
5. Are hospital security personnel trained in handling catastrophic occurrences?
6. Is physical, procedural, and technological security adequate?
7. Are storage facilities warehousing biological, chemical, and radiological agents secure?
8. Are storage facilities warehousing immunizations secure?
9. Does the institution have a catastrophic emergency evacuation plan?
10. Are periodical security surveys performed to evaluate facility risk exposures?

A Final Word

Without a doubt, hospital security has dramatically changed since that terrible day in early September 2001. As we journey through the 21st century, senior hospital security executives are playing a central role in ensuring that all hospital security programs, including disaster protection management follow federal, state, and local legislative mandates. The security executive may very well be the additional eyes and ears corporate America can rely on to help spot and stop future terrorist attacks from immobilizing our healthcare network.

Aspects of Hospital Security: How is Hospital Security Changing in the New Century?

Anthony Luizzo and Bernard J. Scaglione

Hospital security will change dramatically in the new millennium. The 21st century will bring a myriad of initiatives, including violence reduction programs affecting patients, visitors, and staff; heightened security regarding patient's medical information; and a shortage of budgetary funds for protection initiatives.

Legislative Initiatives

In June 1995, the Occupational Safety and health Administration (OSHA) published *Guidelines for Preventing Workplace Violence for Health Care and Social Service Workers*. Their studies concluded that health care workers had the highest incident of assault compared to other professionals. Moreover, the study recommended that hospitals and other health-related organizations consider implementing physical security measures to reduce verbal and physical assaults. In addition, to the federal OSHA guidelines, individual states have legislated the development and implementation of programs to protect workers against violent incidents. This legislation necessitates the implementation of programs to reduce violence in the workplace and requires companies to formulate plans to handle violent situations. Many hospitals have delegated these anti-violence initiatives to the security department. As a matter of course, security personnel are taught to properly respond to disruptive patients, visitors, and staff and are trained to verbally deescalate and physically restrain individuals who become verbally threatening or physically abusive.

Beyond OSHA regulations, the U.S. Congress, along with some states, legislated a *patients' bill of rights* in 1996. This federal legislation, known as the Health Insurance Portability and Accountability Act, addressed the need for enhanced protection of patient's medical information. Among other issues. The Act contained a provision that gave Congress until August 21, 1999, to pass comprehensive privacy legislation. When Congress did not enact privacy legislation by that date, the law required the Department of Health and Human services (HHS) to craft such protections by regulation. The final rule took effect on April 14, 2001. This rule gives patients greater access to their own medical records and more control over how their personal health information is used. The rule also addresses the obligations of health care providers and health plans to protect health information. Hospitals will be required to provide physical security controls for medical information and implement policies to restrict and monitor the distribution and release of medical information. Enhanced protection requisites will most likely mandate that hospital security departments install access control mechanisms and technologies in medical record departments and medical chart storage environments.

In addition, to physical security enhancements, desktop and network computer safeguards and computerized document-tracking systems will be required. By law, covered entities (health plans, health care clearinghouses, and health care providers who conduct certain financial and administrative transactions electronically), have until April 14, 2003, to comply.

Guidance and other technical assistance materials are posted on the HHS 's office for Civil Rights website at www.hhs.gov/ocr/hipaa.

From *Internal Auditing Report* Warren, Gorham & Lamont/RIA /Group (Reuters) – Thomson Publications. (2):4, pp. 9–11. October 2001 – openlibrary@archive.com.

Security Budget Issues and Emerging Technology

Hospital security operations will face increased financial hardship in the new millennium due in large part to Diagnostic Related Treatment Groups and Health Maintenance Organizations that limit the amount of revenue hospitals collect on a specific patient illness. These shortfalls will most definitely affect security budgets. To meet the challenge of shrinking security dollars, security departments will have to rely on technology-driven systems. In the new century, the use of electronic resources such as closed-circuit television, access control, and physical security applications will become increasingly more important than the use of security personnel. From a managerial point of view, security administrators will need to be more knowledgeable in security technology and products. Security services will be geared toward the identification and restriction of persons utilizing hospital services, visiting patients, and workers within hospital entities. Security executives must be capable of identifying and reducing access to patient information and provide protective services with a high level of efficiency at low cost.

Establishing a Proactive Security Initiative

Beyond the expanded utilization of security-related technologies, security executives will have to change their mindset from the reactive model of security and law enforcement to the more proactive model of deterring and preventing potential sources of crime. The establishment of a crime and loss prevention capability gives the security department the capability to evaluate crime risks before they have an opportunity to wreak havoc on the institution and on the security department's budget. In addition, trained crime prevention personnel are often used to spearhead the institution's violence prevention training efforts.

Program Evaluation

As with all programs, a system of evaluation should be designed so that the actual efforts of the security program can be measured. Some measurement parameters might include:

- Developing a series of pre- and post-program studies to ascertain the level of crime reporting in areas where proactive approaches were promulgated
- Designing evaluation models to gauge if the crime prevention message is reaching its intended audience and whether the audience is reacting to the message
- Preparing am institutional data-gathering system to capture information on the levels of participation from past proactive crime prevention initiatives
- Maintaining a statistical mapping system to track crime pattern variations and dispersion data

Measuring Quality Assurance

A structured program of evaluation should be used to measure the security department's response to proactive security initiatives, as well as the overall effect of the strategies put forward. To ensure that security programs are running at optimum efficiency, security administrators often perform security surveys at periodical intervals. A generic definition of a security survey is an on-site physical evaluation of a facility, program, procedure, or other entity to determine its protection status.

The security profiles security-related deficiencies, risks, and hazardous conditions and offers corrective approaches to remedy identified risk exposures.

A Final Word

Conventional wisdom in the security industry classifies hospital security as one of the most difficult protective functions to perform within the gamut of general security operations. One of the major reasons for this is the emotive atmosphere under which hospital security guards perform their duties. When a person visits a hospital, it is often a stressful event- one usually associated with visiting a friend or loved one who is injured or recuperating from an illness. It is often the interpersonal skill of the hospital security guard that prevents emotional episodes from exploding into major incidents. The enhanced emphasis on deescalating workplace violence in health care facilities, coupled with the installation of security technologies, is the key to minimizing security risks in hospitals as we navigate the 21st century.

Hospital Security in the 21st Century: What Should We Expect?

Anthony Luizzo and Bernard J. Scaglione

If we could envision healthcare 20 years from now or even 50 years from now, what would it look like? Will it be different from today? Will the physical structure of hospitals appear familiar to us? Will hospitals operate as they do today? Will the role of security be the same? One thing I think we could all agree upon, it will look quite different.

It can be said with certainty that healthcare costs will continue to skyrocket due in great measure to technological advances. The latest in diagnostic systems will be in high demand. What holds true for technology will hold true for drugs as well. The latest and greatest will be in demand. Hospitals will continue to see drastic swings in available skilled labor. Will tomorrow's youth be interested in cleaning bed pans and lifting the indigent onto x-ray tables? As a result, labor costs will either be low due to an abundance of workers or high because of a continued shortage of labor.

The Impact of New Diseases

Healthcare in the 21st century will surely see decreases in the rate insurance companies reimburse hospitals for care. Although the issue has not been the number one concern for Americans in political circles, the future may hold a different story. Will reimbursement drop even further, closing smaller hospitals across the country? Or will the resurgence of old diseases keep hospital beds full until healthcare can find a quick, adequate cure for these diseases. One thing is for sure; new diseases like SARS or Avian Flu will bring healthcare security changes.

These new diseases have already become catalysts for change in ventilation systems, temperature controls along with environmental and physical isolation capacities within hospitals, urgent care facilities and doctor's offices. Along with the threat of new evolving diseases, the continued threat of terrorist attacks will further help dictate changes in staff training and the hospital's physical environment.

Training Programs to Handle Hazardous Bacterial Incidents

Training programs to teach workers to handle the outbreak of a disease or the massive exposure of chemical or radiological agents will be prevalent in the future. Even now, whether biological, chemical, radiological or explosive, hospitals are required to provide decontamination facilities as well as medical care. Emergency departments are responsible for managing potential chemical disasters, whether they result from an industrial accident or terrorist activity. The Joint Commission on Accreditation of Healthcare Organizations (JCAHO) and the Occupational Safety and Health Administration (OSHA) now require emergency rooms to be prepared for

From *Journal of Healthcare Protection Management.* (22):1, pp. 75–80. 2006.

8 ■ *Healthcare Security*

hazardous material incidents. All hospital emergency rooms must have an emergency response plan for hazardous materials incidents that meets OSHA requirements (29 CFR 1910,120) for both staff training and response. Emergency room personnel, who come in direct contact with victims exposed to a hazardous substance, must be trained as first responders.

OSHA regulations require hospital emergency room personnel who respond to an unknown hazard to don Level B protection, which include a positive-pressure self-contained breathing apparatus and splash-protective chemical-resistant clothing. In addition, any hazardous material response plan must include contingencies for contamination sources within the hospital and emergency room. The plan must contain a procedure to lock down the emergency room quarantining and treating all personnel within the contaminated area and provide appropriate back up facilities to provide emergency patient care.

Unauthorized Access to Medical Records: Third Party Oversight

Recent issues involving unauthorized access to medical records and incidents involving infection control will see continued third party oversight and legislative restrictions on the administration of healthcare. Recent HIPPA legislation and continued monitoring of staff infections demonstrate the increased concern over the management of information and disease in the healthcare industry. In the future, hospitals will have increased restriction and compliance issues from the federal government and other compliance organizations. The administrative simplification provisions of the Health Insurance Portability and Accountability Act of 1996 (HIPAA, Title II), require the Department of Health and Human Services to establish national standards for electronic healthcare transactions and national identifiers for providers, health plans, and employers. It also addresses the security and privacy of health data. For hospitals, the challenge is to ensure that all patient account handling, billing, and medical records are secure.

From Elder to Holistic Care

Society is getting older. Healthcare is focusing more of elder care; Over the next 20 years the "Baby Boomers" will be elderly and will increasingly require healthcare. Notwithstanding, thirty to forty years from now the age of the population in the US will shift to a younger, healthier population. Hospitals, if they want to survive, will have to adjust their services from elder care to holistic care. The population shift along with advances in medical treatments will present a healthcare system vastly different from today

Increases in Violence

Besides the shift in the age of the healthcare population, society will become more violent as the 21st century proceeds. Experts in the field of criminology portend that the crime rate most likely will drop; however criminal acts will increasingly become more violent. Hospitals will deal with various types of violent crimes, crimes against the elderly and kidnapping of infants and other persons. The potential for violent crimes occurring in the emergency room and other areas of the hospital is not going away and may increase. Hospitals will increasingly tackle emotional problems including, but not limited to, domestic disputes, physical and verbal altercations in the ED and other areas, and gang war related violence.

How will these changes affect hospital security?

Changes in hospital protection management for the 21st century will be extensive and primarily include training initiatives in hazardous substances and new diseases, enhanced target hardening and access control innovations, training in crisis intervention and handling of violent persons, emergency response to hazardous material exposures, abductions and serious injuries, and advancements in security technology to assist in the implementation of security services.

Training security officers to recognize symptoms of exposure to hazards and diseases

Security operatives will have to be continuously trained to recognize systems of exposure to chemical substances, biological and radiological agents, as well as different types of diseases. They will need to be able to identify infected people *before* they enter the hospital facility. Protection advocates will be slipping into uniforms that protect from exposure to these agents, as well as learning ingenious methods of isolating victims from the general hospital population and the decontamination processes. Security will have to be able to make the hard, split-second decisions to lockdown the ED and keep all exposed persons within the contaminated area when hospital administrators and other persons within the ED are accidentally exposed to hazardous materials. Security will also need to undergo continual training in crisis intervention, violence prevention, violence prevention and emergency response to natural disasters. As the environment in which hospitals provide services change within society, the security department will have to be better prepared to handle emergencies.

Training in handling new security-related technology

From the security-related technological perspective, detailed training will be needed to pilot tomorrow's security systems. Security operatives will have to knowledgeable in the operation and troubleshooting of the systems. Tomorrow's closed-circuit television technologies CCTV will become smarter, thus requiring more interaction with staff. Access control systems and digital recording systems will in the future be directly tied into the hospital network structure. Protection mavens will have to be knowledgeable in the operation and repair of these systems, which are currently being managed by the information systems department.

The need for more stringent access controls and ED isolation

Looking to the future, securing hospitals will be a big challenge. More stringent access control must be implemented at building access and Emergency Department portals. The Emergency

Department will be structurally isolated and physically separated from the main hospital to isolate potential hazardous substances. More comprehensive access control technologies and physical barriers ill be utilized to screen hospital staff, patients, and visitors to verify their need to be in the inner bowls of the ED.

Partial federal funding of healthcare security

Finance availability will certainly control security services in the future. Most likely, portions of the funds needed to upgrade security services will be coming from the federal government's homeland security budget. Whether or not monies are available to fund services, there will be a progressive reliance on technology over labor.

Investigating financial criminality

Looking even deeper into the state of tomorrow's security, protection specialists will be knee-deep in investigations related to financial thievery. As the government continues to champion a continued crackdown on safeguarding patient information, employees and outsiders will continue to try to breech security's iron curtain for criminal purposes. Tomorrow's security department will be more proactive than its 20th century offspring.

Conclusion: The Look and Feel of Tomorrow's Hospitals

The hospitals of the future will look and feel quite different from the hospitals of today. The role of the security officer will change as compared to today. Security will require extensive training in the identification of the sick and violent. Funding for the identification and direction of the patient, visitors and staff will be prevalent. Security staff will be required to do more detailed investigations and security command centers will have smarter, more technologically advanced security equipment to assist in the restriction of access, identification of visitors and the management of CCTV.

The Changing Face of the Hospital Security: Re-tooling for the Future

Anthony Luizzo and Bernard J. Scaglione

Looking Back to the Future

In a 2006 article by the authors "Hospital Security in the 21st Century: What Should We Expect" which appeared in the *Journal of Healthcare Protection Management* (Vol. 22. No. 1) we discussed in some detail the author's vision of what healthcare security would look like in the years ahead. The article focused on emergency management, healthcare finances and violence, three central issues that continue to play a prominent role in today's healthcare environment. In this article we intend to discuss the impact that new diseases such as SARS and other pandemic flu contaminates have on the system, how proposed budget cuts to Medicare and Medicaid via Obama Care will change the financial landscape, how violence within the healthcare institution can influence patient care, and how natural disasters (hurricanes, tornados, tsunamis, etc.) will begin playing a more active role in healthcare protection management.

Treating Disease

These new and exotic diseases have changed the way patients are treated and the way hospitals engineer their ventilation systems to safely contain airborne contaminates. Since the 2006 publication, we have seen first-hand how H1N1 has impacted regional healthcare markets. A 2008 JHCPM article by Luizzo, A., et al (Vol. 23 No. 2), "Training Security Officers to Recognize the Perils of Weapons of Mass Destruction & Pandemic Flu Contaminates." Thrashes out in some detail the need for security officer training to focus on handling bacterial incidents. The article also went on to mention that there would be a shift in care in the healthcare industry from elder care to holistic care. Moreover, we also noted a shift from "Baby Boomer" care to preventive younger patient care. One prediction offered which unfortunately has drastically come to pass was an escalation of hospital violence. According to a study published by ASIS, "Managing Disruptive Behavior and Workplace Violence in Healthcare," healthcare workers are regularly subjected to verbal and physical abuse from patients, visitors, and other staff. Even though many incidents go unreported, the number of reported cases is on the rise. Another study by the Emergency Nurses Association estimates that about one-fourth of emergency nurses experienced frequent physical violence. One-fifth of emergency nurses reported being the victim of verbal abuse at the workplace. Compared to other working environments, hospitals and adult care facilities are dangerous places to work! Obviously, security officer training must keep pace with this ever-evolving problem. Besides standard protection related enhancements, healthcare security executives should also refer to OSHA publication 3148 and incorporate some of its electronic solutions as well.

From *Journal of Healthcare Protection Management.* (29):1, pp. 1–7. 2013.

Budgetary Issues

In our 2006 article we mentioned that healthcare budgets would be cut. Since Obama Care was passed and approved by the U.S. Supreme Court, both Medicare and Medicaid funding is on the proposed cutting block and most likely will be slashed by congress in the months and years to come.

Taking a realistic look back, recipients of Medicare and Medicaid have increased substantially over the past ten years. Moreover, in our 2006 article we discussed the financial squeeze that hospitals would feel under these projected budget shortfalls, and we stressed the need for efficiency. Here again these place a strain and challenge on security departments to continue to do its job with less resources. One option might be to move from a 100% reactive crime control model to a deeper proactive crime control model. Having a protection program to unearth crime-related exposure sooner than later costs substantially less than dealing with its expensive counterpart.

What's New in Healthcare

Disaster Preparedness vs. Terrorism Prevention?

While speaking on disaster preparedness we believe there should be a modest shift in focus from terrorism prevention to natural disaster management. Disasters such as hurricanes, tornadoes and earthquakes, tsunamis etc., are becoming more prevalent and continue to place a tremendous stress on healthcare institutions. Looking back only a few years ago to hurricane Katrina, hospitals learned first-hand that evacuation preparation is extremely important, and having the ability to be self-sufficient for up to 96 hours without State and Federal government assistance is critical. Another example occurred at St. John's Regional Medical Center in Joplin, Missouri in 2011, the facility was hit by a tornado destroying most of its buildings and infrastructure. These and other disasters only reinforce the need for better preparation so that lifesaving services can be provided for extended periods of time. From a protection perspective, security executives might want to deepen training curricula in this important area as well.

Safeguarding Medical Records: A New Challenge for Security

Unauthorized access to medical records in healthcare institutions is on the rise. Purloined medical and financial information is a major fraud-specific "hot spot" which is often a juicy headline for the print and electronic media. Once this data is obtained, it is often used by fraudsters to create a galaxy of personal ID instruments for sale on the black market. Concomitantly, this has caused the expansion of HIPAA regulations to ensure that electronic information is properly safeguarded. Under this "Red Flag" legislation the law requires that all healthcare institutions report *all breaches of patient financial data, while also providing restitution.* Security executives might wish to consider adding fraud prevention curricula to their training menu. Excellent resources might include: The Association of Certified Fraud Examiners, ASIS and IAHSS.

Access Control Advances

There have been many access control enhancements in hospitals. The Joint Commission along with other organizations has called for tighter access control in hospital emergency departments,

The Changing Face of Healthcare Security ■ 13

and other security-sensitive areas like Pediatrics and Maternity. Moreover, oftentimes these new restrictions call for the complete lockdown of these high security units leaving access to medical staff only. Further, the requirements call for the installation of additional security-specific technologies such as intercoms and buzzers to control visitors and patients' access.

Investigative Advances

Since President Obama was elected in 2008, there has been a marked increase in fraud investigations in medical centers, doctors' offices, and insurance companies. These targeted investigations focus on several fraud-specific crimes including fictitious billing and insurance fraud. Since 2009 this increased focus on medical record oversight has led to well over $4 billion in savings in fraud, waste, and abuse.

Advances in Safeguarding Medical Supplies and Equipment

Larger hospitals and academic medical centers across the country have been experiencing an increase in stolen medical supplies and equipment. These large- and small-scale organized thefts occur because of the high demand for low-cost drugs and medical devices throughout the United States and abroad. Originally this fraud problem focused like a laser beam on stealing expired drugs and medical supplies as well as older medical machinery. In recent years however, these thefts have expanded into stealing new supplies and machinery costing hospitals millions of dollars in losses each year.

Advances in Monitoring Counterfeit Medical Devices

A huge problem in the healthcare industry today is dealing with fake medical products. Oftentimes, these products are produced outside the U.S. and at first glance look the same as the real product, but function quite differently. To our knowledge, the influx of counterfeit products has _not_ caused the death of any patient, but has created difficulties for hospitals, clinics, and out-patient purchasing managers to constantly verify product authenticity both before and after purchase.

Looking to the Next Decade and Beyond

Disease Prevention

With respect to new diseases, as a healthcare becomes more outpatient based to save money; we believe that hospitals will only domicile the extremely sick with diseases that may require isolation and long-term treatment. We envision that the influx of "Baby Boomers" will continue to shrink and be replaced by younger patient medical services. Preventive care will be central to the success of any healthcare system.

Hospitals will only care for the extremely sick, leaving everyone else to recover from home, accessing healthcare from a same day format. Additionally, off-site clinics and wellness centers will dominate the future security services market.

Terrorism vs. Mother Nature

Natural disasters will continue to play havoc within the healthcare industry and continue to expand into areas of the US that have _not_ been hard hit in the past. In our humble opinion, one of

14 ■ *Healthcare Security*

the biggest threats to healthcare security will not be from biological terrorism and related occurrences, but from *Mother Nature herself!* Hurricanes, tornados, floods, and other severe weather occurrences will be healthcare's *major* future challenge. We believe that additional security related training in this area is imperative!!!

Financing Medical Services

The biggest challenge to healthcare in the next decade will be fiduciary in nature. Until the issue of healthcare finances is resolved in the political arena, healthcare institutions will be struggling to meet expenses. With decreases in Medicare and Medicaid funding hospitals will have to learn to live with less while providing better care. With the creation of HCAPS and the National Patient Safety Goals, the quality of healthcare services must improve while income continues to drop. As we see it, finances within the healthcare industry will continue to diminish. Federal and State reimbursement will continue to decline, and competition for limited dollars will reach a feverish pitch. In summary, healthcare institutions will have to provide a better-quality service while reducing costs – or they will not survive. This will affect all medical services including protective services. Security departments will not be immune from this paradigm. Healthcare security executives will have to rely on metrics and other innovative practices to survive and flourish.

Which Challenges Do We Face Over the Next Few Decades?

Reshaping Hospital Security for the Task Ahead

Hospital security departments must become more innovative while working under budget shortfalls. Metrics will be a key component in this process and become an important part of the security executive's toolkit. From a purely financial perspective, security departments will be forced to better justify their existence and learn the 'art and science' of demonstrating their ability to place a monetary value on crime control efforts instituted, and savings realized via their intervention. Moreover, Security will have a greater role in dealing with purloined medical supplies and equipment and in tracking and unearthing counterfeit medical product suppliers. Similarly, hospital security executives will be dealing with increased violence in the healthcare setting. It is our feeling that over the next few decades domestic violence will continue to spill over into hospitals and healthcare facilities. We also believe that higher levels of violence stemming from mental healthcare patients will escalate. Security executives must be up-to-the task of finding innovative methods of reducing violence in and around their institutions. In many cases the amount of violence within a hospital or healthcare institution will affect personnel recruitment and retention. Regulations will continue to increase focusing on cloud data, wireless networks, and patient information security. As electronic medical records move into the 21st century, federal regulation will undoubtedly closely follow. *Security must be ready!*

A Final Word

As we move through the second and third decades of the 21st century, healthcare security professionals will have to re-tool and develop methods of effectively demonstrating their value within their corporate hierarchy. They will need to demonstrate _how_ their department contributes to the organizations overall bottom line. Keeping costs for security under control is fine, but the security executives musty become more innovative and develop programs that capture crime before it becomes cost prohibitive, and an institutional tragedy. Implementing proactive crime control programming will be an important key to achieving this goal. Instituting innovative programming along with cost containment will dominate healthcare security deliberations in both the near and far future.

An excellent local resource for proactive crime control programming can be found by contacting the New York City Police Department's Office of Crime Prevention, or by contacting any larger law enforcement agency nationwide. Other resources include the National Crime Prevention Council (NCPC) @ www.ncpc.org, and the International Centre for the Prevention of Crime (ICPC) @ www.crime-prevention-intl.org.

The Changing Face of Hospital Security

Anthony Luizzo and Bernard J. Scaglione

Introduction

Increases in workplace violence, shootings, and other crimes within the healthcare environment are a siren call to all healthcare protection professionals to devise strategies to combat these horrendous threats. Over the past few years these attacks on workers have escalated and are challenging healthcare security executives to leave the land of the familiar and begin seeking new and more innovative protection blueprints. Many hospital security executives are not sitting idle waiting for their institution to be affected, they are taking the bull by the horns and actively seeking security remedies to adequately handle all fast-coming threats. Sundry strategies under consideration include conjoining in-house surveillance technologies with external public video systems, installing turnstiles, employing magnetometers, arming security personnel, promulgating firearms related "use of force" policies, employing metrics to showcase proficiencies and substantiate expenditures, and involving robotics and drones in standard security machinations. To effectively evaluate institutional crime risk exposure, more forward-thinking security executives turn to the security assessment for guidance. In competent hands, an assessment is analogous to a medical CT scan (computed tomography) a device used by medical experts to diagnose and treat illness. This risk assessment tool helps to diagnose and prescribe remedies for frail security programming while offering creative /corrective solutions to correct shortcomings before they wreak havoc on the institutional setting. Additional information on preparing and effectively utilizing security assessments can be found in two articles authored by the undersigned[1] and detailed further in a book by the undersigned[2].

Conjoining house surveillance with public surveillance systems

It makes good sense for healthcare security executives to reach out to local government and law enforcement officials to discuss joining the municipality's external surveillance network. Connecting to the community's surveillance network would permit the hospital security's eye in the sky surveillance system to monitor access and capture mischievous activity and/or other non-criminal emergencies at the institution's periphery. Interestingly, for the very first time this past New Year's Eve (2019), the New York City Police Department used both public surveillance and drones to monitor access control in Times Square. Obviously, joining these existing networks would be a win-win for all in the never-ending war on terrorism. There are legal and logistical questions associated with conjoining surveillance technologies, but there could be tremendous benefits derived from thinking beyond the standard way security projects are usually packaged.

From *The Journal of Healthcare Protection Management.* (37):1, pp. 1–10. 2021.

Technological enhancement considerations: Turnstiles / magnetometers / arming security operatives / updating use of force policy / employing robotics / drones for patrolling and surveillance / using metrics to showcase proficiencies & substantiate expenditures.

Turnstiles:

The use of turnstiles provides a physical barrier between the entrance and the interior of the hospital. Turnstiles also provide for the screening of all persons entering the hospital.

This process includes the authentication of all visitors and the issuance of an "access device" {pass/card} to provide entry into the hospital. The key to the implementation of a turnstile program is the establishment of reasonable security controls that adequately protect people, property, systems, equipment, and other assets while restricting access where appropriate. Designing a program that considers internal traffic flow and its impact on clinical operations is the desired outcome. It is important that appropriate signage be prominently posted, and security operatives be sensitized and briefed on how to keep visitors and staff moving freely without incident. The screening process should be engineered to quickly maneuver traffic through the turnstile check point as effortlessly as possible. The system should be capable of adequately handling seniors and the disabled as well. As a matter of reality, turnstiles and access control cards that require swiping to pass through the turnstile may be difficult to manage for select individuals. One example that immediately comes to mind is a child visiting a patient with a parent, oftentimes a child would not necessarily be issued an access credential; but must be able to pass through a turnstile. This is precisely why human interaction will likely be required to assist those who do not understand or have trouble navigating these barriers. Finally, some thought needs to be given to turn style jumping and illegally allowing several persons to gain access on the same card.

When using turnstiles, it is suggested that anti-pass back programming be applied. An anti-pass back system can be programmed to allow a credential to open a door or turnstile for a determined period so that an access card cannot be used by _two_ different people. Once the technological issues are addressed, it's time to tackle traffic flow considerations. To get it right, it's important that a traffic study be initiated to determine 'high and low' traffic periods and wait times. Once completed, the new process should be tested to ensure it will flawlessly function under extremely stressed circumstances and that the normal ebb and flow of the facility is not severely interrupted. For example, what happens when one or several of the turnstile portals malfunction? How will this downtime effect wait times? Will security staff be available to screen persons when turnstiles are dysfunctional? These and other eventualities; including cost considerations must be considered when selecting access technology for the turnstile. As with most technological enhancements, the higher the level of security one seeks, the costlier the system. Proximity cards are the costliest and they must be included in your cost/benefit analysis. Should a less costly security technology be used, then consideration must focus on installing two or three different types of card readers, and/or designate specific turnstiles for specific users.

Notwithstanding, most hospitals utilize proximity access cards for staff and a less costly barcode or magnetic stripe cards for visitors and vendors. Obviously, budgetary considerations almost always drive the decision. With respect to budgetary deliberations, turnstile costs vary depending on whether the turnstile project is earmarked as a new construction or retrofit undertaking. A great many institutions engineer a system that offers a lane for visitors and patients, and a separate

18 ■ *Healthcare Security*

lane for staff, as well as an additional lane for eventual breakdowns. Finally, let us not forget that an entry gate may be need for deliveries and/or disabled access.

Magnetometers / screening procedures

In healthcare today, walk-through, and handheld metal detectors are used primarily in emergency departments and in behavioral health areas. There is now interest in utilizing metal detectors at hospital entrances. Protection wisdom theorizes that metal detectors and scan bag X-ray machines help to lessen the opportunity of illegal weaponry finding its way into healthcare facilities. Prior to considering walk-through metal detection devices, it would be wise to survey the installation site, audit the detection device placement schematic, and valuate its effect on access-related traffic flow. In the court of protection wisdom, walk-through metal detectors should be placed in areas where there is the ability to restrict access upon activation; especially when a person activates the detector or tries to by-pass the metal detector. Depending on traffic density, more than one detector may be necessary to reduce wait times. It is suggested that security operatives assigned to pilot these detection systems be armed. *In lieu of arming security staff, many hospitals opt to install a physical barrier to obstruct entry at these strategic check points.* With respect to screening procedures, all persons entering the hospital should be scanned. The scanning process should allow for hand-held scanners so that all medical emergencies can be immediately adjudicated. When metal detectors are used, all entrances into the hospital should be secured and monitored to make sure persons wishing to enter the hospital cannot by-pass the detection system. Finally, when metal detectors are used at emergency department entrances, a procedure must be enacted to handle individuals who arrive by ambulance; but are not seeking medical treatment. It is important to note that metal detectors are not effective if handbags, backpacks, and other carried items are not screened. These items should be sent through an x-ray machine or be physical inspected by a security operative. When inspecting bags, a table must be made available for inspection purposes. Initial inspections should *not* include a detailed review of a person's bags, but simply a quick look-see for weaponry. Security officers assigned can use a handheld scanner before conducting the full-blown inspection to determine if any metal objects are present. To effectively perform full-blown searches, a private screening room needs to be erected to effectively handle these searches. A process needs to be drafted speaking to what to do when a weapon is found? How will weaponry be safeguarded? How will legal weaponry be returned? Finally, a screening procedure is needed to handle special cases such as infants and small children walking through detectors or arriving in a stroller and wheelchair and/or physically impaired access.

Moving from patient and staff access to vendor, delivery, and law enforcement admittance. Procedures need to be drafted speaking to how bags or packages are to be searched? What will the process be for emergency personnel responding to an emergent situation? Will emergency responders be allowed to bypass the security checkpoint without going through the metal detection? What will the process look like for on and off duty law enforcement personnel carrying firearms and other weapons? Finally, the trillion-dollar question, what is the policy re persons that refuse to go through the metal detector? Will service be refused, or will they be allowed to enter the hospital anyway? Questions abound!

Arming hospital security operatives

The decision to arm security personnel should not be taken lightly. This decision can have a major impact on the healthcare institution and its constituency. Arming security staff is an administrative decision that each institution needs to carefully ponder.

Before arriving at a decision, hospital administrators need to decide the purpose for arming security staff. Irrespective of the reason, the process must begin and end with getting legal advice and researching state and local ordinances, along with conducting a comprehensive risk assessment to validate the need for and impact of arming security personnel. Because of the high liability associated with arming staff, alternate approaches to having firearms on hospital property should also be pondered. Possible alternatives might include having an off-duty police officer assigned to the healthcare institution, hiring armed contracted private security, and only arming senior security management personnel. If arming security is the road to be traveled, then selecting weapons of choice need to be considered. When selecting a weapon of choice, there are questions galore. The type of revolver (single shot or semi-automatic) to be purchased? If the revolver selected is a semi-automatic type of firearm than how large of a clip will be allowed? What type of bullet will be used? How much ammunition will be kept on site? Will each qualifying officer purchase and carry their own weapon, or will weapons be issued to each officer during shift changes? Will the Hospital purchase the weapons or ask the officer to purchase the weapon out of their own money? What will the ammunition carry policy entail? In the court of security management opinion, a good strategy to follow is to have the institution purchase all firearms and set the policy and standards. With respect to safeguarding firearms, it is important that the institution provide an isolated and secure location for firearm storage. The room should provide a high level of security and have an ammunition cleaning area. The firearms storage room should have only one entrance and be equipped with a card reader and CCTV camera surveillance system. Access into the room should be restricted to *only qualified armed staff* who have a firearm issued to them.

A firearms instructor / supervisor position should be developed to keep track of all firearms, ammunition distribution, and collection. The supervisor should be an individual who has passed the certification program and who possibly has prior law enforcement experience. A firearms supervisor should be assigned to each shift and/or just work alternate shifts on a regular basis. If one firearms supervisor is selected, then a backup supervisor should be considered as well.

Use of force policy

Obviously if firearm use is added to the healthcare protection envelope, it's imperative that suitable use of force guidelines is enacted. Questions to be considered include:

- state and municipal law requirements
- type and amount of force to be used
- whether aerosols or tasers will be allowed
- training curriculum requirements
- firearm type, distribution, storage, ammunition type, training requirements, instructor availability

The role of robotics and drones

In a 2016 book by Robert J. Gordon a professor in social sciences at Northwestern University[3], speaks of the possible use of robots in a wide variety of applications outside of manufacturing, and warehousing sectors including supermarkets, doctor and dentist offices and hospitals. According to 11/14/2019 article in The Verge: by James Vincent - Security robots are mobile surveillance devices, not human replacements[4] states that security robots are slowly becoming a more common sight in malls, and public spaces.

Moreover, the author goes on to mention that these *friendly* robots are collecting far more data than humans could! Obviously, robotics is becoming a bigger and bigger part of the protection landscape and most likely will play a much broader role in the years to come. It would be wise for security executives to put this new up and coming protection strategy on their radar screens.

In addition to using robotics, security executives need to network with local law enforcement agencies about remote drone surveillance usages.

According to an article by Curt Fleming Remote drone dispatch: law enforcement's future[5] https//www.policechiefmagazine.org/remote-drone-dispatch/, 347 law enforcement agencies in 43 U.S. states are using unmanned aerial vehicle technology (drones) to assist in a wide variety of protection-related applications including search and rescue, traffic control, surveillance crowd monitoring, and active shooter investigations. Ongoing synergism is especially important herein because hospitals play an extremely active role in terrorism-related occurrences helping to treat the injured both during and after catastrophic occurrences.

Cost / benefit considerations

As with all security enhancement endeavors, cost is always a major factor. Once the security scope of work is completed, it is time to consider preparing a cost-benefit study to compare intervention value vs. enhancement costs. This analysis should consider both direct and indirect costs and benefits. Direct costs often include financial and operational costs associated with implementing proposed programmatic initiatives, and the indirect costs often involve productivity, business disruption, management-related diversion, loss of reputation and/or brand value costs. Once the assessment is concluded, it's time for a rigorous benefit analysis. One of the most effective methods of analyzing the degree of crime-risk exposure is to sub-divide risk exposures into "low" – "medium" and "high" risk categories. It is through this analytic process that the amplitude of various risk exposures is valuated. The International Association for Healthcare Security and Safety (IAHSS) has published a set of basic guidelines you should follow. Included in these guidelines is an outline for the development and implementation of a healthcare risk assessment. The IAHSS guidelines state: "Security Risk Assessments will be conducted on a regular and on-going basis. The objective of the Security Risk Assessment is to identify healthcare facility assets, threats and vulnerabilities, and promulgate appropriate mitigation strategies to better protect the institution. Moreover, the Association offers the following advice: "Establish reasonable and responsible security controls and processes that protect people, property, systems, equipment and other assets while restricting access where appropriate!

Applying metrics to validate expenditures

Metrics is a management tool for measuring performance. Using metrics is an effective method of demonstrating security-related programmatic effectiveness and expenditure justification. The authors have written a trilogy of articles[6] and a book[2] highlighting several metric applications. Utilizing metrics helps the security executive speak the language that CFOs (bean-counters) understand. Moreover, using metrics is an extremely beneficial strategy to employ when seeking additional security enhancement dollars and/or to justify programmatic expenditures.

Conclusion

One lesson to be learned from today's healthcare challenges: *"if one is afraid to take chances – one can never get answers"*. Seeing that the security-camera is watching, it is always a good thing to be the *'first to tomorrow'* and begin embracing and experimenting with new security fixes. The techniques and technologies mentioned herein are only the tip of the iceberg; but may be a good fit for your organization.

Finding the right suit of armor to snugly fit your institution's wardrobe is not always an easy task, but a wise security administrator has many advisors, both internal and external, to help him or her find the right suit of protection attire for their institution's wardrobe!

References

1. Luizzo, A. (2018) March/April). The security survey: an investigative tool. *PI Magazine, issue 156,* 28-30.
   Luizzo, A. (2018) March/April). The security survey: an investigative tool – part II. *PI Magazine issue,* 159, 22-25.
2. Scaglione, B. (2019) Security management for healthcare: proactive event prevention and effective resolution. *N.Y. Rutledge, Taylor & Francis Group. Publications*
3. Robert Gordon. (2016) Rise and fall of American growth: U.S. Standard of Living Since the Civil War: *The Princeton University Press*
4. Vincent J. (2019) Security robots are mobile surveillance devices, not human replacements. *The Verge - https://www..theverge.com/2019/11/14/20964584/knightscope-security-robot-guards-surveillance-devices-facial-recognition-numberplate-mobile-phone*
5. Fleming, C. (2019) Remote drone dispatch: law enforcements future? *IACP Police Chief Magazine – https//www.policechiefmagazine.org/remote-drone-dispatch/*.
6. Luizzo, A. & Scaglione B. (2015) An alternative view in the development of security metrics. *Journal of Healthcare Protection Management. 31, 98-104.*
   Luizzo, A. & Scaglione B. (2016) Resources available for applying metrics in security and safety programming. *Journal of Healthcare Protection Management. 32, 27-33.*
   Luizzo, A. & Scaglione B. (2017) Applying metrics to 21st century healthcare security. *Journal of Healthcare Protection Management. 33, 7-13.*

Suggested readings

Luizzo, A. & Scaglione B. (2007) Training security officers to recognize the perils of weapons of mass destruction and pandemic flu contaminates. *Journal of Healthcare Protection Management 23, 1-9.*

Luizzo, A. & Scaglione B. (2017) Aspects of crime and violence avoidance. *Journal of Healthcare Protection Management 33, 21-30.*

Luizzo, A. & Scaglione B. (2019) Training security officers to recognize the perils of weapons of mass exposure contaminates – part II. *Journal of Healthcare Protection Management 35, 32-39.*

Chapter 2

Security Management

The Hidden Cost of Downsizing: Where Loyalty Dies, Fraud Grows

George Van Nostrand and Anthony Luizzo

Brian got the call no one wants at about 4:30 p.m. on a quiet Friday afternoon.

Lately, business has been slow at the firm, but the current month was showing a slight increase in sales. But then Jerry, his friend in the Human Resources Department, called to say that the rumors were true: the company would be laying off another 1,000 employees. Brian spread the word and the tension level in the office rose abruptly.

Who was on the list this time? This would be the fourth cutback in three years, Brian had seen many longtime friends and associates pack up their belongings. They would hear the hollow assurances of "you'll be back before you know it." But no one ever came back. The cutbacks, now infamously known as "downsizing," became permanent paths to obscurity.

Brian wondered if he would be the next to bear the humiliation of saying good-bye, or the embarrassment again of remaining behind with all the inherent insecurities and questions.

The characters and the company are fictitious, but the scenario is very real. In the last decade or so of downsizing, thousands have experienced the uncertainties, the remorse, the despair, and the desire to seek retribution. Emotions brought about by the wholesale firing sometimes can cause the remaining (and past) employees to engage in fraudulent behavior.

Relationship Between Downsizing and Fraud

There appears to be at least two well-established movements affecting business in the late 1990's. There is a clear social price being paid by downsized workers, and at the same time there is a significant increase in fraud incidents among American business entities. Is there a cause-and-effect relationship between these two seemingly unrelated predicaments? No one definitively knows. Despite significant and compelling anecdotal evidence establishing a link between fraud and downsizing, no reliable authority has established a definable bond. The U.S. Department of

---

From *The White Paper* Association of Certified Fraud Examiners. pp. 23–25 – 34–36. September/October 1996.

DOI: 10.4324/9781003215851-2

24 ■ *Healthcare Security*

Labor, Bureau of Labor Statistics, does not maintain any data regarding this topic. The FBI does not subdivide its statistical data for this relationship. The General Accounting Office has not been given the task of studying fraud and downsizing. Though there is little hard data yet, we can analyze the reasons for downsizing.

Downsizing: The Rationale

Downsizing has been a part of business (at least in the United States) since the late 1980s. If you discuss the subject with CEOs of major and mid-sized companies, you will hear a variety of reasons and circumstances that they say mandated reducing staffs: increasing profits, creating a "lean-and-mean" organization, streamlining to be more competitive, eliminating unprofitable aspects, and trimming the "fat." In the article, "corporate Killers," in the Feb. 4, 1996, issue of *Newsweek*, four CEOs said they had no choice but to lay off workers.

And after Robert Allen, CEO of AT&T, announced the layoff of 40,000 employees last January, he said, "Our reduction and other actions are absolutely essential if our businesses are to be competitive." (*Mother Jones*, July-August 1996, "The Wages of Downsizing," by Alan Downs) Downsizing might or might now achieve the desired results but the human costs are always high.

Many economists view downsizing as a necessary correction in the inevitable ups and downs of the normal business cycle. One theory proposes that a company will again hire many of the laid-off workers when it goes through a permanent upturn in economic activity. Social theorists, however, see this phenomenon differently. According to some sociologists, downsizing is a permanent change in the way business conducts its affairs and might even mark a new way that employees view their place in the work force.

Whether the economists or sociologists prove to be right, it appears that business has broken the "social contract" between it and the individual. From the turn of the 20th century to the late 1980s in the United States, there was an unwritten and unspoken "contract" between workers and management. This contract generally recognized that if a worker has a good day's effort consistently and didn't violate any major rules of the company, permanent employment – while not guaranteed – was assured. There were exceptions but to many workers and managers, loyalty to "the company" was an important part of their identities. To say that you were with IBM or Merrill Lynch or McDonnell-Douglas implied that your employment status would remain static throughout your career. The company became more than a source of income. It defined a lifestyle that was a source of pride among its employees.

The contract worked both ways. A stable work force was as much of a benefit to the company as a secure job tenure was to the worker. On-the-job experience was a valued commodity. Training costs were low and searches for replacement employees were rare. Loyalty translated into a concern for the company and ultimately for the quality of its product and service. Now, this all seems paternalistic, but it provided a stable basis for company-employee relationships for many years. Because of downsizing, few companies can claim the kind of loyalty among their employees that was common only ten years ago. The "family" spirit is dead; now company loyalty appears to begin and end with the paycheck.

In the July 1996 issue of *Management Review*, a publication of the American Management Association, Senior Editor Barbara Ettorre wrote that "the new employment contract – the implied relationship between workers and employers – has supplanted the old assumption of lifetime employment. The new implication is that workers will manage their own careers while companies will make them employable in the long run." However, T. Quinn Spitzer, CEO, of the international consulting firm, Kepner-Tregoe, Inc., said in the same article, "there is no social contact. The companies that always had one still do; the companies that never had one are more inclined to talk about it" [1]

AMA's 1996 survey on downsizing showed only 17.2 percent of downsizing firms provided any sort of retaining for displaces workers from July of 1995 to June of 1996. It also shows that other forms of assistance such as outplacement, extended severance pay, and extended health benefits have declined from 1994 to 1996.

What began as a cost-cutting measure now has become a social phenomenon. Nearly half of U.S. businesses reduced their work force during the last decade, according to the Department of Labor (*Newsweek,* March 6, 1995, p. 60)

Lowell E. Hofmann, president of the National Organization of Downsized Employees (NODE), estimates that between January 1991 and April 1994, approximately 2.5 million Americans lost their jobs through downsizing. Hofmann, a dismissed software planner, is among the more that 100,000 people who have been dismissed from IBM since it began downsizing.

A recent *New York Times* survey said that 72 percent of working Americans either had been downsized or had a relative or friend who had been. The same survey indicated that of those full-time workers who lost jobs in 1991 or 1992, only 35 percent had found full-time employment at comparable pay by January 1994. The other 65 percent took jobs at lower pay, were working part time, or were still unemployed.

In 1995, Mahiuddin Laskar of the MBA program at the University of North Florida in Jacksonville, Fla., prepared "A Review of the History and Results of Downsizing."

In his report, he cited the AMA's downsizing survey that found between one-third and one-half of medium- and large-sized firms in the United States had downsized every year since 1988.

Another AMA survey, Laskar says, showed that only 6 percent of companies cut jobs due to short-term business downturns. On the other hand, 44 percent laid off workers in anticipation of an economic downturn. The second reason, with responses at 35 percent, was to make better utilization of staff. The third reason, at 20 percent, was due to automation or other new technology, and the fourth, at 19 percent, was to transfer work to other plants or abroad.

Moving Toward Fraud

The sociological theory of latitudes of acceptance and rejection helps explain how prevailing attitudes are changed by the increase in either positive or negative stimulation. In this theory, each person has his own range of reactions to any situation. A typical employee of a large corporation might begin his career with an attitudinal range that easily includes acceptance of change if it can be shown to benefit the company and ultimately himself. This is called latitude of acceptance.

(Carl I. Hoveland, the late Yale University psychologist, devised the original theory of the latitude of attitudinal change in 1961. Originally published as an explanation of changes in political attitudes, Hoveland, along with social scientist Muzafer Sherif, published a work, "Social Judgment: Assimilation and Contrast Effects in communication and Attitudinal Change." Later, this concept was used to explain a variety of social phenomena dealing with changing attitudes.)

---

*Reprinted by permission of the publisher, from MANAGEMENT REVIEW JULY 1996 ©1996. American Management Association, New York. All rights reserved

26 ■ *Healthcare Security*

The overall scale of reactions to changes varies from ready acceptance to violent reprisal against the company and its officers. Any idea of hurting the company by committing a fraud against it is far down the line of acceptable behavior. This is called latitude of rejection.

However, an employee's range of acceptable attitudes changes when friends are discharged. The employee's attitudes will continue to erode when the company gives him extra duties because of layoffs. And if the employee perceives that management is lying then he will take another important step toward anti-company actions.

As downsizing continues to edge closer to this employee his range of attitudes changes significantly. What he once viewed as unacceptable behavior might now look quite acceptable. His attitude of cooperation might have been replaced by one of the perceived self-survival. The idea of committing a fraud, especially if there are weak internal controls and large profits to be made, now might become a plan. Just one more stimulus added to all the other events might be enough to tip the fragile balance and turn a trusted, loyal employee into an embezzler. Despite the obvious significance of the downsizing phenomena, few studies have been conducted on the effects of this labor force reduction on the lives of displaced workers.

However, Laskar cutes Cole (1995), who lists problems associated with job loss from traditional downsizing: (1) loss of personal relationships between employees and customers, (2) destruction of employee and customer trust and loyalty, (3) disruption of smooth, predictable routines in the firm, (4) increase in employee reliance on rules, (5) loss of cross-unit knowledge of how to respond to non-routine occurrences in the firm, (7) decrease in documentation and concomitant reduction in sharing of information about changes, (8) loss of employee productivity, and (9) loss of a common organizational culture.

Alan Downs, a self-professed former corporate "hit man" and author on downsizing, wrote in the July-August 1996 issue of *Mother Jones* that he discovered what *really* happens after a layoff. "Morale hits bottom. Lines of communication within the company shatter. Productivity ebbs while high-prices consultants try to patch the business back together…" Down said. "During the past decade, studies have shown a mass layoff often does not help a company, and, at worst, it can be the deathblow to a faltering enterprise. The lost time, waning productivity, and devastated morale create hidden costs, which can far outweigh the usual cost-savings predicted from a layoff."

Who Stays, Who Goes, and Why?

Historically, when a company experiences a reduction in staff, the first areas to be affected are those that do not directly increase the sales of "revenue enhancement" aspects of company operations. The most likely places for cutbacks are security, purchasing, management information systems, personnel, and payroll. Generally, sales positions and marketing functions are spared staff reductions if possible. The theory is that the company will try to cut back on expenses (employee salaries and benefits) without putting a damper on the company's ability to market its products or services.

Item: A defense contractor in California manufactured parts for the U.S. Navy's F-14A fighter aircraft. Although the company was profitable, management decided on a cutback of personnel to enhance its short-term profits. Approximately 85 people lost their jobs during this period. Among the reduced areas was the Quality Control Division. This area, the final stage of manufacturing process, was responsible for the inspection and certification of finished aircraft parts.

Once a part was inspected and certified as being in line with specifications, it was shipped and billed to the Navy. The number of people in the area had been cut in half, from 10 inspectors to

Security Management ■ 27

five. One of the five remaining inspectors continually complained to his fellow workers about the increased workload shouldered by him and others. After a period, the Navy inspectors, who were responsible for accepting the finished product, noticed manufacturing defects that any routine inspection should have caught. Upon further investigation, it was determined that many of the parts that had not been accepted had been certified by the same inspector. Based on handwriting comparisons and extensive interviews, the Naval Investigate Service determined that the complaining inspector had been certifying many of the aircraft parts and charging the Navy for the parts that had not been inspected. He had "pencil whipped" the inspection reports without ever looking at the parts. The Navy, of course, was charged for a service that was not performed.

This government contracts fraud had the potential for costing the U.S. government several hundreds of thousands of dollars and risking the lives of Navy pilots. The perpetrator was charged with fraud against the government and was convicted in U.S. district court. The company paid a substantial fine and the former inspector was sentenced to six months in custody and three years' probation. Ironically, the areas where cutbacks are most likely to occur are those in which fraud is either the most prevalent or where fraud protection is practiced. The fraud examination unit or the security departments are, of course, the first lines of defense against fraud. Traditionally, employees of security departments devote most of their time and budget to the physical aspects of security (locks, guards, fences, etc.). However, many modern well-trained security directors are also CFEs, and are aware of the potential for the misappropriation of company assets. Any good security director or head of a fraud examination unit will be intimately aware of the operations and personnel of his company. In many companies, employees are encouraged to entrust confidential information to the company security department. Over time, the bond of trust should mature; the employees eventually might use the department as an early warning system for serious fraud.

To expect a corporate security officer to be able to detect and solve major fraud cases is unrealistic. However, in today's modern corporation, a security director should be trained to spot the early symptoms of a fraud and be able to make a recommendation to senior management on how to examine the situation. If a company downsizes the security department or fraud examination unit is might unwittingly expose itself to greater incident of theft and white-collar crime. The purchasing department of a company is entrusted with the responsibility of spending company funds wisely and obtaining maximum value. Most incidents of inside fraud come from, or are committed with, the complicity of the purchasing department. False invoices, phantom vendors, and kickback schemes are the three most common frauds that originate in the purchasing department. If a company chooses to downsize its purchasing staff it will reduce its ability to perform logical checks, maintain separation of duties, and invite major fraud.

Management information systems (MIS) have become an indispensable function of most companies because there are few business functions that do not involve computers. With all that information entrusted to a few people, the prospects for information theft and other frauds are excellent. And yet this is often one of the first departments to be downsized.

Top management frequently makes the incorrect assumption that if security systems are installed with computer programs, all worries of maintaining sensitive information are dissipated. However, should a fraudster successfully penetrate MIS defenses all operations will be compromised. This department is a poor target for staff reductions that have not been thoroughly analyzed.

Item: A major telecommunications firm located in the industrial Midwest announced a reduction in force of 700 workers. Although all aspects of the company were involved, this reduction primarily affected production line labor and mid-level management. Previously, the company laid off 250 workers and none of them were hired again. In a press release, the company said the latest

28 ■ *Healthcare Security*

round of downsizing would streamline the overall operations of the company and position it for anticipated technological changes. Many of the dismissed workers suspected this statement was a lie. The company cut many employees from the management information systems department including Steve, one of the managers and a nine-year veteran of the company. He had been divorced and remarried four years previously.

He was doing his best to keep up with alimony and child support payments and the financial demands of his new family. Since the job market in general was soft during this period and other companies were not hiring people with his specialty, he was left with few options. Steve was an accomplished computer programmer and part-time hacker. He began to investigate access codes and methods of invading the accounting records of his former employer. With time on his hands and no residual loyalty to his former employer, he was able to devote a great deal of time to his "project." After two months of trial and error, he succeeded in piercing the shield of his former employer's computer security system.

His illegal access to the accounting systems soon developed into a scheme to divert funds to a company that he had set up specifically to receive these payments. He was able to siphon off funds estimated at $20,000 per month from accounts receivables. Of course, the host company failed to reconcile its paid receivable with cash accounts and bank statements and did not detect his fraud for several years. Eventually, Steve actually "caught himself." His business was successful, and he took in a partner. Unfortunately, the partner could not remain quiet and spoke freely about the scheme in a casual conversation overheard by an employee of the defrauded telecommunications company. Federal authorities were alerted, an investigation was conducted, arrests were made, and the former employee-turned-entrepreneur was convicted of fraud by wire. Steve is serving a two-year prison sentence in federal prison and has been ordered to pay restitution. The human resources and payroll departments are additional functions is which reduced staffing (and therefore lessened degrees of diligence) could result in exposure to substantial frauds.

The creation of ghost employees, petty cash defalcations, theft of services, and other forms of employee embezzlement are common frauds that originate from these two departments. The role of the human resources department as a safeguard against dishonest employees cannot be overemphasized. Managers should view this department as the front door of the business that should not be unguarded. Any business that does not thoroughly inspect the backgrounds of its prospective employees is living on borrowed time.

'Good' Downsizing, Less Fraud

Everyone understands that in today's competitive environment, business must run as efficiently as possible. Sometimes this means a business must reduce its work force. But management must know the potential risks of downsizing. Executives must remain alert to the human toll that is being exacted by personnel reductions. Corporate fraud is already a substantial problem.

Downsizing and fraud could be a highly combustible mixture facing corporate leaders who not only do not have the tools to combat the potential threat but in most cases are not even aware of the problem. CFEs are uniquely equipped to advise management of the negatives of downsizing and how to shape the layoff policies to minimize the possibilities of ensuing fraud. If a company cannot immediately institute preventive measures, executives should at least try not to aggravate the problem. They should dismiss employees with tact and a feeling for the human loss. It takes only a little effort to put a compassionate face on downsizing and potentially save millions of dollars from rampant frauds committed by disloyal workers.

Stretching the Security Dollar

Anthony Luizzo

Stretching the security dollar is both an art and a science. The art lies in the security executive's ability to solve protection problems utilizing existing resources. The science lies in the executive's ability to architect protection strategy that meets corporate requisites and industry benchmarks.

Today's Economic Climate

In today's climate of budget shortfalls and shrinking dollars, protection executives would be wise to begin seeking out less expensive solutions to security problems. The trick is knowing where to find this treasure trove of wisdom.

Coping with the Downsizing of Security Programs

As a result of today's fiscal situation, many security programs are being measurably downsized. Some more forward-thinking executives have come to realize that one key to enlarging the protection staff may lie in marshaling support from non-security personnel. Enlisting the assistance of each corporate employee into the protection mosaic, may be the most trenchant approach to squeezing additional security out of the shrinking dollar. The key to this endeavor lies in the executive's ability to bring top management up to speed on the accrual of benefits to such a program.

Strategies to Consider

Several advances that could be put forward include:

- The inauguration of a "security advocate" program to link various departments and security into a two-way pipeline for receiving and disseminating security information.
- The formulation of an in-house crime prevention capability to focus on "proactive" crime control approaches.
- The development of a tailored series of security awareness programs to circulate timely information on personal safety strategies, assets protection measures and general crime prevention techniques.
- The establishment of property marking programs to safeguard corporate assets.
- The institution of employee incentive to thwart internal thievery.
- The preparation and distribution of a daily information bulletin highlighting security deficiencies, crime trends, and hazardous conditions.
- Promoting architectural modification programs such as: closing-off crime prone cul-de-sacs, relocating business operations from "low to high" risk areas to intensify traffic flow, and removing and/or converting existing benches in lobbies/waiting areas to discourage horizontal positioning.

From *The Journal of Healthcare Protection Management*. (7):2, pp. 100–102. Summer 1991.

- Encourage management to install security mirrors in vulnerable locations (stairwells, elevators, etc.), to retrofit critical access portals that rely on privacy locksets mechanisms, and to install adequate security signage in appropriate locations.
- Encourage management to alert department heads to remove calendars, posters, and other paraphernalia from glass doors and partitions.
- Encourage management to computerize visitor/vendor pass policies so that a "red flag" capability is available to alert security of potential problems.
- Encourage management to involve the security department in the corporation's pre-employment screening process.
- The institution of a quality assurance initiative to review security procedures, policies, and technologies to ensure efficiency.
- The institution of a joint program with the facility's management department to periodically review the operation of various security-related systems such as: lighting fixtures, locking systems, automatic door closures, and other security systems and devices.

Conclusion

These and other strategies help deepen and strengthen existing security by fostering the philosophy that security is everyone's responsibility. Oftentimes, it is this skillful display of resourcefulness that influences on approving appropriations for more expensive high-tech systems. Moreover, your inventive ability to stretch the shrinking security dollar will distinguish your operation as an asset, not a liability.

Investigating in a New Environment

George Van Nostrand and Anthony Luizzo

While domestic political issues are getting the most media attention, changes occurring internationally are of equal, or perhaps greater, significance for American companies. Trade barriers are coming down, making international markets more accessible. In response, even corporations once limited to domestic business ventures are answering the siren song of global business. But companies entering these markets must traverse a markedly different, and sometimes dangerous, cultural, and legal landscape. Security directors can play a key role in helping their organizations maneuver safely over this unfamiliar terrain. Experience in the United States has clearly demonstrated the relationship between good security and company profits. Security also plays a crucial role in international business, particularly about investigations of potential locations or investments. Many issues that are taken for granted in domestic investigations must be considered, and everything must be addressed in the context of the country's political, legal, and cultural climate.

Travel planning

A company should begin by checking with one or more of the following U.S. agencies before visiting or setting up investigations in other countries:

- U.S. Department of State (USDS). USDS ensures that passports are current and valid for all countries not off limits to U.S. citizens. (Travel to North Korea, Iraq, and Cuba is currently prohibited.) Some countries require a special visa for a business visit. Other countries require only routine proof of identity such as a birth certificate. USDS passport offices provide this information and assist in obtaining the proper documents.

  USDS also provides fact sheets on 197 countries throughout the world. These fact sheets furnish information such as political stability, commercial activity, and monetary strength. They also include information on local topics such as crime. U.S. embassies and consulates, staffed by experts from the USDS, can provide other useful information to travelers.

  U.S. embassies are always located in the capital city of a particular nation, and consulates are in large urban areas. If an investigation entails travel elsewhere in the country, the appropriate embassy or consulate personnel should be advised of the staff's travel schedule.
- U.S. Department of Health and Human Services (HHS). This agency determines whether travel to countries requires immunization. Although many serious communicable diseases have been eradicated, traveling to parts of Africa, South America, or South Asia, for example, may require vaccinations. The HHS's Centers for Disease Control and Prevention in Atlanta, Georgia, may be contacted (404/332-4555) for current information about required immunizations. This office also publishes a book entitled *Health Information for International Travel*, which contains a great deal of valuable information. Single copies are free.
- U.S. Department of Commerce. Along with the USDS, the Department of Commerce publishes information to alert U.S. citizens to areas of the world that, although not prohibited,

---

From *Security Management Magazine* A Publication of The American Society for Industrial Security. June 1995.

32 ■ *Healthcare Security*

may be dangerous to U.S. travelers. Some countries in the Middle East, for example, fall into this category when tensions in that region cause concern. These alerts, which describe the potential problem and discuss the reasons for the danger, are revised as events warrant.

Legal Systems

Every country has its own legal system, which affects all aspects of the justice process, including investigations. These systems vary greatly from country to country. Permissible investigative approaches in Mexico, for example, may be prohibited in France. Protections that are taken for granted in the United States, including laws pertaining to illegal search and seizure, self-incrimination (Miranda warnings), and illegal imprisonment (through writs of habeas corpus) are limited, if not unknown, in many foreign countries. The major exception to this rule is the United Kingdom. The U.S. legal system, of course, is an outgrowth of the English common law system, and many of the principles of the American justice system are based on the British model. Over the years, differences between English and American rules of procedure have developed, but most investigators from the United States would understand English rules and be able to work in Commonwealth of Nations countries with relatively little adjustment in methodology. In countries with different traditions, however, the security director or whoever is conducting the investigation must first learn the basics of the legal system.

The first rule in conducting a foreign investigation, therefore, is to research the legal system, of the country. It is not necessary to become an expert in the justice system of the host country. But a basic understanding of police procedures is invaluable to a successful operation.

Culture

Although many technical skills are involved in the investigative process, investigations are fundamentally about personal interaction. This premise leads to the second rule of international investigations: understand some of the host culture and try to speak, even on a rudimentary level, the language of the host country. Every investigation includes an interpersonal aspect that cannot be overlooked. Even in some of the most technical fraud audit investigations, the social skills of the investigator determine the outcome of the probe. For instance, those planning to investigate in India have the advantage of a legal system developed from the British model, but it is important to understand the attitude of the Indian people toward the United States, Britain, and its populous and powerful neighbor, Pakistan. If one hopes to enlist the cooperation of foreign nationals, he or she must be careful not to offend those who may be essential to success.

When an investigator plans to conduct an inquiry in a foreign land, he or she should read as much current material as possible about the host country. At a minimum, investigators should try to read available newspapers, magazines, and periodicals, including American, local, and international publications. *The Economist* is a particularly useful source on economic, political, and social issues facing countries around the globe.

The security professional does not need to study history books. Much of that material will not be readily useful, and most good publications will set a current story within a larger historical context anyway. For example, in Mexico it may be helpful to know who Zapata was, but it is far more critical to understand current issues such as Mexico's present economic crisis and political climate. Language is, of course, especially important. Poor communication can undermine an entire investigation. English is widely understood, but the globalization of business is making it increasingly important for U.S. professionals to communicate in languages other than English. If the investigator cannot communicate in at least one foreign language, he or she should consider self-study. Books, audio tapes, video tapes, adult education courses, educational television programs, and many other methods can be used to enhance language ability. One need not become fluent in the country's language if a willingness to communicate in the native tongue comes across. Not only will this effort facilitate communications, but it will also be interpreted as a show of respect for the host culture and language. This show of respect, particularly in Latin America, can assist an inquiry on many levels.

Subcontractors

Without the appropriate license or registration, conducting an independent investigation in a foreign country, either as a contract investigator or as a representative of a U.S. company, is usually prohibited. The image of a U.S. investigator or police officers freely doing investigations in a foreign county is the stuff of Hollywood fantasy. The reality is sovereign nations will not allow foreigners to roam their country investigating their citizens. Doing so invites the wrath of both the host country and the State Department. Investigators unaware of this restriction may find themselves in a local jail cell. One option is to hire a local official under whose name and authority the investigator may conduct an inquiry. This person can be an attorney, government official, local police officer, or some other recognized authority figure.

Mary private investigators in the United States take another approach. They employ subcontractors to conduct investigations for them. The investigator should look for someone who has experience in the region, speaks the language, and has reliable contacts. Even with the best subcontractors, however, confidentiality is difficult to maintain in foreign countries, particularly in sparsely populated areas. In such places, it becomes almost impossible to prevent the locals from discovering that an American is in town asking questions. One way the American investigator can avoid attracting attention is by allowing the subcontractor to conduct the entire investigation. While surrendering some control, this move will ultimately enhance confidentiality.

Firearms

Bringing a firearm to a foreign county could invite trouble. As most U.S. citizens know, the possession of firearms aboard any U.S. airline is a felony (49 USC § 1472 L). Although the law varies from country to country, it is usually a safe practice not to carry any firearms into or in a foreign country. The countries that permit foreign nationals to possess weapons do so only after detailed questioning. Such questions will needlessly highlight the investigator and the mission.

If it is necessary to travel to an area where a firearm is essential – such as some interior areas of Colombia, Peru, and Bolivia – arrangements can sometimes be made with a local contact (especially a local police officer) to borrow a handgun.

Although the authorities will restrict use of the weapon, the investigator will be able to protect him or herself while staying within the bounds of the locality's law and custom.

34 ■ *Healthcare Security*

Local officials

In most cases, the international investigator should contact the local police department on arrival or soon thereafter to discuss the company's purpose within that jurisdiction. It is inadvisable to operate clandestinely for exceptionally long in most foreign countries. Law enforcement personnel will not be reluctant to ask investigators to identify themselves and explain their presence. It does not pay to attempt to mislead or deceive these officials. Many inexperienced investigators have been embarrassed and even detained for not clearly stating their purpose and the company's intention. For example, one young investigator was in Mexico trying to locate a witness in a product tampering case. While driving through the small town of El Rosario, about 250 miles south of Tijuana, the investigator became involved in a minor traffic accident. None of the locals spoke English, and the investigator's inability to communicate with the other driver attracted the local police. When he was questioned by the officer, the investigator refused to disclose the purpose of his visit, seeking to uphold the confidentiality demanded by his employer. Dissatisfied by the investigator's responses, the police placed him in the local lockup. The investigator ended up spending five days in the cell before a consulate officer could obtain his release. This situation could have been avoided had the investigator been tactful and forthright. In most cases, the local constabulary should be one of the first stops in any city or town in the investigative process. The investigator should brief the client about his or her intention to contact local law enforcement and explain the reasons why. Clients who are reluctant to make this contact should be told that failure to do so many results in embarrassment for the company. If handled with the proper tact and decorum, contact with the appropriate officials can pay considerable dividends. Law enforcement officials in many communities virtually own their town and province. Witnesses, persons of interest, documents, books, and a variety of useful information can be promptly identified and located. In fact, the entire investigative process can be streamlined using law enforcement's contacts.

Documentary evidence

If the purpose of the inquiry is to obtain documents, it is important to obtain certified copies of these documents. This is an important aspect of domestic investigations, but even more so in foreign investigations. Some countries may be reluctant to have their officials testify in the United States about the documentation and maintenance of official records. Obtaining certified copies that are likely to be admissible in U.S. courts will probably render the official's testimony unnecessary. Just in case any documents need to be verified, or additional documents become necessary, it is a good idea to record all information about document sources. Such information should include the name, title, address, phone, and fax number of all officials involved in the preparation, recording, or issuance of the documents; contact information for the officials' supervisors; and the days and times of operation of offices. Any information of arguable value should be recorded, lest the investigator must return for it or try to obtain it by other means.

Many of the same basic investigative skills used in domestic investigations can be applied to overseas investigations. But it would be a grave error to assume that *modus operandi* that work in the United States will yield results in other lands.

The many factors that distinguish each country or region must be considered, making investigation a unique and demanding task for any given area. The extra preparation is worthwhile and necessary. Global business is booming. Security professionals must also be prepared to enter this new and challenging arena.

---

*Reprinted with permission: Security Management Magazine

Shoplifter Profiles and Tips on How They Steal

Anthony Luizzo

In the court of security management opinion, experts hypothesize that there are three types of shoplifters:

1. The Amateur
2. The Professional
3. The Drug Addict

The Amateur Shoplifter

It is widely believed in security circles that most shoplifters are amateurs and approximately half are minors, many of whom steal for "kicks" or because of peer pressure. These young people often travel through retail establishments in packs, hoping that their numbers will both confuse and intimidate store management. Too often, it does. Moreover, retailers report that most adults who shoplift are women, frequently 'average' housewives who would hardly arouse suspicion. Many of these offenders often blame their crimes on an uncontrollable—and often unexplainable—impulse.

The Professional Shoplifter

The professional shoplifter is a careful meticulous criminal who knows all the tricks of the trade. They do not commit these crimes on impulse—they plan their crimes down to the minutest detail. Oftentimes carefully casing stores they are planning to loot looking for security cameras, store detectives and escape conduits. Moreover, these miscreants always look for the 'easy mark' and tend to steer clear of stores that have instituted theft control programs. As a matter of course, these thieves are harder to detect, but they can be deterred.

The Drug Addict Shoplifter

This predator is by far the most dangerous of all shoplifters. He or she is often 'wired' on drugs and is out to get cash to support the habit. They usually do not plan their crimes and rarely give any thought to avoiding physical contact. Over the years, many retailers have learned to immediately call local police to deal with these walking time bombs.

How Do Shoplifters Ply Their Trade?

They say that where there is a will, there is a way.

From *Internal Auditing Report* Warren, Gorham & Lamont / RIA Group (Reuters) Thomson Publications. November 2000 – openlibrary@archive.com

36 ■ *Healthcare Security*

Unfortunately, human ingenuity can be brought to bear on tasks as different as walking on the moon and walking out of a store with expensive merchandise. Shoplifters have devised a variety of theft methods—some obvious, some ingenious, however, all-damaging to a firm's bottom line.

Some of the more common shoplifting methods include:

- Palming. The shoplifter merely carries a purloined item out in the palm of the hand, often while concealing it with another object, such as a newspaper or umbrella.
- Bagging. The shoplifter enters the store carrying a bag of some kind—a shopping bag, large purse, briefcase, knitting bag, or diaper bag—and leaves with more than he or she entered with.
- Designer Shoplifting Clothing. Some shoplifters wear special clothing to conceal merchandise—outer garments with 'slits' or 'vents' in the pockets, pants and skirts with elastic expandable waistbands, oversized baggy ski hats, or clothing with pins or hooks sewn into the clothing to conceal merchandise
- The Try-On Method. The shoplifter enters a dressing room to try on several items and casually leaves with one or more concealed items under his or her clothing.
- The Grab and Run Method. A crude but often effective method. The thief finds an unattended section of the store, usually near an exit, grabs several items and beats a path for the door.
- The Team Approach. These shoplifters work in teams, using a variant of the 'Hey, look over there' method of swiping. One person creates a disturbance to occupy the clerk's attention, while a partner steals the merchandise.

Despite the clever techniques and technologies employed by shoplifters, there are strategies that can shift the odds in the good guy's favor.

A cornucopia of strategies to thwart shoplifting might include:

- Check Your Bag at the Door Please. An obvious precaution that many storeowners choose not to follow due to the added labor costs or because they do not want to give the appearance of disturbing their customers. Over the past decade however, many retailers have come to realize that controlling shrinkage saves money whilst lowering prices and increasing sales.
- Prominently Posting Anti-Shoplifting Signage. Signage including the checking of shopping bags, the company's policy anent aggressive prosecution of offenders and the use of electronic camera surveillance to capture thieves sends a strong message to the would-be shoplifter to find another less aware store to ply his or her trade.
- Plan a Smart Store Layout. Retailers should realize that store layout is an important component in making the shoplifter's life difficult. The key is to keep sight lines open, so that would-be shoplifters have few hidden spaces in which to secretly ply their trade.

Effective store layout plans might include

- Keeping store windows free from obstructions.
- Ensuring that in-store displays do not impede visibility.
- Inverting clothes hangers so that shoplifters can only remove single items during 'grab and run thefts.
- Securing high priced items such as jewelry in locked display cases.
- Keeping large expensive items away from the flow of exiting traffic.
- Positioning display counters in broken, random sequences, rather than in one continuous aisle leading to the exit.

There are an endless number of ways in which a retailer can suffer at the hands of criminals. Every retailer is vulnerable, but none are helpless. There are countless ways to stop theft before it can wreak havoc on the company's bottom line. Shoplifting is a crime of opportunity; control the opportunity and you successfully control the crime.

Asking the Right Questions About Fire Prevention

Anthony Luizzo and Joseph Slattery

Fires caused by unsafe acts or conditions can be prevented through rigorous inspection and reporting.

Fire prevention management is one of the most important roles of a company's security department. This role often involves conducting regular inspections to uncover and correct fire-related risks and hazards. The security department must also advocate the participation of all employees in a fire prevention battalion, which is vital to the wellbeing of their company.

Security's Role in Fire Prevention Management

To ensure proper oversight of this important function, security administrators require special skills and certification. In New York City, for example, a fire safety director certificate from the New York City Fire Department's office of fire prevention is required for oversight of fire safety concerns in high-rise buildings. Security's role in fire protection management is to perform periodic inspections of the facilities. Some security companies design easy-to-use checklists for inspection purposes. These checklists should incorporate a check- and-mark format (i.e., a check mark to signify compliance and an x to signify noncompliance). The inspection form should also contain a section for after-action follow-up to ensure that enhancements are swiftly instituted. In addition, the form should leave space for the reporting operative to sign his or her name and should include a section for referring the report to other departments for further action.

The Fire Inspection Report

Many security departments have developed fire prevention inspection reports to capture risk and hazard data. The following checklist questionnaire is often used by security personnel to capture relevant information during building and grounds patrols:

- Are fire extinguishers properly charged?
- Are fire drills held in accordance with local fire department regulations?
- Are sprinkler heads free of paint obstruction?
- Are there at least 18 inches of open space beneath the sprinkler head?
- Are stairwells free of obstructions?
- Are fire exits clear and unobstructed?
- Are standpipe hoses and nozzles in good repair?
- Are emergency exit signs properly illuminated in accordance with local fire and building department regulations?
- Are fire pull boxes in good repair?
- Are fire exit doors equipped with self-opening panic locks?
- Are emergency lights installed and functional?

From *Internal Auditing Report* Warren, Gorham & Lamont / RIA Group (Reuters) Thomson Publications. June 2001 – openlibrary@archive.com

- Are maintenance storage facilities free of oily rags and flammable items?
- Are no smoking signs prominently posted?
- Are no smoking rules enforced?
- Are fire hydrants in good working order, and are vehicles prohibited from obstructing them?
- Are fire-department-approved safety disposal containers used?

Periodic Inspections

Depending on company requirements, inspections can be performed on a daily, weekly, or quarterly schedule. In many jurisdictions, however, the local fire department, the local buildings' department, or OSHA might require differing inspection requirements. It is advisable to confer with all regulatory entities for further guidance.

Targeted Inspection Areas

Beyond regular inspection areas, many security firms also require targeted inspections of specified entities, including company vehicles, fire extinguishers, areas inside of the building, and the building's perimeter. These targeted inspections are normally performed on a periodic schedule (e.g., daily, weekly, monthly, quarterly, semiannually, or annually) set by company management.

Four sample-targeted inspections areas include

- Vehicle inspections. These inspections include checking whether vehicles contain fire-extinguishing equipment, flammable liquid signage is appropriate, and vehicles are parked in non-restricted areas.
- Fire extinguisher inspections. These inspections include checking whether the extinguisher is damaged, the discharge hose is in good repair, and the extinguisher is appropriately charged.
- Building inspections. These inspections include checking whether housekeeping personnel comply with fire safety rules, there are violations of smoking rules, fire extinguishers are in required locations, sprinkler control valves and other fire suppression systems are in good working order, and fire lanes are unobstructed.
- Perimeter inspections. These inspections include checking whether fire hydrants are periodically flushed and are in good working order, fire alarm stations are operational, refuse canisters and dumpsters are located far from building facades and other vulnerable areas, and flammable items (e.g., paper and rags) are properly safeguarded.

Conclusion

The effectiveness of all fire prevention programs depends on the quality of the periodic inspections performed. Company management and employees rest easier knowing that the security department is keeping a watchful eye over fire-related risks and hazards. A well-designed fire prevention program works best when all company employees understand their role in the program and champion the effort.

Putting the Spotlight on Security

Anthony Luizzo

Since the terrorist attacks hit our shore on September 11, 2001, the security industry stepped-up to the plate and began making man-sized advances in protective technologies from locks to surveillance systems, to anti-theft devices used in retail stores keeping internal theft under control, in hospital maternity wards keeping babies safe, and on our borders performing immigration-related surveillance services. It's obviously great to have this new treasure-trove of protective technology at our fingertips, but this would be all for naught if we failed to get the security word out to the audience we protect and serve.

The ABCs of Security Networking

There are a few options that a security administrator can consider helping get security-related information into the hands of every employee in every department. First and foremost, it is extremely important that this information is provided in an easy-to-read newsletter. Some seasoned and knowledgeable administrators already publish an in-house monthly or quarterly newsletter filled with recently published articles and related items of interest; others contract with outside firms that specialize in preparing security-related periodicals for training purposes, and yet others simply have established an extensive in-house library for their internal protection staff to use. This latter option is good, save it fails to reach everyone in the institution who has a role in crime prevention and detection.

Getting Started

The most effective way forward is to begin by selecting an 'Editor" to oversee the project. Experience has shown that a good candidate to fill this position should be an operative who has some background in proactive security administration and understands that it is always advisable to try to uncover crime related deficiencies before they occur, rather than after the damage has been done. Half the battle is won when the right candidate is chosen to fill this position. The right candidate should possess above-average reading and cursive skills, as well as the ability to find timely and relevant periodicals for re-publication. He or she should be versed in copyright and re-publication essentials, be adept at networking with governmental and non-governmental agency representatives; and inter-agency managers and be proficient with computer and internet research capabilities. Moreover, aspirants ought to be capable of adjusting mindsets from the enforcement policing model to the more proactive model strongly associated with the community policing and private security protection paradigm.

From *The Journal of Healthcare Protection Management.* (31):1, pp. 111–116. 2015.

The Art and Science of Proactive Security Programming

One of the central reasons for using this philosophical protection model can be traced back to the early 1970s when major police and private security agencies rarely dedicated resources to preventing crime prior to its occurrence.

In the 1970s however, police agencies following the British policing model began formulating crime prevention / community policing programs via a Law Enforcement Assistance Administration grant awarded to the University of Louisville.

In the court of security opinion these efforts have helped by bringing crime rates down in many municipalities nationwide. Today most major police and private security entities have a crime prevention office within their respective agencies. The benefit in using trained crime prevention staff to spearhead the networking effort is that these specialists have been taught to develop a different mindset than their security brothers and are better able to apply both reactive and proactive crime control strategies simultaneously.

Delivering the Security Message

One of the most effective ways of getting security and safety information out to fellow security troops and institutional employees is via establishing a conduit to deliver the message. Establishing an in-house newsletter is an excellent method to accomplish this task. The proposed publication could include recent articles highlighted in industry journals and newsletters or other relevant information that is germane and relevant. The articles should be selected by the editor in consultation with the security administrator and should include industry-specific topics affecting the security and safety of the entity at hand. As an example, if the entity is a hospital, then the information should be relevant to healthcare security and safety. The newsletter could be disseminated on a monthly or quarterly schedule and periodical "alerts" should be forwarded as needed.

Topic Diversity

Possible Newsletter topics might include:

- Security and safety related topics focusing on target hardening devices, electronic surveillance technologies, alarm system design, crime prevention and related proactive security issues, and white- and blue-collar crime data
- Crime analysis/mapping data from local community sources such as the chambers of commerce, local community boards, political entities, religious facilities, and state and federal law enforcement agencies
- Global research affecting security and safety issues
- Fraud prevention and detection data
- Homeland security updates and terrorism alerts
- Security through environmental approaches
- Cutting edge security advances

Establishing a Security Library

Thinking out of the box for a moment, it would be an excellent idea for all security departments to have an extensive security/safety library for its protection staffs' use and for the use of other employees who might find the info useful. The library might include a book section by topic, and a magazine, journal section for articles, newsletters, etc. The secret is finding the funds for such a project. Stretching the security dollar in today's financial climate is both an art and a science but finding the funds for such a library is well worth the effort. A possible revenue source to get the funds for this project might be found in applying for a grant to stock the library.

Grants can be found at the local level via contacting local development associations, chambers of commerce, politicians' offices, and business development entities. Grants are also available at the national level via contacting www.grants.gov, www.businessgrants.org, www.sba.gov.

It is also a good idea to ascertain if your institution has grant writing capabilities to help in this effort. If not, many municipal agencies and local development agencies may be able to help if asked. Beyond trying to obtain a grant for the funds, another option might be to reach out to local businesses, foundations, and philanthropic organizations for their assistance. Other examples of possible sponsors for your program might be found by contacting businesses that have a vested interest in your firm's services and who might help if only asked. I.e., if your firm is a hospital you might wish to contact pharmaceutical conglomerates, or medical device manufacturers, if your firm is a security guard agency you might wish to contact a security guard uniform or portable radio manufacturer, and if your firm is a financial services entity you might wish to contact banks, mortgage houses, etc. You are only limited by your imagination!

Outsourcing Newsletter Preparation Services

Another method of getting a newsletter published is to outsource the job. Finding the right company is not a difficult task, there are several firms that specialize in preparing print media services. The cost of this service can be kept to a minimum especially if the research and article selection criteria is performed by the company requesting it. The only job being asked of the consultative firm is to put the newsletter together for distribution.

Personalizing your Security Newsletter

Finding the right format for your newsletter involves some thought. First and foremost is finding the right title for the publication. Possible titles might include:

- The Spotlight
- The Security Advocate
- Security and Safety News

Audience Targeting

Seeing that security and safety is every employee's job, it is a good idea to disseminate the security newsletter to other department managers so that the word gets out to all company employees. If feasible, it would be a good idea for the security administrator to include a section in the periodical titled

"The State of Facility Security". This special feature might include new enhancements in security and safety completed and/or contemplated, results of criminal activity within the institution, procedural issues requiring attention, parking security issues, safety, and security related issues etc.

Security Workshops and Special Programs

In addition to disseminating a periodical newsletter, formulating a series of crime prevention related specialized workshops for company employees might also be an excellent method of capturing the employees' undivided attention. Some possible topics might include:

- Personal safety tips
- Auto security and safety tips
- Residential security tips
- Identity theft prevention tips
- Robbery prevention tips
- Burglary prevention tips
- Street safety tips
- Internal theft prevention tips

It is important to note that many of the safety and security brochures listed above are available free of charge from local law enforcement agencies, chambers of commerce, and county, state, and federal public safety agencies. Moreover, many of these agencies also offer speakers and films free of charge.

Aspects of Program Evaluation

As with all programs, a system of evaluation should be designed so that the actual effect of the program can be measured. Some areas to be considered include:

- Before, middle, and after studies should be developed to help gauge the public information effort
- Information-capturing memos should be forwarded to department heads advising them of the initiative and asking for their input re topic selection
- Statistical evaluations should be designed to gauge overall institutional participation in the program

A Final Word

There are an infinite number of strategies to get the word out; formulating an in-house newsletter and library is one of them. If your institution does not already have a venue to get the word out, formulating one makes good sense. All in all, the return on investment is well worth the effort. All things considered, an effective well-run media initiative is limited only by the vision of the person shaping it, and by the practitioner nurturing it!

Improving the Dependability of an ID program

Bernard J. Scaglione

From the Fortune 10 conglomerate securing company trade secrets to the local retailer verifying the authenticity of customer's credit cards, inaccurate identification can lead to lost revenue and increased liability. Identification is the collecting of data to determine who an individual is and what level of security they should possess. This process is conducted through the checking of an individual's background and credentials. When designing an identification program, processes should be considered, to increase the program's effectiveness and reliability. In assessing the implementation of an identification program, consideration should be given to authenticating baseline data and providing continuous data updates.

The authentication of identity has become a complex and sometimes unreliable process. The ability to obtain firsthand information on an individual's background is becoming expensive and available information is increasingly more unreliable. In order to maintain a high-quality authentication program, multiple types of verification should be considered in the identification process. The authentication verification process requires the establishment of standard criteria for the collection and confirmation of the data chosen to establish identification. These standards should be specific and written, outlining the hiring and retention of employees and their access privileges into security sensitive areas.

Authenticating an Identity

Traditionally, corporate entities utilize six potential avenues to authenticate an identity: job application, employment reference check, personal reference check, criminal background check, education check and check of permits, licenses and other governmental records. The key to the successful utilization of these identity checks is personal verification, the personal review of data with the candidate to ensure the completion of all required information and most importantly its accuracy. Specifically, the personal review of name, Social Security number, address, date of birth and all other employment demographics necessary to meet the employment criteria.

Additionally, collected background information should be corroborated through primary source and multiple source verification. Primary Source Verification is the utilization of original source documents to gather background information. For example, when conducting a primary source criminal background check, a court document check would be preferable over the use of a third-party clearinghouse. Multiple Source Verification is the comparison of original source documents with the goal of obtaining consistent demographic information: name, Social Security number, current home address, date of birth, educational degree, etc.

The same holds true when conducting a personal or employment reference check. Primary and multiple source verification should be utilized. Reliance on third party contact should be avoided. Employment reference checks should be directed to the person within the organization that is responsible for providing those checks and all employers listed on the application should be contacted and asked to provide data. When it comes to personal references, the person listed

From *Security E Newsletter, Posted*: March 1, 2009.

as the reference should be contacted – not a roommate, parent or spouse. And again, all the listed personal references should be contacted.

When a reference is contacted, verification should be made on the name spelling and the current address of the applicant. Once all the reference data is gathered, multiple verification should be completed comparing all of the reference data. Using primary and multiple source verification will make the authentication process more reliable. Primary source documentation ensures that the data requested is trustworthy. Using multiple source verification authenticates the identity of an individual. Both practices together provide for a more dependable foundation in which to build an identification and access control program.

Establish ID Standards

In addition to data verification, standards should be established that allow for continuous updates of the original data gathered. A reliable identification program should have the ability to detect and collect changes to the original background and reference data. It is necessary to be advised of changes to criminal convictions, loss or suspension of licenses, major change in credit rating, change of address or name changes. Processes should be developed that establish regular updates to data and provide alerts when changes occur to an employee. Continuous monitoring of an individual's activities is essential in the evaluation of access rights, especially when these rights are based on financial and other confidential criteria. Along with employment data, this data should be primary source verified to ensure it is correct. Updated data (like baseline data) requires personal confirmation with the employee and the agency that is reporting the change.

Working in a major metropolitan hospital, I sometimes encounter medical analogies which reinforce good security practice. In the case of authentication, the healthcare industry offers a good model to consider in the establishment of an identification program. Authentication relies on the collection of substantiated information. Hospitals today exemplify the practice of authentication through compliance with what are called the "National Patient Safety Goals." These goals were developed to increase the safety of patients by instituting practices to reduce the possibilities of errors when providing care. Three Patient Safety Goals demonstrate practices which should be considered in the implementation of identity programs: Accuracy of Patient Identification, Universal Protocol or Time Out, and Effective Communication.

According to the Accuracy of Patient Identification goal, all interaction with the patient from registration through discharge requires the use of at least two patient identifiers. The goals specifically states that every interaction, even if the same healthcare provider interacts with a patient several times during treatment. In each encounter at least two methods must be used to verify identity. That means the provider must ask the patient his or her name and date of birth, look at the patient's bracelet or their identification like driver's license or credit card to confirm they are treating the correct patient. Multiple confirmations and the use of two or more verifiers is an excellent standard to consider when collecting data for any identification program.

The Effectiveness of Communication goal requires the reading back of verbal or telephone orders in the exchange of critical test values to ensure the information stated is correct. In addition, this standard requires a "hand-off" communication protocol. This protocol requires the development of a standard way to exchange necessary information from one care giver to another. This goal sets the standard for conducting personal or work references; continuous verification of data along with constant communication with the applicant sets the standard for reliable data collection. The

46 ■ *Healthcare Security*

third goal is called Universal Protocol. This is used during surgical procedures to verify the correct person, the correct procedural site, and the correct procedure. The key to this goal is the process called Time Out. A Time Out is conducted prior to starting a surgical procedure. During a time-out, all activities are suspended so that all relevant members of the team are focused on the active confirmation of the correct patient, procedure, site and other critical elements.

When reviewing data related to the verification and assignment of access rights a time-out will help to ensure the data is being reviewed and that it is correct. Creating and implementing a successful identification program requires standards that need to be followed each time an identification needs to be verified. In assessing the implementation of an identification program, consideration should be given to authenticating baseline data and providing continuous data updates, which will ensure a smooth system.

Chapter 3

Disaster Preparedness

Training Security Officers to Recognize the Perils of Weapons of Mass Destruction and Pandemic Flu Contaminates – Part I

Anthony Luizzo and Bernard J. Scaglione

Over the years, hospital security officer training included an ever-evolving menu of tasks and procedures covering a galaxy of topics from patient care to asset protection management. As a direct result of that tragic day in September 2001, a universe of new terrorist-related training initiatives has been added to the security administrator's radar screen.

The Art & Science of Training for Disaster

Hospital security operatives need to be prepared in the event of a mass exposure incident; it is the operative's job to protect the hospital, staff, and patients. When an exposure occurs, there is a general *assumption* that hospitals will be notified before victims begin knocking on the door seeking medical services. It is important to recognize that this is only an assumption and that not all emergencies are reported beforehand. One important key to successfully dealing with a disaster is to first recognize that a disaster has in fact occurred. Considering that not all disasters are common knowledge, one acceptable method of disaster management is to inaugurate policies to identify exposed persons before they are admitted for treatment.

Once a disaster victim is identified, it is important to send them to the emergency department entrance from outside of the hospital so that they do not contaminate interior environs of the healthcare facility.

Beyond containment considerations, once a mass exposure incident has been identified it is important to have a clear course of action that controls access into the inner bowels of the hospital, whilst not interrupting the delivery of lifesaving medical services central to all medical centers. To effectively manage disasters, security operatives need to learn the ABCs of diagnosing exposure

---

From *The Journal of Healthcare Protection Management.* (23):2, pp. 1–9. 2007.

DOI: 10.4324/9781003215851-3

models, spotting exposed persons, and donning appropriate contaminate-controlling attire to limit potential exposure.

Identifying Exposure Characteristics

Security operatives need to be taught to recognize the basic symptoms associated with "weapons of mass destruction" so that they are better equipped to gauge catastrophic episodes *before* they can wreak havoc on the medical facilities they are paid to protect. Moreover, operatives need to learn to identify the symptoms of exposure - from the most common biological, chemical, and radiological agents, to recognizing the warning signs associated with flu symptoms emanating from these contaminates.

Biological Agents

Anthrax - **"Bacillus Anthracis"** - Anthrax is an acute infection of the skin, lungs, or gastrointestinal system.

Its related spores can survive for a few days in temperatures as high as 318 degrees Fahrenheit and can remain viable in soil and water for years or even decades. About 8,000 to 10,000 spores are required to cause pulmonary infection and 1,000 spores for intestinal infection. If diagnosed quickly,

Anthrax is treatable with several different types of antibiotics. **Skin contact** - creates sores or blisters that can develop into an infection {generally not fatal}.

Inhalation\Ingestion – bacterial spores are inhaled into the lungs or ingested into the stomach. Victims develop flu-like symptoms within one to seven days of exposure. After two to four days victims have difficulty breathing, they often experience severe exhaustion, and may develop a fever. There is a 90% fatality rate for untreated inhalation, and symptoms begin appearing between the first twenty-four to thirty-six hours of exposure.

Recognizing Virus Symptoms

Ebola is a virus that requires direct contact with the blood or secretions of bodily fluids. It is the most dangerous virus known to science. It causes death in 50% to 90% of all exposure cases. The virus is in incubation for two to twenty-one days. Symptoms include fever, weakness, muscle pain, headache, and sore throat often associated with vomiting, rash, diarrhea, internal and external bleeding.

Smallpox - The Variola Virus- Smallpox is an infection which occurs from contact with blood, secretions of bodily fluids or via inhalation from infected persons. The incubation period is about twelve days. Symptoms include malaise, fever, vomiting, and headaches. Victims develop a rash, which blisters within two to three days. Smallpox is generally not fatal, but a victim must be in isolation for16 to 17 days from the onset of the virus.

Ricin is a toxin made from the left-over mash of the Caster bean, which is processed to produce castor oil. It is easily accessible and is easy to produce. It can be inhaled or ingested. It kills body cells on contact. Death occurs within thirty-six to forty-eight hours after exposure. There is no cure for this toxin. A large aerosol dose is required to be effective, at least 320 mg.

Hazardous Chemical Agents

Cyanide is a common chemical agent used in ore extraction, tanning, and electroplating. Cyanide in a liquid form emits a heavy gas that smells like bitter almonds. It poisons its victims through inhalation of gas. Inhalation of Cyanide blocks the body's cell's ability to consume oxygen, which causes the cells to die. Exposure causes irritation to the eyes, nausea, dizziness, weakness, and anxiety. This is followed by convulsions, unconsciousness then death. The longer the exposure or the higher the concentration of cyanide the quicker a victim will be contaminated and die.

Mustard Gas is a blistering agent; it is an oily liquid that is heavier than water. The vapors and/or liquid are the danger.

The liquid and gas have the odor of mustard, onions, or garlic. Two to twenty-four hours after exposure a victim will notice eye irritation, burning of the skin, and upper airway irritation. High concentrations of exposure will cause blistering of the skin, eyes, and throat. Then it is absorbed into the body where it damages cells and causes death.

Sarin Gas is a nerve gas. It disrupts the mechanism by which nerves communicate with the organs causing over stimulation of the organs. Sarin is a clear, colorless liquid that emits a heavy gas that sinks to the ground. The gas is odorless. Exposure causes a diminishment of the pupils, runny nose, and shortness of breath. Large exposures can cause loss of consciousness, convulsions, and death.

Radiological Exposure

Radiation Poisoning is caused by exposure to irradiated uranium that gives off "Alpha" and "Gamma" rays. Exposure can be caused by exploding a nuclear device, which gives off massive amounts of these rays, or via the exploding of an irradiated source that distributes thousands of finite pieces throughout the explosion area. Exposure to radiation causes body cell disruption or death. The cell disruption generally affects the blood stream and gastrointestinal areas. Symptoms often include nausea, vomiting and malaise followed by a symptom free period. Major organ malfunction occurs from cell death causing body functions to shut down and causing subsequent death. For mild cases of exposure, a victim can take iodine, which will absorb the radiation and help the body to pass the radiation out of the body.

Pandemic Flu All forms of flu present an identification challenge to the healthcare security officer. The difference between a pandemic flu victim and a person with a bad cold may be minute. To protect a hospital from the contamination of pandemic flu, early intervention is important. Notification of the potential of a pandemic event is all that is necessary for a hospital to go on alert and commence screening all persons entering the facility. With respect to this form of flu, security operatives must protect themselves from airborne contamination. To prevent contamination, operatives should slip into water resistant attire, don a M-95 respirator device, and wear protective goggles while screening persons. In the event of a pandemic flu outbreak, the hospital may be required to close their doors to all persons except the sick and internal staff. In the event of such an incident, security officers should be assigned to each access portal to screen all incoming individuals. Like other exposures, once a victim is classified at "risk" it is imperative that they be dispatched to the Emergency Room via walking outside of the hospital and entering in a designated area. The most difficult part of disaster response in a pandemic flu event is identifying flu victims. Although there is no quick sure-fire method of diagnosing the Pandemic

50 ■ *Healthcare Security*

Flu from the common cold or other illness, one efficient method of assessment is through body temperature. The most effective way to determine that an individual has a fever, on a mass scale, is using an infrared thermal imaging device. These instruments are like the devices used by electricians to locate "hot spots" in wiring schmetics; the device is pointed at a person and accurately determines an individual's body temperature. A high body temperature potentially means the individual has the flu.

Personal Protection Equipment

Security Officers must learn to use Personal Protective Equipment {PPEs} when a disaster strike. PPEs are necessary to wear to protect officers from exposure to any dangerous substances. Different PPEs are utilized depending on the type of potential exposure.

Practicing the donning of the different PPE costumes is important in the preparation drills normally associated with mass causality incidents. It is recommended that security staff utilize either Level D or Level C decontamination equipment.

Level D protection - consists of work clothes or in the case of security, the security uniform. The Level D uniform is covered with a light fluid resistant gown, latex gloves, goggles for eye protection, and an M-95 respirator facemask. Level D protection is utilized for biological and flu situations and is worn by security officers at access portals, in treatment areas or when guarding patients.

Level C protection - consists of a "Tyvek" plastic full body suit with a hood embodying a full-face M– 40 respirator, rubber boots or work boots, and heavy rubber gloves. A security officer should wear this level of protection when confronted with a possible exposure to chemical and radiological exposures. *In general, when donning PPEs, the body garment is always put on first. Boots are put on next, followed by the protective mask. Gloves are put on last.*

Removing Personal Protective Equipment

Level D Equipment - the gown is removed first, followed by the goggles, then the gloves. One glove is removed by pulling it off at the end of the glove at the wrist. The glove is pulled off so that it is inside out when removed. That glove is used to grab the other glove at the end by the wrist and that glove is pulled off. Both gloves are discarded. Lastly, the respirator is removed and discarded.

For Level C Equipment - The boots are removed first, the gown second, followed by the goggles, and gloves. Lastly, the respirator is removed.

Lockdown Procedures

It is important that all hospitals have an appropriate "lockdown procedure" in the event of a mass casualty incident. In the event of an incident involving weapons of mass destruction, hospital security personnel must know what procedures to follow in a quick and efficient manner. Operatives must be an integral part of the exposure notification process, they must know whether to institute a partial or full facility lockdown, they need to know when it is necessary to institute an emergency department lockdown, and they must be capable of directing vehicles, visitors, patients, and staff to *"run toward safety and not just away from danger"*.

Notification of Incident

Incident notification is the most important sequence of events in the management of a disaster.

To effectively manage a mass casualty incident, security must be notified immediately of a pending disaster. If an incident is suspected or published, security should be ready to immediately put its respective disaster plan in motion. Irrespective of the plan, all effective plans must embody a process that effectively locks down the facility in a timely and expeditions manner. Whether a full or partial lockdown is called for depends on the severity of the incident at hand.

Directing Vehicles, Visitors, Patients and Staff

Once a disaster is announced or identified, security needs to ensure that emergency vehicles have free and unobstructed access into the emergency department. It is important to continually maintain a clear roadway throughout hospital property, and especially into and out of the emergency environs. Moreover, pedestrian traffic flow needs to be controlled as well. Entrances should be closed and persons wishing to enter the hospital should be questioned prior to entering the inner bowels of the hospital to determine their business-related needs. During disaster scenarios, security operatives posted at access portals should step to the outside of the hospital to physically stop persons whilst searching for potential victims. The hospital disaster plan should include procedures for identification of access portals for hospital staff, disaster victims, disaster victim family members, the media, delivery personnel, and regular in-patient visitors. Experience has shown that each of the above categories should be segregated, and a procedure established to provide entry and cueing guidelines.

Partial Facility Lockdown

When a disaster is announced, the security department should prepare to implement its disaster plan. Depending on the type and extent of the disaster, a partial facility lockdown may be in order. As an aside, if details are sketchy re the magnitude of the exposure, the hospital my wish to only implement a partial lockdown until better info is brought forward. Oftentimes, this entails the closing of *certain* entrances or areas of the hospital. This is done to re-deploy staff and/or supplies, and to control access into and out of the hospital. As an example, a hospital may not want to curtail access to all clinic areas or business offices so that they are better able to re-deploy staff to the emergency treatment areas.

Full Facility Lockdown

In the event of a major incident of mass destruction, a hospital may need to lock down the entire hospital; except for emergency operations to protect the hospital from contamination while identifying and treating disaster victims. Because victims can arrive via cab, bus, or ambulance, it may be necessary to confine access points to one or two specific entrances designated to receive disaster victims.

Emergency Department Lockdown

At some point during a disaster, it may be necessary to lock down the Emergency Room {ER}. The locking down of the ER may occur because of contamination or the need to restrict access into the area by unauthorized staff. If the ER becomes contaminated Security may be required to keep all patients and staff inside of the area and restrict outsiders from entering until the area can be decontaminated.

Decontamination/Treatment Process

All security officers need to become familiar with the decontamination and treatment processes associated with mass casualty or pandemic flu victim incidences. In both cases, victims must be isolated from hospital staff to avoid facility-wide contamination. With respect to mass casualty incidents, victims may be required to disrobe and undergo scrub- down to remove contaminates prior to being treated. Pandemic Flu victims may not require decontamination however, since they will require isolation and segregation in order not to infect hospital staff. During the decontamination or treatment phase of the disaster episode, security officers should be dressed in their personal protective equipment. Again, the correct equipment depends on the type of disaster. Security officers should be made aware of the terms: ***"Hot and Cold Zones"***. A Cold Zone is an area in which <u>no</u> contaminates are present. A Hot Zone is an area of <u>active</u> contamination in which patients are brought into the hospital. Many times, these patients are brought into the hospital in an unconscious state.

Conclusion

The establishment of a WMD training program gives the security department the capability of helping to contain WMD exposures before they adversely impact the institutional setting. The security department's role in keeping hospitals free from contamination is an awesome job, often requiring a dedicated, well trained, appropriately equipped, and highly motivated security contingent that is always keeping a watchful eye over the institution's they protect.

Selected Bibliography

Jane's Chem-Bio Handbook, Jane's Information Group, 1340 Braddock Place Suite 300, Alexandria, Virginia, ISBN 0-7106-1923-5.

Training Security Operatives to Recognize the Perils of Weapons of Mass Exposure Contaminates – Part II

Anthony Luizzo and Bernard J. Scaglione

Our first article featured in this Journal: Vol. 23., No.2., pp.1-9 - 2007 "Training Security Officers to Recognize the Perils of Weapons of Mass Destruction and Pandemic Flu Contaminates" discussed the ABCs of diagnosing exposure models, spotting exposed persons, and donning of contaminate-controlling attire at exposure events. The article spells out how the establishment of a WMD training program gives the hospital security department the capability of helping to contain WMD exposures before they adversely impact the intuitional setting. Over the eleven years since we first wrote this article, terrorism incidents have captured the news at school shootings, church and synagogue massacres, outdoor concerts and at marathons and special events worldwide. Suffice to say that it is extremely important that hospital security departments remain well equipped and ever ready to assist all who come for first aid.

According to an August 14, 2018, website posting by the U.S Department of Homeland Security (DHS), The United States faces a rising danger from terrorists and rouge states seeking to use weapons of mass destruction. DHS goes on to define weapons of mass destruction as a nuclear, radiological, chemical, biological, or other device that is intended to harm many people.

The Changing Terrorist Threats and Tactics

Today, a terrorist's choice of weapons includes trucks, cars, knives, and guns. Not items recognized previously at mass causality incidents. In the past, the weapons of choice included biological, chemical, and radiological instruments. The good news is that potential weapons created from biological, chemical, and radiological sources are often difficult to obtain due to our diligence in securing these types of substances. Notwithstanding, we should always be well prepared for all possible eventualities.

However, diligence also means being prepared for any eventuality. It is security's awesome job to protect the hospital, staff, patients, and visitors. To adequately do this job it is most important that hospital security staff be well versed and trained to recognize the peril they face fighting this seemingly never-ending war on terrorism.

The ABCs of Effective WMD Training

First, it is important to recognize that if an exposure event occurs there is a general assumption that hospitals will be notified before victims begin knocking on the door seeking medical services. Oftentimes, this is only an assumption - not all emergencies are reported beforehand. Frequently, victims' show-up at hospitals before official notification is made to the hospital. As such, it is critical that policies be created and reviewed periodically that speak to properly identifying exposed persons before they contaminate the hospital and staff with unwanted substances. Once it is apparent that an exposure incident has occurred, notification is the most important sequence of events

---

From *The Journal of Healthcare Protection Management.* (35):1, pp. 32–39. 2019.

54 ■ *Healthcare Security*

in the management chain. Seeing that security is always considered the front-line gatekeeper for security and safety issues, they should always be immediately notified. For many hospitals, security is the central point in the implementation of a mass notification scheme. Notification to the rest of the hospital is paramount to the successful implementation of the hospital's disaster plan. Notification should be quick and efficient, allowing security to get the word out, answer calls from inquiring staff and implement their own plan of action. If an incident is suspected or published, security should be ready to immediately put its disaster plan in motion. Irrespective of the plan, any effective plan must embody a process that effectively locks down the facility in a timely and expeditious manner.

Whether a full or partial lockdown is called for depends on the severity of the incident at hand. Beyond containment considerations however, once a mass exposure incident has been identified it is important that a clear action plan is put in place to properly control both ingress and egress into and out of treatment chamber environs.

Handling Vehicle, Visitor, Patient, and Media Issues

It is security's job to direct vehicles, visitors, patients, and staff during a mass causality incident. Their job should be to ensure that emergency vehicles have free and unobstructed access. Likewise, security advocates need to continually maintain a clear and unobstructed roadway throughout hospital property, and especially into and out of the critical treatment environs. Entrances should be closed and all persons wishing to enter the hospital should be questioned prior to entering the inner bowels of the hospital to determine their business-related needs. During disaster scenarios, security operatives who are posted at access portals should step to the outside of the hospital to physically stop persons desiring entry. *This is an extremely important consideration because allowing contaminated persons inside of the facility could prove to be extremely dangerous for all concerned.*

The hospital disaster plan should include Security staff trained on procedures for identifying access portals for hospital staff, disaster victims, disaster victim family members, the media, delivery personnel, and regular in-patient visitors. Experience has shown that each of the above categories should be segregated, and an access procedure established replete with cueing lines.

Facility Lockdown

It is important that all hospitals have an appropriate "lockdown procedure". In the event of an incident involving weapons of mass exposure, hospital security personnel must know what procedures to follow in a quick and efficient manner. Security operatives must be an integral part of the exposure notification process, they must know whether to institute a partial or full facility lockdown, they need to know when it is necessary to institute an emergency department lockdown, and they must be capable of directing vehicles, visitors, patients, and staff to *"run toward safety and not just away from danger"*. To accomplish this Security staff, need to be periodically drilled on this process so when the time comes, they can methodically institute lockdown procedures with relative ease. Depending on the type and extent of the disaster, a partial facility lockdown may be in order. As an aside, if details are sketchy re the magnitude of the exposure, the hospital my wish to only implement a partial lockdown until better info is brought forward.

Oftentimes, this entails the closing of *certain* entrances or areas of the hospital. This is done to re-deploy staff and/or supplies, and to control access into and out of the hospital. As an example, a hospital may want to curtail access to all clinic areas or business offices so that they are better able to re-deploy staff to the emergency treatment areas.

In the event of a major incident of mass destruction, a hospital may need to lock down the entire hospital; except for emergency operations to protect the hospital from outright contamination. Because victims can arrive via cab, bus, or ambulance, it may be necessary to confine access to one or two specific entrances designated to receive disaster victims. At some point during a disaster, it may be necessary to lock down the Emergency Room {ER}.

The locking down of the ER may occur because of contamination or the need to restrict access into the area by unauthorized staff. If the ER becomes contaminated security may be required to keep all patients and staff inside of the area and restrict outsiders from entering until the area is decontaminated.

Personal Protection Devices (PPEs)

Security operatives need to learn to identify the exposure symptoms for the most common biological, chemical, and radiological agents. Once a disaster victim is identified, it is important to send them to the designated emergency receiving point outside of the hospital so that they do not contaminate inner hospital environs.

Security officers need to become familiar with decontamination and treatment processes, and with departmental procedures re how and where to properly isolate infected persons to avoid facility-wide contamination. Moreover, security operatives must be taught how to effectively disrobe and scrub-down potential casualty victims.

Wearing and using PPEs

PPEs are necessary to wear to protect security officers from exposure to dangerous substances. Security personnel need to become familiar with properly utilizing personal protection equipment and learn how to don and disrobe after exposures. Different PPEs are utilized depending on the type of potential exposure. Practicing the donning of the different PPE costumes is important in the preparation drills normally associated with mass causality incidents. When donning PPEs, the body garment is always put on first. Boots are put on next, followed by the protective mask. Gloves should be the last of the items to be donned.

Decontamination Equipment Types

Level D protection - consists of work clothes or in the case of security, the security uniform. The Level D uniform is covered with a light fluid resistant gown, latex gloves, goggles for eye protection, and an M-95 respirator facemask. Level D protection is utilized for biological and flu situations and is worn by security officers at access portals, in treatment areas or when guarding patients.

Level C protection - consists of a "Tyvek" plastic full body suit with a hood embodying a full-face M–40 respirator, rubber boots or work boots, and heavy rubber gloves. A security officer should wear this level of protection when confronted with a possible exposure to chemical and radiological exposures.

56 ■ *Healthcare Security*

Level D Equipment - the gown is removed first, followed by the goggles, then the gloves. One glove is removed by pulling it off at the end of the glove at the wrist. The glove is pulled off so that it is inside out when removed. That glove is used to grab the other glove at the end by the wrist and that glove is pulled off. Both gloves are discarded. Lastly, the respirator is removed and discarded. For Level C Equipment - The boots are removed first, the gown second, followed by the goggles, and gloves. Lastly, the respirator is removed.

Exposure Source Characteristics

As part of the training and education process security officers need to be periodically trained on the basic symptoms associated with the different types of weapons of mass exposure so that they are better able to identify potential victims before they are permitted access into the healthcare confines.

Biological Agents

Anthrax - "Bascillus Anthracis" - Anthrax is an acute infection of the skin, lungs or gastrointestinal system. Its related spores can survive for a few days in temperatures as high as 318 degrees Fahrenheit and can remain viable in soil and water for years or even decades. About 8,000 to 10,000 spores are required to cause pulmonary infection and 1,000 spores for intestinal infection. If diagnosed quickly, Anthrax is treatable with several different types of antibiotics: Skin contact - creates sores or blisters that can develop into an infection. Generally, not fatal. Inhalation\Ingestion – bacterial spores are inhaled into the lungs or ingested into the stomach. Victims develop flu-like symptoms within one to seven days of exposure. After two to four days victims have difficulty breathing, they often experience severe exhaustion, and may develop a fever.

There is a 90% fatality rate for untreated inhalation, and symptoms begin appearing between the first twenty-four to thirty-six hours of exposure.

Ebola is a virus that requires direct contact with the blood or secretions of bodily fluids. It is the most dangerous virus known to science. It causes death in 50% to 90% of all exposure cases. The virus is in incubation for two to twenty-one days. Symptoms include fever, weakness, muscle pain, headache, and sore throat often associated with vomiting, rash, diarrhea, internal and external bleeding.

Smallpox - The Variola Virus- Smallpox is an infection which occurs from contact with blood, secretions of bodily fluids or via inhalation from infected persons. The incubation period is about twelve days. Symptoms include malaise, fever, vomiting, and headaches. Victims develop a rash, which blisters within two to three days.

Smallpox is generally not fatal, but a victim must be in isolation for sixteen to seventeen days from the onset of the virus.

Ricin is a toxin made from the left-over mash of the Caster bean, which is processed to produce castor oil. It is easily accessible and is easy to produce. It can be inhaled or ingested. It kills body cells on contact. Death occurs within thirty-six to forty-eight hours after exposure. There is no cure for this toxin. A large aerosol dose is required to be effective, at least 320 mg.

Hazardous Chemical Agents

Cyanide is a common chemical agent used in ore extraction, tanning, and electroplating. Cyanide in a liquid form emits a heavy gas that smells like bitter almonds. It poisons its victims through inhalation of gas. Inhalation of Cyanide blocks the body's cell's ability to consume oxygen, which causes the cells to die. Exposure causes irritation to the eyes, nausea, dizziness, weakness, and anxiety. This is followed by convulsions, unconsciousness then death. The longer the exposure or the higher the concentration of cyanide the quicker a victim will be contaminated and die.

Mustard Gas is a blistering agent; it is an oily liquid that is heavier than water. The vapors and/or liquid are the danger. The liquid and gas have the odor of mustard, onions, or garlic. Two to twenty-four hours after exposure a victim will notice eye irritation, burning of the skin, and upper airway irritation. High concentrations of exposure will cause blistering of the skin, eyes, and throat. Then it is absorbed into the body where it damages cells and causes death.

Sarin Gas is a nerve gas. It disrupts the mechanism by which nerves communicate with the organs causing over stimulation of the organs. Sarin is a clear, colorless liquid that emits a heavy gas that sinks to the ground. The gas is odorless. Exposure causes a diminishment of the pupils, runny nose, and shortness of breath. Large exposures can cause loss of consciousness, convulsions, and death.

Radiological Exposure

Radiation poisoning is caused by exposure to irradiated uranium that gives off "Alpha" and "Gamma" rays. Exposure can be caused by exploding a nuclear device, which gives off massive amounts of these rays, or via the exploding of an irradiated source that distributes thousands of finite pieces throughout the explosion area. Exposure to radiation causes body cell disruption or death. The cell disruption generally affects the blood stream and gastrointestinal areas. Symptoms often include nausea, vomiting and malaise followed by a symptom free period. Major organ malfunction occurs from cell death causing body functions to shut down and causing subsequent death.

For mild cases of exposure, a victim can take iodine, which will absorb the radiation and help the body to pass the radiation out of the body.

Conclusion

The establishment of a WMD training program gives the security department the capability of helping to contain WMD exposures before it adversely impacts the institutional setting. The security department's role in keeping hospitals free from contamination is an awesome job, often requiring a dedicated, well trained, appropriately equipped, and highly motivated security staff always on guard at the gate protecting us from harm! Continuous drilling and education are key to diligent response when, and if, a mass exposure incident should occur.

Resources / references / suggested reading

Jane's Chem-Bio Handbook, Jane's Information Group, 1340 Braddock Place Suite 300, Alexandria, Virginia, ISBN 0-7106-1923-5

U.S. Department of Homeland Security https://www.dhs.gov/topic/weapons-mass-destruction

Center for Domestic Preparedness: "Hazardous Materials Course on WMD: Attack and Response" This course of study furnishes students an overview of the international and domestic threats whilst focusing a spotlight on identification and decontamination of hazards and evidence preservation https//cdp.dhs.gov/news-media/article/hazardious-materials-course-focus-on-wmd-attack-and-response

The Canadian Center for Occupational health and Safety "Working with Toxic Materials" http://www.ccohs.ca

58 ■ *Healthcare Security*

First Aid Re Certification "Emergency Personal protective Equipment" http://firstaidrecert.com/emergency-personal-protective-equipment

Defense Threat Reduction Agency "Weapons of Mass Destruction Training and Education - http://www.dtra.mil/Mission/WMD-Training-and-Education

Kimberly, N. Treat MD, et al. "Hospital Preparedness for Weapons of Mass Destruction Incidents: An Initial Assessment" Annals of Emergency Medicine: An International Journal – Vol. 38, Issue 5, pp562-565. November 2001.

K. Ganesan MD, et al. "Chemical Warfare Agents" – Journal of Pharmacy and Bio Allied Sciences – 2010.

Disaster Planning: Training for the Perils of Weapons of Mass Exposure 2020

Anthony Luizzo and Bernard J. Scaglione

Introduction

This is the third article authored by the undersigned speaking to handling emergency situations involving weapons of mass exposure contaminates [1] [2]. One of the authors wrote a book [3] speaking to proactive event prevention and effective resolution, and in the spirit of more effective disaster management, the authors have constructed an Emergency Preparedness Readiness Checklist [4] offering a roadmap for security executives to follow. The information herein offers guidance on protecting hospital staff, patients, and visitors from becoming contaminated, as well as tendering suggestions and guidance on risk assessment engineering and design, proactive risk exposure mitigation, and spawning innovative recovery strategies for moving forward once emergencies have passed!

Assessing Risks Associated with Emergent Response

"Necessity being the mother of invention", knowledgeable security executives instinctively know that well structured protection assessments help to deepen and strengthen security response planning strategies. Utilizing lessons learned from actual and planned events, along with best practices, and current trends, helps to make the plan more efficient and effective. Comprehensive assessments include analyzing entry points, security staffing levels, traffic management, physical security systems, policies and procedures, visitor control, media relations, mass notification, and law enforcement support among other critical functions. A complete and thorough assessment always helps to put facility security on solid ground and on the positive side of the protection curve.

Beyond in-house initiatives, government agencies such as The Joint Commission, DNV, Homeland Security and the Federal Emergency Management Agency (FEMA) provide valuable information on current trends and response practices. When assessing risks and response protocols, FEMA breaks down protocols into four phases: mitigation, preparedness, response, and recovery to outline preparedness and response to emergent events. While a healthcare facility's response to an emergent event begins after an incident has occurred, response activities should unfold according to a pre-planned progression determined in the mitigation phase. The response process embodies recognition that a disaster is occurring, expeditious reporting of the disaster to key personnel, activating the emergency operations plan, launching the incident command center, notifying and mobilizing all hospital personnel, and ensuring that all emergency units remain mobilized until the disaster is officially declared over.

From *The Journal of Healthcare Protection Management.* (36):2, pp. 1–10. 2020.

Mitigation Phase

More seasoned security executives should always try to turn a bright RED light into a GREEN light and get in front of oncoming catastrophes before they are allowed to escalate. An excellent approach of getting in front of an oncoming catastrophe is to formulate effective mitigation protocols to lower risk exposure. Mitigation involves proactively identifying potential hazards before it hoists its ugly head. It is often said that effective security is akin *to an assembly line – seek and you shall find*. Mitigation is the most important part of any emergency preparedness process. With respect to emergency management planning, all hospitals are required to have an effective emergency management plan that adheres to all local, state, federal laws, and meets accreditation standards set by TJC, DNV, CMS or the NFPA. Risk mitigation requires using an assessment tool that can effectively do the job. Many hospitals use the Kaiser HVA as their general assessment tool. To further deepen and strengthen risk mitigation efforts, healthcare institutions also place their faith and confidence on external expertise to assist in this important effort.

Formulating a security response program

Common components of a security response initiative include:

- mobilizing and managing security department personnel
- target hardening of the facility
- protecting all utilities
- mass notification of personnel
- collaborating with community resources
- preparing for patient surge
- ensuring regulatory compliance
- monitoring expenses and finances

A main responsibility of the security department is traffic control and implementing institution lockdown requisites during emergencies. Programmatic issues include:

- vehicle restriction and screening
- facility access control
- visitor/patient screening
- building/entry closures
- media/family relations
- emergency department lockdown
- incident Command Center activation
- hot and cold zone security
- mass notification

Preparedness Phase

The Preparedness phase focuses on improving response to and recovery from actual events. The most important activity in this phase is the development of an Emergency Operations Plan (EOP).

This plan should be tested on a regular basis so that security personnel are familiar with the plan and their role in carrying out the plan. Periodical testing of the plan is strongly advised and should be a facility wide exercise. Over and above periodical testing, security personnel should continually receive hands-on training reinforcing their critical first responder role in handling crisis management issues. Training should be continuous so that security knows their role when and if the emergency response plan is activated. A good rule of thumb to follow is to have emergency response training conducted at annual in-service education initiatives, at in-house planned exercises, and intermittently at roll calls.

Depending on Security's role, additional specialized training may also be needed. Training curricula might include:

- hazardous materials identification
- PPE use
- decontamination/treatment process
- FEMA Incident Command training
- Use of thermal or other non-traditional devices

Response Phase

The Response phase is designed to control the negative effects of an emergent situation or event. The main intent of this phase is to help minimize the impact of the hazardous event on facility staff, patients, and operations. Security's central role during a catastrophic event typically includes managing vehicle and pedestrian movement, ensuring that critical notifications are delivered, and implementing institution lockdown.

Controlling Persons and Vehicles

Security is primarily responsible for controlling vehicle and pedestrian access into and out of the hospital buildings, emergency and incident areas. Controlling access may include:

- screening vehicles entering hospital property
- keeping access roads to the emergency department open for ambulance access
- segregating and controlling access for employees, patients and visitors

Hospital Lockdown

In an emergent event the hospital may need to lockdown their institution to reduce the potential for unauthorized access into the facility from potentially exposed persons, the media and/or family members. All buildings need to be secured and access to the facility limited to essential staff, patients, and some visitors. This process may include:

- locking all entrance doors not in use
- assigning additional staff to each entry point to ensure order and to limit and control access

62 ■ *Healthcare Security*

- closing all ancillary buildings and services
- designating an area for media and family members
- facilitating institution locked down procedures

Other security department duties may include:

- activation of a mass notification system to alert all hospital personnel
- inauguration of a hospital command center (HCC)
- institution of a transportation program to pick up off-duty employees
- creation of an emergency "hot and cold" access control procedure
- mandating that staff wear masks related PPE and full Tyvek suits
- establishing liaisons with community groups, law enforcement, fire, emergency management, and other first responders
- facilitating the transport of the deceased and/ or releasing the deceased to authorized individuals
- safeguarding of law enforcement and VIP property
- enacting patient transport regulations
- organizing an effective supply chain security routing procedure
- instituting appropriate lockdown related access control technologies
- expediting access for family members of critically ill patients

Recovery Phase

The Recovery phase begins in tandem with the response phase. Demobilizing staff and supplies once the disaster is over and starting the recovery process by going back to normal operations and recording all financial information pertaining to the disaster and the hospital's response. For many healthcare facilities, returning to normal operations as quickly as possibly is essential for financial survival.

Plans should describe procedures for re-establishing normal operations following an emergency and include the identity of all people involved in the recovery effort. Most important, FEMA should always be contacted for their expertise, resources and assistance. As Walt Disney was quoted saying "the way to get started is to quit talking and start doing". Another words, the more prepared an organization is, the easier the road back to normalcy becomes. Many healthcare facilities underestimate the resources and time necessary to recover adequately from an emergency. Recovery operations should include provisions for staff, facilities, finances and community support. A detailed recovery plan should include recuperation strategies that don't interrupt normal hospital operations and help restore business operations as soon as physically possible.

A well-founded recovery plan should:

- minimize the economic impact of the interruption
- establish alternative means of operation
- train personnel on recovery procedures
- provide for a smooth and rapid restoration
- offer staff support

Recovery planning begins with conducting a risk analysis evaluation report to help identify the most effective method of resuming normal business operations. The analysis should be prepared by competent teams who have business resumption expertise. To help support this evaluation, the following in-house or third-party resources should be made available:

- additional security officers or support personnel
- temporary off-site office facilities
- appropriate technological support (computers, peripherals, communication equipment, software and data)
- vital record availability (electronic and hard copy)
- public service support (power, natural gas, water, sewer, telephone, internet, wireless)
- security-related systems
- specialized training
- third-party service contracting

A wise man once said that there is a unique balance between "Risk and Reward". When developing a comprehensive recovery strategy, it is important to focus any and all recovery efforts to snugly fit the specific needs of the particular hospital or healthcare organization under scrutiny. Choosing the right person(s) to lead the recovery is one of the first steps in developing an effective plan.

Additional steps to consider when piecing together a plan might include:

- ascertaining federal and/or local government reimbursement vehicles
- developing a list of vendors, contact information, and supplies
- locating backup facilities
- formulating an operational recovery process
- identifying security technology requirements
- establishing equipment needs

Testing the plan

It's important to always remember that proper planning always prevents poor performance. Once a recovery plan is finalized, it's time to vigorously test the system. Unfortunately, all too often many organizations never test the recovery plan or train staff in the recovery process. This part of emergent event response is the most important. It can mean the difference between financial stability and bankruptcy.

Conclusion

Considering today's unique circumstances many enlightened Security administrators know that the camera of scrutiny will stop at their desk if their institution is *not* ready when disaster strikes. Hospitals and long-term care institutions need to never exhibit inaction in the face of need. Regardless, whether the disaster is a pandemic event, terrorist attack, active assailant offense, workplace violence incident or a natural disaster, the institution must be ready to tackle the catastrophe.

64 ■ *Healthcare Security*

The key to staying one step ahead of failure is to continually evaluate existing emergency response plans and implement appropriate training to help keep hospital staff current and ready for future onslaughts. Recovery plans need to be reviewed and tested on a regular basis and programmatic enhancements enacted when necessary. It's important that every security executive understand that "quick and innovative security action helps to determine their security departments destiny".

References

1. Luizzo, A. & Scaglione B. (2007). Training security officers to recognize the perils of weapons of mass destruction and pandemic flu contaminates. Journal of Healthcare Protection Management, 23, 1-9.
2. Luizzo, A. & Scaglione B. (2019). Training security officers to recognize the perils of weapons of mass exposure contaminates – part II. . Journal of Healthcare Protection Management, 35, 32-39.
3. Scaglione, B. (2019). Security management for healthcare: proactive event prevention and effective resolution. New York, NY: Routledge/Productivity Press.
4. Emergency Preparedness Readiness Checklist

Emergency Preparedness Readiness Checklist

Review each item check one box for each item, 'Yes', 'No', or N/A' (not applicable). If 'No' is checked off for any item please explain in the comment box provided.

Section 1: Risk Assessment	Yes	No	N/A
1. Has an annual risk assessment been prepared	☐	☐	☐
2. Does the risk assessment include all phases of the emergency preparedness plan	☐	☐	☐
3. Does the risk assessment Include all training updates	☐	☐	☐
4. Does the risk assessment Include drill evaluation compliance	☐	☐	☐
5. Does the risk assessment Include actual event evaluation compliance	☐	☐	☐
6. Does the risk assessment meet regulatory compliance standards	☐	☐	☐
Additional Comments:			

Section 2: Mitigation Phase	Yes	No	N/A
1. Is an emergency management plan available	☐	☐	☐
2. Are potential hazards identified	☐	☐	☐
3. Does the plan meet regulatory compliance requisites	☐	☐	☐
4. Does the plan properly address mobilization strategies	☐	☐	☐
5. Are target hardening recommendations adequate	☐	☐	☐
6. Are utility security concerns addressed	☐	☐	☐

Disaster Preparedness ■ 65

Section 2: Mitigation Phase	Yes	No	N/A
7. Does the plan adequately address personnel and other notification essentials	☐	☐	☐
8. Are community resources included	☐	☐	☐
9. Have fiduciary issues been addressed	☐	☐	☐
10. Are access control strategies included	☐	☐	☐
11. Have media and family relations issues been addressed	☐	☐	☐
12. Other issues:	☐	☐	☐
13. Other issues:	☐	☐	☐
Additional Comments:			

Section 3: Preparedness Phase	Yes	No	N/A
1. Does the plan include an Emergency Operations Plan (EOP)	☐	☐	☐
2. Has the plan been periodically tested	☐	☐	☐
3. Are tests properly evaluated and corrective measures implemented	☐	☐	☐
Additional Comments:			

Section 4: Response Phase	Yes	No	N/A
1. Does the plan adequately control pedestrian and vehicular movement	☐	☐	☐
2. Does the plan address emergency vehicle access	☐	☐	☐
3. Does the plan designate employee, patient and visitor access particulars	☐	☐	☐
4. Does the plan adequately address institutional lockdown measures	☐	☐	☐
5. Does the plan include beefed up staffing at strategic access points	☐	☐	☐
6. Does the plan address ancillary building and service closures	☐	☐	☐
7. Does the plan earmark media and family member billets	☐	☐	☐
8. Does the plan define institution locked down maneuvers	☐	☐	☐
Additional Comments:			

66 ■ *Healthcare Security*

Section 5: Recovery Phase	Yes	No	N/A
1. Is a recovery plan available	☐	☐	☐
2. Does the recovery plan spell out when the institution can return to normal operations	☐	☐	☐
3. Does the plan contain disaster-related fiduciary documentation	☐	☐	☐
4. Does the plan contain economic impact interruption data	☐	☐	☐
5. Does the plan contain alternative institutional operational models	☐	☐	☐
6. Is the staff adequately trained to handle recovery procedures	☐	☐	☐
7. Does the plan address restoration prerequisites	☐	☐	☐
8. Does the plan offer staff support	☐	☐	☐
Additional Comments:			

Chapter 4

The Security Survey

Beyond "Target Hardening" – Approaches in Applying Crime Risk Management Principles and Techniques in Community Surveys

Anthony Luizzo

Introduction

The specific form of crime risk management counseling offered clients in conventional crime prevention is the security survey. A survey is the on-site examination of a physical facility (home, business, industrial plant, hospital, etc.) and its immediate surroundings, the purpose of the survey is to advise clients of risks and weaknesses observed and measures they can take to improve overall security.

The Community Crime Control Plan

In single-client surveys, the facility is analyzed as a whole and recommendations for improved security are systematic. The basic idea is to design a crime risk management system that makes the facility secure and that is consistent with the client's interests and lifestyle. To do this, the practitioner must analyze existing security elements in relation to profit (in the case of a business) or lifestyle (in the case of a residence).

In providing security advice to single clients, the practitioner may deal with a multitude of crime risks (e.g., theft, fraud, forgery, arson, burglary, robbery, malicious damage, personnel screening and investigation, theft of trade secrets, industrial espionage, executive protection, kidnapping, extortion, bomb threats and bombings, emergency, and disaster planning issues). Generally, solutions offered are of the "target hardening" variety. By and large, the philosophy is essentially to maintain a private interest viewpoint.

From *Practitioner Magazine* A Publication of the International Society of Crime Prevention Practitioners. 1988.

DOI: 10.4324/9781003215851-4

68 ■ *Healthcare Security*

Over the last twenty years, a new breed of civilian security specialist has begun to emerge. These people have their roots in various fields, including economic development, city planning, academia, engineering, and architecture. They also include citizen volunteers seeking to create safer neighborhoods and commercial/industrial centers. They should be welcomed into the ranks of the security profession, as they bring to the profession an awareness of the cooperative basis of security.

Quite a different mindset is required when preparing a multi-client or community survey. The single client is still important, but the object of the survey is to improve the security of the community and its facilities. In this form of survey, the specialist is interested in reducing the risks of personal injury and property loss due to crime for everyone who occupies or uses the environment. The philosophy in these studies shifts dramatically from essentially a private to a public interest viewpoint. In 1985, while completing graduate studies in Criminology, I coined the term: Community Crime Control Planner" (CCCP) and a form of crime risk management based on a "Crime Impact Statement" (CIS). The CCCP practitioner focuses on crime risks related to the characteristics of the physical environment and to the behavior of persons who use ad are part of that environment.

In this wider study, the specialist examines land use data, canvasses users, interviews public service providers, and gathers and evaluates other pertinent information.

A checklist of areas requiring attention includes:

- Obtaining and evaluating community profile data. At a minimum, data should include a population breakdown by ethnic group, age, income, housing, and employment.
- Obtaining and evaluating land use, traffic flow, and building construction data, including a structural analysis of the entire area.
- Coordinating and/or preparing single-client security surveys.
- Linking single-client surveys into the overall study.
- Evaluating local police agencies' crime statistics.
- Reporting discussions, informal/formal conversations, and interviews with local retailers, customers shopping, pedestrians traversing the area, community residents, service providers, community groups, organizations and agencies (youth groups, schools, health care providers, etc.) and local elected officials.
- Evaluating the strength and effectiveness of the local merchants and community organizations (commercial, industrial, and residential).
- Ascertaining the strength and effectiveness of any crime prevention programs, prior or present.
- Observing and making intuitive interpretations.

It is in this mass of data where the resourceful practitioner will be able to pinpoint the various problem areas and where the art and mechanics of solution lie.

Framing the Survey

Crime impact statements are prepared in three phases:

Introduction – Problem Statement

   I. Problem Assessment
   II. The Search for Solutions Summary Statement
   III. The Plan for Implementation Appendixes – Support Data

Introduction – Problem Statement

A. Identifies the project site and time frame
B. Indicates crime-related problems
C. Identifies the primary objectives of the project
  I. Problem Assessment
  Researches the study area to identify weaknesses and other risk-related factors
  II. The Search for Solutions
  Enumerates various approaches to ameliorate and solve the problems. May include a list of suitable case studies and examples of other successful programs across the country

Summary Statement

Discusses various positions reached after consideration. May also include information on needed follow-up visits to the site for evaluation, and a list of possible alternative approaches

The Plan for Implementation

Expository method (including a timetable) for executing the recommended solutions. May also include a timetable for revisiting the site after implementation

Appendixes

Documents needed to help support the study include:

- Community profile- maps, charts, graphs, diagrams, photographs, etc.
- Minutes of meetings, interviews, etc.
- Memorandums
- Relevant subsidies prepared (client-user perceptions, attitudes, shopper surveys, etc.)
- Other pertinent information

These studies may take from two to four months (or more, depending on the target area) to prepare. The single-client survey, on the average, takes from one to five days to complete. For the practitioner, the transition from single-client to community environments is often a mammoth leap- like moving from stream to ocean. Although the ocean waters are somewhat uncharted, a considerable body of knowledge is available to guide the journeyman. The challenge is to find innovative and creative ways to apply this knowledge. Crime prevention in the community environment is an exciting, open-ended field of activity. Community Crime Control Planners are limited only by their imaginations.

Problems and Solutions

The following are some ideas that have been proposed in previous studies involving a wide range of environments. They offer a realistic picture of the various approaches that could be set in motion to resolve security issues.

✓ Mitigation of safety/security issues in municipal parking garages. Often, the public views these garages as unsafe and unprotected (surveys in various neighborhoods have verified

70 ■ *Healthcare Security*

this); thus, they are fear-inducing and unattractive areas. This view affects the volume of shoppers and users who normally would drive into an area and hurts neighborhood business activity and job availability.

Possible Solutions

- O Installing improved lighting and security surveillance closed-circuit television (CCTV) capabilities
- O Adding staff and improving security staff training
- O Buying identifiable uniforms and related support equipment (portable radios, scooters, etc.) for security staff
- O Instituting architectural modifications, such as closing off blind spots; eliminating dead-end corridors; shunting elevators

NOTE: Previous studies have shown that in many municipal garages, security operatives do not wear identifiable uniforms, supervision of personnel is poor, and communication equipment is not available. Further, many municipalities lease these garages to private vendors who pay little attention to contract language regarding security requirements. Another solution is to have the private corporate and public sector (corporations, universities, hospitals, etc.), which have a vested interest in the community, help by extending their security influence from their own doors out into the community. Agreements have been negotiated to have private and/or public agency security operations involved in providing random patrols in parking garages, shopping centers, designated safety/security corridors, etc.

- ✓ Mitigation of safety/security issues in municipality operated subway/rail stations. Subway stations, like municipal parking garages, are among the strongest fear-inducing places in an urban center.

Possible Solutions

- O Installing improved lighting and security surveillance capabilities
- O Installing prominent exit signs
- O Installing "conductor indicator boards" to tell passengers where the subway car on which the conductor is riding will stop on the platform
- O Installing above-ground light indicator globes to tell passengers which station entrances are open, and which have token clerks on duty
- O Closing off cul-de-sacs on station mezzanines
- O Increasing police presence where appropriate

NOTE: In some neighborhoods, private corporations have installed CCTV capabilities in subway stations near their plants. The corporation's security department monitors are the CCTV system, and patrols exterior station entrances. This program is known as "adopt-a-station."

- ✓ Reducing incidents of street crime (mugging, robbery, etc.) and the fear of crime during evening hours. In many industrial and commercial centers, employees leaving work at day's end often fall prey to street crimes. Many of the streets are poorly lighted, and employees who use public transportation (many do) fearfully flee the area to catch their train or bus. Rarely do any of these people linger in the area to shop or dine.

The Security Survey ■ 71

Possible solutions

The formation of strategically designed lighted corridors (pedestrian routes) linking business centers to mass transit points – in association with directed police surveillance programs along these routes at peak times.

NOTE: Funding for this program has come from neighborhood businesses, as well as other sources.

✓ Modifying street traffic flow patterns to overcome various crime problems

Possible Solutions

- O Closing, narrowing, or "one-waying" streets to change traffic patterns
- O Creating cul-de-sacs where appropriate
- O Modifying traffic signal synchronization to encourage vehicular concentration at certain intersections at critical times
- O Relocation bus stops from undesirable intersections to more appropriate locations and changing subway entrances to coincide with lighted corridor routes
- O Working with area business leaders to coordinate employee work release schedules with bus and train schedules

✓ Reducing neighborhood perceptions of crime

Possible solutions

- O Working with local law enforcement officials on innovative approaches to assigning police resources
  - O Establishing mobile crime prevention services
  - O Creating satellite police stations
  - O Using mounted police in commercial centers
  - O Forming special programs such as senior citizen escorts, lighted corridor patrols, and community patrol officer programs
  - O Developing community-based crime prevention networks linking residential, commercial, industrial, institutional, private, and public sector security and law enforcement into a cohesive neighborhood-wide system of crime control

These and other solutions are used to stimulate social attitudes and behavior that can help reduce both opportunities for crime and fear of crime through:

- O Intensified use of streets, parks, commercial and industrial centers, neighborhoods, and communities
- O Increased visibility of intruders to legitimate occupants and users
- O Increased sense of shared interest of improving and maintaining the quality and of the physical and social environment.

---

*Reprinted with permission: International Association of Crime Prevention Practitioners

72 ■ *Healthcare Security*

The Access Control Security Survey

Anthony Luizzo

Reviewing the Facility Survey

Hereunder, the surveyor must peruse the entire survey document prior to arranging to interview key staff at the facility. Interviewees may include department heads, managers, and other relevant staff.

Cross-Examination of Risk Exposures

This segment of the analysis is by and large the most time consuming. The process begins by logging each risk. The information is then divided into "low, medium, and high" risk categories. Further, this base-line data is subdivided and codified to form two polar columns – "vulnerability" vs. "criticality" matrix.

It is through this analytic process that the amplitude of various exposures is valuated.

Cost-Benefit Analysis

Once a list of possible solutions has been identified, it's time to move on to the comparative analysis segment of the process. The tent here is to draw a parallel between each proposed solution and its cost-productiveness.

In the main, posited recommendations should always:

1. Be consistent with the mission of the entity.
2. Expenses should never exceed intended benefits.
3. Programmatic costs should always conjoin with budgetary constraints.

As an aside, when costs are unrealistic, the consultant will quickly lose credibility and most often the assignment.

Availability of Resources

Determining what is available and how to use it is itself a task. This segment of the process involves a thorough review of the facility's security staffing plan. (If a plan is unavailable, it should be prepared as part of the project.) Beyond staffing, there are various other adjoining factors that need to be taken under advertisement. Some of these side issues include: a review of security workload and crime incident data (a two-year snapshot), an examination of post description and location specifics, and the exploration into the efficacy of substituting security technology in lieu of conventional staffing.

From *Journal of Healthcare Protection Management*. (6):1, pp. 25–29. Fall 1989.

Analytical Exposition

When all the data is ready for examination, it's time for rigorous analysis. At this juncture, the important information needs to be extricated and criticized. Thenceforth, an inventory of possible recommendations should be drafted and recorded. In time, the information will help to awaken the memory while writing the final report.

Levels of Access Control

There are various levels of crime control approaches that can be put in motion to frame an access control program. The approaches can be summed up in the following groups:

- Completely restricting access
- Partially restricting access
- Control and monitoring of access
- Monitoring of access
- Selectively controlling and monitoring of access
- Architectural security and access control

Completely restricting access

This approach involves complete curtailing of access into an environment. In most instances, this method is almost always associated with "extremely high security" environs. Most often, only top executives and their designates are authorized access privileges.

Partially restricting access

The approach involves partially curtailing of access into an area. Often, this method is associated with "high security" environs. In this application, top executives, department heads, and key employees have access privileges.

Control and monitoring of access

This approach involves a "free-flow" model of access control. The area is monitored either by personnel or surveillance capabilities (CCTV), exclusive of physical obstruction. These control measures are most strongly associated with lobbies, hallways, elevators, and entrances and exits.

Selectively controlling and monitoring of access

This is like the monitoring approach, except that only selected points are surveilled. Many times, the areas selected are chosen by design and/or without definite method or purpose (randomly selected).

Architectural security and access control

This method of access control planning involves putting forward various structural changes to influence criminal behavior.

Here the surveyor works with architects, designers, and builders on security design or redesign issues at the facility. A brief list of frequently discussed issues include: a review of the building's floor and electrical plans, location and number of access points, positioning of shipping and receiving operation, and the consistency of various materials.

Applying Control Approaches

Access control strategy is set apart into two applications:

- Procedural Application
- Technological Application

Procedural application – Identification by document

Procedural strategies normally put forward include:

- The design and issuance of "identification badges." Special consideration is always given to the size, color, and information displayed on the various documents.
- The issuance of "daily visitor passes." Like identification badges, visitor passes come in a variety of sizes, shapes, and color combinations. Oftentimes, color coding is used in tandem with electro-mechanical systems (readers and other technology), and to designate authorization for levels of areas of access. ID passes are also available which are light sensitive and, over a measured time, tend to darken and become illegible when exposed to light.
- Daily logging of employees, visitors, vendors, and janitorial staff.
- Daily logging of follow up inspections of door and window closures, equipment and file security, alarm system malfunctions, suspicious occurrences, etc.
- Designation of employee access points.
- Configuration of office space to control access more efficiently. Many agencies designate "security advocates" – an employee who sits closet to the office entrance to challenge (may I help you) incoming visitors.
- The initiation of well-founded "package inspection" policy.

Technological application

- The installation of computerized control systems (alarm, CCTV, locking, etc.)
- The installation of computerized card access control systems:
  1. *Proximity Readers.* Entry is regulated by a reader sensor that can be installed behind a wall or glass partition, making it both more aesthetically pleasing and more tamper resistant. A badge, key-tag, or card is "waved" or passed near the sensor, without removing the card from its holder. This system is most appropriate for the health care environment.

The Security Survey ■ 75

Devices can be worn on the wrist to control the whereabouts of patients, nursing home residents, and infants. The system can meet both short- and long-range needs – short range (0"-6") and long range (6"-6').

2. *Magnetic Stripe Readers*. Like most credit cards, magnetic stripe cards have a strip of magnetic recording tape that can be programmed, and machine read. This technology is extremely popular and well developed. The cards are easy to encode and read, but they are also easy to erase and recode, making them one of the more versatile card types.

3. *Wiegand Readers*. This is a plastic card that has a series of specially treated short wires embedded within. These wires produce a change in the strength and polarity of the surrounding magnetic field when the card is inserted into the reader. A sensing coil picks up the unique pattern in the card. Wiegand cards are virtually impossible to copy and are not vulnerable to weather pr vandals.

■ The installation of detecting systems:
1. Walk-through scanners
2. Hand-held scanners

■ Retrofitting of elevator banks to include floor shunting capabilities.

Conclusion

No one standardized instrument will adequately cover the many varieties of situations or security needs of all environments. Each survey must be individually tailored to fit the specific task. Intuitively, the adept practitioner knows how to set about arranging the survey to suit the client's needs. All things considered, planning, training, and communication are the central components in all successful programs. When everyone understands the policy, it works!

The Security Survey: A Prescription for Enhancing Security

Anthony Luizzo

In the medical profession, physicians diagnose and prescribe remedies for human ailments. By the same token, security professionals diagnose and prescribe remedies for frail security programs.

In essence, what a "cat scan" is to a physician, the "security survey" is to a security diagnostician. The survey is the fulcrum from which prescribed security remedies are formulated.

By definition, a security survey is an on-site physical examination of a facility to determine its protection posture. In professional hands, the survey profiles deficiencies, risks, and hazardous conditions, and offers creative/corrective approaches to remove and/or mitigate identified exposures.

Developing the Survey: "The Examination"

Organizing a survey is easy to understand when taken in a step-by-step process.

1. The surveyor needs to meet with top management to discuss:
   a. Project parameters,
   b. The term of the project,
   c. Subcontracting issues, if warranted,
   d. Budgetary requirements.
2. The surveyor needs to gain insight into the mission and special functions of the entity to be surveyed.
3. Documents authorizing the survey-such as letters of introduction, facility ID cards, etc. – must be made available to the survey team.
4. Construction documents such a floor plans, architectural drawings, electrical blueprints, etc., mut be reviewed.
5. The survey site needs to be visited on all work shifts so that each facet of the operation is examined.
6. Department heads, managers, and employees need to be interviewed to ascertain their views, concerns, and special requirements. *Note:* It is also useful to solicit their ideas on strengthening security.
7. Crime incident data relating to the facility need to be examined.
8. Local law enforcement (police, transit, housing, etc.) crime statistics need to be scrutinized. In addition to perusing law enforcement statistics, community organizations should be canvassed to ascertain whether they also maintain crime-related statistical samples. *Note:* As an aside, a great many adept surveyors believe the statistical catchment area should include a one-mile radius of the survey site.
9. Risk exposures and hazardous conditions need to be noted.
10. The facility's security staffing and technological blueprints (CCTV, alarms, etc.) need to be analyzed.
11. Asset's protection policies and procedures need to be reviewed. *Note:* Questions that need answers include: Does the security department have "inventory control" responsibilities? If not, should they? Does the facility have an operation manual?

From *Journal of Healthcare Protection Management.* (7):1, pp. 32–35. Fall 1990.

The Security Survey ■ 77

12. Security awareness initiatives need to be canvased. *Note:* Questions that need answers include: Does the security department have a canned series of security /safety lecture programs? Does the department have a skilled trainer on board to spearhead the effort. If not, should a program be developed?

Professional Evaluation: "The Diagnosis"

Once the examination is concluded and all pertinent data gathered, it's time for rigorous analysis.

The process begins by logging each risk and subdividing the various risks into "low," "medium," and "high" risk categories to form a risk grid. It is through this analytic process that the amplitude of various risk exposures is valuated.

A good rule of thumb, often applied in formulating protection wisdom, is to fashion judgements on sustentative data extrapolated from the risk grid inventory, coupled with the diagnostician's intuitive abilities.

Framing the Survey: "Writing the Prescription"

Regardless of form and style of the survey document, it is really the content that is important.

A well-structured survey should include: An Introduction, a Core, a Summary of Findings, an Implementation Plan, and a Closing Statement. The report should be easy to read and understand. Conclusions put forward should be realistic, and the surveyor should confer with the client to review the entire report upon completion.

Introduction

This section of the report should begin by stipulating who authorized the survey and why it's being requested. It should describe the survey site and provide an overview of the parameters of the survey.

Core

The core segment of the report, often referred to as the body, staple, or bulk portion of the document, should address: "Problem Assessment" – identification of risk exposures, and security program weaknesses, and "Interpretive Solutions" – an inventory of approaches to mitigate and/or remove risk situations.

Summary of findings

The summary statement presents a menu of solutions for consideration, a list of alternatives approaches and a cost appraisement for the overall project. *Note:* A prioritized inventory of risks uncovered, correlated to a prioritized listing of recommendations, should be attached.

Implementation Plan

This section of the report includes a timetable for executing the recommended solutions, and a schedule for revisiting the site after implementation.

Closing statement

The closing statement should rivet attention to those individuals (department heads, employees, etc.) who assisted during the survey by acknowledging their contribution. Herein, the surveyor should highlight the importance of follow-up on implementing *all* recommendations – especially all priority references. He should further point out that instituting a modicum of enhancements will measurably contribute to uplifting global security.

Note: Appendices could also be attached to support the overall study. Such documents could include:

- Memoranda
- Relevant subsidies
- Minutes of meetings
- Crime statistics
- Community profile data (maps, charts, diagrams, photographs, etc.)

Conclusion

Writing the correct prescription for an ailing security operation is often an arduous task. The professional diagnostician spends a great many hours probing, examining, researching, and pondering before he tears a page from his "Rx" pad to give to a client company.

Aspects of the Security Survey: Distinctions Between: Single-Client, Multi-Client, Access Control, & Community-Wide Security Surveys

Anthony Luizzo

Since that dreadful day in early September 2001, a great many security executives have been scrambling to inaugurate new and innovative approaches to crime control. The U.S. government has also stepped-up to the plate by establishing the Office of Homeland Security and by allocating millions of dollars to fight the war on terror. Fighting this new war requires that security executives begin to place more emphasis on detecting crime risks <u>before</u> they occur. This is often not an easy task especially for the more seasoned old school security executive who most likely has <u>not</u> been oriented in using security surveys to gauge crime risk exposures. Many security executives are retired law enforcement professionals who have little or no experience in applying pro-active crime risk management principles and techniques to mitigate crime risk exposures. Oftentimes they come to the job with a single mindset - gate it, lock it, and alarm it. One of the tenets in pro-active crime control planning is using the security survey to gauge crime risk exposure. The security survey is much like a diagnostic "cat scan" used in healthcare, in that it offers security diagnosticians an opportunity to see into the inner environs of the protection envelope. In professional hands, the survey profiles deficiencies, risks, and hazards, and offers creative/corrective approaches to remove and/or mitigate identified exposures.

The New Breed of Security Executive

Over the last twenty years, a new breed of civilian security specialist has emerged. These people have their roots in various fields including economic development, city planning, academia, engineering, and architecture. They also include citizen volunteers seeking to create safer neighborhoods and commercial and industrial centers. These non-law enforcement security practitioners should be welcomed into the profession as they bring to the profession an awareness of the cooperative basis of security. Some of these new practitioners are also coming from law enforcement and are being taught pro-active crime control basics via crime prevention courses and symposia inaugurated over the past two decades or so by police agencies and security organizations nation-wide.

Types of Security Surveys

The Single-Client Survey is used when analyzing stand-alone entities such as hospitals, apartment buildings, commercial stores, or residences. In this form of assessment, the facility under review is analyzed as a whole and recommendations for improvements are systemic. The basic idea herein is to design a crime risk management plan that makes the facility secure and is consistent with the client's interests and lifestyle. To do this, the practitioner must analyze existing security elements in relation to profitability (in the case of business) or lifestyle (in the case of a

---

From *The Journal of Healthcare Protection Management*. (24):2, pp. 90–94. 2008.

80 ■ *Healthcare Security*

residence). Security related recommendations offered in these forms of assessments include but are not limited to:

- Installation of security gates and alarm systems
- Installation of closed-circuit television (CCTV) and electronic article surveillance technologies
- Installation of 'bandit barriers"
- Promulgation of cash control and check cashing policies

The Multi-Client /Commercial Strip Security Survey

The philosophy in a multi-client /commercial strip survey differs significantly from the single-client survey in that the focus of the assessment is to identify crime exposures that affect both the individual client and the commercial strip they are located in. The mindset of the practitioner requires that he or she understand that the individual entity and commercial strip are one interrelated unit, and that simply recommending a single-client quick fix like target hardening their store against break-ins will not effectively deal with the more complex commercial strip crime problems such as roof top break-ins, organized shoplifting gangs, congregating youths in front of stores and on street corners, and poor illumination during evening hours. Security related recommendations offered in these forms of assessments include but are not limited to:

- Placement of lighting on store roofs to protect against roof burglaries
- Placement of address identifying signage on roof tops that offer visibility and recognition from neighboring buildings and passing law enforcement aircraft
- Installation of alarm and CCTV systems in all stores featuring monitoring by a local hospital and/or other community-based entities. In many instances, communal monitoring helps to bring all entities on the strip together into a cohesive crime control consortium. In some instances, grants may be available from local political organizations for this type of initiative.

The Access Control Security Survey – this form of survey is completed after an incident has occurred to help shore-up security in a specific environment post occurrence. In many instances, the survey endeavors to bolster protection requisites at critical access points and environs in and around the breached area. Security related recommendations include but are not limited to:

- Installation of security-related technologies in and around the affected area
- Assignment of temporary or long-term security presence in the area
- Formulation of security/safety seminars to keep employees informed and in the loop

The Community-Wide Security Survey – the philosophy in a community-wide survey differs significantly from the single-client, access control, and commercial strip surveys in that the focus of the assessment is to identify surrounding community concerns that affect *everyone* who legitimately uses the area such as store owners, shoppers, and neighborhood residents, etc. The mindset of the practitioner herein requires that he or she understand that the individual entity, commercial center, and surrounding neighborhood are one interrelated unit, and that security-related enhancements must focus on reducing and mitigating the more complex "signs of disorder/quality of life" crime problems that often plague entire communities.

Oftentimes, these crimes include but are not limited to public street sale of drugs and alcohol, streetlights, park benches, and vacant lot fences in disrepair, abandoned buildings left unsecured and not patrolled, and dirty streets and graffiti plagued buildings. Security related recommendations offered in these forms of assessments include:

- Installation of improved street lighting neighborhood-wide
- The formation of strategically designed lighted "safety corridors" for use by pedestrians, shoppers during evening hours
- The installation of security-related enhancements in mass transit stations and parking garages
- The formulation of neighborhood volunteer neighborhood watch programs
- The designation of neighborhood "safe-havens" for children and seniors in approved and supervised locations
- The promulgation of community-based crime prevention networks linking the commercial, residential, industrial, and institutional sectors into a cohesive community-wide crime control safe streets program.

It is important to note that community-wide assessments are intended to bring the commercial, residential, and institutional communities together in a pro-active crime prevention consortium that helps to enhance the quality of life for all who live, work, and legitimately use the neighborhood.

Conclusion

In the court of protection opinion, security executives need to reach out to security consultants that specialize in drafting security surveys and have their facilities diagnosed on an annual schedule. Having security reviews completed on a periodical schedule helps to unearth frail security policies, procedures, and technologies, and helps to substantially reduce security-related crime risk exposures before they wreak havoc on the institutional setting. One of the best resources to use when soliciting the services of a surveyor is to contact the local law enforcement agency's crime prevention office, or professional security organizations such as the American Society for Industrial Security for guidance.

The Security Survey: An Investigative Tool – Part I

Anthony Luizzo

Investigators use many tools to do their job. Some of these specialized tools include recorders, surveillance-capturing technologies, radios, computers, tracking/forensic software, logbooks, and cameras. The security survey is one of the many tools in the investigator's toolkit. Since most investigators lack the expertise to prepare security surveys, they usually opt to engage a professional surveyor to tackle the task. Most surveyors receive their specialized knowledge and training from academia and/or working as crime prevention specialists for major city, state, federal law enforcement agencies.

What is a Security Survey and How Does it Function?

The security survey is analogous to a medical CT scan (Computerized Tomography) which is an important device used by medical experts to diagnose and treat illness. Similarly, security executives use the security survey to diagnose and prescribe remedies for frail security programs. What a CT scan is to a physician, the security survey is to a security diagnostician. In professional hands, the survey profiles deficiencies, risks, and hazardous conditions, and offers creative/corrective approaches to correct these shortcomings.

Types of Security Surveys

- **The single client security survey** is a facility-wide assessment of a residence or business. These assessments are often extremely lengthy reports and touch on all aspects of facility security. The philosophy behind this form of survey is that the entire focus of the assessment is to identify crime exposures that affect the individual client only.
- **The after-incident security survey** is prepared as follow-up to an incident (burglary, robbery, assault). These assessments are usually extremely brief reports and strictly focus like a laser on the incident under scrutiny. The philosophy behind this form of survey is that the entire focus of the assessment is to identify incident-specific crime exposures only.
- **The access control security survey** is prepared as follow-up to incidents affecting ingress and egress points. This assessment is only intended to shore-up security at critical high trafficked points without restricting access into and out of the access portal
- **The multi-client/community-wide security surveys** – the philosophy behind this form of survey is that the focus of the assessment is to identify crime exposures that affect both the individual client and the overall community. These surveys are usually prepared at the request of organizations such as residential groups, gated communities, industrial parks, business improvement districts, etc. It's important to note that in these broader assessments the surveyor's mindset requires that they understand that the individual entity and the community are one interrelated unit.

From *PI Magazine*: Issue 156, pp. 28–30 – March/April 2018.

The ABC's of Organizing the Security Survey

A great way to understand how a security survey is structed is to frame the discussion using medical terminology:

1. Physicians examine patients
2. Physicians diagnose ailments
3. Physicians write prescriptions

The Examination

- First and foremost, the investigator must know whether the survey is a standard *overt* security survey assessment or a *surreptitious endeavor,*
- In some instances, surreptitious surveys are performed to capture internal thievery and on-site visitation by a surveyor is unadvisable. All work on this form of assessment is done during non-work periods.
- In standard overt type surveys, the surveyor meets with top management (CEO, VP, security director, facilities management director), to discuss project parameters, time-frame constraints, sub-contractor issues, budgetary issues, etc.
- The surveyor then examines company construction related documents (blueprints, floor plans, architectural drawings, electrical schematics, site maps, etc.)
- The surveyor obtains authorization letters to gain access to the survey site and its environs
- The surveyor visits the survey site on all work shifts so that each facet of the operation is examined.
- The surveyor obtains written authorization to interview department heads, managers, and employees.
- The surveyor examines company related crime incident data.
- The surveyor examines and reviews crime incident data from local law enforcement agencies (municipal and federal).
- The surveyor examines neighborhood crime incident data. An acceptable rule of thumb in to check crime incident rates occurring within a one-mile radius of the facility. Oftentimes, this info can be obtained by visiting local development corporations/industrial parks/business improvement district facilities and/or local political office of elected officials.
- The surveyor examines the facility's security staffing grid and security technology grid – where alarms, cameras, etc. are located
- The surveyor examines the facility's asset protection and inventory control programs.
- The surveyor examines the company's security awareness program.

The diagnosis

Once the examination is concluded, it's time for rigorous analysis. This process begins by logging each risk exposure and sub-dividing them into "low" "medium" and "high" risk categories, forming a risk grid. It is through this analytic process that the amplitude of various risk exposures is valuated. A good rule of thumb is to fashion judgements on sustentative data extrapolated from the risk grid, coupled with the diagnostician's intuitive abilities.

84 ■ *Healthcare Security*

Writing the Prescription

Regardless of the form or style of the survey, it is really the content that counts. A well-structured security survey should include:

- Introduction
- Core (body of the report)
- Summary of findings/enhancements
- Implementation timetable
- Closing statement
- Appendices

Introduction

This section of the survey stipulates who and why the survey is being prepared, the overall parameters of the study, who will be interviewed, and the start date and end date of the undertaking.

Core

This section of the assessment includes a list of departments visited, individuals interviewed, and security deficiencies noted.

Summary of Findings/Enhancements

The summary statement presents a menu of deficiencies coupled to an enhancement strategy listing. It is always a good idea to prioritize this listing so that percentage comparisons can be put forward.

Implementation Schedule

This section of the report includes a timetable for executing the recommended solutions, and a schedule for revisiting the site to review progress and non-progress.

Closing Statement

The closing statement should rivet attention to those individuals (department **heads**, employees, etc.) who assisted during the survey by acknowledging their contribution. Moreover, the surveyor should also champion the importance of implementing all recommendations.

Appendices

This section of the report includes all support documentation including, but not limited to:

- Memoranda
- Relevant studies

- Minutes of meetings
- Crime statistics
- Community profile data (maps, charts, diagrams, photographs)

The ABCs of Preparing Community Wide Assessments

Often, investigative firms are asked to evaluate security and safety issues for an entire community and/or a residential complex. It is important that investigators have some knowledge of how these broader studies are prepared.

The specific form of crime risk management counseling offered clients in conventional crime control differs significantly from the philosophy applied in preparing community wide studies. Quite a different mindset is required when preparing community wide survey. In these broader assessments, the surveyor needs to examine community data sources and conduct area-wide interviews with residents and retailers. Some of the tasks involved in drafting these wider studies include:

- A thorough review of community wide profile data (population, ethnic, income, age, housing, and employment breakdowns).
- A thorough review of land use, traffic flow, and building construction data.
- A thorough review of community-wide crime analysis data from police, community groups, elected officials, chambers of commerce, etc.
- Interviews with residents, retailers and legitimate users of the strip.
- Interviewers with delivery personnel, mail carriers, delivery truckers, utility company personnel who regularly service the area.

The ABCs of Preparing a Community Wide Security Survey

Essentially, these wider studies follow the same structural format as standard surveys. There is a big difference in the assortment of security measures put forward to help mitigate identified risk exposures. Protection measures used in these wider assessments include:

- **Problem:** Street crime control (muggings, robberies, etc.)
- **Solution:** The formulation of strategically designed lighted corridors (pedestrian routes) linking business centers to mass transit hubs.
- **Problem:** Crime incidents at bus stops and high crime intersections.
- **Solution:** Synchronizing signal lights at high crime intersections to encourage vehicular concentration; relocating bus stops from undesirable high crime intersections to more appropriate lower crime areas.
- **Problem:** Work-related muggings at quitting time.
- **Solution:** Encourage businesses to better coordinate work release schedules with local bus and train schedules. Coordinate police coverage to correspond with work release schedules.
- **Problem:** Poor coordination between the local police and residents.
- **Solution:** Establishment of mobile crime prevention services. Creating satellite police facilities, using mounted police for special events, creating senior citizen escort programs.
- **Problem:** Crime incidents at municipally operated subway and rail stations.

86 ■ *Healthcare Security*

■ **Solution:** Installation of state-of-the-art lighting, installing prominent signage, installing conductor boards to tell passengers where the subway car will stop on the platform, installing subway entrance lighted globes to alert passengers of entrance closures. Oftentimes, globes are either Red or Green. Red means the subway entrance is closed and green means it is open for use.

Conclusion

In the court of protection wisdom, the Security Survey is the right tool to use when measuring crime risk exposure. Surveyors spend countless hours probing, examining, researching, and pondering before they tear a page from their "Rx" pad. Many larger police agencies offer *free* security surveys and private firms specializing in this area can be found by searching the world wide web. It makes good sense for investigators to add this unique service to their company's roster of services.

---

*Reprinted with permission: PI Magazine

The Security Survey: An Investigative Tool – Part II

Anthony Luizzo

As with all professional endeavors, progress drives change, In the March/April 2018 edition of PI Magazine authored an article, "The Security Survey: An Investigative Tool" which laid out the ABCs of effectively drafting a security survey. The article walks the reader through the internal processes and intuitive strategies employed by experienced practitioners seeking to uncover criminal risk exposures. At times, changes to existing survey protocol are driven by factors that have been developing for decades. In this article, one specific factor is solely responsible for revising the existing security survey.

Reason for Revisiting the Security Survey

In 2015, an excellent book hit my desk written by Samuel I. Schwartz: *"Street Smart: The Rise of Cities and the Fall of Cars": Public Affairs Books.* Looking back to the middle of the 20th century, most Americans who resided in large urban cities such as NYC, witnessed firsthand the mass exodus to rural communities for a better life in the spacious suburbs. Obviously. The population shifts and the rise of crimes in urban cities helped to directly frame how security surveys were written to meet the risk exposures faced. The term "target hardening" became the protection management philosophical strategy of the day. Solid steel external gates and burglary bars on residential windows became the new décor. The book goes on to discuss how today's new millennials prefer bicycles to cars and short commutes to restaurants and are moving back to urban centers in droves.

The New 21st Century Security Survey

Today's professional surveyor understands that yesterday's strategies and technologies are NOT appropriate for today's environment. Gone are the solid steel gates and window bars – relaced by see-through mesh external portals, large full-view windows, and full display counters visible from the street. Surveyors understand that marketing and security are one interrelated strategy. Yesterday's gondolas (merchandise counters) did not allow for free and unobstructed access throughout the store. The major reason why yesterday's gondolas were restrictive (random left and right turns) is because it was believed that allowing customers to freely roam throughout the store could expedite their exodus from the store with purloined merchandise in-hand. Today's protection philosophy is quite different in that gondolas still feature random left and right turns, but the reason is because it improves item display and marketing promotions. Another example can be found by looking at the boardwalk in Coney Island New York. Years back, targeted police coverage was required to keep crime at bay under the boardwalk – today sand fills this vacant space which serves as both a berm from storm surge as well as restricting access to this crime prone sensitive area. Ingenuity at work I might say!

From *PI Magazine*: Issue 159, pp. 22–25. September/October 2018.

The Evolution of the Security Survey

The evolution of the private security industry from the Romans using geese to surround and protect battlefields during evening hours, to the sophisticated technological systems of the 21st century, is quite something indeed!

One of the most important innovations born out of the march to excellence in protection management was the realization that security practitioners needed to have a solid foundation in proactive security engineering. It was not until 1971 that the United States followed Great Britain's lead and formalized crime prevention training via law enforcement assistance administration grant awarded to the University of Louisville. Since the founding of the National Crime Prevention Institute, thousands of students in academia and law enforcement have honed their skills in the art and science of crime control planning. One of the pivotal tools used in this proactive crime control discipline is the security survey.

Security Survey Rationale

The rationale behind why security surveys are prepared can be tracked back to a 1968 paper by Shlomo Angel: "Discouraging Crime Through City Planning" – Berkley Institute of urban and Regional Development: University of California. The article describes in some detail how: *crime rates are related to the social and physical environment to territoriality, accessibility, and to victim behavior.* Seeking out crime exposures before they strike is truly a prescription for sound crime control planning, and the security survey is the go-to tool used to examine, diagnose, and proscribe crime-related remedies.

Looking to the Past

There are a variety of security survey models used to diagnose crime exposures in residences, commercial and industrial entities and for wider studies of entire communities. A discussion of the various survey models can be found in a 2008 article authored by this author "Aspects of the Security Survey: Distinctions between Single Client – Multi Client – Access Control and Community Wide Surveys" – Journal of Healthcare Protection Management: A Publication of the International Association for Healthcare Security and Safety – Vol. 24, No. 2 pp 90-94. From a protection management perspective, standard survey models for single entities rarely need major change – possibly only slight tweaks. Notwithstanding, considering the seismic shifts in population from suburb to urban center – community-wide surveys need continual tweaks to keep pace with the ever-changing demographics of today's urban centers. We need to move beyond standard "target hardening" approaches to applying new crime risk management techniques in future surveys.

In 1988 in an article authored by the undersigned, "Beyond Target Hardening: Approaches to Applying Crime Risk Management Principles and Techniques to Community Surveys" – featured in: The Practitioner: A Publication of the International Society of Crime Prevention Practitioners, lists several corrective strategies that could be applied in community-wide assessments. The article goes on to mention that over the last 20 years, a new breed of civilian security specialist has emerged who has his or her roots in various fields including: economic development, city planning, academia, engineering, and architecture. Moreover, the article speaks to the fact that these new practitioners should be welcomed into the ranks of the proactive security profession. Further change will be coming.

Looking to the Future

As in the past, new proactive crime control research will most likely come from future federal grants earmarked for crime control planning. One area that I believe will be a major part of this new research will involve using metrics as part of future crime control planning.

I strongly believe that security executives need to begin speaking the language that CFOs understand when pursuing their security enhancement wish lists. One of the important keys to obtaining needed security dollars from CFOs is to develop metric equations that are relevant and measurable.

Using Metrics in Security Planning

In an October 15, 2013, article by Scott Greaux featured in PhishMe.com, "Use of Metrics to Measure and Improve Security Awareness" whilst discussing the important of using metrics to improve security awareness programming, hypothesizes that unfortunately most security awareness programming fails to use metrics as part of the protection mosaic. In 2014, the ASIS Foundation issued a report "Persuading Senior Management with Effective, Evaluated Security Metrics" which summarized that security metrics support the value proposition of an organization's security operation; and without compelling metrics, security professionals continue to rely on the intuition of company leadership. Finding the right suit of metrics to snuggly fit a firm's protection wardrobe is both an art and a science. Choosing the right metric equation is the challenge!

In November 2006, Elizabeth A. Nichols and Andrew Sudbury authored an article: "Implementing Security Metrics Initiative" published in Information Security and Risk management Magazine. The article offers several suggestions on using metrics and discusses the challenges associated with their use. Moreover, the article also offers a seven-stop integration implementation guide to help guide the new protection practitioner.

The seven-step guide includes:

1. Defining goals and objectives
2. Determining information goals
3. Developing metrics models
4. Establishing a metrics reporting format and schedule
5. Suggestions on implementing a metrics program
6. Commentary on setting benchmarks and targets
7. Enacting a formal review cycle

Further information on using metrics can be found in a trilogy of articles authored by the undersigned:

- "An Alternative View in the Development of Healthcare Metrics" Vol. 31 No. 2. 2015 – The Journal of Healthcare Protection Management
- "Resources Available for Applying Metrics in Security and Safety Programming" Vol. 32 No. 1 2016 – The Journal of Healthcare Protection management
- "Applying Metrics to 21st Century Healthcare Security" Vol. 33. No. 2 2017 – The Journal of Healthcare Protection Management

A Final Thought

Over the past 40-plus years, the security survey has been a large part of the proactive crime control initiative. Over these years, many major police agencies have begun offering crime prevention programming.

Many of the larger law enforcement agencies offer a full menu of services including offering pamphlets on personal, residential, business security and safety tips, specialized services featuring neighborhood watch, identification etching of valuables, etc. Many of the larger departments offer free security surveys to residences and businesses. In addition to law enforcement agencies, many private investigators, and security firms offer security survey assessments as a part of the menu of services. Another service offered by some security firms involve surveying neighborhoods, gated communities, amusement complexes, business improvement districts and enterprise zones, industrial parks, and the like. These broader studies require that the surveyor have unique understanding of standard crime control techniques and technologies, as well as a firm grasp of concepts associated with understanding crime prevention, understanding design against crime and defensible space initiatives, understanding security through environmental design concepts, and understanding safe neighborhood design engineering concepts.

These and other solutions are used to stimulate social attitudes and behaviors that help reduce both opportunity for criminality and the fear of criminality. One excellent resource that should be read by all proactive crime control planners is the excellent book by C. Ray Jeffery "Crime Prevention Through Environmental Design" – Sage Publications, 1977. The book offers several studies on applying environmental design concepts which have become a major part of the foundation upon which proactive security programming is erected.

---

*Reprinted with permission: PI Magazine

Revising the Security Survey

Anthony Luizzo

Why Revise the Security Survey?

In an excellent book by Samuel I. Schwartz "**Street Smart: The Rise of Cities and the Fall of Cars**": Public Affairs Books, 2015, the author recounts how urban life has been resurrected since the beginning of the new millennium. Looking back to the 1940s and 1950s the trend was to jump into the family automobile and leave the large cities for a better life in the spacious suburbs. As the exodus continued coupled with the abrupt loss of industrial jobs to foreign countries many neighborhoods in industrial U.S. cities have become desolate crime infested baron wastelands. Many of these communities were left without jobs and economically devastated. As the new millennium dawned, the pendulum began to shift back to where it all started. Suburban dwellers AKA millennial(s) longed for shorter commutes to work, healthier lifestyles (bicycling to and from the workplace) and having easy access to mass transit systems for both long and short business and non-business commutes. They also recalled the countless hours spent buckled and strapped into car seats eventually leading to a general distaste for auto travel in general. For many of today's new urban dwellers it is a relief indeed to be living in the large city once again. Beyond the population explosion, 9/11was also a big game changer forcing many protection specialists to put security and terrorism prevention on their front burners. Considering that both population shifts, and terror threats directly impact public safety and security, it is important that new and innovative protective strategies are put forward to ensure that optimum public safety is preserved.

Looking Behind the Survey

In the court of crime deterrence, the diagnostic tool used to gauge safety and security appropriateness / effectiveness is the security survey. The standard survey models include single-client, multi-client, access control, and community wide security surveys. Considering the lifestyle changes we have undergone since 1940, it is imperative that our survey models keep pace. One innovative thought might be to consider developing a terrorism-specific survey for use by our local law enforcement and private security surveyors. If such a survey is adopted, it would be wise to seek the assistance and cooperation of the Office of Homeland Security in developing the appropriate survey model that snugly fits each community's structural and demographic skeleton. The rationale behind why security assessments are prepared can be found in a paper by Shlomo Angel: **"Discouraging Crime Through City Planning"** – Berkeley Institute of Urban and Regional Development, University of California, 1968 when he describes in some detail how crime rates are related to: the social and physical environment, to territoriality, accessibility, and to behavior of victims. Proactively seeking out crime exposures before they strike is truly a prescription for good crime control planning.

From *The Journal of Healthcare Protection Management*. (34):2, pp. 106–112. 2019.

The Standard Security Survey

Crime control planners specializing in drafting security surveys have been plying their trade for well over 40+ years.

The security survey is an onsite examination of a physical facility (home, business, hospital, factory, or neighborhood) which helps to gauge crime-related risks and weaknesses; while also proffering preventative measures to remove and/or mitigate these risks. Taking a page from the medical lexicon, what a *"cat scan"* is to a physician, the security survey is to a security diagnostician. In professional hands, the survey profiles deficiencies, risks, and hazardous conditions, and offers creative /corrective approaches to remove and/or mitigate identified exposures. Physicians and security diagnosticians do have much in common; they both are in the examination, diagnosis and prescription dispensing business proscribing remedies for both human and criminological ailments.

The Evolution of the Security Survey: Single Client to Multi Client to Community-Wide Assessments

In a 2008 article featured in the Journal of Healthcare Protection Management: Vol. 24 No. 2: **"Aspects of the Security Survey: Distinctions Between Single-Client, Multi-Client, and Community Wide Surveys"** tenders a description of the various types of surveys available and how they are prepared. In the early days, the security survey was a simple less complicated instrument which only focused on the security needs of the single entity such as: dwellings, hospitals, stores, and other stand-alone entities. Over the years, surveyors began preparing multi-client security and safety studies involving many different stores in commercial centers nationwide. The focus of these new more complex multi-client assessments differed significantly from the single-client assessment in that the surveyor's mindset needed to drastically shift. In these broader in-depth studies, the single client continues to remain important, but the object of this survey is to improve the security of the commercial center. Herein, the surveyor is interested in reducing crime risks for each individual business but is also looking to reduce incidents of street and personal crime exposures for everyone who occupies and/or legitimately uses the environment. As time passed, the need arose to begin preparing community-wide security assessments. These even more sophisticated studies required a more drastic shift in mindset. In these much broader and complex assessments security and safety for everyone (residents, dwellings, pedestrians, automobile operators, business facilities, etc.) is the overall goal.

Survey Specifics

The following is a roll call of security specific recommendations furnished in single-client, multi-client, and community-wide security assessments:

- In Single Client Surveys recommendations are often limited to target-hardening devices such as metal gates, improved locking systems, closed circuit, alarm and point-of-sale loss prevention internal theft reduction technologies, and robbery deterrence devices
- In Multi-Client Surveys recommendations include all the above enhancements plus special tailor-made options for each specific project. As an example, if robberies and burglaries were

found to be the most prevalent crimes of record plaguing the commercial center, installing alarm and closed-circuit systems in each store would be a viable option and a wise strategy. To deepen and strengthen security in this venue, the surveyor might consider reaching out to an anchor partner within the community such as a hospital and ascertain whether they would consider furnishing free alarm monitoring services for all participating in the project. The next step might be to reach out to the local merchant association and ask them to consider reaching out to their members participating in the in project and ascertain whether they would be willing to make a periodical voluntary tax-deductible contribution to the anchor facility to cover the monitoring service fees – herein everyone wins! (These types of programs are *"Network Projects"*.)

- Over and above the financial incentives, network alliances help to deepen and strengthen the bonds between the residential, commercial, industrial, and institutional sectors, while also establishing a multi-faceted crime fighting network that benefits all. It is important to note that over the years "network" alliances have been established for roof lighting projects and mobile patrol projects. The surveyor is only limited by his or her imagination.
- In Community-Wide Surveys recommendations include all the above plus land use statistics, traffic flow, building construction, population, housing, and employment data. In this form of analysis security recommendations put forward are for all who legitimately use, live, work, pass through, and legally and/or illegally stumble into the environment.

Fashioning a Terrorism Prevention Survey

Half of the battle is won when the right representatives are chosen to develop a template for the survey. Once a template is developed, it is time to identify the actors and players who will be involved in performing these assessments. Will these surveys be prepared by local law enforcement specialists, such as crime prevention experts, or will they be outsourced to outside firms? Will surveyors be required to undergo specialized training and certification? What will be the fee structure for these assessments? It is important to note that presently, local law enforcement agencies offer security assessments free of charge, while private security firms charge a fee. Once the logistics are finalized, it is time to begin structuring the report.

The following information needs to be included in this form of assessment:

- Community profile data: including a population breakdown, by group, age, income, housing, and employment
- Immigrant profile data
- Land use, traffic flow, building construction data: including a structural analysis of the entire catchment area, pedestrian, and customer shopping habits,
- Local and federal government crime and terrorism statistics
- Strategic information re prior security surveys prepared in the past
- Local school, healthcare and elected official data

This information helps to form the sum and substance of the survey. Sum and substance alone is worthless without sitting down with all this data and tying it all together and turning it into a cohesive set of strategies to help keep the community safe. Coordinating such an effort is a monumental task but quite necessary if terrorism is to be kept at bay. Like all surveys METRIC equations should also be included to adequately measure and improve security awareness. An excellent

94 ■ *Healthcare Security*

discussion of why METRICS should be used in security assessments can be found in an article in the Journal of Healthcare Protection Management: Luizzo / Scaglione **"An Alternative View in the Development of Healthcare Security Metrics"** - 2015.

Framing the Survey

These assessments should include:

1. **An opening statement** – describes the survey target (movie theatre, concert hall etc.)
2. **Deficiency / Recommendation Section** – lists deficiencies and recommended enhancements
3. **A Prioritized List of Recommendations** – a list of all risk exposures in priority order (High Priority, Medium Priority or Low Priority)
4. **A Closing Statement** – a summary of the findings
5. **After Action Review Schedule** – a review and inspection schedule

Evaluating the Assessment

As with all programs a system of evaluation should be designed so that the effect of the study can be measured. Some areas to be considered include before, middle and after studies - to help determine crime reporting levels, and statistical evaluations - to gauge public information efforts. All in all, a structured program of evaluation should measure the community's response to the terrorism prevention efforts and the specific effect of the strategies put forward.

Looking to the Future

As our urban population and terrorism-related threats increase, a central question that needs to be answered is whether our protection capabilities are up to the job? And does it require retooling? Do our hospitals, shopping centers, residential and industrial complexes, and mass transit systems need to be re-evaluated? Questions abound. Much of the initial research in crime prevention and control was completed in the 1960s and 1970s during a period when large city population was on the decline. The funding for this research came from federal grants from the "The Omnibus Crime Control and Safe Streets Act of 1968". In 1986, the National Crime Prevention Institute, a division of the University of Louisville's School of Justice Administration – College of Urban and Public Affairs published "Understanding Crime Prevention" which offered several proactive security techniques, technologies, and solutions. In my humble opinion, I believe it is again time for us to seek federal, state and/or private sector funding for new research on crime control for the second half of the 21st Century.

A Final Thought

Over the past forty plus year's crime prevention theory and environmental design applications have become part of security assessment process. Many of today's firms perform security surveys on an annual schedule to ensure that their company is a safe and secure workplace.

C. Ray Jeffery in **"Crime Prevention Through Environmental Design"**: Sage Publications 1977 offers several studies on applying environmental design crime control concepts which have become an important part of the security survey process.

What is needed today is additional research into how terrorists ply their trade and how we should respond? Private security needs to do its homework and work diligently with federal law enforcement mavens to frame a security assessment that can be applied locally for each community throughout our great nation. Security and safety diagnosticians spend countless hours probing, examining, researching, and pondering before he or she tears a page from their "Rx" pad to give to their respective clients. Getting started is the hard part!

Selected Bibliography

- C. Ray Jeffrey: "Crime Prevention Through Environmental Design" – Sage Publications: 1977
- National Crime Prevention Institute: "Understanding Crime Prevention" – Butterworth 1986
- Samuel I. Schwartz: "Street Smart: The Rise of Cities and the Fall of Cars" – Public Affairs New York Publishers 2015.

The Many Faces of the Security Survey

Anthony Luizzo

Over the years, I have written several articles on the art and science of preparing single-client, multi-client, access control, and community-wide security surveys (1-8). This article details how this diverse set of surveys is applied. The rationale behind why security assessments are crucial can be found in a paper by Shlomo Angel, "Diagnosing Crime Through City Planning" - Berkeley Institute of Urban Planning and Regional Development , University of California, 1968, when he describes in some detail how crime rates are related to the social and physical environment, to territoriality, accessibility, and to behavior of victims. Proactively seeking out crime exposures before they strike is truly a prescription for good crime control planning". Further reinforcing the age-old adage: "an ounce of prevention is worth a pound of cure".

Innovation drives change

It is said that innovation is the engine that drives change. Looking back to the early days of our nation, our founding Fathers used newspapers to get the word out to the public about national issues of importance. In the 1940s, President Theodore Roosevelt used Radio (Fireside Chats) to get his message out. In the 1960s, President John F. Kennedy used television as his media carrier. In the new millennium, President Donald Trump took our nation totally digital and the tweet became the new media venue. Like media innovation, the security field has also undergone tremendous change as well. Just a few short years ago, the only way to lock and/or unlock a door was by physically doing so, the only way to surveil a premise was to physically watch a video replay, and the only way to take a photo was via camera. Today, remote locking and unlocking, real-time video surveillance and instant photo availability via smartphone is a way of life. With all this innovation abound, the security survey has joined the march to tomorrow. Yesterday's simple single client often straight-forward security survey of buildings, hospitals and businesses has expanded into full blown security assessments of multi-client commercial centers and community-wide surveys of neighborhoods, gated communities, industrial parks, business improvement districts, and enterprise zones.

The birth of a new breed of security surveyor

Over the last fifty years, a new breed of civilian security specialist has emerged. These people have their roots in various fields, including economic development, city planning, academia, engineering, and architecture. They also include citizen volunteers - community organizers and activists seeking to create safer neighborhoods and commercial /industrial centers. Prior to these specialists joining the crime control continuum, security surveys were almost always performed by law enforcement and private security.

From *PI Magazine*: (21):173, pp. 16–19. January / February 2021.

Evolution of the security survey

The actual birth date of the security survey is difficult to ascertain since many forms of crime related risk assessment studies have been ongoing for centuries.

Early references to crime deterrence efforts can be traced to the Roman Empire when during field battles roman centuries surrounded their camp with geese to forewarn of an impending encroachment. In the 1960s, the more modern security survey was born championed by research conducted by the National Institute of Law Enforcement & Criminal Justice (NILE), the Law Enforcement Assistance Administration (LEAA) – U.S. Department of Justice. In 1968, LEAA issued its report, "The Challenge of Crime in a Free Society" – which led to funding for community not-for-profit organizations, anti-crime studies and related academic research. These texts and Monographs from LEAA and NILE eventually led to the establishment of the National Crime Prevention Institute.

In 1971, The National Crime Prevention Institute (NCPI) – a division of the University of Louisville's School of Justice Studies, College of Urban and Public Affairs, was established to serve as the nation's educational and technical resource for crime prevention programming. Over the past half a century, NCPI has been hard at work teaching law enforcement, corporate security, community organizations and private citizenry the art and science of proactive security programming techniques and technologies. Writing security surveys has been and continues to be an important tool used in the proactive crime control discipline.

What is a security survey?

A security survey has many meanings to many protection practitioners. To some it is a tool used _after_ a security initiative has failed. To others, it is a tool to evaluate existing programmatic initiatives. To the more seasoned security professional however, the survey is a medical CT Scan (Computed Tomography) that can scientifically diagnose frail security programming.

Definition of the security survey

The generic definition of a security survey is an onsite examination of a physical facility (home, business, industrial plant, hospital, community complex. In practice, trained surveyors from both public and/or private entities search for crime related risks, hazards and weaknesses and devise preventative measures to remove and/or mitigate frail security inequities. The security survey is the fulcrum on which proficient security is erected.

The science behind the survey

Writing a security survey is not rocket science, one needs only understand that there is a methodology behind effectively writing security studies. Most standard security officers can be sent to the scene of a security breach to document a problem, but it requires years of study in the proactive security discipline to sit down and draft full-blown multi-client and/or community-wide /neighborhood crime impact statements (aka security surveys). Writing these broader studies starts with first knowing what types of data will be needed for each type of survey prior to commencing the

98 ■ *Healthcare Security*

endeavor. In single client studies the surveyor needs only have some knowledge of how security technology functions.

In the broader studies however, surveyors need to examine land use and crime analysis data, ethnic and age breakdown studies, canvass business owners and legitimate area users, traffic flow patterns, building construction schematics, and area housing and employment statistics. All in all, the surveyor spends hours examining and reexamining this treasure-trove of data before taking pen in hand to begin piecing together his or her report.

The single client security assessment

By and large, the philosophy behind drafting a single-client assessment is for the surveyor to maintain a private interest viewpoint. For the most part, the focus is very straight forward, and solutions offered are almost always of the 'target hardening' variety.

In single-client security surveys, the facility under scrutiny (business, hospital, store) is always analyzed as an independent entity and the wisdom applied is to design a strategy to make that structure more safe and secure. To do this the surveyor analyzes existing security in relation to profit for business and/or lifestyle for residences. In these surveys, the surveyor considers a multitude of crime risks including but not limited to theft, fraud, forgery, arson, burglary, employee safety, executive protection, etc. Once a strategy is devised, it is time for promulgating remedies.

The multi-client security assessment

A multi-client security survey involves piecing together a security package for a number of independent stand-alone facilities such as a residential complex, a strip of commercial retailers, a shopping mall, and retail outlets. Herein, the single-client's security concerns are still important, but the object of the survey is to collectively improve the overall security and safety of the entire cluster of clients. In these wider studies the surveyor is interested in reducing both property and personal crime for everyone who occupies or uses the complex. The philosophy in these broader studies shifts dramatically from a private to a public interest perspective. One of the biggest differences between performing a single client vs. a multi-client survey is that the focus of the assessment is to identify crime risk exposures that affect both the individual client and the commercial strip they are all located in. *As such, the practitioner's mindset requires that he or she understand that the individual entity and commercial strip are one interrelated unit, and that a quick fix target hardening upgrade will not make the cut.*

The access control survey

An access control survey is a very narrow form of assessment and is usually triggered after a security breach has occurred at one or more ingress and/or egress portals. Once the extent of the breach is determined, it is usually rectified.

The community and/or neighborhood security assessment

A community-wide neighborhood assessment in many ways is similar to the multi-client survey, save that the main focus of these assessments is to try to engineer strategies that zero in on high-risk neighborhood crime hot spots. Oftentimes these locations include crowded bus stops in remote locations, commercial corridors with long histories of assaults, burglaries, robberies and related crimes, desolate areas often used as "lovers' lanes", and other commercial and industrial high crime risk locations like methadone clinics and marijuana sales stores, etc. On average, single client surveys may take about a week to complete, multi-client surveys about two months to complete and community-wide assessments between three to six months or longer to complete.

The mechanics of performing the security survey

The single-client security survey: *Step one:* the surveyor performs an onsite examination of the entity under review (business, residence, etc.). *Step two:* the surveyor diagnosis the security issue. *Step three:* the surveyor writes the prescription to correct the problem. *Step four:* enhancement strategies often include "target hardening devices" such as: alarm systems, locking systems, steel store curtains, etc.

The multi-client security survey: *Step one:* the surveyor meets with the project manager or official representative to discuss project parameters, obtain letters of authorization, acquire construction blueprints and site maps. *Step two*: the surveyor performs both day and night site inspections, interviews all project participants, determines project essentials. *Step three:* the surveyor diagnoses the existing security problem, approves security installations, obtains governmental approval letters, performs final step-test inspections. *Step four:* enhancement strategies often include lighting upgrades, establishing centralized monitoring networks, erecting anti-crime signage, hiring external security guard services, establishing an ongoing liaison between merchants, mobile security patrols and local police.

The community-wide or neighborhood survey *Step one:* the surveyor obtains community profile data (land use, age and employment), traffic flow schematics, mass transit schedules, current and future construction investitures, local police and area FBI crime reports. *Step two:* the surveyor performs both day and night inspections, canvasses property owners, legitimate users, interviews public service providers. *Step three:* the surveyor diagnosis the crime problem. *Step four:* enhancement strategies often include: installing improved community-wide lighting, improving security on mass transit systems, relocating bus stops to well lighted areas, synchronizing traffic signals to better control vehicle concentration at vulnerable high crime incident intersections, creating safety cul-de-sac termination points, installing municipal surveillance systems, conjoining municipal CCTV systems and local CCTV merchant systems, changing traffic flow patterns to increase vehicle concentration and visibility, encouraging local mounted police patrols in high crime business sectors, devising community based crime prevention networks linking residential, commercial, industrial, institutional, private and public law enforcement into a cohesive neighborhood-wide system of crime control, establishing strategically designed lighted corridors (pedestrian walkways) linking business centers to mass transit points.

Diagnosing and prioritizing crime risks

Once the examination phase of the survey is concluded and all pertinent data is catalogued, its time for rigorous analysis. The process begins by logging each risk and subdividing the various risks into "low", "medium" and "high" risk categories - forming a risk grid. It is through this analytic process that the amplitude of various crime-risk exposures is valuated. Oftentimes, surveyors list risk and enhancement strategy side-by-side in priority order. This helps to ensure that critical data is always front and center and never lost in the details!

A final word

In the court of protection wisdom, private investigators would be wise to reach out to their corporate clients to ascertain if they perform annual security assessments on a regular basis. Pulling that thread even further, they should advise their clientele that security is fragile, and it needs to be treated with extreme care!

References

1. Luizzo, Anthony. Beyond Target Hardening: Approaches in Applying Crime Risk Management Principles and Techniques in Community Surveys – Practitioner Magazine: A publication of the International Society of Crime Prevention Practitioners - July 1988 pp. 4-7
2. Luizzo, Anthony. A Checklist to Audit the Security Survey – Internal Auditing Alert: Warren Gorham & Lamont – RIA Group – Reuters: Thomson Publications – Vol. 18 No. 2 - October 1998 - pp. 5-8
3. Luizzo, Anthony. Aspects of the Security Survey – Internal Auditing Alert: Warren Gorham & Lamont – RIA Group – Reuters: Thomson Publications – Vol. 26. No. 6. - June 2000
4. Luizzo, Anthony. How is Crime Risk Measured and Managed - Internal Auditing Report: Warren Gorham & Lamont – RIA Group – Reuters: Thomson Publications – Vol. 2. No. 11 - May 2002
5. Luizzo, Anthony. Aspects of the Security Survey: Distinctions Between Single-Client, Access Control, and Community Wide Security Surveys – Journal of Healthcare Protection Management: Rusting Publications – A Publication of the International Association for Healthcare Security and Safety – Vo. 24 No. 2. - 2008 pp.90-94
6. Luizzo, Anthony. The Security Survey; an Investigative Tool – PI Magazine - Issue 156. – March / April 2018 pp. 28-30
7. Luizzo, Anthony. The Security Survey; an Investigative Tool – Part II - PI Magazine - Issue 159. – September / October 2019 pp. 22-25
8. Luizzo, Anthony. Revising the Security Survey - Journal of Healthcare Protection Management: Rusting Publications – A Publication of the International Association for Healthcare Security and Safety – Vo. 34 No. 2. - 2018 pp.106-112

Suggested reading

1. C. Ray Jeffrey Crime Prevention Through Environmental Design – Sage Publications – 1977
2. Understanding Crime Prevention – National Crime Prevention Institute – 1986

*Reprinted with permission: PI Magazine

Chapter 5

Practical Crime Prevention

An Alternate Perspective on Healthcare Crime Prevention

Bernard J. Scaglione

To be more effective in providing healthcare security, security departments need to focus more on the prevention and/or prediction of crime, identifying criminal activity before more crime can occur rather than reacting to crimes as they occur. Crime prevention today is analytical and predictive. Criminologists and law enforcement experts have found scientific methods that prevent and even predict crime. These theorists use "Evidence-Based" modeling to quantify the effectiveness of crime prevention theories, identifying criminal activity, predicting future activity, and tracking criminal behavior through trending and pattern recognition. Collecting relevant data and analyzing it to identify trends and recognize emerging patterns in criminal behavior. Evidence-based crime prevention uses the 80-20 rule in the prediction of crime. The 80-20 rule, in theory, states that 20 percent of some things are responsible for 80 percent of the outcomes. It is never exactly 80-20, but it is always a small percentage of something, or some group involved in a large percentage of outcomes. Criminal justice theorists have demonstrated that a small number of events produce most of the crime. In crime prevention that means crime is highly concentrated to particular people, places, and things, and by using models that focus on repeat location, repeat offender, repeat victim, hot products and high-risk areas, practitioners can predict crime patterns before they occur.

Predictive Models That Work

Crime prevention practitioners use several models that are effective in the prediction and prevention of crime. These models have been proven to work in the law enforcement field and can work effectively in the healthcare environment. "Mapping" is place based crime prevention. Mapping utilizes frequency-based charting of crime locations to determine where future crimes will occur. Research has found that crime occurs in a small number of locations within a city, town or even hospital, the 80-20 model. By plotting locations security personnel see where crimes are occurring and predict future occurrences based on the 80-20 rule.

From *LinkedIn* Blog Post, July 31, 2015.

DOI: 10.4324/9781003215851-5

101

102 ■ *Healthcare Security*

Place-based prevention includes what are called "Hot Spots." Hot Spots are specific locations identified through Mapping and signify those areas where crime is occurring and more likely to occur in the future. Through detailed analysis of Hot Spot incidents, incident rates can be trended and targeted to reduce crime. Studies within the criminal justice field have shown that victim and perpetrator recidivism does exist. These studies show that once a person or place becomes a victim of a crime, they are more likely to become a repeat victim than a person or place that has never been a victim. The same holds true for offenders. Persons who commit crimes are a small number and will repeat committing crime until they are caught or in some cases even after they are caught. Therefore, when looking to reduce crime in a Hot Spot area, attention should be given to previous offenders. As most know who work in the security and law enforcement fields, the 80-20 rule also works for property crimes. When a product becomes a hot target, it is more likely to be stolen than other products that reside in the same location.

Practitioners know that this is true from experience, like the IBM Executive Electric Typewriter, MP3 Players, the I Pod and of course the I Phone. Once a hot product is identified, resources should be focused on reducing the opportunity for theft. Once a pattern or trend is developed with a particular place, victim or product, future crimes can be reduced. Focusing resources where crime is concentrated yields the greatest preventive benefits. Techniques like directed patrol, CPTED, community-based policing and Broken Windows theory all can help to reduce crime within the healthcare environment. Directed patrol is utilized to provide a security presence in identified Hot Spot areas. When data identifies a concentration of crime, a patrol officer can be present in a particular area during high crime times and days to identify and reduce crime activities.

Crime Prevention Through Environmental Design (CPTED) provides techniques that reduce the potential for crime in Hot Spot areas by changing the physical environment. CPTED techniques increase surveillance capacity, harden high-risk targets, and reduce the opportunity to commit crime by altering the design of the physical environment to become crime free.

Community-Based Policing reduces crime by placing police within the community and allowing them to solve problems within that community that create crime. When a police officer spends time in a Hot Spot area getting to know residents and patterns of behavior like mail delivery, school hours, etc., police can assist in identifying crime patterns while working with residents to reduce crime through the community's involvement in solving crime problems. This process works in the healthcare environment as well. Having security officers that are engaged with staff, learning patterns of business-like discharge times, transport services and visiting hours helps to identify potential crime problems before they occur.

Broken Windows theory suggests that communities or environments that become worn down, contain vandalism, broken windows and abandon cars attract crime. When the community is cared for, graffiti is quickly removed, vandalism is immediately repaired and the community is well kept, residents are engaged and not only look out for crime but make a proactive effort to keep crime low. This process of community engagement works in hospitals. For example, in-patient units that are well maintained and contain staff that care about their work areas notice unauthorized persons, door locks that are broken and even supplies that have gone missing.

By collecting data, analyzing it and identifying concentrations of crime related to time, date location, person and product, hospitals can reduce the potential for crime by implementing and maintaining basic crime prevention techniques.

A Clinical Approach to Crime Detection

Anthony Luizzo

Licensed private investigators play a vital role in helping their clientele decipher both reactive and proactive crime-related risk exposures. Investigative firms that do not have a strong background in proactive crime control planning and security simply offer reactive solutions to identified crime problems. Alternatively, investigative firms with extensive expertise in proactive crime control planning offer a much broader selection of services from both the reactive and proactive universe of security services. Having the capacity to offer both proactive and reactive crime solving techniques is a much wiser business model, especially in today's turbulent world. This is especially true for corporate security in the business sector where security-enhancement dollars are scarce.

One of the central reasons why security dollars are scarce is because oftentimes in the business sector security is <u>not</u> considered a profit contributor, but rather an expense that CFOs must keep in check. Contradicting this premise however is an age-old truism: **"an ounce of prevention is worth a pound of cure"**. Companies may be saving money at their peril!

The technical definition of proactive crime control planning

Proactive crime control planning aka crime prevention is commonly defined as the anticipation, recognition and appraisal of a crime risk and the initiation of an action to mitigate identified risks. Security firms and corporate entities that employ community crime control planners (CCCP) have a step-up on their competition in that they have an internal capability to capture crime exposures before they have an opportunity to wreak havoc and possibly devastate a company's reputation and standing within the mercantile community. Three recent articles authored by the undersigned speak to how the security survey is the go-to investigative tool often used by investigative firms to uncover business-related crime risk exposures, and the third article offers a menu of low-cost security enhancement strategies to help in the never-ending war against criminal wrongdoing:

- "The Security Survey: An Investigative Tool – Part I & II": Issues 156 /159 – PI Magazine
- "Squeezing the Most from you Security Dollar" – The Texas Investigator Magazine: Spring 2018

Is there a need for proactive crime control?

The simple answer is a resounding YES! Contemporary issues such as budget cuts, revenue short-falls, terrorism, computer hacking, social unrest, and political tribalism among other issues, have left many security administrators searching for new and innovative approaches to crime control.

Fashioning a proactive security program

The building process begins by the investigative company pulling either one or two investigative operatives from the investigative assembly line and properly school them in the ABCs of proactive crime risk management.

From *PI Magazine*. (18):161, pp. 12–14. January / February 2019.

104 ■ *Healthcare Security*

During their studies operatives are taught to evaluate crime risk exposures and formulate strategies to mitigate identified exposures. (This is an especially difficult aspect of training since many operatives are quasi-law enforcement/security-oriented candidates who work in a reactive role and are rarely asked to come up with proactive crime reduction remedies – it is simply not their job.) Over and above education in theoretical proactive security axioms, operatives are taught to apply crime prevention and environmental design concepts and strategies utilizing today's sophisticated security technologies and machineries. The process begins by selecting the right candidate to work in this role. Selection criteria should include candidates who possess above-average reading and cursive skills and have the ware withal to get up in front of small and large audiences and effectively deliver the proactive security message effectively.

Sample proactive security curricula might include but should not be limited to:

- Introduction to today's new millennium security technologies
- Introduction to crime prevention 101
- Introduction to physical security 101
- Aspects of applying environmental design concepts
- The role of the crime prevention specialist
- Developing employee and/or citizen participation
- Using metrics in security evaluation and planning
- Evaluating programmatic impact

Tasks and responsibilities of proactive security advocates

In the main, proactive security advocates perform the following tasks:

- Preparation of security surveys
- Reviewing and analyzing incident reports, employee hot-line missives, complaints and other relevant correspondence
- Preparing and presenting lecture programming and special exhibitions
- Networking with facility engineers and architects on security design issues
- Reviewing the functionality of existing security systems
- Maintaining and/or establishing a security / safety library
- Conducting and/or updating facility security surveys. *It is important to note that security surveys be prepared on an annual schedule to ensure that security and safety issues remain adequate*
- Maintaining accreditation by taking required continuing education credits

Programmatic evaluation

A system of evaluation needs to be promulgated so that the actual program effect is accurately measured. It is most important that a schedule of before and after studies is developed to help determine actual crime level reporting numbers, decipher crime patterns, promulgate / maintain crime mapping initiatives, and help decipher crime dispersion patterns.

All in all, a structured program of evaluation should accurately measure the entity's response to proactive crime control planning and the long-lasting effects of the promulgated strategies.

Using metrics in security planning

To better understand the role that metrics can effectively play in security and safety planning, the undersigned coauthored a trilogy of articles that directly address this issue: "An Alternative View in the Development of Security Metrics" -Vol. 31., No 2 - 2015 / "Resources Available for Applying Metrics in Security and Safety Programming" – Vol. 32., No. 1 – 2016 / "Applying Metrics to 21st Century Healthcare Security" - Vol. 33. No. 2 -2017: Journal of Healthcare Protection Management: a publication of the International Association for Healthcare Security and Safety. These three articles offer a roadmap to follow when using metrics in the security and safety habitat.

The financial value of using metrics

It is only recently that many security executives have begun speaking the language that all CFOs know and understand when going hat-in-hand asking for additional security dollars for their facility. In competent hands, metrics can vividly show fluctuation in service delivery variations, enhancement options, and service curtailment calamities among other yardsticks. As a practical matter, CFOs understand numbers very well (they usually are bean-counters), and security administrators need to make their case for additional dollars by showing simple verifiable facts to support their case. Support documentation includes response time inconsistencies, incident report upsurges, criminal activity spikes, calls for service hikes, square footage comparisons vs. other similar facilities, conjoining incident rates to visitations, and conjoining incident rates to response durations. These and other yardsticks will go a long way in justifying security expenditures to the individuals who control the company's purse strings.

The role that robotics might play in security management

Robert J. Gordon a professor at Northwestern University in his excellent work "Rise and Fall of American Growth: U.S. Standard of Living Since the Civil War": Princeton University Press, 2016 – whilst speaking of the possible use of robots in a wide variety of applications outside of the manufacturing and warehousing sectors including: supermarkets, restaurants, and hospitals; hypothesizes that the sixty million dollar question we should be pondering is: what role will robotics play in all industries in the coming decades? If innovation is said to drive commerce, I expect that robotics will have a central role in the coming decades simply because security technologies are becoming smarter and smarter. Just think how far we have come when the simple doorbell and smart phone can bring us into the inner environs of our home or business, whilst we are thousands of miles from the scene!

Looking to the future

Private investigators and corporate security administrators should strongly consider establishing a proactive crime control operation that can effectively diagnose crime risks *before* they are able to breed further devastation. Community crime control planners serve as the agency's advocate to spread the gospel that "security is every one's responsibility". CCCPs also help senior security management make the financial case to CFOs that security is a profit center and not simply a cost contributor.

A final thought

Security executives always have an extremely hard time trying to champion how much crime they averted, using Metrics could help make your case!

References

- National Crime Prevention Institute: "UNDERSTANDING CRIME PREVENTION" – Butterworths – 1986
- C. Ray Jeffrey: "CRIME PREVENTION THROUGH ENVIRONMENTAL DESIGN" – Sage Publications – 1977
- K brown – Blog Entry "5 Steps for Creating a Proactive Security Plan": http://ibm.conres.com – June 2, 2016
- T Scholtz – "Seven Techniques for More Proactive Risk and Security Management" – https://cdn.ttgtmedia.com – 2014
- G Connell – "5 Benefits of Having a Proactive Incident Response Plan" – http://info.garlandheart.com/blog/5-benefits-of-having-a-proactive-incident-response-plan - May 20, 2016

*Reprinted with permission: PI Magazine

A Clinical Approach to Hospital Security

Anthony Luizzo

In the medical profession, it is said that having an annual check-up helps to keep the human body healthy. By the same token, periodic check-ups by knowledgeable security experts is considered the best prescription for maintaining a healthy protective program.

Like medical professionals, security experts must keep current with today's minute-by-minute advances in the security management field. Looking back just a few short years ago, a "chief of security" was simply asked to oversee protection of assets and personnel. Today's executive shoulders broader responsibilities, often including engineering of security and fire systems, protecting inventories, screening of personnel, designing of emergency preparedness programs, managing information security, and promulgating quality improvement initiatives which meet both facility and industry standards.

Considering this new world order in the security management profession, is today's security executive expected to be a specialist or general practitioner? For that matter, it is possible for one person to a specialist in all areas? It is generally accepted that being an expert in all fields is contrary to reason. How then does the security executive go about maintaining a healthy security program? Some more forward-thinking executives are tackling this problem by marshaling the expertise of both in-house and external resources.

Prior to addressing how to best utilize these two resources, it is important to distinguish between "reactive and proactive security." Reactive security maintenance is the conventional environment in which the lion's share of manpower is expended on general protection functions (post/ sector security, closed circuit surveillance, escorts, etc.) Proactive security deals with addressing crime/safety risks before they occur. Personnel normally assigned to this side of the security function are referred to as Crime Prevention Specialists.

In the health care environment, these specialists can be referred to as security diagnosticians. Their training and orientation focus on learning to anticipate and mitigate crime risk situations. By and large, this breed of security officer is rarely found on the "front lines." He or she is often in the background, keeping a skillful eye over how best to design a protection mosaic to snugly fit the entity's continually changing environment. It is sometimes said that these officers are more comfortable carrying a set of blueprints and conducting lecture programs than monitoring personnel and assets.

Fashioning a Hospital Security Crime/Loss Prevention Program

The building process begins at the top. The security manager needs to demonstrate to management that in these financially lean times, one manner of stretching the shrinking health care security dollar lies in anticipating crime-related expenditures before litigation costs wreak havoc on the institution's budget.

In the court of security opinion, experts would agree that litigation costs can be substantially reduced if it is demonstrated that security protection either met or exceeded industry standards. A yardstick often applied in measuring security acceptability hinges on whether the entity had a program in-place to periodically evaluate its protection capability. A well-founded crime prevention

---

From *The Journal of Healthcare Protection Management.* (8):2, pp. 1–6. Summer 1992.

108 ■ *Healthcare Security*

program is one of the many tools which a security manager can apply to ensure that protection availability is adequate. In some hospitals, the crime prevention specialist is considered the manager's clinical and diplomatic arm. He or she maintains crime analysis statistics, conducts facility-wide and department specific reviews, diagnoses weak security policies and procedures, prescribes remedies to cease the internal hemorrhaging of missing inventories, and acts as the departments security advocate to ensure that all health care personnel are educated to the rules of good security and safety. Once a crime prevention policy is promulgated, the next step depending on the magnitude of the facility, is to select the right personnel for the job.

Selection Criteria

The right candidate should possess above-average cursive and oral skills, as well as the ability to communicate effectively to both individuals and large groups. He or she should be a career-minded professional who is interested in the techniques and technologies exercised in the crime prevention discipline. Aspirants ought to be capable of adjusting mindsets from the enforcement security model to the more proactive posture more strongly associated with the security management model.

Training Requirements

Training in crime/loss prevention differs substantially from conventional private security training curricula. The two areas are totally dissimilar. Study in this specialized discipline is intended to introduce students to a host of areas on the more technical side of security.

Upon completion of the standard 80-hour basic program, students should be expected to:

■ Understand the principles of crime/loss/fire prevention.
■ Master the basics of the crime analysis process.
■ Develop the skills required to prepare a security survey.
■ Develop the skills required to evaluate and recommend security technologies (locks, CCTV alarms, etc.)
■ Become familiar with municipal and regulatory agency specifications such as: fire, building, JCAHO, U.L., landmarks preservation, etc.
■ Gain an understanding of the importance of integrating crime risk management concepts and architectural needs.
■ Comprehend how to read blueprints.
■ Become proficient in applying assets protection strategies and technologies to shrink property and inventory loss.
■ Become proficient in packaging and presenting crime prevention exhibits and safety seminars.

Tasks and Responsibilities of Crime Prevention Staff

An inventory of tasks and responsibilities include but are not limited to:

■ Preparing facility-wide and department-specific security surveys.
■ Reviewing and analyzing incident reports.

Practical Crime Prevention ■ 109

- Formulating engineering scopes for security technology.
- Networking with facility architects and engineers on security design/redesign issues, As well as assisting the Capital Budget Department on formulating long and shot-range projections for capital expenditures;
- Networking with the facility's Internal Audit Department on tightening security in conjunction with audit findings.
- Providing tailored training programs as needed.
- Presenting crime prevention exhibits; and
- Establishing and maintaining the institution's crime/loss prevention library.

Program Evaluation

A system of evaluation should be designed to measure the effectiveness of the program. Some considerations may include:

- Development of a series of interim studies – before, middle, and after reviews – to determine the actual level of crime reporting in areas where proactive approaches have been instituted.
- Design of a statistical gathering process to gauge whether the crime prevention message is reaching its audience, and whether of not the audience reacts to the message.
- Development of a data-capturing instrument to record the level of institutional participation from past proactive efforts.
- Maintenance of a data base to log changing patterns of crime so that both actual and anticipated dispersion can be measured.

Selecting External Consultants

As in all fields including the health care profession, "experts" abound. How does one embark upon finding the right expert? This is not a tough question to ponder. When should outside consultative services be commissioned? In the security management profession, experience has shown that some security administrators use the "barn door" approach to consultant selection – calling in the carpenter to repair the barn door after the horses have fled. In today's climate of skyrocketing litigation, the age-old adage, "an ounce of prevention is worth a pound of cure," may well be the security executive's guiding beacon to maintaining a healthy protection program. A good rule of thumb to follow is periodically call on outside expertise to review in-house initiatives. As an example, since one of the major assignments of the crime prevention function is to piece together a facility-wide security survey annually, it would be an excellent idea to have this report reviewed biannually by an objective and independent resource.

This approach helps to ensure that the in-housework product is an accurate representation of the institution's state of security, while also helping to contain consultative costs. This is not to say that expert advice should be restricted to a biannual schedule, but that if these services are not required for other projects – such as security design/redesign for new construction, cost containment initiatives such as inventory and cash management audits, etc. – this approach could contain these costs over the long haul.

Selecting Qualified Experts

Like other fields of endeavor, selecting a health care consultant requires that the candidate/firm be appropriately credentialed and knowledgeable in health care operations. Many consultants who contract their services have had career positions as security executives in the health care field. Some suggestions on assessing qualifications include:

- Does the consultant/firm have experience in the germane facets of the discipline including: expertise in managing health care security competence in security, fire and loss prevention management; and technical efficiency in the engineering of security-related systems?
- Is the consultant/firm licensed and/or certified in various aspects of the security/loss prevention discipline? Licensing and certifications may include:
  - ○ Locksmith Licensing
  - ○ Engineering Licensing
  - ○ Professional Certifications may include Healthcare (CHPA), Physical Security (CPP), Security Training (CST), Loss and Fraud Prevention (CFE, CPA).
- Is this consultant firm an authority in the field? An accepted method of assessing expertise in this area might be to ascertain whether the consultant/firm has been published in the field (books, articles, etc.)
- Is consultative reference available?
- Always review their work product to measure performance standards.

Conclusion

The establishment of a crime/loss prevention capability to diagnose crime risks before the adversely impact on the institution's operation and budget. Likewise, utilizing consultative services wisely helps to ensure that the quality of security and safety is consistent with industry expectations. All things considered, having an in-house diagnostic team on board coupled with periodic examinations performed by qualified experts is the best prescription for keeping health care centers safe, secure, and healthy.

The Art and Science of Proactive Security Programming
Anthony Luizzo

Security administrators need to cast an investigative eye on whether the security department has a proactive cadre of specialists that actively labor on searching out crime-related exposures before they wreak havoc on the global facility. Prior to September 11, 2001, protection mavens rarely addressed crime problems before they occurred. One of the reasons for this philosophical protection approach can be traced to the fact that prior to the early 1970s, major U.S. police and security agencies rarely dedicated resources to preventing crime prior to its occurrence. Since that horrible September day that will forever be held in infamy, many things have changed in the security-programming arena. First and foremost, an Office of Homeland Security was formed, and businesses had to add "terrorism" to their protection grid. Taking a page from the medical profession, "an ounce of prevention is worth a pound of continued good health." Similarly, in business, security experts counsel that one of the most effective methods of diagnosing crime risks is to have a security survey completed annually. Drafting a security survey is most definitely an art and is one of the cornerstones of the crime prevention security model.

The Origins of Proactive Security

Great Britain is known as the world leader in fostering the modern crime-prevention model of policing. In the mid-18th century, Sir Henry Fielding, a British magistrate, and criminologist, organized the forerunner of today's policing methods by settling two goals: stamp out existing crime and prevent outbreaks of crime in the future. He further identified three objectives necessary for the achievement of these goals: the development of a strong police force, the organization of active citizens' groups to assist law enforcement, and the initiation of strategies to remove the root causes of crime and the conditions in which they flourish. Due in large part to the vast number of criminals that continued to ply their trade, the British constabulary was soon forced to abandon the proactive policing model championed so passionately by Fielding. By the 1950s, British law enforcement realized that dealing with crime reactively was not sufficient, and again revisited the preventative model. In 1963, the British police force formulated a mandatory one-month "crime prevention" training program for all its officers.

In 1971, the United States followed Britain's lead, formalizing crime-prevention training using a Law Enforcement Assistance Administration grant, which was awarded to the University of Louisville. Since the founding of the National Crime Prevention Institute, thousands of crime prevention specialists (e.g., law enforcement officers, investigators, corporate security executives, and loss prevention advocates) have graduated with specialized skills in detecting crime risks before they wreak havoc on company assets. One of the most important skills taught to all graduation crime prevention specialists is how to decipher criminality using an assessment tool known as the security survey. In competent hands, the security survey helps to determine when, where, how, and why crimes occur. In essence, the survey acts like a CAT scan, in that it provides a global view of the entity under scrutiny by highlighting security- and

From *Journal of Healthcare Protection Management.* (24):1, pp. 91–96. Summer 2008.

112 ■ *Healthcare Security*

safety- related abnormalities and offering preventative enhancements to remove and/or mitigate identified risk exposures.

By the mid-1970s, all major U.S. police agencies had established crime prevention programs. As a rule of thumb, depending on the size of the department, usually between one and three percent of a department's investigative resources are dedicated to proactive assignments. In the early years, all investigative staff assigned to crime prevention duty was sent to the National Crime Prevention Institute for certification as crime prevention specialists. Today, larger municipal police agencies train their own via internal training initiatives. As an example, the New York City Police Department's Crime Prevention Unit offers a 40-hour "Basics of Security and Crime Prevention Program" twice annually. The course is open to qualified personnel and attendees earn up to three college credits.

The Art and Science of Proactive Security

In addition to standard law enforcement training (e.g., patrol and investigative approaches), crime prevention specialists learn to develop a different mindset than their counterparts; in short, they are taught to think beyond the galaxy of contemporary police work. This new proactive mindset, often called the environmental model of criminology, teaches students to address both the criminal and the environment in which the criminal act is committed. Criminologists of this school theorize that crimes are committed when three conditions exist (two of which are uncontrollable): 1) Desire – an uncontrollable factor in the crime equation, 2) Ability – also an uncontrollable factor, 3) Opportunity – a predictable and controllable variable. Protection experts suggest that opportunistic misdeeds can be effectively controlled via eliminating the ease with which the prize (e.g., property) is taken illegally and instituting crime-deterrence initiatives that help to up-the-odds of identification and capture of the transgressor.

Fashioning a Proactive Crime Control Program

As a matter of course, the building process begins by pulling a small contingent of the security force off the patrol assembly line and schooling them in the abc's of crime risk management. During their studies they are taught to anticipate crime risks and to initiate strategies to mitigate risk exposures. Over and above education in the theoretical application of conventional and environmental crime prevention fundamentals, they are also schooled in the technical skills normally associated with security systems design and engineering.

Tasks and responsibilities of crime prevention operatives

In the main, an inventory of tasks and responsibilities include but are not limited to:

- Preparing facility-wide and targeted security assessments
- Reviewing and analyzing crime incident reports
- Formulation crime mapping systems to showcase "hot spots"
- Laboring shoulder-to-shoulder with facility architects and engineers on general security issues
- Framing timely proactive security workshops for in-house staff and corporate employees
- Maintaining an on-going liaison with the local law enforcement agency's crime prevention office

Evaluating the proactive security initiative

As with all programs, a system of evaluation should be framed so that the effect of the program is appropriately measured. Considerations on instituting such a program might include:

- Design of before, middle, and after studies to determine the actual level of crime reporting in areas where proactive approaches have been put forward
- Design of a statistical model to gauge whether the proactive message is reaching its intended audience

All in all, a structured program of evaluation will help security administrators to better measure the department's response to their organization's proactive policing program.

Innovative Environmental Security Approaches

Mitigating crime risk exposure via target elimination

There are several crime reductions projects around the country that have solved problems using the environmental crime control model. As an example, some years back many people were using the Coney Island Boardwalk in New York City during the day and early evening hours as a main thoroughfare to the seaside amenities. After dark, however, the environs under the boardwalk became dangerous crime-prone locations used by miscreants to trap their prey. For many years prior to the acceptance of environmental security and proactive crime control, the age-old approach to mitigating these crime risks was to saturate targeted locations with protective personnel. Oftentimes patrolling was limited because the cost of assigning sufficient protection personnel was not fiscally feasible. Moreover, trying to devise an effective protecting blanket over the entire boardwalk was totally out of the question. To mitigate the crime problems, the underbelly of the boardwalk was filled with sand thus completely removing the crime risk without expending one penny of the entity's protection budget. Beyond the crime prevention benefit achieved, this strategy also helped to establish a flood control carrier protecting the surrounding community from surging tides. Other beachfront communities would be wise to follow suit where appropriate.

Mitigating crime risk exposure via altering traffic control patterns

Security initiatives often used to better handle street and bus stop mugging and larcenies at crime prone locations is to re-synchronize traffic light patterns during "high incident" periods to concentrate additional eyes and ears at the locations. Where there are no traffic control devices available, crime control planners have been known to recommend that the department of traffic consider installing these devices as a crime deterrent tool and/or to relocate bus stops to locations that have traffic control devices. Likewise, crime control planners have on occasion recommended that public street traffic patterns be re-directed from one-way to two-way, or from one direction to another direction to increase traffic concentration at crime prone locations. In rural communities, crime control planners have asked traffic control agencies to establish "cul-de-sacs" to better control access.

Mitigating crime risk exposure by modifying seating design, carrying illumination and heating levels

Many corporate entities are architecturally retrofitting waiting areas, atriums and public leisure areas with seating configurations that discourage horizontal slouching and sleeping by those who use the facilities. Oftentimes, seating fixtures are constructed of less than comfortable type materials with seating surfaces and backs that dissuade long-term habitation. Over and above seating re-design, another strategy often put forward is to vary illumination and heating levels to further discourage long-term habitation (playing loud music to discourage sleeping during evening hours and setting temperature levels to defy logic such as offering air conditioning in summer and heating in the winter). Many establishments have tackled the problem of moving the homeless and other less desirables from strategic facilities via these methods.

Securing the Future

As we enter the 21st century, security is on every security executive's radar screen in all-mercantile sectors from airports to shopping centers to hospitals. Security wisdom strongly portends that the most effective method of controlling crime exposure is to diagnose it before it has a chance to wreak havoc on its institutional host. In the court of security opinion, security executives would be wise to ensure that proactive crime detecting capabilities are an integral part of their asset protection cosmos. Crime prevention courses are offered gratis by many law enforcement agencies nationwide. As an example, in the New York City security executives can contact the New York Police Department's Crime Prevention Office for training information and assistance in formulating a proactive security program. Outside of NYC, contact your local police department for assistance.

The Varied Roles of the Crime Prevention Expert

Anthony Luizzo

There are many experts who labor in several medical and non-medical specialties in the healthcare environment. Since that dreadful day in 2001, consultants offering protection-related services from security devices and procedures to anti-terrorism technologies have exponentially increased numerous times. Crime Prevention is one of several consultative services being offered to help security executives better protect their facilities. Crime prevention is quite candidly an amazingly simple strategy that helps to keep both the employee and corporate entity free from present and future criminal exposures.

The Definition of Crime Prevention

The formal definition of Crime Prevention is "the anticipation, recognition and appraisal of a crime risk and the initiation of some action to remove or reduce it". The word anticipation is the key phrase to understanding the main difference between reactive and proactive security services. The great preponderance of security strategy in most protective entities is dedicated to reacting to crime related exposure. Crime prevention practitioners however usually only deal with proactive crime risk management strategies to help identify crime exposures before they occur and wreak havoc on the institution and its employees.

Differing Job Titles

Over the years, crime prevention experts found their way into the corporate sector as loss prevention specialists. Their assignment was to evaluate crime risk exposure and frame policy to mitigate said exposures. In the public sector of government agencies term these experts crime control planners. Irrespective of title, all do similar labor - they apply proactive risk management principals to reduce crime-related exposures. In law enforcement these practitioners are called crime prevention specialists and their role is to work with corporations and citizens on crime reduction efforts. Over the past 35 years, most major police agencies have active crime prevention programs that offer proactive services and programs.

What is Crime Risk Management?

In the court of proactive security planning and implementation, crime risk management is designing crime deterrent systems that are not cost intensive and do the job with optimum efficiency. In a business sense, crime risk management involves promulgating protective strategies that provide optimum benefits at reasonable expenditures. Another more recent strategy used in the crime risk management toolkit is crime incident "Hot Spotting". This relatively new strategy involves deciphering and prioritizing crime prone locations and furnishing protective strategies to

---

From *The Journal of Healthcare Protection Management*. (38):2, pp. 84–89. 2012.

116 ■ *Healthcare Security*

"Cool Down" critical areas. Hot Spotting is sometimes called Crime Mapping, and for decades past called crime analysis targeting involves collecting and collating crime incident data from security operative's field reports gathered during their daily patrols.

Some incident data is collected from internal employees and visitors who have been previous victims of crime on company property, and some info is received via anonymous tips. Moreover, other information is collected from previously completed security surveys by both internal and external consultants. Upon receiving that data, the security department usually prepares cluster maps for targeted review by security patrols. Oftentimes, the practitioner includes these crime-prone locations in the periodical security survey or in some instances, the hot spotting data is included in a stand-alone report for a specific area for a specific time frame. In summary, the crime control planner, crime prevention specialist, loss prevention director is all concerned with improving protection availability and corporate profitability.

The Definition of an Expert

From a legal point of reference an expert assists juries to better understand subjects that are not common knowledge. Courts must qualify a candidate as an expert based on a review of his or her credentials and expertise. In the criminal justice system, there are two types of witnesses: Lay Witnesses and Expert Witnesses. The Lay Witness is restricted from testifying in the form of opinions, conclusions, and characterizations. The Expert Witness is permitted to offer professional opinions and judgments. In the case of Crime Prevention, an expert should have an in-depth understanding of both reactive and proactive crime control models. The Crime Prevention Expert often testifies to the efficiency of existing security approaches in both civil and criminal litigation.

The Expert's Role in Crime Prevention

Like experts in other fields of endeavor, a crime prevention expert may serve as a witness in support of a position, as a rebuttal witness, or to critique the opposition's position. Sometimes an expert will not be asked to testify, but to serve as a trail consultant, assisting counsel handling the litigation. An expert can become involved during the various stages of the case including but not limited to:

- The examination of before trial depositions, photographs, investigative reports
- Interviewing witnesses
- Evidence examination (police reports, incident reports and related documents)
- Perusal of other experts' findings
- The execution of site inspections
- Review of opposing experts' assertions

During case preparation, the expert furnishes a verbal or written report to counsel speaking to conclusions extrapolated from his or her research. During testimony preparation the expert and barrister ponder anticipated court testimony, during which the expert furnishes sworn testimony.

Reactive vs. Proactive Crime Control Models

In addition to the standard reactive security model that often includes monitoring security-related technologies, (alarm systems, CCTV) patrol, investigative approaches, etc., crime prevention practitioners are also thoroughly schooled in applying strategies that help measure crime exposures before they occur. One of the control tools used by all crime prevention experts is the Security Survey. A survey can be considered a medical diagnostic device; it allows the security diagnostician to measure a facility's crime exposures so that a prescription can be written to make frail programs healthier.

Selecting In-house or External Experts

It really depends on the facility's budget. As with most security operations, dollars are quite scarce.

In-house Operatives

The internal building process begins by selecting one or two or more (depending on the size of the institution) well-seasoned security operatives off-of-the patrol assembly line and schooling them in the ABCs of proactive security management theory and practice. The aspirants ought to be capable of adjusting mindsets from the enforcement policing model to the more proactive community policing/private security models.

Program Evaluation

A system of evaluation should be established to adequately measure the programs effectiveness. Some areas to be considered include but are not limited to:

- Establishing before, middle and after studies to determine program efficiency
- Establishing statistical evaluations to gauge whether the program's message is reaching its audience and whether the audience is reacting to the message
- Establishing an in-house monitoring system to determine the levels of institutional participation from programming put forward
- Establishing a system of capturing changing patterns of crime displacement so that both actual and anticipated dispersions are addressed.

External Consultants

If outside experts are to be used, it is imperative that the consulting firm has a proven track record of providing proactive security services for institutions such as yours. References should be carefully checked, and a review of prior consultative assignments should be reviewed. The staff performing the work should be properly credentialed to perform the task at hand.

Training Prerequisites for all Crime Prevention Operatives

Generic courses of study that all crime prevention practitioners are required to attend include some of the following modules of instruction:

- The history of crime prevention
- Introduction to physical security (perimeter, interior and interior protection)
- Introduction to security technology 101 (alarm, closed circuit television (CCTV), locking system design and functionality
- Introduction to protective glazing techniques 101
- Introduction to lighting design 101
- Introduction to access control planning and design
- Introduction to safe, metal detector & biometric security
- Introduction to security survey preparation
- Introduction to crime risk management 101
- Introduction to crime analysis programming 101
- Introduction to crime prevention through environmental design 101
- Aspects of effectively packaging crime prevention programs for employees, visitors and legitimate users of the space.

Oftentimes, this is a standard 40-48 hour – 3 college credit courses of instruction offered by several organizations including the New York City Police Department's Crime Prevention Division. When the student completes the training, he or she is issued a crime prevention certification. It is important to stress that beyond classroom exercises, the great preponderance of expertise in this discipline comes from years of working in the field.

Locating Crime prevention Experts

Since the Savings and Loan crisis and those terrible days following 9/11, security continues to be on every security executive's radar screen. Over these many years the proactive side of security has exploded. Corporate entities are either employing their own in-house experts or reaching out to consultants who specialize in this discipline. There are several security and investigative organizations that can be called to obtain proactive services. A short list might include:

- The American Society for Industrial Security
- The International Association of Crime Prevention Practitioners
- The Academy of Security Educators and Trainers
- The National Crime Prevention Institute
- Local Colleges offering Security Management Programs
- Larger Law Enforcement Agencies Nationwide
- The International Association of Healthcare Security & Safety

Keys to Selecting the Right Consultant

Selecting the right consultant is made easier when you know what questions to ask in the selection process.

Five questions to ask when searching for a crime prevention expert:

- What specific expertise is needed for the assignment?
- Does the consulting firm possess proper credentials?
- Is the firm properly licensed?
- Have any of the experts ever been court qualified?
- Are firms insured?

Looking Toward the Future

As we enter the early years of the 21st century, selecting the right expert to perform specific tasks is not an easy endeavor. All things considered, an effective crime prevention program is limited only by the vision of the security administrator shaping it, and the practitioner nurturing it.

How Is Crime Risk Measured and Managed?

Anthony Luizzo

Because *internal* auditors are frequently called upon to review and monitor the effectiveness of corporate security operations, it is extremely important that the audit professional have some knowledge of how such programs function. This month, we look at the crime risk management operation.

Capturing and Evaluating Crime Risk Data

Most crime analysis utilizes facility incident reports of past crimes and records of observations by patrol operatives, employees, residents, pedestrians, or other witnesses. Such information usually includes the time the crime occurred, the type of crime, the location of the crime, the perpetrator's description, and other relevant data associated with the crime or crime scene. This data forms the foundation upon which crime patterns are developed. A "crime pattern" is a string of single incidents that occur with regularity in a concentrated cluster grouping. Once crime risks are identified, evaluated, and logged, they are divided into low, medium, and high-risk categories. It is through this analytic process that the amplitude of various risk exposures is evaluated.

Crime Risk Mapping and Risk Exposure

The "crime analysis mapping system" is a mechanism used to identify risk exposure. Before the development of today's computerized tracking programs, large area maps and colored pins served as the tools for recording and tracking criminal events. As the number of crimes recorded on the maps mounted, the maps were transformed from rather bland landmass mosaics into multicolored clusters of crime locations. By simply looking at the various crime maps, a knowledgeable crime analyst can often forecast with some degree of accuracy where both existing and future criminality could occur.

Dissecting Crime Risks

In the universe of crime risk management, crime-related risks are often divided into two categories:

- *Pure crime risks* affect businesses daily (e.g., fire or flood).
- *Dynamic crime risks* are often associated with advance purchasing of merchandise for sale at a future date.

From *Internal Auditing Report* Warren, Gorham & Lamont /RIA Group (Reuters) – Thomson Publications. May 2002 – openlibrary@archive.com

In practice, security administrators most often deal with pure crime risks in their normal day-to-day operations. The management of dynamic crime risk is more strongly associated with retail security operations involving purchasing or merchandising operations.

Finding Security Weaknesses and Solutions

Some of the most effective ways to pinpoint security exposures are regular reviews of crime statistics, daily incident reports, and previously performed security surveys. All three serve as roadmaps to follow when searching for security risks and protective solutions.

Protection Methodologies

There are three principal methods of "target hardening" a facility to protect it from criminal endeavors:

1. *Mechanized security approach.* This involves using both security personnel and technologies (e.g., alarms or locks) to protect crime-prone areas. Conjoining both human and technological security approaches in a *mechanized* scheme is both wise and efficient.
2. *Non-mechanized security approach.* This security application involves using a single, non-mechanized protective strategy (e.g., a security guard or a standalone security device such as an alarm or security camera) to protect the affected area.
3. *Environmental mechanized approach.* This approach involves making structural or procedural changes to the physical environment, coupled with human and technological security enhancements to influence criminal behavior. (For example, assume that reports have been received that homeless people and other uninvited guests are using your hospital's waiting room as their living area. This problem could be dealt with via the environmental mechanized model by (1) redesigning the seating arrangements in the waiting room by removing existing benches and replacing them with single-occupancy seats that discourage stretching out or loitering for extended periods; and (2) utilizing security cameras or guards to augment the environmental strategies by keeping a watchful eye over the problem area.)

Applying Protection Strategies

The most effective method of strengthening frail physical security programs is by reinforcing the perimeter-the exterior and interior environs of the entity under scrutiny. From a professional point of view, this often means reinforcing perimeter security with such basic items as fencing and lighting systems, adding industrial-strength doors and windows to the building's exterior facade, and buttressing interior protection with alarms, access control, and closed-circuit television technologies.

Beyond security hardware, it is most important that proactive security assessments are performed on a periodic basis so that crime risks are uncovered before they have an opportunity to cause human tragedy or affect the firm's fiscal health.

Measuring Cost Considerations

Once a list of possible security solutions has been prepared, it is time to begin calculating the cost-effectiveness of each proposed solution.

Most security executives will realize that:

- Proposed solutions should be consistent with the mission of the entity.
- Expenses should never exceed expected benefits.
- Programmatic costs should mirror budgetary constraints.

Auditing the Security Department

When auditing a security department's crime-risk countermeasures, an internal auditor should consider the following:

- Does the security department have a crime risk management program?
- Are crime risk exposures regularly mapped?
- Are crime patterns disseminated to the appropriate personnel?
- Are past crime risk management files available for review?
- Are identified crime risks immediately adjudicated?
- Are security surveys regularly performed?
- Do experienced security personnel perform the surveys?
- Are previous copies of security surveys available?
- Are security expenditures justified by the results achieved?
- Does the security department function in a proactive rather than a reactive atmosphere?

Managing Crime Risk

In summary, the nature of crime risk management systems and programs requires the security professional to look systematically at all points of possible criminal attack and devise protective solutions to mitigate all identified risk exposures. Crime risk management is clearly within the security manager's purview, and it is extremely important that he or she take every opportunity to become familiar with the various state-of-the-art crime mapping approaches. During the preliminary survey, an internal auditor faced with the task of auditing the security department should familiarize himself or herself with crime risk management and its costs and benefits.

Using Access and ID Control to Prevent Workplace Violence

Bernard J. Scaglione

On June 3, 2010, The Joint Commission, the accreditation organization for healthcare issued what they call a "Sentinal Event Alert," which is an affirmation of a serious event issued by the Joint Commission to educate healthcare institutions on recent data, collected by them, that denotes a significant increase in a serious or deadly situation. In this case, The Joint Commission recently noted an increase in the number of reported assaults, rape and homicides that have occurred in healthcare institutions.

Workplace violence within healthcare is not a new phenomenon. In 1994 the Bureau of Labor Statistics (BLS) Census of Fatal Occupational Injuries (CFOI) reported that healthcare providers had the highest rate of fatal injuries due to workplace violence compared to all other industry. In response, the Occupational Safety & Health Administration (OSHA) published "Guidelines for Preventing Workplace Violence for Health Care & Social Service Workers" in 2002.

The primary purpose of the OSHA document is to assist in the development of a comprehensive program to reduce the opportunity for violence to occur within the workplace. The key component recommended by these authors to reduce workplace violence happens to be the control of access and the identification of violence. Specifically, the OSHA document and other workplace violence reports and guidelines call for the manipulation of the environment to control or restrict access and the training of staff to identify potentially violent persons through behavior recognition.

All the reports recommend the completion of a workplace analysis to start the process. This analysis is a security risk assessment or survey focused on the control and prevention of hazards related to violence. They recommend that the analysis focus on the use of engineering controls to reduce violence. That means restricting access through the manipulation of the physical environment, using physical barriers placed between people and hazards that allow for the screening of persons or the restriction of access and creating a work environment where people are continuously controlled and screened throughout the organization, where workspaces are designed to keep physical structures between staff and others.

As recommended, institutions can use the physical environment to reduce potentially violent acts. Physical barriers like doors, walls and partitions should be installed to restrict entry. Once persons enter a facility, they must be screened to determine who they are going to visit and the purpose of their visit. A solid visitor management system can take a photo of the visitor and collect images of identifying documents as well as allow for the option of placing flags within the database, so screeners are alerted to potentially dangerous persons. Once inside of the building visitors should be restricted to where they can go. Access control can keep persons from straying into unauthorized areas and allow for authorized, announced entry into work areas. Installing doors, counter partitions, glass window or screens, installing door locks and card readers help to restrict unauthorized access.

Access control within individual work areas is paramount as well. Physically separating waiting and reception space from staff workspace is important in violence reduction. In addition, the

---

From *Security E Newsletter*, July 1, 2010.

setup of an individual's office can help to reduce violent acts. Workers should arrange desks and other furniture so that there is a physical barrier between visitors and the employee and so that they can leave their office without meeting the violent visitor.

To successfully prevent violence within the workplace, it is imperative that all organizations establish workplace violence prevention programs. Every program needs to include the control of access and identification of violent behavior along with a zero-tolerance policy and the implementation of criminal background checks for all employees to determine if a potential employee has previous violent behavior.

Workplace Violence Prevention: A Guide to Active Shooter and Workplace Violence Resources

Bernard J. Scaglione

Introduction

Healthcare related organizations have recently published information to educate the healthcare industry on the risks associated with workplace violence and active shoot, and to aid in developing and implementing reduction programs. The Occupational Safety and Health Administration (OSHA) in 2015, published a revised version of their healthcare workplace violence document, entitled, *"Guidelines for Preventing Workplace Violence for Healthcare and Social Service Workers.* "This document was reintroduced because of the increasingly high number of workplace violence incidents occurring within the healthcare industry.

The document indicates that in 2013, the Bureau of Labor Statistics reported more than 23,000 significant injuries due to assault at work. More than 70 percent of those assaults were in the healthcare and social service settings. According to the Bureau of Labor Statistics health care and social service workers are almost four times as likely to be injured because of violence as the average private sector worker. In addition, OSHA recently published, "Caring for Our Caregivers, Preventing Workplace Violence: A Road Map for Healthcare Facilities. This document outlines the process in developing and implementing a comprehensive workplace safety program.

In a viewpoint article published in March of 2015 in the Journal of the American Medical Association, entitled, *"Hospital-Based Active Shooter Incidents: Sanctuary Under Fire,"* the authors indicated that the number of active shooter incidents in U.S. hospitals has increased over the last decade to a frequency of more than one a month. In 2014, the FBI along with Texas State University and the Justice Department released a national study on active shooter in the work sectors since 2000. The FBI found an increasing trend in active shooter incidents and reported that the average casualties per year had risen as well.

There are numerous published resources available for the prevention and mitigation of workplace violence and active shooter response. Throughout these resources are similar themes that are useful in developing programs that can reduce the potential for violent acts. These strategies are not new, but often absent in healthcare security strategies. These strategies include the control of access, providing a strong security presence and educating staff to the risks and processes involving workplace violence and active shooter response.

Access Control

Many security experts believe that the single best method for minimizing the risk of violence within a facility starts with the control and restriction of access. Restricting access into the hospital and surrounding buildings and locking interior spaces to control access within the hospital environment. One method for restricting access is the use of Crime Prevention Through Environmental Design (CPTED) techniques or target hardening.

(Unpublished)

126 ■ *Healthcare Security*

These are physical changes to the environment, like fencing, doors, locks, and card readers that control, restrict or minimize access into and around the healthcare facility. The use of CPTED principals can effectively control the interior environments as well, and access into high-risk areas like Emergency Department, Maternity, Pediatrics, ICUs, and other areas designated as high-risk by the healthcare facility. However, the installation of door locks and fencing are only effective when they are functioning as intended, operating at manufacturer standards. Many times, access control becomes ineffective when access control doors are compromised. For example, propped open by a person to smoke outside and then regain entry into the hospital. Additionally, many times exit doors are found unlocked, broken, or not closing properly because they are not checked on a regular basis. It is important to check exit and entry doors on a regular basis to ensure they are locked and in proper working order. Interior access control doors should be checked, as well, to ensure their proper operation. Most times access users swipe their card, get a green light, and open the door. Never does anyone check an access control door when it is indicating locked to make sure it is locked not ajar or malfunctioning.

Security Presence

Security presence is a major part of violence reduction. Security officer visibility along with visible aspects of the security program all contribute to violence reduction. Continuous security officer patrols and officer presence at entrances provides security visibility to persons wishing to gain access for inappropriate reasons. Increased surveillance capacity is another way to reduce the potential for violent activity. Using windows, glass partitions and CCTV cameras can increase the ability for staff to view and recognize the beginnings of violent activities. Security presence or visibility also means response, not only a security officer rushing to an emergency, but the repair of security features like door locks, lighting and CCTV cameras which provide an environment where staff and visitors see and feel a security presence.

Many times, security officers are hired with the intent to screen visitors or just be present in an entrance lobby. However, all too often the officer is posted off to the side, behind a desk or posted so far inside of the lobby that they are not noticed by patients or visitors entering the hospital. In addition, officers posted in lobbies or patrolling a hospital and its surrounding buildings are many times used for patient watches. This significantly reduces security presence within a hospital and creates a security program viewed by patients and visitor as inconsistent or non-existent. Leaving patients, visitors, and staff with an unsecure feeling.

Security Perception

The perception that a security program is present, and operating is often missing within a hospital. Today, people expect to see security present wherever they go. The lack of security only increases their feeling of insecurity. When the security program is perceived as being inconsistent, that perception is even greater because patients, visitors and staff can visually see and feel that the hospital does not care about their security program, only going through the motions of providing a secure hospital. The perception of a security program does not only include the use of security officers posted in lobbies or patrolling the hospital. It is the overall actions of the hospital staff and their continued execution of security processes that influence the perception of security within the institution. For example, staff wearing their ID card or following infant security protocol.

The issuance of security passes to everyone not just a few. Even approaching persons and directing them to their designation. These are all examples of how staff can demonstrate the perception of security within their hospital and workplace.

Surveillance Capacity

A major part of the CPTED philosophy is the use of surveillance to deter crime. Surveillance capacity is the use of windows, mirrors, low walls, or shelving to increase one's ability to observe another. This includes CCTV surveillance as well. However, often healthcare facilities will install camera and purchase recorders by not actively view CCTV images. Mostly, CCTV is used for review after an incident has occurred. In addition, those hospitals that do provide live surveillance usually do so on small computer monitors, viewing sixteen two-inch across images is an ineffective way to provide surveillance. Additionally, these officers are often performing a vast majority of other tasks which gives them little time for surveillance. If CCTV cameras are installed within the healthcare institution, they should be monitored live and on large screens so that images can be view in detail. Healthcare institutions that have IP addressable cameras and video management systems should be programing their systems to detect motion and provide a pop-up image on a security monitor in specific high-risk areas. For example, the stairwells leading to the Maternity unit during the off hours. This way the security officer's attention will be drawn to the image when someone is present within the view of the camera and a security officer can be dispatched to further investigate the situation, if necessary.

Security Response

Security response is not just the security officer rushing to a location after a duress alarm has been activated. Just as important, is the hospital's reaction to security issues and their quick and thorough resolution. For example, when an exterior light burns out or Day Light Saving Time is underway, light should be replaced immediately and the timers controlling the lights should immediately adjusted to match the level of darkness. When an exit door is broken, it should be repaired immediately so that the hospital remains secure. When burnt out lights and broken doors remain out of service hospital staff along with patients and visitors notice it and it increases their feeling of insecurity.

Education

Education is an important part of violence reduction as well. All hospital staff should be trained on the hospital's policy and processes relating to workplace violence and active shooter. More concentrated training should be provided in high-risk areas, like the Emergency Department, Maternity and Pediatrics, and the ICUs. In high-risk areas, policies should be continually reviewed with staff and processes should be drilled so that staff feels comfortable responding to acts of violence or an active shooter event. Workplace violence and active shooter training should take place at new employee orientation and reviewed during annual in-service training.

Education of security staff is important as well. Security staff should understand their role in responding to violent incidents and work with local police on a regular basis to ensure both the

128 ■ *Healthcare Security*

hospital and police understand the processes when a violence incident occurs. Security officer training should include basic information on workplace violence and active shooter, training on crisis intervention along with all hospital workplace violence and active shooter policies and procedures. This review should take place annually and include the specific processes that Security is responsible for.

The Key to workplace violence and active shooter response is the cooperation and understanding of police and fire response. The Security Department should meet with the local police and/or fire departments to learn and compare notes on response to a workplace or active shooter incident that may occur at the hospital. This meeting should occur annually and include a tour of the hospital so that responders know where they are going.

Workplace Violence and Active Shooter Resources

Dealing with emergencies like workplace violence or active shooter requires a focused approach. Guidance that prepares, prevents, and directs response.

Homeland Security groups response to emergency events into four phases: (1) Mitigation, (2) Preparedness, (3) Response, and (4) Recovery. The grouping of these functions is useful for classifying and conceptualizing activities used in the preparation and response to violent incidents. As indicated above there are numerous published resources available for the prevention and mitigation of workplace violence and active shooter response. Here are a few broken down within the four stages of response as outlined by Homeland Security.

Mitigation

Mitigation is the first of the four approaches. Mitigation activities entail identifying risks and hazards to either reduce or eliminate the impact of an incident. Mitigation activities often have long-term or sustained effects. Some examples of mitigation include:

- Developing and implementing a work policy on violence and violent incident response
- Conducting assessments on high-risk work areas
- Target hardening work areas to prevent workplace violent incidents

Resources for the mitigation of workplace violence and active shooter include:

1. OHSA Document - Guidelines for Preventing Workplace Violence for Healthcare and Social Service Workers: https://www.osha.gov/SLTC/workplaceviolence/
2. OHSA Website of Workplace Violence: https://www.osha.gov/SLTC/workplaceviolence/
3. CDC - NIOSH Publication - Violence Occupational Hazards in Hospitals: http://www.cdc.gov/niosh/docs/2002-101/
4. Florida Hospital Association Workplace Violence Tool Kit: http://fha.org/health-care-issues/emergency-preparedness/workplace-violence-toolkit.aspx

Preparedness

Preparedness is distinct from mitigation because rather than focusing on eliminating or reducing risks, the general focus of preparedness is to enhance the capacity to respond to an incident by taking steps to ensure personnel and entities can respond to a wide range of potential incidents. Preparedness activities may include:

- Conducting drills and exercises so that staff can respond effectively and safely
- Continually training staff so that they are always prepared to handle violent situations
- Procuring resources Intelligence and surveillance activities to identify potential threats

Resources for the preparation of workplace violence and active shooter include:

1. Training video: Armed: Are you ready active shooter training video: http://vimeopro.com/lmpgeneral/armed-are-you-ready
2. Department of Homeland Security on-line training program for active shooter: http://www.nationalterroralert.com/2013/01/20/dhs-launches-new-active-shooter-preparedness-webpage/
3. FBI: Active Shooter Planning and Response in a Healthcare Setting: https://www.fbi.gov/about-us/cirg/active-shooter-and-mass-casualty-incidents/active-shooter-planning-and-response-in-a-healthcare-setting/view
4. The Office of the Assistant Secretary for Preparedness and Response - Incorporating Active Shooter Planning into Health Care Facility Emergency Operations Plans: http://www.traumacenters.org/news/205038/Incorporating-Active-Shooter-Planning-into-Health-Care-Facility-Emergency-Operations-Plans.htm

Response

Response activities are comprised of the immediate actions to save lives, protect property and the environment, and meet basic human needs. Response involves the execution of emergency plans and related actions, and may include:

Handling victims

- Deployment of response teams, medical stockpiles, and other assets
- Establishment of incident command operations

Resources for the response to workplace violence and active shooter include:

1. Department of Homeland Security - How to Respond to an Active Shooter: http://www.dhs.gov/publication/active-shooter-how-to-respond
2. FBI: Active Shooter Planning and Response in a Healthcare Setting: https://www.fbi.gov/about-us/cirg/active-shooter-and-mass-casualty-incidents/active-shooter-planning-and-response-in-a-healthcare-setting/view
3. Healthcare and Public Health Sector Coordinating Councils - Active Shooter Planning and Response in the Healthcare Setting: http://www.google.com/url?sa=t&rct=j&q=&esrc=s&source=web&cd=2&ved=0ahUKEwjcvqiOv7bKAhUEPD4KHdz2B90QFggiMAE&url=http%3A%2F%2Fwww.floridahealth.gov%2Fprograms-and-services%2Femergency-preparedness-and-response%2Fpreparedness-planning%2F_documents%2Factive-shooter.pdf&usg=AFQjCNFOtWCfM8Jus8bfsUpm_O_WQk1BkQ&sig2=LuONbZlhK4EacHqqrXx68w

Recovery

Recovery activities are intended to restore essential services and repair damages caused by the event. Recovery activities may include:

- The reconstitution of operations and services
- Assist with the victim and organizations staff mental health
- Replenishment of stockpiles

Resources for the recovery to workplace violence and active shooter include:

1. Center for the Study of Traumatic Stress Recovery - In the Aftermath of Workplace Violence: Guidance for Supervisors: http://www.google.com/url?sa=t&rct=j&q=&esrc=s& source=web&cd=9&ved=0ahUKEwiZnrapwbbKAhWDWD4KHYhsBisQFghQMAg&u rl=http%3A%2F%2Fwww.cstsonline.org%2Fassets%2Fmedia%2Fdocuments%2FCSTS_ aftermath_workplace_violence_supervisors.pdf&usg=AFQjCNHA-DYyYz1CodumNysU w1FYn40rWw&sig2=D8uJLt8EQFLJhJL0XUD92Q&bvm=bv.112064104,d.dmo

Aspects of Crime and Violence Avoidance

Anthony Luizzo and Bernard J. Scaglione

The Problem

The disastrous effects of terrorism, shooting and other violent acts striking our shores since 2001 has been a siren call to protection professionals to devise strategies to combat these horrendous threats. In the healthcare sector, several governmental and non-governmental studies have been promulgated to help guide security executives to devise a blueprint to better educate and deter risks associated with workplace and gun-related violence (shooting). As an example, in 2015 the Occupational Safety and Health Administration (OSHA) published a revised version of their healthcare workplace violence document, entitled, *"Guidelines for Preventing Workplace Violence for Healthcare and Social Service Workers."* It is important to note that this document was reintroduced because of the increasingly high number of workplace violence incidents occurring within the healthcare industry.

The study indicates that in 2013, the Bureau of Labor statistics reported more than 23,000 significant injuries due to assault at work. Moreover, more than 70% of those assaults were in the healthcare and social service settings. According to the Bureau of Labor Statistics, healthcare and social service workers are almost four times as likely to be injured because of violence as the average private sector worker. Speaking further on the issue, OSHA also published a road map for healthcare executives to follow, *"Caring for Our Caregivers, Preventing Workplace Violence."*

This document outlines the process in developing and implementing a comprehensive workplace safety program. In a viewpoint article published in March of 2015 in the Journal of the American Medical Association, entitled, *"Hospital-Based Active Shooter Incidents: Sanctuary Under Fire,"* the authors indicated that the number of active shooter incidents in the U.S. hospitals has increased over the last decade to a frequency of more than one a month. In 2014, the FBI, Texas State University and the Justice Department released a national study on active shooter in the work sector since 2000. The FBI found an increasing trend in active shooter incidents and reported that the average casualties per year had risen as well. According to the "2016 Hospital Security Survey Report," published by Health Facilities Management, 75% of hospitals surveyed report that maintaining security has become more challenging in the past two years due in part to the rise of behavioral issues and opioid abuse among patients. The article goes on to mention that promulgation of appropriate de-escalation training programming to manage this aggressive behavior should be considered. The complete study can be found at www.hfmmagazine.com/articles.

Solutions and Strategies

By simply going to the Internet anyone can find an infinite number of published resources speaking to the prevention and mitigation of workplace violence and firearms-related terrorism.

Notwithstanding, from a practical perspective, diagnosing crime risk exposures should begin and end with reaching out to an expert with proactive crime control and violence avoidance

---

From *Journal of Healthcare Protection Management.* (33):1, pp. 21–30. 2017.

132 ■ Healthcare Security

expertise and ask to have a comprehensive crime risk impact assessment (security survey) prepared. The surveyor should be asked to diagnose and offer sound strategies to mitigate unearthed exposures.

Some areas that should be included in the security assessment might include but should not be limited to:

- Enhancing access control strategies
- Bolstering security presence and perception
- Employing Crime Prevention through Environmental Design (CPTED) strategies
- Propping up security's response to emergencies
- Deepening and strengthening protection education initiatives
- Instituting an effective background screening process

Enhancing Access Control Strategies

Many security experts believe that the single best method for minimizing the risk of violence within a facility starts and ends with the control and restriction of access. One novel method for restricting access is to employ Crime Prevention through Environmental Design (CPTED) techniques including target hardening initiatives. These strategies are intended to physically alter the access flow so that security or technology can capture potential breaches before wreaking havoc on the institution under review. In addition to CPTED strategies, target hardening hardware such as fencing, doors, locks, and card readers can be introduced to further target harden the environment. The use of CPTED principals can effectively control the interior environments as well, and access into high-risk areas like Emergency Department, Maternity, Pediatrics, ICUs, and other areas designated as high-risk by the healthcare facility.

The installation of door locks and fencing are only effective when these devices are allowed to operate as designed. Oftentimes, access control policies and procedures become ineffective when compromised. For example, an exterior portal propped open by a person to smoke outside and then regain entry into the hospital, etc. Additionally, many times exit doors are found unlocked, broken, or not closing properly because they are not checked on a regular schedule. It is important to check exit and entry doors on a regular basis to ensure they are locked and functional. Interior access control portal doors should also be included. Beyond hardware considerations, software technologies such as access card readers must also be included in the inspection process. Like traffic signals GREEN means go and RED means stop, it is important that these devices are checked to ensure that they are functioning as intended.

Bolstering Security Presence and Perception

Security presence is a major part of violence reduction. Security operative visibility along with visible aspects of the security program all contribute to violence reduction.

Random patrols and fixed protective presence at select critical ingress and egress portals provides a strong preventative message to miscreants. Increased surveillance is another strategy to reduce the potential for violent activity. Using windows, glass partitions and CCTV cameras can increase the ability of staff to view and recognize danger and violence. In essence, these high-visibility technologies can help the institution enlist everyone (worker, salesperson, contractor, patient, visitor, etc.) and turn them into "security advocates".

Often security officers are hired with the intent to screen visitors or just be present in an entrance lobby. However, all too often the officer is posted off to the side, behind a desk or strategically located so far inside of the lobby that they are not noticed by patients or visitors entering the hospital. All too often officers posted in lobbies or patrolling hospital surroundings are reassigned to patient watches. These re-assignments reduce security presence and help create the perception that security presence and help create the perception that security is nowhere to be found and absent from duty!

Security Perception

In these days, post 9/11, feeling secure is especially important. Whether a person is at an airport, attending a ballgame or simply walking on the street; we are always taught to be ever vigilant. But walk into a hospital and most people believe they are in a safe haven – healing zone. When the healthcare security program is perceived as being nonexistent, then patients, visitors and medical staff feel that the hospital does not care about their security and safety. The perception of a sound security program does positively influence the perception of security within the institution. Examples of strong security might include hospital staff wearing their ID card; the institution issuing security passes to everyone, not just a select few; the institution following infant security safeguards; and the institution having security operatives (ambassadors of security and safety) on duty to direct pedestrian traffic. These strategies enhance the image of security and safety and send a strong message to all potential wrongdoers that security is on the job and hard at work.

Employing Crime Prevention through Environmental Design Strategies

A major part of the CPTED philosophy is the use of surveillance technologies. Systems design criteria should include an in-depth review of the surveillance area so that windows, mirrors, low walls, or shelving are used effectively to observe the scene. Often, healthcare facilities install cameras and purchase recorders but may not be utilizing them effectively. Most surveillance systems are used for review of after incident occurrences a not for live monitoring. Those select hospitals that do live surveillance do so using small computer monitors, viewing sixteen two-inch wide across images which is an ineffective way to provide surveillance. Professionally speaking, surveillance staffs are often asked to perform a vast majority of other tasks which substantially limits overall surveillance capabilities. It is important to remember that if CCTV cameras are installed within the healthcare institution, these systems should be monitored live; and on large screens so that images can be viewed in detail. Healthcare institutions that have IP addressable cameras and video management systems should be programming their systems to detect motion and provide a pop-up image on a security monitor in specific high-risk areas. Effective camera positioning might include surveillance of stairwells leading to the Maternity unit during the off hours so that security will be drawn to the image when someone is within the view of the camera allowing for the immediate dispatch of an operative to further investigate.

A 1988 article[1] offers some guidance on how CPTED strategies can be included in the security survey.

Propping up Security's Response to Emergencies

Security response does not just include a security officer rushing to a location after a duress alarm has been activated. Equally important is the hospital's reaction to security issues and their quick and thorough resolution of the incident.

As an example, when an exterior light burns out or Daylight-Saving Time arrives, defective or inadequate lighting should be replaced immediately and the timers controlling the lights should immediately adjusted accordingly. When an exit door is broken, it should be repaired immediately so that the hospital remains secure. When burned-out lights and broken doors remain in disrepair hospital staff, patients and visitors notice it and it increases their feeling of insecurity and overall vulnerability.

Deepening and Strengthening Protection Education Initiatives

Education is an important part of violence reduction as well. All hospital staff should be trained on the hospital's policy and processes relating to workplace violence and shooting incidents. More concentrated training should be provided in high-risk areas, like the Emergency Department, Maternity and Pediatrics, and ICU units. In high-risk areas, policies should be continually reviewed with staff and practice drills held so that staff feels comfortable responding to acts of violence or an active shooter event. Workplace violence and active shooter training should take place at new employee orientation sessions and reviewed during annual in-service training programs. Education of security staff is important as well.

Security staff should understand their role in responding to violent incidents and work with local police on a regular basis to ensure that both the hospital and local law enforcement understand the processes when a violent incident occurs. Security officer training should include basic information on workplace violence and active shooter training concerning crisis intervention along with all hospital workplace violence and active shooter policies and procedures. This review should take place annually and include the specific processes that Security is responsible for. Key to workplace violence and active shooter response is the cooperation and understanding of police and fire response. The Security Department should meet with the local police and/or fire departments to learn and compare notes on response to a workplace or active shooter incident at the hospital. This meeting should occur annually and include a tour of the hospital so that responders know where they are going. It is also important to ascertain staffing level shifts within the local police agencies (some police agencies have special events happening during the year which require the hiring of additional staff) so that if major changes do occur either at the law enforcement agency or healthcare institution immediate training is instituted.

Instituting an Effective Background Screening Program

Good security does not happen by accident. It begins with not hiring and associating with high-risk individuals (employees, contractors, salespersons, etc.). Background checking is an excellent diagnostic tool to decipher deception before it can wreak havoc on your institution. A 2014 article[2] highlights the importance of background checking and its relationship to avoiding crime and violence related victimization.

Workplace Violence and Active Shooter Resources

Dealing with emergencies like workplace violence or active shooter instances requires a focused approach.

Homeland Security groups respond to emergency events in four phases:

1. Mitigation
2. Preparedness
3. Response
4. Recovery.

The grouping of these functions is useful for classifying and conceptualizing activities used in the preparation and response to violent incidents. As indicated above there are numerous published resources available for the prevention and mitigation of workplace violence and active shooter response. Here are a few broken down within the four stages of response as outlined by Homeland Security.

Mitigation is the first of the four approaches. Mitigation activities entail identifying risks and hazards to either reduce or eliminate the impact of an incident. Mitigation activities often have long-term or sustained effects. Some examples of mitigation include:

- Developing and implementing a work policy on violence and violent incident response
- Conducting assessments of high-risk work areas
- Target hardening work areas in order to prevent workplace violent incidents

Resources for the mitigation of workplace violence and active shooter incidents include:

- OSHA Document – Guidelines for Preventing Workplace Violence for Healthcare and Social Service Workers: https://www.osha.gov/SLTC.workplaceviolence/
- OHSA Website of Workplace Violence: https://www.osha.gov/SLTC/workplaceviolence/
- CDC – NIOSH Publication – Violence Occupational Hazards in Hospitals: http://www.cdc.gov/niosh.docs.2002-101/
- Florida Hospital Association Workplace Violence Tool Kit: http://fha.org/health-care-issues/emergency-preparedness/workplace-violence-toolkit.aspx

Preparedness is distinct from mitigation because rather than focusing on eliminating or reducing risks, the general focus of preparedness is to enhance the capacity to respond to an incident by taking steps to ensure personnel and entities can respond to a wide range of potential incidents.

Preparedness activities may include:

- Conducting drills and exercises so that staff can respond effectively and safely
- Continually training staff so that they are always prepared to handle violent situations

Resources for the preparation of workplace violence and active shooter include:

- Training video: Armed: Are you ready active shooter training video: http://vimeopro.com/lmpgeneral/armed-are-you-ready
- Department of Homeland Security on-line training program for active shooter: http://www.nationalterroralert.com/2013/01/20/dhs-launches-new-active-shooter-preparedness-webpage/

136 ■ *Healthcare Security*

- FBI:ActiveShooterPlanningandResponseinaHealthcareSetting:https://www.fbi.gov/about-us/cirg/active-shooter-and-mass-casualty-incidents/active-shooter-planning-and-response-in-a-healthcare-setting/view
- The Office of the Assistant Secretary for Preparedness and Response – Incorporating Active Shooter Planning into Health Care Facility Emergency Operations Plans: http://www.traumacenters.org/news/205038/Incorporating-Active-Shooter-Planning-into-Health-Care-Facility-Emergency-Operations-Plans.htm

Response activities are comprised of the immediate actions to save lives, protect property and the environment, and meet basic human needs. Response involves the execution of emergency plans and related actions and may include.

- Handling victims
- Deployment of response teams, medical stockpiles, and other assets
- Establishing of incident command operations

Resources for the response to workplace violence and active shooter include:

- Department of Homeland Security – How to Respond to an Active Shooter: http://www.dhs.gov/publication/active-shooter-how-to-respond
- FBI:ActiveShooterPlanningandResponseinaHealthcareSetting:https://www.fbi.gov/about-us/cirg/active-shooter-and-mass-casualty-incidents/active-shooter-planning-and-response-in-a-healthcare-setting/view
- Healthcare and Public Health Sector Coordinating Councils – Active Shooter Planning and Response in the Healthcare Setting: http://www.dhs.org

Recovery activities are intended to restore essential services and repair damages by the event. Recovery activities may include:

- The reconstitution of operations and services
- Assist with the victim and organizations staff mental health
- Replenishment of stockpiles
- Resources for the recovery to workplace violence and active shooter include:
- Center for the study of Traumatic Stress Recovery – In the Aftermath of Workplace Violence: Guidance for Supervisors: http://www.cstonline.org

A Final Word

There are an endless number of ways in which a hospital or other businesses can suffer at the hands of criminals. All are vulnerable, but none are helpless. There are countless ways to thwart workplace violence and firearms related terrorism before it devastates your institution. Just instituting only some of the suggestions outlined will undoubtedly help to further shield your institution from criminal activity. The key to success is to get started.

References

1. Anthony Luizzo. *Beyond Target Hardening: Approaches in Applying Crime Risk Management Principles and Techniques in Community Surveys* published in The Practitioner Magazine, a publication of the International Society of Crime Prevention Practitioners
2. A. Luizzo, et el, *Background Checks: a Diagnostic Tool to Decipher Deception* (Vol. 30. No. 2: 2014, Journal of Healthcare Protection Management)

Squeezing the Most from Your Security Dollar

Anthony Luizzo and Philip Luizzo

The Dilemma

In this new millennium forward thinking security executives know that it is virtually impossible to purchase security technologies on the cheap. This is especially true since terrorism hit our shores in early September 2001 – when virtually every American began buying security-related technologies by the bushel and the prices began to skyrocket. How does a security administrator proceed? One possible approach to solving this dilemma might lie in learning to think outside of the proverbial box and seek to implement less costly security strategies that can do the job effectively. In today's budget conscious atmosphere, stretching the security dollar is both an art and a science. The art lies in the company's ability to solve protection related deficiencies using existing resources, whilst the science lies in architecting protection strategies that meet and/or exceed industry benchmarks. Obviously, if security enhancement dollars are readily available then all is well. But in most cases such dollars are scarce and the secret to achieving success in this endeavor may lie in finding low-cost initiatives that can further strengthen and deepen protection availability without blowing up the budget.

What is Proactive Security?

Simply put – proactive security approaches and technologies involve devices and techniques that address crime exposures BEFORE they occur. The standard policing and private security model have been and continues to be a REACTIVE model. It was not until the 1970's that crime prevention and proactive security strategies entered our law enforcement and private security lexicons. One of the most cost-effective strategies developed during the evolution of the proactive security revolution was the birth of the SECURITY SURVEY. Information on how surveys are drafted and how they play a role in uncovering risk exposure can be found in an article written by the undersigned: "THE SECURITY SURVEY: AN INVESTIGATIVE TOOL", featured in the 2018 Spring issue of this magazine, pp. 39-42. The article offers a roadmap on how security surveys are structured.

The Origins of Proactive Security

Great Britain is known as the world leader in fostering the modern crime prevention model of policing. Sir Henry Fielding, a British magistrate and criminologist in the mid -18th century organized the forerunner of today's policing methods by setting goals and objectives to assist law enforcement to identify and remove the root causes of crime and the conditions in which they flourish. In 1971, the United States followed Britain's lead formalizing a course of study in the ABCs of crime prevention via a Law Enforcement Assistance Administration grant awarded to the University of Louisville. This later helped to spawn The National Crime Prevention Institute which

From *The Texas Investigator Magazine*. Summer Issue, pp. 30–33. 2018.

138 ■ *Healthcare Security*

over the years has helped to train thousands of crime prevention practitioners in law enforcement and in the private security industry. One of the most important skills taught to all graduates is how to decipher criminality using the security survey.

Advancing the Proactive Security Agenda

Security administrators need to cast an investigative eye on whether their security departments have a cadre of specialists that labor on searching out crime related risk exposures within the entities they work in. Oftentimes, these specialists are trained to conduct security surveys and search out preventative strategies for their specific institutions. Crime Prevention training programs are normally offered by many larger police agencies and state criminal justice entities free of charge. As a matter of course, the program includes training in a few sub-topics including but not limited to history and theory of crime prevention, aspects of drafting security surveys, alarm and locking system applications, crime mapping techniques and technologies. The alternative to having a crime prevention team on board is to reach out to professional surveyors which can become quite expensive indeed! Seeing that security wisdom suggests that security surveys should be prepared on an annual schedule, hiring outside experts could be quite cost intensive.

Thinking Out of the Box: Some Low-Cost security Initiatives

Security executives might wish to consider marshalling support from in-house corporate personnel and begin a campaign to champion proactive crime prevention measures to bolster security. Several programs to consider include:

- Establishing a "Security Advocate" program that links all corporate personnel into a direct pipeline for receiving and disseminating timely security and safety information. A security advocate is an employee who is charged with keeping a watchful eye over all incoming visitors, and others entering their area of responsibility. The security advocate has a simple task to CHALLENGE unknown individuals by simply asking CAN I HELP YOU. In many instances, corporate security executives follow the advice of their security surveyor when positioning their advocate staff. Advocates are usually selected from among peers and their desks strategically relocated to an area that offers direct unobstructed sight of access and egress portals. As such, anyone entering the area is immediately challenged by the advocate.
- Formulating crime prevention initiatives that champion proactive crime control approaches. These approaches include conducting security surveys to help diagnose frail security deficiencies, enrolling company employees into local law enforcement programming such as "operation identification" – etching company property with serial numbers, neighborhood watch programming, and other programs normally offered by most law enforcement agencies
- Asking local law enforcement agencies to design a series of personal safety programs for company employees
- Encouraging in-house employees to work more closely with facility security
- Promulgating a periodical security/safety bulletin highlighting security deficiencies, current crime trends, hazardous conditions, and other cautionary security-related directives for dissemination to all employees
- Establishing financial incentive programs to thwart thievery

- Promulgating architectural initiatives that help deter criminal behavior such as: relocating business hubs from low to high-risk environs, reconfiguring waiting room furniture to restrict prolonged horizontal positioning (sleeping). Using air conditioning, heating, and music systems as deterrents to extended loitering episodes
- Installing exterior and interior critical access portals with secondary industrial strength locking mechanisms to help bolster perimeter security and safety
- Erecting security specific signage in critical areas that offer safety tips such as: always walk with a neighbor or two in dangerous environs, listen to your instincts when feeling uncomfortable, remember to use the street landmarks such as parked cars and fire hydrants, etc., to accurately judge a possible perpetrator's height.
- Inaugurate package inspection programs to reduce internal thievery and shoplifting episodes
- Ensure that all department administrators remove calendars, posters, and other paraphernalia from glass doors, and partitions to enhance overall visibility
- Inaugurate comprehensive background screening initiatives to help weed out miscreants
- Encouraging security and facility maintenance departments to work together to find facility lighting and locking systems in disrepair and other safety and security hazards before they wreak financial havoc.

The Role of Metrics in 21st Century Security Planning

Security executives instinctively know that profit is what drives the business model. When a company needs to financially downsize, security is one of the first areas to be cut. One of the most important reasons why this is usually true is because security in general is NOT considered a profit center, but rather an expense. Showing how much money was saved because of good sound proactive security approaches such as: injuries and crimes avoided is extremely difficult to substantiate. More forward-thinking security mavens have begun applying metric measurements in their security survey assessments to better help spell out the financial value and programmatic effectiveness of proactive security initiatives.

An excellent discussion on how METRICS can be applied to help make the financial value case can be found in a trilogy of articles co-written by the undersigned and featured in the Journal of Healthcare Protection Management – a publication of the International Association for Healthcare Security and Safety:

- 'AN ALTERNATIVE VIEW IN THE DEVELOPMENT OF SECURITY METRICS" VOL. 31., NO.2. -2015
- "RESOURCES AVAILABLE FOR APPLYING METRICS IN SECURITY AND SAFETY PLANNING" VOL.32., NO. 1. – 2016
- "APPLYING METRICS TO 21ST CENTURY HEALTHCARE SECURITY" VOL. 33., NO. 2. – 2017.

Asking the Right Questions

The following is a list of questions that a security executive should ask when evaluating their company's proactive security and safety programming:

1. Does company management champion proactive security initiatives?
2. Are all company employees enrolled in the firm's proactive security and safety initiative?

Healthcare Security

3. Are both low budget and high budget security strategies employed?
4. Are security advocates assigned protection duties?
5. Are security surveys prepared by in-house or external specialists?
6. Are security surveys prepared after all serious crime-related incidents?
7. Are security surveys prepared on an annual schedule?
8. Does the security department maintain a crime analysis and crime mapping program?
9. Does the company have an in-house bulletin to disseminate security and safety directives and announcements?
10. Does the company security department maintain an ongoing liaison with local law enforcement?

The ABCs of Evaluating Security Initiatives

As with all programs, a system of evaluation should be promulgated so that the overall effect of the initiative can be accurately measured. Structuring such a program might include:

- Designing an instrument that evaluates before, middle, and after studies to help determine the actual level of crime reporting in areas where proactive approaches have been put forward
- Designing a statistical instrument to help gauge whether the proactive message is reaching its intended target audience

All in all, a structured program of evaluation will measurably help security administrators to better gauge their organization's proactive crime control initiative.

Looking to the Future

These and other low budget strategies help to strengthen existing protection availability via fostering the philosophy that *"SECURITY IS EVERYONE'S RESPONSIBILITY"*. Oftentimes, this skillful display of resourcefulness influences top management to consider and approve more expensive protection specific systems. The security administrators' inventive ability to stretch the ever-shrinking security dollar often distinguishes him or her as a company asset and not a corporate liability.

---

*Reprinted with permission: The Texas Investigator Magazine

Chapter 6

Metrics and Data Application

An Alternative View in the Development of Healthcare Security Metrics

Anthony Luizzo and Bernard J. Scaglione

In an October 15, 2013, article by Scott Greaux featured in PhishMe.Com, "Use Metrics to Measure and Improve Security Awareness," while discussing the overall importance of using metrics to improve security awareness, the author goes on to mention that most security awareness programming fails to gather and/or use metrics as part of its protection mosaic. Greaux goes on to discuss the importance of gathering as much information as possible about an institution's services so that appropriate metrics can be developed and applied to properly meet todays and tomorrow's challenges. In "Persuading Senior Management with Effective, Evaluated Security Metrics" published by the ASIS Foundation in 2014, the report summarizes the need for effective metrics as follows: "Security metrics support the value proposition of an organization's security operation. Without compelling metrics, security professionals and their budgets continue largely on the intuition of company leadership. With metrics, the security function grounds itself on measurable results that correlate with investment, and the security professional can speak to leadership in a familiar business language. Security metrics are vital, but in the field and in the literature, one finds few tested metrics and little guidance on using metrics effectively to inform and persuade senior management." Metrics is a management tool that provides a measure of performance for a given project or entity. Business Dictionary.Com defines metrics as a standard of measurement by which efficiency, performance, progress, or quality of a plan, or process, or product can be assessed. To derive the most benefit from using metrics, it's important that security administrators understand the benefits of using metrics in their daily endeavors and make them part of their managerial toolkits.

The use of metrics to evaluate the effectiveness of healthcare security services and staff has been widely debated. Several security organizations including: The International Association of Hospital Security and Safety (IAHSS) have conducted surveys and studies to determine which metrics work best to evaluate a given service.

From *The Journal of Healthcare Protection Management*. (31):2, pp. 98–104. 2016.

DOI: 10.4324/9781003215851-6

142 ■ *Healthcare Security*

To date however, no real consensus has been obtained on what works best. On the contrary, many different ideas have been brought forth and many different types of metrics are used by healthcare organizations. Oftentimes, most security executives rely on individual security expertise when developing metrics. These metrics are understood by the security professional but have not gained ground outside of the healthcare security field. Consultants and senior executives alike have not seen real value in security metrics, and in general dismiss them as being ineffective or demonstrating no real value to the evaluation process. In "Persuading Senior Management with Effective, Evaluated Security Metrics" the authors discuss the criteria for evaluating an effective security metric. They state that a security metric should be reliable, have validity and have generalizability. They should operationally demonstrate cost, timeliness and be manipulative. They should be strategic demonstrating return on investment, organizational relevance and be easily communicated.

Herein Are a Few Ideas that Deserve Consideration.

Productivity Indicators: Clinical Length of Stay/Discharge Rate

On the surface, it appears that there is no real value in the use of length of stay or discharge rate when evaluating security services; and in general, that is true. Alone this metric holds no real value in the determination of service relative to the security of patients, visitors, and staff. But, when we compare these rates with the long-term evaluation of incident rates or calls for service, we can compare the effectiveness of monthly or quarterly service by monitoring its highs and lows. This metric works because when length of stay is low, and discharge rate is high, the number of patients and visitors within the hospital is greater. In theory, the number of incidents and calls for service should be accordingly higher as well. When compared over time, the security department can demonstrate value by showing a decrease in the incident rate when more people are using the hospital. Comparing security-related incident rates or calls for service with length of stay or discharge rates; illustrates the effectiveness of security services as compared over time and to other hospital departments that utilize the length of stay metric in evaluating service.

Square Footage

Although square footage alone is not a valuable metric in the evaluation of security services, it is a statistic that many consultants rely upon in evaluating healthcare support services. For security services, the amount of square feet does _not_ wholly determine the amount of staff necessary to provide a safe and secure environment. Still and all, this statistic can be useful in demonstrating the effectiveness of services. The value of using square footage as a metric is its acceptance with consultants and the C-Suite alike. This metric demonstrates its value when compared to security data over time, or with other facilities of similar square footage. If the call for service rate is higher in comparison to other facilities, or increases over time, the metric demonstrates an increase in the level of service andsuggests the need for more staff. If the incident rate is lower over time, or lower than other similar institutions, the security service is efficient in its delivery.

Workload/Calls for Service "TOUCHES"

Generally, security departments report the number of incidents that occur, the number of patrols conducted, or the number of visitors passes dispensed. These statistics no matter how they are presented demonstrate the amount of work that the security department produces in each period. It does _not_ show the value of the service provided. However, if the data collected shows how many times the security department interacts with patients, visitors, and staff, coupled with the type of interaction furnished, then the security department can demonstrate its value and effectiveness-based upon the patients, visitors and staff served. So, what metric is important in the evaluation of calls for service? _Ergo, then "Touches" is the metric that should be used!_ Touches are not the number of patrols conducted, or the hours that an officer held a post, it is the interaction with the customer and the results of that interaction.

Reporting the number of times security accompanied and/or assisted staff to their designation, provided directions or escort them to their vehicle is a more definitive evaluation of the service as compared to the number of patrols conducted or the hours an officer stands post.

Many times, security departments will document and report the number of doors they unlocked or the number of doors that were found unlocked and/or opened. With respect to these types of assignments, opening a door for a staff member is a touch. In this case, a staff touch can be both a positive and negative metric. Having a high number of touches to assist staff in a non-patient related way may not be a positive metric when it is compared to patient and visitor touches. Comparing the number of staff touches with patient and visitor touches can demonstrate the need to reduce staff interaction or increase patient and visitor interaction, translating to less door openings and more facility patrols.

Near Misses

The term, "Near Miss" is used in the healthcare setting to indicate the intervention or discovery of an incident or event that <u>could have been adverse</u> but was averted. This concept can be used in healthcare security since it is more readily identifiable than a door found open, a behavioral health patient that tried to leave the hospital and was stopped or the continued denial of an access card being presented to a storeroom or high security door. In lieu of reporting the number of doors found open, reporting a near miss related to a purse left unattended or a computer that could have stolen is a better more understandable metric. Not reporting the patient who almost left the hospital or the employee who is continually trying to access a door that they have no access to, negates the effectiveness of the security services provided to the institution. A near miss is an evaluation tool that risk management, nursing and administration can relate to.

Interventions

An intervention is a term that isused in the healthcare profession generally in the behavioral health arena. An intervention is a planned or unplanned interaction with a patient or client because of negative or potentially negative behavior. A patient restraint is an intervention; a patient watch is an intervention; a disruptive patient or visitor is an intervention. An intervention is a metric that can describe aspects of the execution of the security operatives' job that is not demonstrated by reporting basic workplace violence. Using interventions as

144 ■ *Healthcare Security*

a metric demonstrates actions taken to improve a declining or detrimental situation and can be used to categorize the workload conducted by security staff in the prevention of violence within the hospital. This phraseology helps behavioral health administrators better understand the use of this metric by security and can provide a more defined application of security services.

Staff Configuration/Work Force Management

Staff configuration and/or work force management is the evaluation of staffing requirements and the costs associated with labor and other expenses and are another metric that can be used to evaluate the effectiveness of security services. Generally, the security professional sees work force metrics as the cost by officer post or hours worked, two metrics that provide little insight into the financial value of security services as seen by the fiduciary administrator. In finance, the value of service is determined by the expense, or the cost compared to patient care data or industry known metrics. As such, to show value within financial metric circles, expenses should be compared by square foot or discharge rate. Comparing labor expenses or overall security expenses with square footage or discharge rates alone has no real value in determining the effectiveness of security services; but when compared over time or with like facilities, these metrics can demonstrate the value of security services over time. These metric measurements speak the language of the fiduciary aficionado.

Experience demonstrates that the best metrics to use in fiduciary-related situations varies from entity to entity. Besides labor or expenses compared to square footage or discharges, financial data should be determined based on exceptions. In finance, exception reporting paints a true picture as to the state of expenses and overages that plague budgets. So, items like overtime, sick time, injury time off, accidents or breakdowns in vehicles and extra training are all examples of exceptions that influence budgets.

Other Metrics

From a programmatic perspective, the best metrics for security executives in the healthcare environment to employ are those metrics that hospital administrators know and understand. These may include demographics related to employment/background checks, equipment outages, emergency responses, and policy and/or procedural violations. Finding the appropriate metric to exploit is limited only by the security administrator's imagination.

Conclusion

Metrics are an effective way to validate the business of security to the C-Suite. By speaking the language of clinical and administrative personnel, metric use and evaluation can better position the security department in the evaluation of services and its value to the organization. When using metrics, it is imperative that a dashboard be developed to appropriately monitor and evaluate whether programmatic standards and metric applications are within acceptable, defined compliance standards. A dashboard consists of a series of graphs or data points presented on a single sheet of parchment, or on a computer screen that furnishes a clear picture of the task at hand. Applying effective mathematical metric measurements gives the security professional the capability of deciphering adverse incidents before they have an opportunity to adversely impact the intuitional setting.

Selected Bibliography

"Persuading Senior Management with Effective Evaluated Security Metrics": ASIS Foundation 2014.

146 ■ *Healthcare Security*

Resources Available for Applying Metrics in Security and Safety Programming

Anthony Luizzo

A 1991 article by this author "Stretching the Security Dollar" (Vol.7. No.2). - Journal of Healthcare Protection Management highlights the major fiduciary-related issues security executives' face endeavoring to substantiate protection program proficiency. How does a security administrator take credit for crimes that HAVE occurred, and/or <u>MAY</u> have occurred and were deterred? This is obviously a difficult mountain to climb for any administrator. Further compounding this dilemma is the harsh reality that security and safety cost money and <u>does not</u> contribute to the company's immediate bottom line. Moreover, the company's bottom line <u>may</u> be positively affected in future budgets via litigation-related cost reductions due to exceptional security strategies or other factors but may not be immediately apparent. Notwithstanding, stretching the security dollar is both an art and a science. The art lies in the security executive's ability to solve protection problems utilizing existing resources, the science in the ability to keep protection programming healthy and current. In today's climate of budget shortfalls and ever shrinking dollars, protection mavens should be seeking new strategies to better protect their institutions. The trick is finding where these elusive strategies and approaches reside. Looking even further into this problem, in a 1990 article by this author "A Clinical Approach to Crime Detection" – Campus law Enforcement Journal (Vol. 20), while discussing contemporary issues such as budget cuts and revenue shortfalls and its effect on security in general, championed a need for security directors to begin searching for new and innovative approaches to crime control.

In the 25 years since this article was published, little has changed, security executives are still fighting for additional protection dollars; whilst crime risk exposures coupled with the new Terrorism related threats have exponentially increased tenfold. One possible solution may lie in using *Metrics* to substantiate program-related effectiveness and expenditures. In security management, one of the central methods of evaluating the effectiveness of security programming is to prepare a security survey. The survey is the fulcrum upon which security evaluation is built. Surveys have been around for well over 40 years, rarely if ever has Metric-related strategies been part of the equation.

Modifying the Standard Security Survey

Two previous articles by this author featured in Vol. 7, No. 1: 1990: Journal of Healthcare Protection Management "The Security Survey: A Prescription for Enhancing Security", and in a June 2000 article in the Internal Auditing Report Vol. 20, No. 6 "Aspects of the Security Survey" published by Warren Gorham and Lamont/ RIA Group – Thomson Publications define the security survey as an onsite inspection of a facility to determine its protection posture. Both publications speak to survey structure and include information anent which security-related risk exposures need to be evaluated. Beyond the standard high-risk areas such as building structure, access control and internal procedural security issues, etc., it's important that security administrators begin devising a comprehensive list of metric-related applications that they would like included in their facility's assessment.

From *The Journal of Healthcare Protection Management.* (32):1, pp. 27–33. 2016.

Over the past few years much research into the use of metrics to gauge efficiency has been brought forward. One example is the excellent research by the International Association of Hospital Security and Safety that conducted numerous studies to determine which Metrics work best in the healthcare environment. Security administrators would be wise to conduct their own research within their field as well. It is most important that security administrators from all walks of life and surveyors who specialize in preparing security assessments consider including these new strategies in their firm's offerings.

Some examples of these applications include but are not limited to:

- Tracking ID Compliance
- Tracking the time security operatives spend on various assignments (checking IDs, greeting patrons, spot checking select staff, etc.)
- Tracking clinical length of stay and discharge rates
- Tracking calls for service (touches) performed
- Tracking and including square footage data and its correlation to service effectiveness

The Value of Using Metrics

Finding the right suit of metrics to snuggly fit a firm's protection wardrobe is also both an art and a science as well. With ever shrinking dollars available for security endeavors, it's imperative that security administrators apply strategies that help to further stretch the security dollar even further. Choosing the right metric to apply is critical to keeping your security and safety programming healthy. In a June 2012 article by Bernard Scaglione - "Metrics: The Evaluation of Access Control and Identification" published in Security Magazine, mentions that using metrics provides a quantifiable way to measure the effectiveness of security programming. Moreover, the article highlights the importance of identifying the objectives, structures and goals of the program under consideration; concomitant with applying the precise metric to demonstrate the effectiveness of the objectives and goals of the program under evaluation. Another excellent resource to better understand how to effectively use Metrics can be found in a 2006 article by George K. Campbell "How to use Metrics" – published in CSO Online.com. The article touches on several central issues that should be soothing music to any security executive's ears. When looking toward research in this new discipline, there have been a plethora of publications championing the benefits of effectively applying metrics; conjoined with additional information highlighting the challenges associated with implementing such a program. Amid the many articles on this exciting topic, is a November 2006 article by Elizabeth A. Nichols and Andrew Sudbury - "Implementing Security Metrics Initiatives" published in Information Security and Risk Management Magazine which offers a few suggestions in this specialized field of endeavor. The article speaks to the value of using metrics, the challenges associated with using metrics, including a seven (7) step implementation guide.

The guide includes information re:

1. Defining goals and objectives
2. Determining information goals
3. Developing metrics models
4. Establishing a metrics reporting format and schedule
5. ABCs of Implementing a metrics program,
6. Setting benchmarks and targets, and
7. Enacting a formal review cycle.

148 ■ *Healthcare Security*

Moreover, the publication goes on to mention that the real challenge is to effectively integrate security techniques and technologies into existing IT management, governance, and business structures.

Joining Metrics and the Community Security Survey

In a July 1988 article by this author "Beyond Target Hardening: Approaches in Applying Crime Risk Management Principles and Techniques in Community Surveys" – published in the Practitioner Magazine: a publication of the International Society of Crime Prevention Practitioners discusses the philosophy behind preparing a community or neighborhood wide assessment and how it differs from other survey types. The focus of these broader assessments is to identify surrounding community concerns that affect everyone who legitimately uses the area such as store owners, shoppers, residents, and motorists. The practitioners' mindset in these broader assessments requires that he or she understand that the individual entity, commercial center and surrounding community are one interrelated unit. In these studies, the surveyor examines land use data, canvasses users, interviews public service providers, and gathers and evaluates other information germane to the community as a whole. Possible solutions to crime related problems might include installing new street lighting, installing public area cameras to keep a watchful eye on public areas, and modifying traffic flow patterns for security purposes. Beyond these strategies, surveyors might wish to include Metric applications to the survey recommendation mixture as well.

Determining Metric Applications for Community Wide Assessments

The following is a list of possible Metric equations that surveyors might use in community or neighborhood wide security assessments:

- Working with chambers of commerce, local and national political leaders, local development agencies, area law enforcement, and other community organizations to devise metrics that focuses on tracking shopper habits and its correlation to protection requisites
- Working with the traffic agency personnel to devise metrics to track motorist related protection issues
- Working with mass transit agencies to devise metrics to track straphanger issues and security requirements
- Working with local law enforcement, federal law enforcement, and other community agencies to devise crime mapping programming to discern crime-related patterns and staffing requisites.
- Devising metrics that effectively link commercial, residential, institutional, and industrial entities into a crime control network and staffing grid.

Metric Related Jargon (TOUCHES – DASHBOARD)

A 2015 article "An Alternative View in the Development of Healthcare Security Metrics" published in summer edition of the Journal of Healthcare Protection Management by A. Luizzo & B. Scaglione, offers insight into how metrics might be used in security related applications.

Seeing that security departments use numbers to report and measure crime and non-crime related data, it would be wise to also use such a system in security assessments to gauge protection wherewithal. In the universe of metrics, using numbers to record select activities is called TOUCHES. Likewise, surveyors should advocate the use of dashboards to record program efficiency and deficiency. A dashboard consists of a series of graphs or data points that helps to paint a clear picture of the facility's program. As an example, an excellent CCTV system might be valuated at a 5, while a weak application, a 1. Correspondingly, all security related techniques and technologies should also be labeled accordingly. Applying mathematical measurements gives the security entity the capability of deciphering adverse incidents before they have an opportunity to become catastrophic events. Moreover, using such a system will be an extremely valuable tool when making programmatic comparisons from year to year.

Fiducially Speaking

Standard survey solutions are used to stimulate social attitudes and behavior that help to reduce both opportunities for crime and the fear of crime. Where these strategies often miss their mark relative to stretching or adding to the security dollar is that senior management and security administrators do not speak the same language. Metric-related solutions are music to the CFOs ears, thus possibly causing earmarked security dollars to begin flowing more easily and readily. Security executives need to learn the right jargon so that everyone is happily on the same page.

A Final Word

In the court of protection wisdom, security executives need to tackle two important issues sooner than later. First and foremost, security executives need to begin using metrics to substantiate their protection grids, and second, they need to reach out to security consultants that specialize in drafting security surveys and ask that they incorporate metrics into their work product. Further, security executives should be pondering new and innovative metric applications and begin applying the mathematical metric approaches in all areas within their sphere of influence. It's evident that security related Metrics are a valuable resource – implementation however continues to be a problem. Security administrators should begin building a closet-full of possible metric applications for all possible scenarios. Likewise, security executives should ensure that Metrics is included in their facility's operations manual so that regulators realize that applied science is at work and on the job. The age-old adage "knowing what to look for and how to analyze it" spells success, success, and success. And success is what all security executives strive for and what every malefactor fears and detests! The key is to get started!!!!!

Applying Metrics to 21st Century Healthcare Security

Anthony Luizzo and Bernard J. Scaglione

In their third article for the Journal of Healthcare Protection Management on the subject, the authors spell out why and how Metrics will have to be used in the years ahead to demonstrate the financial value and program effectiveness of healthcare security.

Healthcare security professionals have the awesome task of trying to justify the value of the protective services they provide. The primary goal of every healthcare security executive is to keep hospital staff and visitors safe. The evaluative tool used to do this job is the security survey. In professional hands the security-survey functions like a diagnostic CT scanner seeking protection deficiencies and other abnormalities requiring adjustment and or repair. In today's budget conscious times, all security executives face the stark reality of trying to adequately deal with these budget shortfalls and ever shrinking protection dollars whilst offering optimum protective services within their respective institutions. Many more informed security executives have begun moving into the 21st century and are using Metrics to justify protection-related expenditures. They have finally learned that the key to obtaining needed dollars for security related expenditures is to learn the language that CFOs know and understand when pursuing their wish list. Two recent articles[1, 2] written by the undersigned authors for this publication help to cast an eye on both the benefits of metric utilization and its immense value in substantiating programmatic costs to management.

Developing Metrics to Demonstrate Value

The key to obtaining needed dollars for security related expenditures is developing metrics that are relevant to the operations being performed by the security department. When metrics are applied over time, they show fluctuation in service delivery, enhancement options and/or deteriorations in service levels. A galaxy of different metrics is employed in the healthcare sector to determine the value of security services. Unraveling which Metric applications are the most effective has been exhaustively debated for many years by numerous organizations and individuals.

We believe that the following Metric applications should be added to the list of options:

- Officer response time to emergent situations
- The number of security department generated incident reports presented monthly or weekly
- The amount of reported crime presented within a specific period (monthly, weekly, annually)
- The number of calls for security service over a given period
- The institution's square footage

As a matter of course, some institutions compare security specific metrics to hospital-based metrics so that senior management can better relate to the security program at hand. For example:

- Conjoining the security incident rate to patient length of stay or bed census
- Conjoining incident rate, crime rate, service call and officer response durations

---

From *Journal of Healthcare Protection Management*. (33):2, pp. 7–13. 2018.

Metrics and Data Application ▪ 151

An alternative metric that demonstrates value to the security program can be determined by how security officers perform their duties compared to the costs associated with the program and how patients, visitors and staff perceive the security program and how safe they feel. These metrics are often not utilized in the evaluation of value and should be considered when demonstrating the true worth of the security program and its effectiveness in providing a safe and secure environment.

Demonstrating Financial Value of Security Services

What does it cost the hospital to provide security services and how effective are the services compared to their cost? By attaching a cost to security services and evaluating the effectiveness of these services, value to the hospital for those services can be determined. Individual programs like patrol, visitor screening, employee escort or patient restraints, can be reviewed to determine the individual cost to furnish said services. Then individual metrics related to that service can be developed to help measure the program's effectiveness. Together, both metrics demonstrate the value of said security programs to the hospital. Using a cost-metric equation allows for an evaluation based on a quantifiable number that the C-Suite can understand. Determining program financial value must include adequately defining the scope of the initiative to be undertaken, appraising services, collecting/cataloguing property, evaluating patrol and visitor screening. Once this is competed then the labor and operational costs can be established. Further, costs can be determined by the average salary of the officers assigned to the task or program – if the same officer holds a specific job regularly, then their actual salary can be used. With respect to service calls - the average time the officer is assigned to the call can be used.

Determining Program Effectiveness with Metrics

A set of metrics must be developed to evaluate the program effectiveness. This starts with establishing the purpose, scope or any goals associated with the program and a breakdown of the program functions. For example, when evaluating visitor screening services, effective metrics may be the average length of time a person waits for a pass, the number of passes issued in a specific time frame, the results of a security audit on how many visitors surveyed were wearing their pass as opposed to the number that were not. The number of passes issued each day, week or month, or the number of persons that enter each post broken down by time. The time it takes to produce a pass for each visitor. These are all metrics that can help in determining program effectiveness. Once all the metrics are gathered, they need to be compared to the program's expense. This comparison will determine service value to the hospital.

Calculating Costs

If an entrance is staffed with two (2) officers from noon to 8 PM at an average expense of $50 per hour, and from 12 PM to 4 PM only 20 visitors are screened, then the total expense to screen visitors is $200 or $10 per visitor. From 4 PM to 8 PM 100 visitors are screened, then the expense per visitor is $2 per visitor. However, if the wait time for a pass from 4 PM to 8 PM is 5 minutes, but at 12 PM to 4 PM it is 1 minute, then the value of the service changes. From 4 PM to 8 PM the

152 ■ *Healthcare Security*

expenses are lower; but the service metrics are higher, resulting in a lower value service. From this example, it can be determined that visitor screening has a lower customer value from 4 PM to 8 PM when lines are longer as compared to 12 PM to 4 PM when lines are shorter.

This example shows how financial evaluation can demonstrate value as well as help to identify potential service issues. For this program, it might be better to even out the costs by reducing staff to one officer from 12 to 4 PM and having three officers from 4 PM to 8 PM. With respect to this example, the expense from noon to 4 PM would now be $25 dollars an hour or $100 for the four hours, or $5 per visitor. From 4 PM to 8 PM the expense for the officers would be $75 an hour or $300 for the four hours, or $3 per visitor. Screening time increased to about 1 minute from noon to 4 PM and reduced to 2 minutes from 4 PM to 8 PM. Thus, the cost of the screening program from 12 PM to 8 PM is $400 with an average cost per visitor of $3.50. Screening time now averages 1.5 minutes. It is important to note that the true value of developing and monitoring services by expense as compared to service is when budget reduction or program evaluation is needed. For example: If security is asked to decrease their budget by a specific amount of money, then service changes can be evaluated from a financial perspective. The security department can save $700 a week by eliminating the third screening officer from 4 PM to 8 PM daily. This will decrease the cost per visitor from $3 a visitor to $2 per visitor but increase waiting time from 2 minutes to 5 minutes. It's all in the numbers!

Monitoring & Measuring the Perception of Security

It is well known in the security industry that the perception of security can be different from the actual amount of security available. Oftentimes however perception dictates security availability. The perception of poor security, insecurity or fear often takes precedent over a strategically placed security initiative. Perception of security tends to be reactive as opposed to planned or evaluated service execution. Seeing that perception can be such a strong driver of service placement - it is important to monitor perception so that service changes are anticipated and not a knee jerk reactive exercise. Monitoring the feelings or perception of patients, visitors, and staff only helps to improve overall security. How can perception be measured? It can be measured several different ways, but mainly it should be accomplished by simply asking patients, visitors, and staff, on a regular basis, how safe they feel both at their work location and within the hospital setting overall.

Surveys should be short and to the point; asking only a few questions at a time like: How safe do you feel in the hospital? How safe do you feel in your workplace or patient room? How safe do you feel visiting at night or after 8 PM? Do you feel safe walking to your car at night?

The survey should be limited to two or three questions at a time and should use a rating scale or yes/no answer format. A comment area should be made available so that patients, visitors, or staff can give examples of why they feel or do not feel safe. Surveys can be conducted by e-mail, mail or in person. For patients and visitors, it is best to conduct surveys in person while they are on site so that information is obtained in a timely fashion and response rates are higher. Perception can also be determined by the number of service calls for a specific hospital location: department or nursing unit. High rates of specific types of calls may indicate a perception of poor security or a higher feeling of insecurity by patients, visitors, or staff. For example, a high number of calls for disruptive patients or visitors to a nursing unit may indicate the perception of insecurity of visitors and staff may have a higher rate of fear compared to units that do not have a high rate of disruptive patients or visitors.

Additional Metric Considerations

Perception can also be determined by the number of incident reports generated for specific departments or nursing units. The use of specific Metric applications such as unearthing the number of exterior lights in disrepair in a specific location at night, the number of broken door locks found, the length of time a reported broken door is discovered and then repaired, the number of escorts provided to parked cars or bus stops during evening hours all play a role in the overall exercise. Perception is another metric that can be compared to security services like escorts or physical security installations of CCTV. Perception can also be compared to the overall crime rate, incident report rate or any other metric that helps to determine the value of security services.

Looking to the Future: What Role Can Robotics Play in Security/Safety Planning

Robert J. Gordon a professor in social sciences at Northwestern University[3] speaks of the possible use of robots in a wide variety of applications outside of the manufacturing and warehousing sectors including supermarkets, restaurants, doctor and dentist offices and hospitals. The sixty-four-billion-dollar question that healthcare security executives should be pondering is whether robotics has a role to play in the healthcare security and safety environment and how it might be utilized.

Conclusion

The use of Metrics in security planning and programming allows the hospital security administrator to find that unique balance between furnishing optimum security at a modest and acceptable cost. Everyone wins!

Resources

1. Anthony Luizzo, and Bernard Scaglione: *An Alternative View in the Development of Healthcare Security Metrics (Vol. 31 No. 2 2014-2015-* Journal of Healthcare Protection Management)
2. Anthony Luizzo, and Bernard Scaglione: *Resources Available for Applying Metrics in Security and Safety Programming* (Vol. 32 No. 1: 2015-2016 - Journal of Healthcare Protection Management)
3. Robert Gordon, *Rise and fall of American Growth: U.S. Standard of Living Since the Civil War:* The Princeton University Press, - 2016.

Chapter 7

Physical Security Applications

The Man Behind the Security Camera

Anthony Luizzo

Security professionals spend a great many hours tailoring CCTV systems to snugly fit an organization's profile. Engineering the right blueprint requires the tactful commingling of protective personnel and technology. By contrast, seldom is equal time devoted to the human engineering issues associated with piloting these systems. As an example, rarely do environmental issues such as: noise levels, lighting design and temperature variance, as well as human physical factors: stress, eye strain, and fatigue, ever receive the same vigorous attention.

Informative Findings from CCTV Studies

Various studies focusing on the human element in CCTV operations have brought to light some informative findings:

Engineering findings

- As the quantity of CCTV screens in the workplace increase, the potential for error and stress increase.
- As the quantity of CCTV screens increase, vigilance levels tend to decrease.
- Monitor screen size, as well as the distance the operator sits from the console, affects vigilance levels.
- The workload factor is rarely a consideration in CCTV engineering.

Environmental findings

- Noisy environments may cause operators to reduce vigilance levels as a means to avoid stress and fatigue.
- Too little light often promotes drowsiness.

From *Journal of Healthcare Protection Management*. (6):2, pp. 106–110. Spring 1990.

DOI: 10.4324/9781003215851-7

Procedure and policy findings

- Personnel selection is rarely a consideration in CCTV engineering.
- Keep-busy type tasks and effective supervision tend to enhance vigilance.
- Planned supervisory spot checks with relation to monitoring techniques are not being conducted.
- Performance standards are higher in a moderate workload configuration, than in either a small, or enlarged arrangement.

Medical findings

- Evidence indicates that the effects of light, screen size, viewing distance, and duration of tour promote eye strain.
- In complex programs, evidence indicates that noise, temperature, poor ventilation, and extended stints in front of the console often promote stress related headaches.
- The single most common body pain experienced in CCTV monitoring is lower back pain, believed to develop as a symptom of stress.

Psychological findings

- Evidence indicates that vigilance degrading symptoms disappear once the operator is reassigned to other than monitoring tasks.

General findings

- One of the general findings that surfaced in much of the research suggests that loss of vigilance is a common phenomenon in complex surveillance monitoring operations.
- The three major aspects of the work environment that adversely impact monitoring capabilities include:
  1. Monitoring load.
  2. Presence of environmental stress factors.
  3. The absence of presence of peers, and supervisors (the isolation factor).

Some suggestions to Enhance CCTV Effectiveness

Monitoring criteria

In the final analysis, if it is the ability of the systems operator to perform surveillance that determines effectiveness. As with all things, there is a limit to the number of cameras that can be effectively monitored. The key to achieving counterbalance amid staffing commitments and technological demands can often be found in addressing this issue while the project is still on the drafting table. This is the stage of the process normally set aside to thrash out various issues. By and large, it is the perfect time to seize the opportunity and make a pitch for additional resources for staffing and/or training needs. Likewise, it is also an ideal time to open the door to discussion and bring to focus the importance of setting aside appropriations to establish a fully detached monitoring function.

Operations center

Start by selecting a suitable location to house the operations function. Choose an area that is relatively noise free, temperature controlled and adequately lighted.

Note: Many computer driven/assisted systems require air conditioning.

Monitor size, staffing issues and supervision

- In general, a 9" inch monitor is considered the narrowest screen size that will allow the operator to recognize image characteristics.
- The maximum vertical angle between observer and monitor should not be greater than 30 degrees. A maximum horizontal viewing angle of 45 degrees in both directions is necessary to reduce distortion.
- Maximum and Minimum Viewing Distances

Tube Size (Inches)	Maximum Viewing Distance (Feet)	Minimum Viewing Distance (Feet)
9	7.0	3.0
12	10.0	3.25
14	12.0	3.6
17	14.0	3.75
19	17.0	3.85
21	19.0	4.85
23	19.5	5.0

Staffing considerations

Depending on the complexity of the assignment, it is a good rule of thumb to limit monitoring stints to two-hour frames. During the off-time, other related assignments can be performed. Observing a monitor can become quite a boring chore. It can also be quite a stressful and fatiguing assignment. As such, it is not advisable to have an officer sit and monitor these systems for extended periods of time.

Training considerations

The Greek Philosopher Aristotle has been quoted as saying "All men by nature desire knowledge." This desire as well as the need has not lessened in the more than 2,400 years since Aristotle made

158 ■ *Healthcare Security*

this statement. In fact, the need has become increasingly more important over the years because information and knowledge are now so vital in our modern, complex, technology-oriented society. From the technological perspective, I can't say enough about the importance of training, especially with regard to piloting security systems. Oftentimes, the simplest system is intimidating to the novice as well as the seasoned officer. Just imagine the level of intimidation one experiences when sitting in front of a seemingly awesome-looking security console. Like purchasing a computer these days, it is a good idea to see to it that a proviso is written into the scope, inviting the various bidders to furnish both basic and follow-up training. Beyond vendor training, it is important to supplement this instruction with informal on-the-job exercises as well as formal classroom education. To further strengthen this effort, it would be advantageous to use the talents of the crime prevention specialist (if available) to shepherd the training program.

As an aside, special training programs are also available through professional organizations, consultants, and at various universities that offer academic programs in security management.

Supervision

Good supervision is an important part of the security manager's protection blueprint. With relation to CCTV operations, supervisors should make sure that the control rooms and consoles are kept clean and free of impediments. The control room should be a place of business rather than a gathering place. Spot checks should be scheduled to monitor the efficiency levels of the operators, as well as to conduct practice runs to enhance their ability to recognize events, individuals, and other activity. Moreover, simulated practice drills such as planned intrusions and other activities to gauge response reaction time and competency levels could be instituted.

Conclusion

Wow! There is a person behind the security camera. His job is not an easy one, but it is an important one. He is responsible for keeping a watchful eye over the institutions he works in. Most employees, patients, and visitors may not see him, they may not know his name, but they rest easier because the "man behind the camera" is looking out for their safety and security.

Shell Hardening

Kevin A. Cassidy and Anthony Luizzo

The approach suggested here is to deepen and strengthen security around Acme's perimeter as well as in the interior of the facility. The system of controlling and monitoring doors and windows must interface with access control, fire suppression, and detection systems.

The electronic control and management systems needed will include intrusion detection, CCTV, access control, emergency and duress reporting, and sensor annunciation and monitoring. Specific areas to be alarmed and monitored include

- administrative offices,
- vertical and horizontal conduits (stairwells and elevators),
- shipping and receiving areas,
- archival storage areas, and
- computer rooms.

All technological systems should be tied to one command center and staffed 24 hours a day. All points of entry to the facility should be alarmed and monitored. An ID card key system should interface with the access control system. Doors to the previously listed areas should provide access only to selected egress and ingress portals.

All windows that are at least 18 feet above ground level should be protected with industrial-strength screening shields. Windows on the lower two stories of the building should be coated with a burglary-resistant glaze. On the first two floors and in offices with glass windows wire mesh safety glass should be used as well. All windows in the basement, on the first two floors, and on the eighth floor should also be alarmed.

All entries to and exits from specific areas should be recorded by computerized access control system. When access is denied to a specific location, the card key system will seize the card until security has investigated the incident.

Doors and windows, the first line of defense, should be made of industrial strength materials. Industrial-strength doors, windows, and locking devices should meet industrial standards.

Solid steel roll-down doors should be used in the shipping and receiving areas. When the departments are closed, the solid doors should remain closed. Due to Occupational Safety and Health Administration specifications regarding ventilation, a set of mesh curtains should be installed in the interior of the loading dock. These provide adequate ventilation as well as restrict access.

When the building is secured, these doors should be secured with padlocks. The shunting of the motorized switch that operates these doors should be controlled after hours by security personnel.

The doors to the front entrance should be made of glass. Two revolving doors should be situated on each side of the doors. All glass on the doors should be glazed and the locking mechanisms should tie into the card key system. This system should be shunted during busy hours and activated during off hours. All doors and windows should be acceptable according to the provision's set by the National Fire Protection Association.

From *Security Management Magazine*, – June 1991.

160 ■ *Healthcare Security*

Critical interior access portals requiring after-hour availability should be equipped with access control devices to allow monitored movement. Such systems may include standard access systems or biometric type accessing modes. Other critical doors throughout the facility should be on the monitoring system.

Building and fire codes specify that all exits should provide egress from all parts of the building. Also, locks or fastening devices should not prevent escape from the interior of the facility.

These codes make Acme extremely vulnerable; however, electromagnetic locks should incorporate a fail-safe locking system that ties into the fire safety and access control system.

All office doors in the interior of the building should be constructed of solid filler – hollow core doors should not be used. The doors will be equipped with double-cylinder dead bolt locks, which unlock from both the outside and inside with a key.

All executive offices, computer rooms, and archival storage areas should be incorporated into the card key system. The doors to these rooms should be constructed of industrial-strength material. These special areas should also be monitored by CCTV cameras. After hours, a video camera can record the events in these areas.

The archival storage area in the basement should have sprinklers along with CCTV camera and card access capability. Duplicate records should be maintained at a second storage area off-site in case the main area is destroyed.

All doors should be surveyed to ensure that door hinges are not exposed, and door frames are strong. Many times, hinges are installed on the wrong side of the door. This incorrect installation allowed the hinge pins to be accessible from the outside.

The two internal stairways in the building should not allow access to the computer room on the fourth floor and the executive offices on the eighth floor. Keypads should be installed on these doors in the stairwell, with a four-digit code to gain access. All access to these areas will be recorded by the computerized access control system.

Elevators should stop on the fourth and eight floors. On exiting the elevator locked glass doors with keypads should prevent individuals from proceeding unless they have the four-digit code. These systems will be tied into the fire system.

Doors to areas of lesser importance should be secured with mortise locks. Most mortise locks have both the convenient latching feature and the deadbolt security feature. If the knob of a door is vandalized, most likely the vandal will not gain entry since the knob is not part of the locking mechanism.

The one flaw of the mortise lock is the cylinder is held in place with a single-set screw. If this screw is removed by an intruder during the day, he or she can return remove the cylinder from the outside and operate the bolt and latch with his or her fingers. Acme should maintain optimum key control procedures and put putty and nail polish on these screws to make removal more difficult.

The security system and subsystem integration should be effective and operational. As a result, doors and windows will be adequately protected, alarmed, and monitored to prevent intrusion.

---

*Reprinted with permission: Security Management Magazine

Digital Security Technology Simplified

Bernard J. Scaglione

Digital security technology is making great strides in replacing analog and other traditional security systems including CCTV card access, personal identification, and alarm monitoring applications. Like any new technology, the author says, it is important to understand its benefits and limitations before purchasing and installing, to ensure its proper operation and effectiveness. This article is a primer for security directors on how digital technology works. It provides an understanding of the key components which make up the foundation for digital security systems, focusing on three key aspects of the digital security world: the security network, IP cameras and IP recorders. Physical security applications have resurrected. They are now a component of the digital universe. More and more security devices and systems are converting to IP or digital technology. Digital technology has some real advantages over conventional security systems, but to be effective end users need to understand how it works and its limitation if they want digital installations to work effectively.

Digital security technology has many distinct advantages over analog and traditional security systems. First, digital data can travel great distances without signal degradation and loss of video quality. During new construction, digital technology can be installed for a third of the cost of conventional security systems, digital data can be distributed and presented in a variety of different formats, digital data can be stored with a minimal of space and cost, and digital data can be retrieved quickly and efficiently.

In the security field, digital technology refers to CCTV, card access, personal identification, and alarm monitoring applications.

Once these applications are converted to a digital format, they can work together to provide a converged, single integrated application: hence the term convergence. The digital world allows all security devices to communicate collectively providing a truly integrated system. In addition to security devices, digital security applications can interface with digital mapping, GPS or WIR to collect; organize and distribute information. Digital security can interface with different data bases which can provide information like photos, street addresses, fingerprints, and any other information an end user may require. All this information can be integrated into one single distributed data base that can be presented on a single or multiple PCs. But before embarking into the digital universe it is important to understand key components which makeup the foundation for digital security systems. It is important to understand how digital technology works and what limitations it may have. Like any new technology it is important to understand its benefits and limitations before purchasing and installing, to ensure its proper operation and effectiveness. This article will discuss three key aspects of the digital security world: the security network, the IP camera, and the IP recorder, and provide basic information on their operation and performance.

Networks

Probably the most significant element of the digital world is the "Network." A security network carries digital signals between security devices utilized in physical security applications. A digital network or Ethernet is a series of computers or devices wired together to exchange information

From *Journal of Healthcare Protection Management*. (23):2, pp. 51–60. 2007.

162 ■ *Healthcare Security*

within the group of devices. Also refer to as a LAN or WAN. A LAN or "Local Area Network" is a network of several devices linked together in an immediate area: usually in the same building or on one floor of a building. A WAN or "Wide Area Network" is a network of computers or devices that cover a building or campus. It refers to a multi-building or multi-site configurations connected.

Network protocols

All networks are set up with a set of rules or a "Protocol" which provides standardized communication between computers. The "rules" are guidelines that regulate how data is transferred from one computer to another. Typically, networks utilize an IP/TCP configuration which stands for Internet Protocol/Transport Control Protocol. This type of configuration is the most utilized protocol and is a packet-switch network configuration. This means that data is transmitted in two packets of data. One packet is the information being sent. The second packet is the network protocol, it describes how the information is received and understood by the receiving computer.

Bandwidth

There are specific aspects of a network that are important to understand when deciding to use security systems in a network configuration. Bandwidth is probably the most important aspect to consider for security applications. Bandwidth refers to how much data can be sent through a transmission medium or wire. When you refer to bandwidth, or bit rate, you are referring to bits of data transmitted every second through a transmission medium. This is commonly referred to as bits per second or "bps." As an example, a full page of English text is about 16,000 bits of data, a fast modem can move data at about 57,000 bits per second, and full motion/full screen video requires a bandwidth of roughly 10,000,000 bits-per-second. Bandwidth or bit rate capacity depends on the size of the physical wire and the devices the wires are connected to. To understand the concept of bandwidth, think of a wastewater drain pipe system. The pipe diameter (bandwidth) can support only so many sinks, toilets, and other devices to effectively drain waste. In the design of the waste system, the drainpipe must be wide enough to allow drainage when all the devices are at full capacity and working simultaneously. If designed incorrectly the drain will backing up or stop draining. In the case of a digital network, overload can cause devices to slow down, shut off, or reduce their bandwidth causing signal degradation and/or data loss.

Switches

The wires that come out of the back of each computer or network device are connected to a Switch. Switches enable the communication between multiple computers, printers, and other devices within the network. A Switch organizes and distributes data packets from the networked devices and transmits them throughout the LAN or WAN. Switches vary in size, from 4 ports and up. Switches can also be connected to additional Switches to increase the capacity of the network.

Physical Security Applications ▪ 163

A Switch cannot access the Internet or other LANs, this requires a device called a Router. A Switch connects to a Router and a Router selectively transmits data according to an IP address to another computer, Switch, or other Router.

Cables

For data to be transferred from computer to computer and switch to switch there needs to be cable which will transfer the data packets from place to place. There are six categories of transmission medium which can be utilized in a network configuration. The six categories are: Coaxial Cable, Twisted Pair cable, Unshielded Twisted Pair, Shielded Twisted Pair, Category Program cable and Fiber Optic cable. The most frequently utilized wiring types are: Coaxial Cable, Twisted Pair cable, Unshielded Twisted-Pair or (UTP), Category Program cable or CAT cable and Fiber Optic cable.

Coaxial cable is a copper-based cable type which can support up to 100 Mbps of data. It is inexpensive, and cable can be run up to 500 meters before a signal boost is required.

Twisted-Pair is a pair of wires twisted together to form a circuit that transmits data. Twisted-Pair cabling is made from copper wires. There are two basic types: Shielded Twisted Pair and Unshielded Twisted-Pair.

Unshielded Twisted-Pair or UTP is the least expensive of all wire types. It is the fastest copper-based medium and requires signal boosts every 100 meters. UTP is used in most networking architectures. Today's UTP is referred to as Category Program cable or CAT for short. CAT cable usually has a numerical designation which refers to the transmission capacity or production generation. Currently CAT-6 cable is utilized in new construction and can carry a bandwidth of 1000-T Base or 1000 Mbps.

Fiber Optic cabling supports transmission speeds of more than 1 Gb/ps (a Gigabit per second) making it the fastest cabling choice. It can also be run for longer distances than UTP. It can transmit 40 miles with off-the-shelf equipment. UTP and coaxial cabling use copper wire, which is susceptible to electrical interference. Fiber Optic works differently by converting data (bits) into beams of light, which do not carry electrical impulses. The major downside of Fiber Optic is the cost; it is more expensive than any other type of network cabling available. Fiber Optic cabling is often and selectively, alongside a cheaper form of cabling to create a backbone of a network (drain-pipe). Fiber can be used for both analog and digital transmissions.

The best configuration for a security network is a fiber backbone with CAT 5 or 6 cables connecting each device. Fiber is used to connect all of the Switches and Routers together. CAT 5 or 6 cables is used to connect each device to the Switch. The fiber provides the largest diameter pipe or transmission capacity. CAT 5 or 6 is a smaller and cheaper pipe, just large enough to support the flow of data for any single device into the main drainpipe. If an existing network is going to be used for the security system, the transmission medium should be investigated.

Older networks may be running CAT 3 or 4 cable with little or no fiber. Remember the Program Category cable number defines the bandwidth and if it is an older installation, it may be too restrictive to work on newer security devices, or the security device may need to reduce the quality of the signal it transmits so that it can transmit on a smaller pipe. Too small a pipe may delay alarm signals or dramatically reduce the quality of video. Even CAT 5 or 6 cables utilized without a fiber backbone can restrict the bandwidth of some IP security devices.

New or existing network?

The first hurdle to overcome when committing to networked security systems is deciding between developing a new, separate network or to use the existing hospital network. The major stumbling block associated with a separate network configuration is the cost of the installation. The cost of running fiber is more expensive than installing coax cable. However, several strands of fiber are all that is necessary to transmit the signals from multiple cameras and alarm points. This cost may be necessary if the existing hospital network's bandwidth does not meet the requirements of the security devices. With the rapid changes occurring in IP CCTV, it is best to consider using a separate network to transmit the video signal. The newer cameras utilize a high rate of bandwidth and as IP cameras increase in resolution, i.e., high definition, their bandwidth may become greater. Large bandwidth is also necessary if analytics are going to be used. If your institution does not utilize a high volume of cameras than an existing network may work successfully.

To make the conversion to IP, it may be advantageous to make the transition slowly combining analog and networked cameras together and build the new network through renovations or during new construction. In between construction project a fiber backbone can be constructed slowly through new or upgraded security installations, strategically placing network switches throughout the facility to be utilized in the future.

Network redundancy and reliability

Before finalizing the decision to create a new or use an existing network, two other issues need to be considered: network redundancy and network reliability. If you are going to utilize a new network, then redundancies should be built in so that communication can continue if the network should fail. Redundancies include building a "Sonic Ring" network configuration with network servers attached remotely to local Switches. When utilizing an existing network research should be done on its down time history or reliability. If the existing network is not reliable and has large periods of down time, then the security system may be unreliable as well. Again, some of the downtime can be eliminated by installing network servers at the local Switch and ensuring that all Switches and servers are plugged into emergency power. In addition, some IP cameras have built-in memory which will store video when the network goes off-line and then transmit video when the network comes back online.

IP cameras

Besides providing a digital plat form, IP cameras offer some real advantages over analog cameras. IP cameras can be wireless, PTZ can be controlled over the network requiring less cabling. IP cameras can be powered over the network utilizing one cable for both power and video signal. IP camera systems are scalable, flexible and allow for open architecture. IP camera video is easily transferable to hard drives so searching and retrieving video is faster and easier. They have adjustable resolution, pixels, and bit rate to fit network demands. IP cameras can have built in memory or removable memory cards, key to reducing video loss from network downtime. IP cameras come with high definition or mega pixel capacity. Analytics can be programmed into cameras freeing up network bandwidth and improving storage and processing capacities. Some of the analytics currently available include setting up the cam era to operate upon motion or scheduled into a time zone. Camera can generate an alarm condition with a virtual trip wire or when someone loiters, or an object is left behind. Viewers can digitally move across the picture without the camera physically moving and portions of the digital picture can be physically blacked out.

IP recorders

When assessing a video recording system several features need to be reviewed before purchasing and utilizing a digital recorder. There are two types of digital recorders on the market today, Digital Video Recorders or DVRs and Network Video Recorder or NVRs. DVRs were developed to replace video tape recorder, and they convert analog video into digital video then compress the video for storage. When retrieved from storage the video is uncompressed and converted back to a n analog video signal. Current DVRs can record both analog and digital cameras. When converting analog video to digital and back again there will be loss of picture quality, that is why NVRs are the preferred recorder technology. However, to obtain the full benefits of NVRs it is best to be completely digital utilizing IP cameras connected to a network. Both units can be remotely located in the field and networked back to a command center or any PC for reviewing or recording.

DVRs generally are produced to input a specified number of cameras and record a specified or fixed number of frames per second. Generally, the more cameras used in each box, the less frames per second pcr camera are available for recording. For example, if a recording box can record a total of 200 frames a second and is equipped to handle 20 camera inputs, when 20 cameras are installed, each camera can only record up to 10 fps. If fewer cameras are used in each box, then the recording rate will increase. For example, if 10 cameras are plugged into the recording box then each camera can record up to a maximum of 20 fps.

Storage capacity is also a consideration when evaluating a DVR or NVR. Generally, a recording unit will contain a single, large volume hard drive to store video data. Some units come equipped with back up internal hard drives; others use a drive array as built-in redundancy in the event the main drive fails. Using a hot swappable RAID set-up provides several swappable hard drives setup in an array. The array records video one drive at a time. If a drive fails, the system will automatically transfer recording to the next drive in the array.

The bad drive can be quickly replaced so the system can continue to record at capacity. When selecting a recording system, make sure the hard drive is large enough to store all of the cameras for the time frame requested. Recording time is based upon the number of cameras, the camera pixels, movement in the field of view of each camera and the amount of pan, tilt and zoom used by the camera operator. The last item to consider is the systems networkability. Can recording boxes be combined so that they can be viewed together on one software program? To simultaneously view video images from different boxes, the video recording software should interconnect all the cameras and recording boxes so that they all can be seen and/or be retrieved from any location or PC.

Viewing software

Viewing software should also be evaluated when purchasing a recorder. Some systems need to connect directly to the recording box and can only be viewed with vendor specific software. Other systems are web based and only require a web browser to view and retrieve stored video from the recording system.

166 ■ *Healthcare Security*

Assessing Digital Video Components

When assessing the viability of an IP camera or video recorder, compression technology, image presentation technology and frame rate should be evaluated before purchasing. These three aspects of the digital products determine the bandwidth utilized and the quality of the image that is either recorded or presented on a monitor.

When deciding to use IP cameras, along with digital video recorders or network recorders, it is important to understand video compression. To send a video signal effectively across a network the video file size must be reduced, like the idea of "zipping" a file so that you can send it in an e-mail. Compressing streaming video data is necessary to ensure the network is not overwhelmed by large amounts of data being sent through the network at the same time. If the video is not compressed, a network could easily shut down or crash due to an over flow of digital traffic.

Video compression

Video compression is used to transmit streaming video from a camera to a monitor or recorder. Recorders compress video, as well, to increase video storage capacity. The higher the compression ratio the smaller the amount of bandwidth that is used, however, the higher the degradation of the image once uncompressed for viewing. Video can be transmitted or stored as either full frame or conditional storage.

Conditional storage is known as either Lossless or Lossy compression. Lossless compression means that the original data is reconstructed exactly as it was before it was compressed. Lossless compression means that certain data is lost during the conversion. The loss occurs mostly in the picture resolution. Compressing video can cause reduced color nuances, reduced color resolution, it can remove small, invisible parts of the picture and may not record parts of the picture that do not change as the picture sequences.

One of the most common forms of compression technology is called JPEG4 or M-JPEG which stands for Joint Photographic Experts Group or Motion - Joint Photographic Experts Group. JPEG compression technology records every video frame and compresses each frame by combining pixels into large blocks which are transported over the network and then reconstructed when the video is displayed. JPEG can reduce file size to about 5% of its normal size. Another aspect of compression technology is the picture presentation. When retrieving video from a recorder or directly from an IP cam era the size of the video picture that appears on the computer screen is called CIF or Common Intermediate Format. CIF appears in four formats or sizes, CIF through 4 CIF. CIF or 1 CIF presents a picture about the size of a post-It note, approximately 4 inches long by 3 inches high. 4 CIF, the largest format, is approximately the size of a full computer screen. The smaller the CIF the less disk space or bandwidth is utilized. The problem with 1, 2 or 3 CIF presentation is the picture becomes blurry and distorted when it is blown up to a 4 CIF size.

Frames per second

The next consideration in evaluating an IP camera or recorder is the frames per second or fps. This refers to how many video frames are sent per second from the camera or are recorded on the recorder's hard drive. In the video tape days, a typical security installation recorded 3 to 7.5 fps. To compare digital technologies, a TV picture transmits at 30 fps and the human eye perceives

Physical Security Applications ■ 167

full motion at 16 fps. Again, the lower the frame rate the less bandwidth and the less disk space is utilized.

When it comes to compression technology, frames per second and CIF presentation, the best way to assess what works for your needs is to see different application in an actual field setting. There are several different compression technologies on the market each compressing and uncompressing video differently. When accessing a system remember that a low compression rate in a 4 CIF format at 30 fps produces a very high-quality video image and it is going to require a high amount of bandwidth.

Some Things to Evaluate Before Installing Digital Devices

There are many aspects of digital security that should be evaluated before installing digital devices into your physical security systems. The key to a successful installation of a digital security system is the network. Ensure that the network has the bandwidth capacity necessary to operate the devices and products purchased for the security application. Also, ensure that the network has room to grow so future devices can be installed and work correctly within the guidelines of the network. Remember to question the specifications of the cameras and recorders being purchased to ensure they provide the picture quality you are looking for not only in the live picture but the recorded video as well. Make sure the camera and recorder video are viewed from an actual application not from a showroom set-up. Last of all, make sure video recorders are storing video for the time frame specified and redundancies are present so if the recorder fails, important video is not lost.

Determining and Implementing Successful Access Control Solutions

Bernard J. Scaglione

Today, the key phrase in security is convergence: the convergence of physical security systems, the convergence of logical and physical security and the convergence of corporate processes to ensure compliance. CSOs in every industry must protect massive amounts of electronic and paper information, secure virtual as well as physical infrastructures, and monitor the actions of employees, vendors, and visitors for regulatory compliance. The control of access and the authentication of identity play a key role in security convergence. However, all too often, the fundamental principles associated with access control and identification are overlooked.

These fundamental principles are not always emphasized in the design and implementation of security programs. I am reminded of this myself when I periodically guest lecture at a local college for introduction to security and security management classes. I enjoy not only the opportunity to stand up in front of a group and educate them on security practices, but teaching basic principles gives me the opportunity to reflect upon and review my own programs to ensure basic principles are adhered to.

Assess and Establish Access Control

All security practitioners should conduct a survey to determine if basic access control principles are present within their security program. These principles are important to consider because they establish a strong foundation for all other programs incorporated into the access control process. Establishing programs with a weak foundation can only lead to weak systems, which can become overly complicated and ineffective – something to strongly consider in this current economy of shrinking budgets and increasing crime. The access control process can be broken down into four basic components: people, policy, procedure, and physical security systems. Each component is important to consider in the creation of a comprehensive access control program. So, whether protecting digital information on a network or identifying visitors as they enter a facility, the management of these four elements helps to establish a solid foundation for the access control process. They will facilitate the restriction and monitoring of access, the detection of unauthorized users and the proper channeling of authenticated personnel into authorized areas.

The single most prominent principle to consider when designing or evaluating access control is the notion of "Concentric Circles," security systems constructed in layers. Layers can be physical barriers like fences, doors, windows, walls, or door locks. They can be electronic systems like card readers, intercoms, or security video.

Layers can be security officers posted at an entrance, a receptionist behind information desk or armed personnel patrolling the grounds with an attack dog. They can also be the creation of a policy statement and the implementation of a procedure. What is important to remember is no one single component can effectively control access; it is the coordination of several systems or components working together that create a controlled security infrastructure.

From *Security E Newsletter*, Posted January 1, 2009.

Development and Implementation

When developing and implementing physical access control layers, the principle of "Crime Prevention through Environmental Design" or CPTED should be utilized. CPTED looks to change the physical environment to stop or channel people to monitor, restrict or control their access. Utilized correctly, CPTED controls the physical environment to create barriers that can be difficult to breach. The advantage to using CPTED is that environmental manipulation provides consistent control within the parameters of the physical elements being utilized to control access.

Layered security also means policy and procedure. As part of any solid access control program, a strong policy statement along with a tested procedure adds value to the security strategy. Policies should be written to make a statement about the security philosophy and the process being instituted. A procedure should be outlined within the policy statement that details the elements of the process being implemented. The process should be designed to coordinate and support the physical design elements being utilized through CPTED. It is important to have alignment among process and physical security.

The most important element in the implementation of basic access control is compliance. Are the layered systems put into place working as designed? Compliance is the confirmation of processes, the verification that policy and physical security work to provide the designed access control consistently and effectively. Compliance practices should be instituted that continuously monitor access control systems to ensure they are working as specified. Ensure that your security staff consistently screens visitors as outlined within the policy, and make sure the procedure is written within the policy correctly, stating the process being carried out by the security staff.

Finally, the installation of layered security should be done with one philosophy in mind - Keep It Simple. The proliferation of layers can create a complicated and ineffective system in which end-users look to bypass security features so they can function effectively within the corporate environment. Security systems should not conflict with the corporate culture. The installed processes must provide security without supporting a prison like environment.

Chapter 8

Customer Service Initiatives

The Patient Wish List: Getting Customer Service Right

Bernard J. Scaglione

In October 2015, US News and World Report published an article entitled, "The Patient Wish List: Let me sleep, keep my room clean, Listen to me. Sound familiar?" In this publication author Peter Pronovost reviews a panel discussion conducted by John Hopkins Hospital related to patient satisfaction. This article examined the ten things that patients would like hospitals to provide for high quality clinical care and safety.

The ten things include:

1. Let me sleep
2. Keep the noise levels down at the nurse's station
3. Do not lose my personal belongings
4. Knock on the door before entering
5. Please keep the white board current and up to date
6. Update me and my family if you notice changes in my condition
7. Keep my room clean
8. Listen to me and engage me in my care
9. Please orient me to my room and the hospital
10. Please maintain professionalism

What was amazing to see is number three, *"Don't lose my personal belongings"* Of all the things that could presumably go wrong during a hospital stay, the issue of valuables being part of a top ten list is remarkable. Remarkable because many times patient valuables take a back seat to other more pertinent clinical objectives. The fact that patient belongings made the list of patient satisfaction, signifies the importance of collecting, safeguarding, and returning patient belongings. Because of its importance to patient satisfaction, re-evaluation of the patient belongings program should be conducted, ensuring that belongings are properly collected, stored, and returned. Even within the Emergency Department where emergency medical care is the highest priority, patient belongings

---

From *LinkedIn* Blog, Posted: July 23, 2018.

DOI: 10.4324/9781003215851-8

171

should be properly inventoried, stored, and returned to patients or patient family members. Often this responsibility falls upon the security director with extraordinarily little support from the clinical and administrative staff. Of note, are some of the other performance drivers included in the top ten list, like knocking on the door before entering and the general noise level at the nurse's station. Many times, security officers interact with clinical staff at the nurse's station and should be mindful of the noise level when doing so, no matter what time of day, but especially at night. Additionally, security officers should make sure that they knock before entering a patient room whether to collect valuables or take an incident report. Let me sleep is another driver that should be considered by Security and clinical administrators. Hospitals today provide 24-hour visitation. Many times, visitation is necessary because of a family member's work and life schedule, or the patient's medical condition.

However, Security and clinical staff need to be mindful that patients require sleep to help them recover and feel better. Off hour visitation should not be restricted but visitors should be screened to those persons that require late night visitation.

Visitors who are loud or not considerate of other patients at night should be asked to quiet down or leave. Lastly, being professional in all areas of the hospital. How patients perceive Security is often how they perceive the hospital and the care being administered. It is important to remember that in most cases Security is the first, or close to the first person, that a patient or visitor encounters when entering the hospital. So, whether on break, entering or leaving the hospital. Security staff reflect the hospital and the perception of the care given to patients.

Attention to these five satisfiers can make an average hospital stay a great one and provide a high level of patient satisfaction for the patients and visitors housed within the hospital. Adjusting security protocol to address these five satisfiers can not only bring up the satisfaction level of the Security Department but the hospital. In addressing these satisfiers, security departments should consider the use of a third-party expert to help determine needs and develop best practices. An objective third party can provide a clearer perspective and armed with years of experience in security customer service and healthcare consultative expertise, they can help to establish best practice in the service of patient care and security procedure.

Creating a Customer Service Program for Healthcare Security

Bernard J. Scaglione

With the new focus on customer service, it's more important than ever that the Security Department – often the first department with which hospital patients and visitors engage – present a strong first impression.

In October 2012 healthcare patient satisfaction scores were tied to Medicare reimbursement, as measured through the Hospital Consumer Assessment of Healthcare Providers and Systems (HCAHPS) survey. HCAHPS scores reflect patients' perspectives on several key aspects of care including their overall satisfaction of hospital services. While the Security Department is not directly involved in the HCAHPS process, the overall satisfaction of the hospital experience is considered a summary of the entire visit for each patient or visitor no matter who the patient or visitor meets during their hospital stay. Many hospitals rely on their Security Department to provide customer service since they are usually the first person a patient or visitor interacts with when they enter the hospital. It may be the officer posted at the main entrance or in the Emergency Department. It may be the officer on patrol, the officer that responds to take a report for missing property or another event, or the officer who approaches a patient or visitor who seems lost. A strong customer service program for security may be the difference between a high or low patient satisfaction score, ultimately determining a hospital's reimbursement.

A Model to Follow

A solid customer service program goes a long way in providing quality security services and customer satisfaction scores. Although most literature on the topic of healthcare customer satisfaction revolves around clinical staff and clinical outcomes, lessons learned through clinical studies do present a viable model for security services. This model promotes patient satisfaction through a caring and concerning environment. This care and concern for patients is exemplified by staff attentiveness, dignity, respect, effective communication, and shared decision-making. The characteristics of the care and concern begin with attentiveness. The demonstration of dignity and respect results in a patient feeling understood and accepted as a person.

Customer service programming requires looking through the customer's eyes. It is important for security staff to understand that the only time patients are happy within the healthcare setting is when a baby is born. Otherwise, their minds are preoccupied with the status of their own health or the health of a loved one.

An Attitude to Present

As a department, Security should anticipate patient and visitor's needs, acknowledge, and apologized for mistakes made by themselves and others, respect an individual's confidentiality and privacy, and represent the hospital in a positive light by acting in a professional manner. Security

---

From *Facility Care: Serious Solutions for Healthcare Facility Managers*. September 2013.

174 ■ *Healthcare Security*

staff needs to understand differences in the cultures of the population they service to relate to different cultures, especially when dealing with a potential volatile situation. Security staff needs to create a positive first impression by smiling and making eye contact.

In addition, staff needs to make sure they maintain proper hygiene, have a happy upbeat attitude and that their surrounding environment is clean and presentable. Security officers need to work together within their department and with other departments to quickly resolve patient issues. They need to be able to give correct directions the same way every time, know operating hours for all clinics, doctor's offices, knowing the visitation policy. Officers need to dress appropriately and maintain a consistent look. They need to make sure their ID is in plain view. Do not underestimate the importance of officer appearance. It shows respect and engagement. Security officers should stand during high volume times, as it demonstrates engagement as well as a friendly, inviting presentation. They need to pay attention to persons as they enter the hospital and to persons that approach them with a question or concern. Security officers should have defined scripts with which to work. They need to know what to say when they greet patients and visitors, and that message should be consistent between shifts.

Putting all these aspects of customer service together will provide a positive environment for all patients and visitors that enter and reside within the healthcare environment. Customer service training and the promotion of a customer service culture should be standard operating procedure for all healthcare security departments.

Chapter 9

Auditing and Forensics

Auditing Proactive Security Programs

Anthony Luizzo

In today's atmosphere of shrinking security dollars, corporate downsizing effects all departments, including security. In this decade of fiscal awareness, how does a security executive continue to provide effective protection with fewer eyes and ears to watch over its company assets? Stretching the security dollar is an art and a science. Internal auditors should be familiar with both. The art lies in the security executive's ability to solve protection problems utilizing existing resources. And the science lies in the executive's ability to design a protection strategy that meets corporate requisites and industry benchmarks. Many security executives tackle this problem by instituting in-house crime prevention programs to champion proactive security approaches. Proactive security approaches deal with addressing security and safety risks – and preventing crimes from occurring.

Managing the Initiative

The security representative assigned to manage this initiative is tasked with keeping employees aware of crime risks, diagnosing facility security needs, writing security surveys, and maintaining a liaison with local law enforcement. The tenet of this program is to champion the philosophy that company security is everyone's job. In essence, company employees are taught the ABCs of crime prevention and are asked to work shoulder-to-shoulder with the security department in keeping a watchful eye over global security. When auding crime prevention programs, it is important that the internal auditor be familiar with the qualifications of management personnel and how crime prevention programs are structured. Most security departments assign a trained crime prevention specialist to manage the overall program. Ideal candidates for this job should possess above average writing and oral skills, as well as the ability to communicate to both individuals and large groups. He or she should be a career minded employee who is interested in the techniques and technologies exercised in the crime prevention discipline. Moreover, he / she should be able to adjust mindsets

---

From *Internal Auditing Alert* Warren, Gorham & Lamont / RIA Group (Reuters) Thomson Publications. (18):8, September 1998 – openlibrary@archive.com.

DOI: 10.4324/9781003215851-9

176 ■ *Healthcare Security*

from the traditional enforcement security model to a proactive posture which is strongly associated with the proactive security model.

Training

With respect to crime prevention training, most local police departments offer free training programs for area companies and agencies. The training often includes from 40 to 80 hours of instruction, and a certificate of completion is issued to successful graduates. In addition, external consulting firms also offer training programs for industrial, commercial, and institutional entities.

Students attending crime prevention programs are taught:

- The principles of crime and loss prevention management
- To master the basics of crime analysis
- To write security surveys
- To evaluate and recommend security technologies (locks, closed circuit television, and card access, alarm, fire systems)
- To become familiar with municipal and regulatory agency requirements (building, fire, etc.)
- To formulate and present security awareness programs
- The basics of applying asset protection strategies to thwart property and inventory loss

Consultants

If the security department does *not* have an in-house crime prevention program, are external consultants being utilized? As with other industry specialties, selecting qualified experts is not hard. Consultants should furnish evidence that they have completed crime prevention courses and that they possess industry credentialing such as appropriate licensing (locksmith, alarm installer, etc.), and hold professional certifications including, Certified Protection Professional (CPP), Certified Fraud Examiner (CFE), Certified Security Trainer (CST), In addition, the consulting firm should be asked to furnish references and a client listing.

The Night Has a Thousand Eyes

Proactive security programs help to deepen and strengthen security by fostering the philosophy that company security is every employee's responsibility. Moreover, in today's fiscally lean times, enlisting additional eye and ears to the company's protection team helps to stretch the shrinking security dollar even further.

Interrogation 101

Seven questions an auditor should ask when auditing crime prevention programs:

1. Does the security department have a crime prevention program?
2. Is the administrator of the program qualified?

Auditing and Forensics ■ 177

3. Are external consultants being utilized?
4. Are external consultants qualified?
5. Are security awareness programs offered?
6. Are security surveys being completed?
7. Are adequate internal controls maintained to evaluate the effectiveness of the program?

Auditing Investigative Techniques

Anthony Luizzo

Interviews or interrogations: The debate between internal auditors continues.

When *auditing* security department operations, *internal* auditors should be familiar with all aspects of the investigative process including how interviews and interrogations are conducted. The interview is often called the cornerstone of the security management process. A well-structured interview helps to paint a picture of what occurred and who was involved.

Interview vs. Interrogation

An interview is a structured question and answer session designed to elicit specific information from the interviewee. Most often, the interviewee is ready and willing to tell what he or she knows. The interview helps the interviewer gather facts about what happened and who might have committed the infraction. In competent hands, the information extrapolated from the interview helps the interviewer zero in on who should be interrogated.

The objectives of an interview include:

- Gathering facts about when, where, how, and why the incident occurred
- Gathering facts about who might have been involved

The interrogation is a structured question and answer session designed to test the validity of the information gleaned from interviews previously conducted. Oftentimes, the interviewer must probe and draw out information by asking precise, trenchant questions.

The objectives of the interrogation include, but are not limited to:

- Learning additional facts about the incident
- Developing details about the interviewee's involvement
- Extracting truthful information from reluctant, evasive, or hostile interviewees
- Locating physical evidence

From *Internal Auding Report* Warren, Gorham & Lamont/RIA/Group (Reuters) Thomson Publications. (18):10, November 1998 – openlibrary@archive.com.

Auditing and Forensics ■ 179

- Developing new leads
- Obtaining corroborating testimony
- Recovering purloined property or other fruits of the crime
- Ascertaining specific information relative to hideouts, weapons, etc.
- Establishing guilt or innocence

Qualifications of Interviewers

Investigative interviewers often have prior investigative training in the ABC's of conducting interviews and interrogations. Local police departments often offer specialized courses in the art and science of conducting interviews and interrogations. Security consulting firms also offer specialized courses on conducting interviews and interrogations. Most courses of study are 40-to-80-hour programs and certificates of completion are often given to graduates.

Types of Interviews

- **Spontaneous field interviews**—this type of interview is often conducted early in the investigative process with persons somehow associated with the crime scene or related in some way to the incident at hand.
- **Planned interviews**—this type of interview is often with persons who have direct involvement with the issue at hand. As an example, if a theft was reported from the purchasing department, interviewees might include departmental heads, employees or other persons who are affiliated with the purchasing operation.

Interview Locations

Interviews can be conducted in a variety of locations including interview rooms, the interviewee's office, restaurants, automobiles, in the field, and at the scene of the incident.

Tips for Successful Interviewing

1. Appropriate interview locations should be selected
2. Sufficient time should be allocated for the interview—20 minutes to 45 minutes
3. Interview notes should be safeguarded
4. A complete record of evidential facts and data should be maintained

The Pre-Interview Checklist

Most security departments maintain a pre-interview checklist for their investigative personnel. The checklist helps ensure that the interviewer is ready to conduct an effective interview.

180 ■ *Healthcare Security*

A sample checklist might contain the following:

1. Does the interviewer know what information must be learned?
2. Has the interviewer framed appropriate questions for the interview?
3. Has the interviewer selected an appropriate interview location?
4. Has the interviewer researched information about the target of the interview?
5. Has the interviewer ascertained which investigative technologies will be used to capture information? Technologies might include tape recorder, hidden camera, etc.

Utilizing Interpreters

If an interpreter is required it is important to remember that all communication should take place between the interviewer and the interpreter, not between the interpreter and interviewee.

Utilizing Investigative Statements

Maintaining written and/or oral statements are extremely important when conducting interviews and interrogations.

Written statements often help to:

1. Support documentary evidence that oral disclosures were made
2. Preserve the oral testimony in permanent written form
3. Provide a verbatim written record for legal proceedings
4. Protect the information from loss or recall problems
5. Solidify the interviewee's story
6. Provide a summarized verification of the facts

Helpful Investigative Tips

Many investigators like to conduct interviews in the interviewee's office environment, since it gives the seasoned investigator hidden insight about the interviewee. Many successful investigators feel that valuable clues can be found in the decor of a person's office and the person's mode of corporate dress.

As an example, if the interviewee's office is posh, and replete with a top ten view of the city, he or she is most likely entrusted with much corporate power and/or decision-making responsibility. Likewise, it is often said that a neat desk is indicative of an organized person. Moreover, some investigators feel that the way a person dresses is somewhat indicative of their philosophical viewpoint. A tweed sport jacket with elbow patches, a buttoned-down collared shirt and leather oxfords may suggest that the person is an academician, and/or possibly of the conservative philosophy. Suspenders may be indicative of a staunch established professional and a bow tie may be characteristic of a non-conformist or liberal philosophical nature. These and other clues in expert hands help to shape an investigators "gut" feeling about possible involvement or non-involvement in the incident at hand.

Questions an Auditor Might Ask When Performing an Audit of the Interview Process

1. Does the security department have a written policy regarding performing interviews and interrogations?
2. Are written statements used to support interview information?
3. Are interviewers adequately trained?
4. Are interview records maintained?
5. Are interview rooms available?
6. Are pre-interview checklists available?

182 ■ *Healthcare Security*

Auditing Hospital Security

Anthony Luizzo

How does a security executive piece together a security program for a facility that is open to the public 24 hours a day, seven days a week!

With cars and people moving about all the time, conventional security technology such as motion detectors and alarm systems are of little value in monitoring general site conditions. When auditing hospital security operations, internal auditors should begin by asking to view the institution's "Security Operation's Manual." Perusal of the manual often termed the "bible," can help the auditor to better understanding how the security program is structured. Moreover, the manual will help the auditor evaluate how the program is managed and whether internal control strategies are being followed.

A comprehensive manual often includes:

- mission statement
- table of organization
- institution demographics.
- emergency procedures
- specialized security policies and procedures
- general security policies and procedures
- theft prevention initiatives
- employee safety awareness initiatives
- legal requirements
- risk management (insurance) requirements; and Security survey reports

Upon auditing the above, the auditor might also wish to review the following functions for compliance:

- Access control security. Does the hospital have an access control policy? Many hospitals monitor and control access by issuing ID badges to incoming and outgoing personnel — employees, visitors, vendors, other legitimate invitees. As an example, ID badges are issued to employees and visitor passes are issued to visitors and vendors. Beyond badges and passes, auditors should be aware that separating the entrances for administration, medical personnel and visitors/patients is an approach often championed by seasoned security executives.
- Patient security. Are patient areas protected by either security patrols and/or security-related technology including but not limited to closed circuit television systems, panic alarms at nursing stations and emergency telephone communication's systems?
- Employee Security. Are employee lounges and "on-call" rooms (rooms used by medical staff awaiting call) adequately patrolled?

From *Internal Auditing Report* Warren, Gorham & Lamont / RIA Group (Reuters) Thomson Publications. December 1998 – openlibrary@archive.com

Auditing and Forensics ■ 183

- Medical Supply Security. Are inventory storage rooms alarmed and are inventory controls such as "control logs" used to monitor the removal of items such as medications, gauze pads, medical gowns, bandages, etc.?
- Property Security. Are machines, computers, desks, etc., adequately protected? An excellent method of securing machinery such as computers, adding machines, calculators, telephones, etc. is to affix a locking device to prohibit easy removal. In addition, etching the hospital's ID number onto the item is an excellent theft prevention strategy.
- Pediatric Security. Does the hospital have an infant abduction policy? Infant abductions in hospitals continue to be a major security concern for healthcare administrators. In recent years, many institutions have begun to use electronic monitoring devices to track infant whereabouts. Like electronic devices used in retail stores to track shoplifting —electronic tags are affixed to an infant 's clothing and/or to an infant's nametag which annunciates when the infant leaves the confines of the pediatric department. In addition, closed circuit television systems and stationary security guards are also used to augment global security.
- Construction/Modernization Security. Does the security department have input into the construction process? From a security management perspective, designing security safeguards into a project prior to its completion —helps to ensure that overall security issues are adequately, and cost effectively addressed. Retrofitting security after a project is constructed is often quite expensive (e.g., walls may have to be opened to run wiring, etc.), while also causing extensive delays in inaugurating coverage upon opening the building for services.
- Employee Awareness Security. Does the security department offer periodical security awareness programs to staff? The auditor should ascertain whether on-going security awareness seminars, meetings, briefings, etc. are offered to hospital staff on a regularly scheduled base. The tenet of such a program is to ensure that important safety and security information is periodically disseminated to all employees.
- Database Security. Does the hospital have an effective computer security program? The safety and protection of a medical center's database in the event of catastrophe or intrusion is important. Vital information such as research, patient records, financial data, etc., must be kept secure. The auditor should ascertain whether protection safeguards are in-place and if computer terminals are physically safeguarded. Physical safeguards might include issuing user codes and PIN numbers, encrypting sensitive data, and restricting access into sensitive terminal areas. In addition, the auditor might also inquire whether copies of files are maintained in off-site storage areas.
- Periodical Security Assessments. It is said that an "ounce of prevention is worth a pound of cure" Auditors would be wise to inquire if annual security surveys are completed. A security survey is an on-site evaluation of the institution's overall security posture. A survey helps the security administrator to keep a watchful eye over the safety and security of everyone that works or visits the facility.

Questions an auditor might ask when auditing hospital security

- Does the security department have an official security operation manual?
- Does the manual contain all security-related initiatives and programs?
- Is the manual authorized and signed by a senior hospital administrator?
- Is the manual current?

184 ■ *Healthcare Security*

- Does the manual reflect with some degree of accuracy the state of security for the institution as a whole?
- Is employee ID badges and visitor passes used?
- Are patient areas patrolled?
- Are employee lounges and on-call rooms patrolled?
- Are medical supply storage areas protected?
- Is hospital property kept secured and properly marked for identification?
- Are pediatric areas properly protected?
- Does the security department have a role in the design and construction process?
- Are security awareness programs offered on a periodical basis?
- Is database information properly protected?
- Are periodical security surveys completed?

Getting the Best Results

Internal auditors should understand that no method of protection is perfect, and no security plan can be 100 percent effective. However, auditors do know that one of the best methods of improving program performance is to perform compliance audits on a periodical basis. Results of the audit can help security administrators to better measure the effectiveness of in-place security initiatives while also offering guidance re improvements.

Auditing Crime Analysis Programs

Anthony Luizzo

Most security departments maintain a crime analysis function to define and measure the recurrence rate of crime. Tracking the time and location of crimes committed against a company offers security management personnel a detailed snapshot of weak areas in a company's protective shield. In many companies, crime analysis gathering is coupled with a routing plan to distribute distilled information to various departmental groups to mend security inequities. Most crime analysis data is collected from crime-related incident reports prepared by field security operatives (guards and investigators) during their daily patrols and inspections of the protected property. Crime analysis data is also collected from complaints from employees and visitors who have been victims of crime while on the company's property. In addition, crime analysis data is collected from internal security surveys prepared by in-house crime prevention specialists or by security surveys prepared by external consultants.

Analysis Targeting

Upon receiving an incident report, the security department issues a control number (incident report number). The incident information is reviewed and either forwarded to a specialized investigative unit for follow-up or logged in the department's incident file. Beyond simply logging and routing the incident report through channels, forward thinking security executives have opted to institute a Crime Analysis Program, which includes maintaining a detailed flow chart of major crime. Major crime types include burglary, robbery, auto theft, theft of employee property, and theft of company property. In practice, a pin map or computer program is often used to highlight the type of incident, the time of the incident and the day the incident occurred. Maintaining this type of visual chart helps the security administrator to immediately identify crime trends and potential crime target locations.

Analytical Factors

There are several factors that may be central to a particular crime type. The specific crime factors represent the information that the analyst uses to connect the crime to unique characteristics and to offender patterns. Various factors in the analytical process include crime type, geographic factors, chronological factors, victim, suspect, and vehicle or property loss descriptions.

Geographical analysis is the examination of crime type and location data via using maps, charts or other manual-visual techniques or computer mapping programs (crime scene chronologies). It is through these analytical methods that the experienced crime analyst identifies crime trends and possible locations of future criminal activity.

From *Internal Auditing Report* Warren, Gorham & Lamont/RIA/Group (Reuters) Thomson Publications. July 2000 – openlibrary@archive.com.

186 ■ *Healthcare Security*

Communication of Information

Crime pattern information and investigative lead reports form the fulcrum upon which an effective crime prevention effort is erected. Since crime prevention is the responsibility of every employee, it is important that crime prevention information extrapolated from crime analysis data is quickly disseminated to operational user groups. Many security departments disseminate this vital information via formal reports, crime alert bulletins and one-on-one meetings with departmental employees. In some instances, security departments sponsor periodical crime prevention workshops and training programs for company employees.

Framing the Crime Analysis Program

Selecting the right person to administer a crime analysis effort is not difficult. The selected person should have successfully completed a 40-hour basic course on the methods of crime prevention and have a proactive, rather then reactive, crime control philosophy. Many local police agencies nationwide, including the New York City Police Department, offer crime prevention training programs. In many areas, local police departments will assist private companies to formulate effective crime analysis programs free of charge. For further information on crime prevention training programs or to obtain information on formulating a crime analysis program contact the New York City Police Department's Crime Prevention Division at 212 646-5000.

Eight Questions an Auditor Might ask when auditing a company's crime analysis program

1. Does the security department have a crime analysis function?
2. Is the crime analysis staff adequately trained?
3. Is crime analysis data of major crime maintained?
4. Are pin maps or computer programs used to track major crime incidents?
5. Is information extrapolated from crime analysis data disseminated to departmental units on a regular basis?
6. Does the security department adjust its security-staffing grid to address crime pattern information?
7. Is the security department aware that local law enforcement agencies offer crime prevention training programs and assistance in formulating crime analysis programs?
8. Does the security department sponsor periodical crime prevention workshops and seminars for company employees?

Auditing Warehouse and Loading Dock Security

Anthony J. Luizzo

How to ensure against cargo crime

Ask business owners whether they have ever suffered warehouse or loading dock theft, and most will respond "yes." Whether the products are computers, salami, clothing, or stereos, finding a consumer to buy hot merchandise is not difficult. Experienced security managers know that theft usually occurs where the goods are received, stored, or shipped.

The Magnitude of Cargo Theft

Law enforcement officials estimate that $12 million worth of goods are stolen from factory floors, warehouse shelves, or in transit in the United States each year.[1] However, cargo theft often goes unreported because companies do not want their insurance company notified. Hot items on the thieves' hit list include sports and designer apparel, liquor, perfume, currency, gold bullion, and jewelry and gemstones. More than half of all cargo crimes are inside jobs. Theft rings gather reconnaissance while working as temporary employees at warehouses. Warehouse and loading dock criminals prefer truck theft, and according to FBI data, the ports most affected are in New York, New Jersey, Miami, Long Beach, and Los Angeles. San Francisco, San Jose, Memphis, and Chicago have also noted an increase in cargo crimes.

Cargo theft could exceed more than 100 billion worldwide. Theft of cargo has become so widespread that it constitutes a serious threat to the flow of commerce in the United States.[2] Organized crime is an area where they can carry out profitable illegal activities with a low chance of apprehension and prosecution.[3] The average loss experienced by a high-tech company from theft of any kind surpasses $750,000, up from only $5,000 in 1991.[4]

Internal auditors performing audits of warehousing security operations should be aware of the terminology, procedures, and technologies commonly employed in warehousing and loading dock operations.

Warehouse and Loading Dock Terminology

The following is warehouse and loading dock jargon:

- **Aggregated shipments.** Several shipments from different shippers to one consignee, which are consolidated and treated as one consignment.
- **Bill of lading**. A written transportation contract between shipper and carrier or agent.
- **Blocking chocks**. Supports used to prevent cargo from shifting during transport.
- **Bulk freight**. Freight not stored in packages or containers.
- **Cargo**. Freight carried by a vehicle.

From *Internal Auditing* Warren, Gorham & Lamont/RIA/Group (Reuters) Thomson Publications. March/April 2001 – openlibrary@archive.com

188 ■ *Healthcare Security*

- **Claimant**. A person or company filing a claim.
- **Clearing house**. An organization that processes and collects bills for participating freight hauling firms.
- **Concealed loss**. Loss or damage that cannot be determined until the package is opened.
- **Consignee**. The cargo recipient.
- **Consignor**. The cargo shipper.
- **Dock**. A platform where trucks are loaded and unloaded.
- **Dock pass**. A numbered pass issued to identify freight carriers.
- **Dispatcher**. An employee who dispatches trucks from a terminal to pick up cargo.
- **F.O.B.** Free on board.
- **Forklift**. Also known as a hi-low, it is a vehicle with two large metal blades used to move goods on pallets or skids.
- **Freight seal**. A numbered metal or plastic device attacked at time of loading or when freight is checked in transit.
- **Line driver**. A driver qualified to operate large rigs on long hauls as opposed to a local delivery driver.
- **Packing list**. A detailed listing of packed goods.
- **Pallet**. A wooden platform upon which cargo is carried, stacked, moved from location to location by forklift. Depending on the type and weight of freight, pallets can be single, double, or triple stacked (also known as palletizing).
- **Rig.** Truck, tractor, semi-trailer and full trailer, or other combination.
- **Shrink wrap**. A thin clear plastic wrapping paper used to wrap freight.
- **Sleeper**. Truck with sleeping quarters in its cab.
- **Tare weight**. The weight of the vehicle without freight.
- **Trailer**. Also known as a box, it is the portion of the vehicle used to store freight during transport.
- **Waybill**. Description of goods sent with a common carrier freight shipment.
- **Yard jockey**. A person who operates a yard tractor or mule.
- **Yard mule**. Small tractor used to move trailers around the terminal yard.

Twenty Auditing Warehouse and Loading Dock Security Questions

1. Is the warehouse alarmed for security?
2. Are security cameras installed?
3. Are physical security devices (e.g., locks, lights, and fencing) adequate?
4. Do security guards regularly patrol the warehouse during all shifts?
5. Is employee parking prohibited near loading platforms?
6. Are trash control initiatives employed to discourage theft?
7. Are security advocates assigned to loading dock security duties?
8. Are loading dock security logs maintained?
9. Are loading dock security logs adequate?
10. Are truckers escorted to and from dispatching facilities?
11. Are cargo seals used?
12. Are lavatory and rest areas available outside of storage environs for incoming truckers?
13. Are truckers restricted from freely roaming distribution areas?

14. Are background checks of warehouse and loading dock personnel completed?
15. Is nondescript cargo packaging being used to thwart theft?
16. Are cargo crimes being reported?
17. Does the company maintain a liaison with local and federal law enforcement agencies?
18. Do appropriate prosecutorial agencies investigate cargo theft?
19. Does the company know which ports-of-call are considered high theft terminals?
20. Does the company enhance security when shipping cargo to these high theft ports?

Auditing Warehouse Security

When auditing a warehouse, check to see whether the facility is protected with alarm and surveillance technologies or has security guard personnel assigned. It is important to note that intrusion detection devices (e.g., alarms and cameras) are often used as a supplement to, but not a substitute for, the facility security force. These technologies are intended to alert security personnel to an intrusion or attempted intrusion into the facility. The effectiveness of intrusion technology depends on the reaction time of the guard force once an alarm is transmitted.

Only items that cannot be easily physically moved should stored near exits. Employee entrances and exits should always be segregated from areas where inventories are stored. Other security areas an auditor should consider include:

- Whether security guards regularly patrol the facility?
- Whether undercover security operatives are used to investigate thefts?
- Whether security logs are maintained?
- Whether locking systems are manufactured of industrial strength materials?
- Whether a key control system is in place?
- Whether facility lighting is adequate?
- Whether a package inspection policy has been promulgated?
- Whether a search and seizure agreement with respect to checking employee lunch pails, locker and automobiles has been promulgated? It is important that legal counsel be contacted for assistance in drafting guidelines that meet legal and regulatory requirements.
- Whether a fire safety procedure is in place?
- Whether a trash control policy is in place, which allows for inspection of trash dumpsters on a regular basis. Some companies use clear plastic refuse bags to curtail thievery; others install compactors to crush trash.

Auditing Shipping or Receiving Operations

The shipping and receiving functions at a warehouse or terminal are particularly vulnerable to theft and pilferage. Companies should have the following prevention initiatives in place to thwart internal thievery at loading platforms:

190 ■ *Healthcare Security*

- Background checks should be completed for all employees working in sensitive positions including dispatchers, shipping, and receiving clerks, and inhouse truck drivers.
- Distribution areas and platforms should have functional electronic surveillance systems in place.
- Vehicle parking should be prohibited near shipping and receiving platforms.
- Incoming and outgoing freight should always be inspected and counted.
- Truckers should never be allowed to freely roam the platform environments without a security escort. Many companies erect restrooms and waiting room faculties for truckers outside of the company environments. To offset the cost of erecting such facilities, many companies make vending machines available to waiting truckers.
- Security guard personnel should regularly monitor and control access into and out of loading areas. Personnel should also perform the following tasks:
  - O Guide trailers into the loading platform.
  - O Escort incoming truck drivers to and from the dispatch office.
  - O Inspect incoming and outgoing shipments.
  - O Verify the count of incoming or outgoing cargo against bills of lading.
  - O Countersign incoming and outgoing bills of lauding.
  - O Ensuring that the trucker exits the platform without extra cargo.
  - O Ensure that freight seals are properly attached and recorded.

Platform Security Logs

A generic daily security log used by security advocate operatives should contain:

- The security guard's name, tour date, or loading dock number.
- The time trucker entered or exited the platform
- The trucker's name and license plate number.
- The description of cargo being handled.
- The cargo totals being shipped or received (e.g., number of items and pallets).
- The dispatcher's name or the forklift driver's name.
- The type of seal and seal number affixed to the vehicle.
- Any discrepancies.

Investigation and Prosecution of Cargo Thefts

Because cargo theft may involve national or international jurisdiction requisites, the following agencies often have a direct stake in the investigation of thefts:

- **State and local law enforcement agencies.** Usually prepare local theft reports and respond to thefts in progress.
- **Office of the United states attorney and the FBI**. Investigates cargo thefts associated with white-collar crimes, organized crimes, foreign counter-intelligence offenses, and narcotics-related crimes. The FBI also provides wiretaps and, if local laws are not sufficient, applies federal statutes.
- **The United States Customs Service**. Investigates cargo thefts associated with import and export shipments.

- **State and local District Attorney**. Investigates and prosecutes cargo thefts not handled by federal agencies.

Cargo Theft Prevention Management

The FBI and cargo industry association, which includes the National Electronic Distributors Association, suggests shippers use the following basic precautions to protect cargo:

- **Know your employees.** Companies should run credit and criminal history checks on all employees.
- **Establish a secure work environment**. Companies should deepen and strengthen physical and procedural security requisites (e.g., guards, CCTV, alarms, lighting, and access control).
- **Do not advertise your cargo**. Dress-down eye-catching packaging designs. Use nondescript packaging.
- **Always control cargo shipping documents**
- **Carefully select transportation partners.** Select freight carriers that champion theft prevention management programs.
- **Report theft**. According to the FBI, a lack of detailed crime-related information is the biggest hurdle to catching cargo thieves.

Conclusion

The relationship between security and company profits has been clearly demonstrated. Theft or shrinkage and cargo crime numbers will continue to increase, however, if internal security related controls are not championed and instituted. Experienced internal auditors know that familiarity with the basic techniques and technologies employed in various security environments is often a catalyst for improvement and change within the corporate marketplace. Who better to lead the siren song of enhanced security than the trusted internal and external auditor?

Notes

1. Minahan, Tim. "How Sound is Your Cargo Security Plan?" *Purchasing Online Magazine,* May 1988.
2. "Cargo's Security Blanket." *The Journal of Commerce On-Line,* 2001/
3. The National Cargo Security Council Chairman Edward Badolato, while being interviewed for "Cargo's Security Blanket." *The Journal of Commerce On-Line,* 2001.
4. Mary Lu Korkuch, Chubb Insurance Group, while being interviewed for "Cargo's Security Blanket." *The Journal of Commerce On-Line,* 2001.

Bibliography

Jones, Lawrence S. "Cargo Security: A Nuts-and-Bolts Approach." Butterworth Publishers, 1983.

Luizzo, Anthony J. and George Van Nostrand. "Investigating in a New Environment." *Security Management Magazine,* June 1995, pages 43-45.

Luizzo, Anthony J. and George Van Nostrand. "the Hidden Cost of Downsizing; Where Loyalty Dies, Fraud Grows," *The White Paper,* September/October 1996, pages 22.36.

192 ■ *Healthcare Security*

Auditing Access Control Procedures

Anthony Luizzo

Proactive companies use access control to lower security risk

Access control security involves designing procedures for the safe and orderly flow of people, vehicles, and property (i.e., inventory) into, and out of, an entity (e.g., factory, warehouse, or office building). Access control systems are locking or procedural systems that ensure people, vehicles, or property safely pass through a designated entry point. Entrances, such as doorways, are equipped with either a combination lock that can be opened with a code or a door fitted with an industrial-strength lockset that features either passkey or identification card access. The plastic wallet-sized card, the most popular device, is used in 75% of access control systems. Entrances not fitted with locksets are often monitored by security television surveillance systems or posted security personnel.

Security Through Environmental Design

Before making access control judgments, it is important to understand security-related architectural design and engineering concepts (also known as "security through environmental design") and their relationship to criminality. A health care entity offering geriatric services, for example, should not locate its front entrance next to a building offering a methadone assistance program, where senior citizens might be at increased risk of mugging. The healthcare entity should locate its front entrance in a lower risk area of the building. In addition, entrances should not be in ill-lighted, un-trafficked areas.

Preparing an Access Control Survey

Forward-thinking companies enlist the services of security consultants who specialize in preparing access control surveys. If in-house or external consultants are used, auditors must ascertain whether a global security survey has been completed and results put in place. Besides checking for locking security devices, the survey should examine various procedural issues, including security staffing, workload, and crime incident data.

Cross-Examination of Risk Exposures

Engineering an access control plan begins by identifying and categorizing (i.e., as low, medium, or high) risk. The survey process calls for carefully logging risk according to categorization. This

---

From *Internal Auditing Report* Warren, Gorham & Lamont/RIA/Group (Reuters) Thomson Publications. April 2001 – openlibrary@archive.com

baseline data is then subdivided into two contrasting columns, forming a vulnerability-versus-criticality matrix. Identifying vulnerabilities exposes critical risk. A high-risk exposure requires security technologies that restrict access to everyone except top executives and designates.

A medium-risk exposure requires less-sophisticated technologies that offer access to a wider group of people. A low-risk exposure usually requires little access control technology, such as closed-circuit television.

Cost/Benefit Analysis

Protective solutions must be weighed against their budgetary impact. It is often less expensive to move an entrance from a vulnerable location than to erect an elaborate security system to thwart potential criminality. When costs are unrealistic, the security initiative can quickly lose credibility. When determining the budgetary impact of protective solutions, recommendations should:

- Be consistent with the mission of the entity.
- Ensure that expenses do not exceed the intended benefits.
- Ensure that programmatic costs fit within budgetary constraints.

Analytical Exposition

Once risk-exposure information is extracted and analyzed, access control strategies must be framed. An effective method for instituting access control wisdom is to divide protective strategies into the following groupings or levels of access:

- Complete Restriction. Usually associated with high-risk security environments, this approach restricts access to everyone except key personnel. Sophisticated access control technologies are required, possibly coupled with security surveillance systems, and posted security operatives. A sophisticated access control system operates as one element in a total protection envelope and must function in conjunction with other protective devices, including physical barriers, alarm traps, turnstiles, portal hardware, and security guards.
- Partial Restriction. Partially curtailing of access to everyone except executives, department heads, and key staff, this approach is usually associated with medium-to-high-risk security environments. Less-sophisticated access control technologies may be instituted along with posted security operatives, industrial-strength portal hardware, and alarm traps.
- Control and Monitoring. Allowing access privileges to authorized personnel, this free-flow approach may or may not be off-limits to the public. If the public is restricted, low-security access technologies may be used, possibly with surveillance oversight.
- Monitoring. This approach involves a free-flow model of access control and may or may not be monitored by surveillance technologies. Personnel or surveillance exclusive of physical obstruction may monitor the area. These control measures are most often used with lobbies, hallways, elevators, entrances, and exits.
- Selective Control and Monitoring. This is like the monitoring of access approach, except that selected points of access are carefully monitored.
- Architectural Security and Control. Various structural changes are made to deter criminal behavior. Businesses, for example, remove the backs of benches in waiting areas and construct waiting areas outside of shipping and receiving platforms.

194 ■ *Healthcare Security*

Procedural Access Control Approaches

Procedural access control strategies include:

- Designing and issuing identification badges and visitor and vendor passes. Special consideration should be given to size, color, and information displayed. Visitor and vendor passes should be 8-by-10-inch laminated documents that are far too large to fit in a coat or pants pocket. These passes should be color-coded to restrict access within the facility. Color-coding is often used in tandem with electromechanical systems (e.g., card readers and surveillance systems).
- Separating employee access from customer access portals.
- Inaugurating logging procedures at selected portals.
- Designating security advocates to challenge visitors (i.e., asking visitors "May I help you?") and to champion company safety and security initiatives.
- Instituting package inspection policies.
- Installing electronic detection systems (e.g., metal detectors).
- Retrofitting elevators to block access to select floors during specified periods.

Conclusion

An effective access control program neutralizes threats and risks and pieces together a protection quilt that shields a company from criminal attack. No one standardized access control strategy will adequately cover the security needs of all environments. Each technological and procedural system must fit in with the other elements of the company's security plan. Planning, training, and communication are the central components in all successful access control programs. An access control policy works when everyone understands the policy and when access codes and keys are appropriately safeguarded.

Eleven Questions to Ask When Auditing an Access Control Program

1. Are access control strategies based on the company's global security survey?
2. Are risk exposures cross-examined?
3. Does the security department maintain a list of vulnerable and critical access points?
4. Are risk exposures categorized as low, medium, and high?
5. Are in-house or external consultants used to perform access control surveys?
6. Are both procedural and technological systems used in the access control program?
7. Are employee identification cards used in the access control program?
8. Are visitor and vendor passes distributed?
9. Are card access codes changed when employees are dismissed or when cards are lost or stolen?
10. Are visitor and vendor passes too large to be hidden in pants or coat pockets?
11. Are high-security environments protected with state-of-the-art access control systems, such as signature verification, retinal eye scanning, and voice printing?

Auditing Loss Prevention Programs

Anthony J. Luizzo

When auditing loss prevention programs, what should the internal auditor keep in mind regarding the risks associated with internal theft?

In general, security is not viewed as a moneymaking operation. The exceptions to this rule should include loss prevention programs. These programs are generally evaluated on how well they keep the level of employee theft within acceptable industry averages; total elimination of employee theft is probably an unrealistic goal. Internal auditors may be called upon to evaluate the effectiveness and efficiency of such programs, particularly because loss prevention's overall contribution to a company's bottom line is often difficult to measure and evaluate.

Measuring the Internal Theft Problem

Shrinkage. It is the retail industry's euphemism that describes corporate profits walking out the door. According to the University of Florida's *2001 National Retail Security Survey Final Report*, inventory shrinkage cost U.S. retailers approximately $33.2 billion last year, up from $29 billion the year before. The survey data also revealed that internal theft now accounts for an estimated 46 percent of inventory shrinkage, costing U.S. retailers approximately $15.2 billion annually, compared to shoplifting costs of about $10.2 billion. The *Final Report* also points out that "there is no other form of larceny that annually costs the American public more money than employee theft." Employee theft and shoplifting combined account for the largest source of property crime committed annually in the United States. Other alarming statistics regarding internal theft abound. For example, the National Restaurant Association estimates that employee theft amounts to 4 percent of food sales, at a cost more than $8.5 billion annually, and that 75 percent of inventory shortages can be attributed to employee thievery. Various other studies also estimate that employee theft costs between .5 percent and 3 percent of an average company's gross sales. Even if the correct figure is just 1 percent, it would mean that employees in the United States steal over a billion dollars a week from their employers.

Why Do People Steal?

Most employers pay their employees a fair wage, so why do some steal It is believed that there are as many reasons for theft as there are incidents. Some employees simply do not consider taking an item or two stealing—they would rather think of it as one of the perks of the job. Still others point to spur-of-the-moment impulse, the same reason cited by some shoplifters. Thieves are often attracted to any location that is known to house something of value.

From *Internal Auditing* Report Warren, Gorham & Lamont/RIA/Group (Reuters) Thomson Publications. September 2002 – openlibrary@archive.com

196 ■ *Healthcare Security*

The infamous Willie Sutton (a glamorized bank robber) told law enforcement officials that he robbed banks because—that was where the money was.

Reducing Internal Thievery

The most effective and efficient method of reducing internal thievery is to prevent it from occurring in the first place. Because preventing *all* thefts is an unrealistic goal, most security and loss prevention programs incorporate strategies that are aimed at reducing or mitigating thievery while also seeking monetary restitution to help offset losses.

Beyond the standard security techniques and technologies normally employed in asset protection programs, companies should strongly consider:

- Conducting background screening of all employees (e.g., verification of past employment history and criminal conviction checks).
- Enlisting all corporate employees in the fight against thievery (e.g., loss prevention awareness programs and anonymous telephone hotlines).
- Rewarding employees for theft prevention information (e.g., rewards for calls to ethics hotlines).
- Performing periodic security evaluations to test internal controls intended to thwart theft. Controls might include such measures as refund and void controls, employee package checks, and controlled access to cash, among others.

Security Surveys

One excellent method of evaluating a company's anti-theft capabilities is to test the program against various crime-related scenarios. The security survey is the diagnostic tool of preference used by most security executives to accomplish this task. Informed protection experts suggest that security assessments be performed on a regular schedule to ensure the continued success of the company's anti-theft measures.

Restitution

The practice of requiring an individual who has harmed another to reimburse the injured party has been an integral part of jurisprudence since the beginning of the civilized world. Throughout history, the concept of repayment or restitution has been inseparable from the principles of crime and punishment. Virtually all states have adopted laws with respect to collecting restitution as a standard remedy for crimes committed. Restitution can be quite effective when the offender has assets that can be converted to satisfy the obligation.

The types of losses for which victimized organizations may obtain restitution vary from jurisdiction to jurisdiction. Many jurisdictions allow the courts to garnish offenders' wages. In some relatively minor cases of employee theft, court intervention may not be needed—such offenders may remain on the corporate payroll and enter into a mutually acceptable restitution agreement with the corporation.

Reviewing A Company's Internal Theft Program

During an internal audit of a loss prevention program, the auditor should ask the following:

- Are the organization's internal theft prevention strategies adequate?
- Are shrinkage levels consistent with industry averages?
- Are statistics regarding internal theft maintained?
- Are copies of previous internal theft studies available?
- Are internal and/or external restitution programs used?
- Are periodic theft prevention assessments performed?
- Are recommended protection enhancements implemented?
- Are the monetary savings derived from crime reduction programs tracked effectively?
- Are the company's anti-theft initiatives cost-effective?
- Are the proper asset controls in place?

Such controls might include:

- Refund controls.
- Void controls.
- Employee package checks.
- Trash removal controls.
- Security cameras in key locations.
- Inter-store transfer controls.
- Bar coding and bar code scanning (both in inventory and at the point of sale).
- Price change controls.
- Detailed merchandise receiving controls (including separation of duties).
- Building entrance and exit controls.
- Cash handling controls.

198 ■ *Healthcare Security*

The Environmental School of Criminology: Proactive vs. Reactive Security

Anthony Luizzo

An experienced security professional discusses the benefits of addressing security proactively and provides tips for internal audits of corporate security programs.

Asset protection has become a central issue on every executive's agenda. When auditing a firm's security program, internal auditors need to cast an investigative eye on whether the security department actively searches out crime risks before they occur. In reality, prior to the terrorist attacks of September 11, 2001, protection mavens rarely addressed crime problems before they occurred. One of the reasons for this philosophical protection approach can be traced to the fact that prior to the early 1970s, major U.S. police and security agencies rarely dedicated resources to preventing crime prior to its occurrence.

The Origins of Proactive Security

Great Britain is known as the world leader in fostering the modern crime-prevention model of policing. In the mid 18th century, Sir Henry Fielding, a British magistrate, and criminologist, organized the forerunner of today's policing methods by setting two goals: stamp out existing crime and prevent outbreaks of crime in the future. He further identified three objectives necessary for the achievement of these goals: the development of a strong police force, the organization of active citizens' groups to assist law enforcement, and the initiation of strategies to remove the root causes of crime and the conditions in which they flourish. Due in large part to the vast number of criminals that continued to ply their trade, the British constabulary was soon forced to abandon the proactive policing model championed so passionately by Fielding. By the 1950s, British law enforcement realized that dealing with crime reactively was not sufficient, and again revisited the preventative model. In 1963, the British police force formulated a mandatory one-month "crime prevention" training program for all its officers.

In 1971, the United States followed Britain's lead, formalizing crime-prevention training using a Law Enforcement Assistance Administration grant, which was awarded to the University of Louisville. Since the founding of the National Crime Prevention Institute, thousands of crime prevention specialists (e.g., law enforcement officers, investigators, corporate security executives, and loss prevention advocates) have graduated with specialized skills in detecting crime risks before they wreak havoc on company assets. One of the most important skills taught to all graduating crime prevention specialists is how to decipher criminality using an assessment tool known as the security survey. In competent hands, the security survey helps to determine when, where, how, and why crimes occur.

In essence, the survey acts like a CAT scan, in that it provides a global view of the entity under scrutiny by highlighting security- and safety-related abnormalities and offering preventative

From *Internal Auditing* Report Warren, Gorham & Lamont/RIA/Group (Reuters) Thomson Publications. January 2004 – openlibrary@archive.com

enhancements to remove and/or mitigate identified risk exposures. By the mid 1970s, all major U.S. police agencies had established crime prevention programs. As a rule of thumb, depending on the size of the department, usually between 1 and 3 percent of a department's investigative resources are dedicated to proactive assignments. In the early years, all investigative staff assigned to crime prevention duty was sent to the National Crime Prevention Institute for certification as crime prevention specialists. Today, larger municipal police agencies train their own via internal training initiatives. As an example, the New York City Police Department's Crime Prevention Unit offers a 40-hour "Basics of Security and Crime Prevention Program" twice annually. The course is open to qualified personnel and is worth three college credits.

The Art and Science of Proactive Security

In addition to standard law enforcement training (e.g., patrol and investigative approaches), crime prevention specialists learn to develop a different mindset than their counterparts; in short, they are taught to think beyond the galaxy of contemporary police work. This new proactive mindset, often called the environmental model of criminology, teaches students to address both the criminal and the environment in which the criminal act is committed. Criminologists of this school theorize that crimes are committed when three conditions exist (two of which are uncontrollable):

1. Desire—an uncontrollable factor in the crime equation.
2. Ability—also an uncontrollable factor.
3. Opportunity—a predictable and controllable variable.

Protection experts suggest that opportunistic misdeeds can be effectively controlled via eliminating the ease with which the prize (e.g., property) is taken illegally and instituting crime-deterrence initiatives that help to up the odds of identification and capture of the transgressor. There are several crime reductions projects around the country that have solved problems using the environmental crime control model. As an example, some years back many people were using the Coney Island Boardwalk in New York City during the day and early evening hours as a main thoroughfare to the seaside amenities. After dark, however, the environs under the boardwalk became dangerous, crime-prone locations used by miscreants to trap their prey. For many years prior to the acceptance of environmental security and proactive crime control, the age-old approach to mitigating these crime risks was to saturate targeted locations with protective personnel. Oftentimes patrolling was limited because the cost of assigning sufficient protection personnel was not fiscally feasible. Moreover, trying to devise an effective protective blanket over the entire boardwalk was totally out of the question. An ingenious solution was devised: filling the underbelly of the boardwalk with sand helped to completely remove the crime risk without expending one penny of the police department's budget. Moreover, filling the areas under the boardwalk with sand also helped to establish a flood control barrier protecting the community from surging tides.

Questions to Ask When Auditing Security Programs

- Does the security department have a crime prevention program?
- Are crime prevention personnel professionally trained and certified?
- Are all employees trained in the ABCs of crime prevention?

200 ■ *Healthcare Security*

- Does the firm maintain an ongoing liaison with local police agencies' crime prevention units?
- Are security surveys being conducted on a regular basis?
- Are security survey recommendations being implemented?
- Are records of previous surveys being maintained?
- If the security department does not have an in-house crime prevention initiative, are external consultants being used? If so, are they properly credentialed?

Securing the Future

As we enter the 21st century, internal auditors as corporate watchdogs are being asked to play a central role in ensuring that all corporate programs, including security, meet industry benchmarks. Informed security executives would agree that terrorism having reached our shores has forced us to go back to the drawing board to reevaluate the way we secure our assets.

Auditing Hospital Security: Is Your Security Program In Compliance?

Anthony Luizzo and Bernard Scaglione

Historically the responsibility for auditing security and safety in the mercantile community is shared among the security executives, accounting, and auditing professionals. The security executive's role is to create effective protective policies to blanket their respective facilities and ensure compliance with those policies. With respect to regulatory requirements, security administrators strive to meet security industry and JCAHO mandates, while audit professionals labor on assuring shareholders, upper management, and regulatory agencies that the firm's financial records are compliant with accounting industry standards.

Behind the Call for Increased Oversight in the Security Industry

What events have driven the call for increased oversight in the security industry? Beyond terrorism hitting our shores, fiduciary oversight by the accounting industry has increased ten-fold due in large part to the savings and loan fiasco and the recent Wall Street debacle of 2008. These events have demanded greater accountability from the security and fiduciary communities and have been the driving force behind security executives in all industries not wanting to get caught in the "jaws of program compliancy" within their respective entities. With the surge if corporate compliance coupled with the necessity to ensure proficiency with in structures and policy, security practitioners need to ensure that security-related processes work as promulgated. Ensuring compliance and value of physical security systems and programs is key to providing effective security services. Security executives must strive to minimize program deviation, to expeditiously identify program failures and to ensure that proper training is offered to guarantee the overall success of the initiative. Moreover, program-related failures need to be minimized and back-up systems need to be installed.

Four Key Issues of an Audit/Compliance Program

Writing an effective audit/compliance program requires that security practitioner's focus on four key programmatic issues: program functionality, program deviation, program failures and program compliance.

1. Program Functionality

Protection executives need to develop a process to ensure policies and procedures are working the way they are outlined within the written policy or designed within the process. The most efficient method of monitoring functionality is to ensure that systematic checks and/or inspections are regularly administered. More forward-thinking security executives instinctively know the value

From *Journal of Healthcare Protection Management.* (25):2, pp. 9–15. 2009–10.

202 ■ *Healthcare Security*

of having these checks organized by shift and day of the week. The data should also include the individual supervisor's pedigree. It is important that these checks are spread over a defined time. For example, when checking to make sure that all security officers are in fact doing their job and checking IDs, the access control inspection for should include all the security officer's names plotted on a master spreadsheet. This helps security administration to quickly check on when, where and who completed inspections at any given time. In this way periodical and annual compliance audits are readily available

2. Program Deviation

An important part of program compliance is being able to quickly identify and curtail deviation. Deviation refers not to inconsistency of policy, but an individual's own change in the process. To minimize deviation, a procedure needs to be designed and implemented to immediately stop the deviation, while also allowing for corrective mechanisms to be put in place as expeditiously as possible. Beyond correcting the deviation and offering an alternative solution, it is a good idea to also re-educate all involved (officers, vendors, management, employees, etc.) on the process breach. As an example, if a policy states that all visitors must sign in before entering a building, but a review of the inspection process reveals that one vendor is not following the rule – the officer and vendor should be admonished and educated on the spot to the correct policy. As a matter of course, it would be a prudent idea to reinforce the importance of the access rules with all security operatives and vendors including the deviated policy as a learning point.

3. Program Failure

Generally, failure rates refer to equipment that is not working at acceptable standards. Ensuring that physical security systems function at 100 percent, it is important that backup, temporary systems are put on-line without delay. All security departments should be monitoring equipment failure rates. When a camera stops working or an alarm contact is torn off a door, the level of security is diminished. What makes failure rate monitoring so important is not just the immediate identification of the failure, but also the process of maintaining the same level of security until repairs are put in place. What happens when a device fails? Device or system loss must be identified immediately. Temporary systems should be instituted, and a pre-determining plan must be established which will address and all failures of physical security devices. These plans need to be reviewed and tested at least yearly. A down time procedural review should be carried out on a periodical schedule to insure optimum performance. Drills or tabletop exercises should also be conducted and the results of the inspection including any resolutions for change in procedures should be properly noted for future review. Device checks should be conducted periodically through visual inspections and organized according to their importance, i.e., panic buttons more frequently than door contacts, etc. In addition, devices should have regularly scheduled maintenance to insure optimum operation and long-life availability.

4. Program Compliance

When we talk about policy compliance, we mean the alignment of policy and procedure to actual practice. How often when involved in litigation does the question come up: Are We Following Our Own Policy? Compliance also means consistency. Is the implementation of security procedures consistent across the organization, shift and amongst staff? Is the service we provide to our customers reliable and constant? Is there minimal deviation in service? Most importantly, are there checks and balances in place to ensure compliance? Policy compliance is especially important and central to the successful functionality of the security program. The first step to ensuring compliance is staff education. All staff should be intricately aware of all corporate policies and procedures. This involves not only having an in-depth knowledge of policies employed daily, but also having a working knowledge of those policies used in random instances in select situations. In addition, when policies or procedures are changed or updated, staffs' needs to be reeducated on the entire policy; with specific emphasis on the modifications put forward.

What is an Audit and How is it Applied?

An audit is oftentimes defined as in inspectional process to evaluate program performance and compliance using standards within the regulatory sector. In competent hands, an audit should measure with a fair degree of accuracy a firm's adherence to regulatory and corporate mandates. When performing an audit of a company's security policies and procedures, one of the most effective ways of measuring program effectiveness is to periodically test the program against a set of potential exposures. The auditor should ascertain if such tests are regularly performed and whether corrective measures are instituted accordingly.

Aspects of training and competency testing

Security mavens know that the foundation for any strong security program is proper training. The more training that is done the better-equipped security staff are in providing a safe and secure environment. Taking a page from academia, training programs need to convert the content presented in the classroom into practical information used in the field. It is widely believed that security operatives find it much easier to retain immediately following training than three, six or eight months after training sessions have concluded. To ensure top-notch training exercises, training coordinators should use competencies to ascertain effectiveness. Competencies are learning points that are vital to the understanding of training material. They allow trainers to determine the amount of knowledge that was absorbed by an individual and the level of memory retention associated with that training six months after it has occurred. The three- or six-month assessment is crucial to any successful training program; it provides officers with a continual assessment of their knowledge and the consistent application of security processes and procedures.

How do competencies work? During the development stages of any training program key features or objectives are developed in the subject training. Not much different than learning objectives, competencies are learning objectives broken down into the actual process that is being taught. For example, when teaching about customer service some key components of the program would be to smile, maintain eye contact, greet people with the words, "good morning", etc. Competencies are the core objectives that the instructor wants the student to understand. At the conclusion of training there should be some level of assessment to confirm that the student understood and retained the information present in class. The most common type of post-training competency is a written test.

204 ■ *Healthcare Security*

A written test or exam is composed of questions that the student must answer to show that they retained the information presented in the training session. Another type of assessment or test is an observational assessment. This is where a student must physically demonstrate the processes, they learned in the classroom (role playing). It is often said that the best exercise for security-based competency assessment is the observational method. Making sure that an officer can physically demonstrate and speak about what was learned is a better technique than a written test, which provides no direct learning feedback between the teacher and the student. The successful use of an observational competency assessment is the breakdown of the key components of the process or processes that are being taught and the transfer of those key components onto an assessment form which can be used to review with each student and document their success or failure.

Observational competency assessments should be used as a post test strategy upon completion of classroom training and again three to six months after classroom training has ended. This allows for reinstruction and reminds a student of the components necessary for the correct implementation of certain process or procedures.

After-action follow-up

It is imperative that a quality improvement process be implemented to insure consistent implementation of the overall compliance program. Metrics should be developed that will monitor procedural and failure rate compliance. Metrics should include standards for auditing of procedural steps, midterm competencies, annual or regular training, the surveying of end users and observations or spot checks. Setting up metrics will ensure that the compliance program is being monitored and that all aspects of the program meet management standards.

Conclusion

Auditors should understand that no one method of protection is perfect and no one-security plan is 100 percent effective. Auditors can say with some certainty however that the best methods of improving program performance are via employing compliance techniques on a periodic basis. Results of these audits can help security administrators to better measure the effectiveness of in-place security initiatives while also offering guidance re future enhancements.

Security Auditing: A Prescription For Keeping Protection Programs Healthy

Anthony Luizzo

Keeping security programs healthy is an arduous task that requires constant vigilance and dedication. Security administrators instinctively know that internal security controls are <u>not</u> in place, or do not work, protection is diminished. The trouble with most explanations of security auditing is that several security experts see the audit function as an accounting exercise. Auditors and accountants among other duties draft audits for a living, but so do select security professionals who specialize in security auditing services. Their mission is simple they search out frail protection strategies and make suggestions to remedy them. These proactive protection specialists labor under different job titles in both the private and public sectors.

Differing Job Titles

In the law enforcement profession security auditors are called "crime prevention specialists". Since the mid 1970's, many police agencies nationwide assign their operatives to work with individuals and businesses on crime control programs. In the private sector these operatives are labeled "proactive security specialists" and labor on a galaxy of assignments from performing periodical and annual security audits to formulation corporate-wide crime prevention training programs for employees, customers, and visitors. In the governmental and engineering sectors they are called "community crime control practitioners" and work shoulder-to-shoulder with architects, engineers and builders on security-related design and redesign issues. In the economic development sector, these security operatives are called community crime control planners" and work on preparing crime-impact studies and other specialized crime evaluation programs for business improvement districts, industrial parks, residential complexes, and enterprise zones. These highly specialized practitioners usually have their roots in the criminal justice, business administration and/or sociology disciplines and have been cross trained in crime control theory and practice.

Why is Security Auditing Important?

One of the most important functions of the security department is to keep employees and assts safe and secure. Since that terrible day in early September 2001, security has been on every protection executive's radar screen. All too often security executives are taken to task when internal protection controls are deficient. Moreover, judicial-related litigation costs have skyrockets forcing many corporate entities to fail. Security administrators', who do not champion the proactive security model, do so at their peril.

From *Journal of Healthcare Protection Management.* (26):2, pp. 24–30. 2011.

What is security auditing?

Security auditing is defined as furnishing inspection services of existing security programs. Traditionally, any well-structured program should provide four basic protection tenets:

1) **Asset protection** – ensuring that inventories, employees, electronic devices, building, and cash are safeguarded
2) **Information management** – ensuring that security-related crime analysis information is trustworthy
3) **Operational efficiency** – ensuring that security does not hamper day-to-day business operations
4) **Programming adherence** – ensuring that corporate policies and procedures are followed

Tasks and responsibilities of security auditors

Auditor responsibilities include but are not limited to:

1) Preparation of periodical audit reports
2) Preparation of regulatory audit reports
3) Reviewing and analyzing incident reports
4) Preparation of engineering scopes for security-related technologies
5) Networking with facility architects on facility design and/or re-design issues
6) Preparing capital budget plans for short and long-term security expenditures
7) Promulgating proactive crime control training programs, exhibitions, and seminars

Aspects of formulation an effective security audit program

A critical component to launching a security audit initiative is finding the right professionals for the job. Skilled security audit operatives should have completed studies in crime control planning and have demonstrated knowledge in writing security surveys and audit reports. They should be able to evaluate crime risk exposures, promulgate strategies to mitigate risk exposures, and have a unique understanding of how security system's function. Once the right staff is assembled, it is time to establish a task list and after-action evaluation system of oversight. The day-to-day job of a security auditor should be to formulate a schedule of audits for his institution.

This often involves identifying critical facility functions and scheduling both annual and periodical audits throughout the calendar year. By year's end, all the critical areas should have been audited. If any areas were left out of the schedule, the annual audit should catch the discrepancy.

Types of security audits

Security audits are sub-divided into four distinct categories:

1. **The annual audit** – this form of audit is usually a facility-wide evaluation of the institution, building or entity. In this type of exercise, the auditor examines the entire facility from the

outside environs to the inner bowels of the entity. After review, the auditor is tasked with drafting a comprehensive report detailing his or her finding and enhancement recommendations for improvement.

2. **The periodical audit** – this form of audit differs from the annual audit in that the auditor is tasked with examining select sections of the entity that have been identified as crime-sensitive locations. In many institutions' crime analysis data and incident reports help identify these "hot spots". In many circles this form of crime analysis programming is termed crime mapping. Irrespective of how it is termed these hot spots need to be audited on a regular basis and kept under the auditors' watchful eyes. Many more forward-thinking security executives devise a schedule for their institutions that capture each hot-spot location withing the calendar year. By the time the auditor returns to hot-spot number one; it is time for the annual audit once again.

3. **The emergency audit** – this form of security audit differs from its two predecessors in that the auditor is tasked with examining locations that have been the scene of criminal incidents. This form of audit is far less sophisticated than both the annual and periodical audits and is meant to only highlight immediate security fixes for existing crime problems.

4. **The regulatory audit** – many institutions such as hospitals, banks, and government entities are governed by regulatory agency audit mandates This form of security audit is regulated by industry guidelines and requires that many institutions always be prepared for a "no prior notice audit". This form of audit requires that the auditor be detailed to work on this audit project all year long and be ready for all exigencies.

Security audit lexicon

The following is a short list of security audit-related definitions:

- **Crime Prevention** is defined as the anticipation, recognition and appraisal of a crime risk and the initiation of an action to remove or reduce it
- **Security audit** is defined as an on-site physical inspection of an entity (business, institution, building, factory, residence, etc.) to discern security related deficiencies and provide enhancement strategies to mitigate these deficiencies
- **Perimeter security** is defined as the first layer of the security envelope and includes all landmass, excluding buildings, which help form the corporate complex
- **Exterior security** is defined as the second layer of the security envelope and includes the building's exterior façade and all access portals therein (windows, doors, hatches, etc.)
- **Interior security** is defined as the third layer of the security envelope and includes all items, departments, and operations within the inner bowels of the corporate complex (machinery, security systems, security guard operations, shipping/receiving operations, due diligence screening, etc.)
- **Global security** is defined as the fourth layer of the security envelope and includes programs associated with terrorism prevention, executive protection, overseas facility protection, intellectual property security, etc.
- **Target hardening** is defined as applying industrial strength materials (metal plates, window guards, etc.) to portals and vulnerable points of ingress and egress to bolster facility security
- **Technological security blueprint** - is a detailed security-related technological schematic of electronic and non-electronic security systems including but not limited to: alarm, television, locking and fire protection contrivances

208 ■ *Healthcare Security*

- **Security department table of organization** – a physical drawing listing the chain of command and assignments of all protection personnel
- **Protection Blueprint** – a detailed listing of all protection personnel assigned within the facility (post assignments, etc.)
- **Corporate table of organization** – a detailed listing of <u>all</u> employee assignments within the corporate complex and at external satellite facilities
- **Crime risk exposure grid** – a detailed explanation of how crime risk incidents are valuated and catalogued

Audit Review and Oversight

Audits are completed on a regular basis to ensure that protection wisdom is adequate and up-to-speed. Most security audits of companies are performed by in-house personnel, rarely if ever, is an outside security firm called upon to do the work. Obviously, it is expensive, but well worth the expense. Casting an objective eye on security by an outside firm often helps to ensure that in-house personnel are up-to-the-job and on target with their work products. Moreover, conducting outside audits can also reduce exposure to security-related litigations costs as well.

Ten Tips for Auditors to Follow when Writing a Security Audit

1. Formulate a security audit/survey numbering system
2. Include neighborhood community profile data (population/land use statistics)
3. Include both FBI and local police statistics
4. Include minutes of meetings and photographs taken during the audit
5. Formulate a prioritized listing of risk exposures
6. List deficiencies and enhancement recommendations together in priority order
7. Include a paragraph in the final report highlighting which functions are being audited and excluded from the audit exercise
8. Include a paragraph in the final report thanking employees for their assistance
9. Stamp all pages of the audit report "confidential"
10. Hand deliver the completed audit report and obtain a signed receipt

Summary

The establishment of a proactive security program gives the security department the capability of nailing down crime risks before they adversely affect global security and safety. It is often said that what a "cat scan" is to a physician, the "security audit" is to the security diagnostician. There are many benefits to be derived from implementing adequate security audit programs especially when terrorism, financial uncertainty and skyrocketing security-specific litigation costs are knocking on every executive's front door. Many more forward-thinking administrators have heard the *Science of Survival (SOS)* signal and are either actively employing experienced proactive security diagnosticians or contracting with outside firms for these services. Many larger police departments nationwide have training programs in this diagnostic discipline and would be happy to assist with technical support and training expertise. In the private sector IAHSS or ASIS could also be contacted for assistance.

Aspects of Preparing for a "No Prior Notice" Regulatory Audit

Anthony Luizzo and Bernard J. Scaglione

As a matter of course many hospital executives rush to prepare for regulatory surveys from several different agencies; including The Joint Commission (JCAHO). Oftentimes the process embraces policy/procedure compliance verification, the auditing of medical equipment, doors, walls, etc., re code acceptability, and verifying that training standards for hospital security and safety programs meet acceptable standards. To pass these compliance exercises, hospitals spend thousands of dollars in overtime and related construction and reconstruction expenditures, leaving many healthcare institutions in financial ruin and unable to sustain that perfect fine-tuned environment indefinitely. Recently, this pressure-packed process has become even more challenging in that The Joint Commission, as well as CMS and other regulatory agencies, no longer give prior notice before arriving. This has created quite a quagmire for many hospital administrators in that their institutions are now required to be compliant-ready 24 hours a day, 7 days a week, as opposed to only once every few years. To meet this new requirement many hospitals have adapted a 24 by 7, always-ready approach to management, ensuring that staff is always prepared for a survey event. The 24 by 7 philosophical model may be simplistic but can be complex and quite cumbersome.

Creating an organization that is always on top of its game takes planning, commitment, and dramatic changes within the organization's culture. However, the benefits clearly out-weigh its shortcomings. Implementation of 24 by 7 readiness forces organizations to operate more efficiently, ensures optimum response to emergency situations and helps to reduce the financial burden associated with scrambling to ensure compliance once every three years or so. It would be a cost-effective move to have all departments within the hospital organization adopt the 24 by 7 approach to operational compliance and readiness.

Document Availability

One of the basic tenets in converting to the 24 by 7 model is the availability of documents. Policies and procedures, training information and compliance reports need to be available in the event of a regulatory audit. This means that if the department head is out sick or on vacation, there is other staff available to represent and provide documents that may be requested by a surveyor. It is central to the success of the endeavor that all documents are always accessible and safeguarded in a central location. Documents should be kept in locked facilities that are secure from outside availability but always offer easy accessibility. In addition to availability and security, documents should be well organized, properly labeled and placed in 3 ring binders for easy reference. This binder should contain documents that are no more than a year old. Older documents should be stored in a different location. The length of time that all documents are kept by the hospital is based on the individual hospital's requirements.

From *Journal of Healthcare Protection Management.* (26):1, pp. 14–20. 2010.

210 ■ *Healthcare Security*

Safeguarding Training Records

Beyond training institutional mandates, securely maintaining training records also helps to facilitate readiness and compliance. All training records need to be up to date so that both in-house and external auditors can determine the level of training completed during their visit.

Training reports should include the outline and training objectives, the sign-in sheets and all competencies utilized in the training process. Correspondingly, document availability helps to facilitate tracking of license expiration and re-certification dates as well as other program documentation. Presenting a report that highlights deficiencies such as expired security officer licenses or certifications does not make a good impression at audit time and could cause the hospital to be penalized during regulatory review.

Policy and Procedure Compliance

The most important documents that a regulator will review are department policies and procedures. As a rule of thumb, policies should be updated every two to three years. Typically, policy review is limited to only a quick scanning of the policy seeking out misspelled words, title changes, and addresses and/or phone number updates. A 24 by 7 readiness review requires a complete audit as well as an exhaustive review of the policy to ensure that implementation mimics written statements. To achieve 24 by 7 status, policies should be tested every two to three years. With respect to testing, a small number should be critiqued each year to ensure compliance. The Compliance process should include a review of the written documents to help catch penmanship discrepancies, as well as holding meetings with all involved parties via tabletop or mapping exercises to monitor the procedural operations in action.

Physical Security Systems

Processes should be developed and implemented that allow for the regular auditing of equipment to ensure proper operation. For example, the National Center for Missing and Exploited Children recommends weekly checks of the infant banding system to make certain it is operating properly. All security equipment should be inspected on a regularly scheduled basis to ensure optimum functionality. As a matter of practice, items from flashlights to card readers to camera recorders need to be inspected. It is vital that all physical security systems are inspected regularly.

Equipment compliance requires that management institute an inspection schedule that is spread out over a finite period listing specific mandates re which pieces of equipment are to be checked, when they are to be checked, and how they are to be checked. For example, if all the cameras in Building "A" are checked in January, the cameras in Building "B" should be checked in February, etc. Equipment checks can encompass 100% of the total or a percentage of the total number of in-place devices. If it is decided to check a percentage of the total number of devices, then these same devices should not be tested again until 100% of the devices are checked. As an example of a detailed inspection of an infant abduction system would be to test every, or a percentage of every, transmitter, portal, and ceiling receiver to ensure proper activation. Portal checks would include the locking of the doors and the activation of alarms at all portals.

Training Compliance

Training is critical to the readiness process. It is paramount that all staff working on all shifts is knowledgeable in every single policy and procedure that relates to security.

For that to become reality, training must be a continuous on-going exercise. Training must occur on an annual basis at minimum, with a midyear test or competency added thereto.

In addition, when procedures change, immediate action must occur to ensure that staff is appraised for all systems-related modifications. One of the major obstacles to successful training facilitation is retention. Security officer retention over a long period of time is normally limited at best. One method to address and resolve this problem is the use of competencies. Competencies are tests that highlight the key components of the training program and are used by educators to improve retention levels. Competencies can be written tests, observations, drills, or any combination of the three. It is important to remember that training alone may not be enough. Procedures may have to be framed that will support the initial training and reinforce the key learning points between training sessions. The best methods of accomplishing this is either via observation testing and review, or through drill and exercise critiquing. Both methods allow for hands-on review and educational reinforcement of the initial training framework.

Program Implementation

So, what does it take to become truly 24 by 7 compliant? It takes easy access to documents, instituting a process to ensure that the documentation is current, formulating policy review procedures, instituting a regimented physical security system testing program, and more importantly, drafting a process that will ensure continuous readiness. The key to the successful implementation of the readiness program is the development of monitoring processes, which will ensure that the program is always in compliance. The use of departmental standards and metrics to monitor and measure compliance works best for the implementation of a monitoring program. Department standards are developed to set a minimal level of readiness, while metrics are utilized to measure performance alacrity.

Creating Departmental Standards

Standards are developed to set an acceptable level or minimal level of compliance. Standards need to be developed for all department readiness components and then monitored regularly. This will make certain that all readiness components are on track 100% of the time. For example, components for a developed standard to ensure that CCTV cameras are functioning as installed should note:

- Whether cameras are presenting a picture when turned on,
- Whether the picture quality is acceptable, both day and night,
- Whether the cameras are viewing their defined areas,
- Whether the cameras are recording at specified levels,
- Whether cameras are securely mounted or have been compromised, and
- Whether camera pictures appear on all defined monitors.

Establishing Metrics

Metrics is a management tool that provides a measure of performance for a given entity. With respect to our CCTV standard above, a metric should be developed to measure technological compliance and standards levels. The technological metric should include a requisite to inspect a percentage of the total number of CCTV cameras during a thirty-day cycle. In turn, by months end, all the cameras set in the standard should have been checked.

In addition, levels of performance established for each camera should be evaluated as well. For example, when determining recording levels, 15 fps at 4 CIF for 14 days would be an adequate metric, meaning that recording level could exceed that metric but never fall below it.

Implementing a Dashboard

To manage program readiness and performance, a dashboard should be developed to appropriately monitor whether program standards and metric applications are within compliance. A dashboard consists of a series of graphs or data points presented on a single sheet or computer screen that helps to summarize standard compliance and program performance. Looking at our CCTV example, when the dashboard is utilized on a monthly or quarterly basis it will show that the CCTV standards were met, and the performance metrics were met. In this case the CCTV metric would be green in color exemplifying the met standard and metric. Moreover, the dashboard will also underscore the number of inspections conducted during the month or quarter, while enforcing the fact that the system complies and is in the green mode.

A Final Thought

Preparing for a regulatory agency audit is a pressure-filled mentally challenging experience; it can make even the most seasoned security executive frazzled. The secret to keeping cool and meeting the challenge of passing the audit with flying colors is to formulate a process in which your institution can examine, diagnose, and proscribe remedies to make frail security programs healthy once again. The age-old adage: "prior planning prevents poor performance" should be the fulcrum upon which every security executive designs his institution's protection defenses.

Forensic Accounting and the Criminal Justice Process

Anthony Luizzo

Internal auditors and accountants who perform white-collar investigations should be familiar with terms commonly used in criminal and civil litigation.

Beyond performing the standard audit, forensic accountants are often given the task of evaluating environments susceptible to fraud, drafting preventative measures to thwart fraudulent behavior, and assisting law enforcement officials in bringing criminals to justice Therefore, it is important that non-law enforcement numerical detectives understand the internal mechanics of the criminal justice system.

Warrant of Arrest

Criminal proceeding usually begins with an arrest. An arrest is the taking of a person into custody by law enforcement for the purpose of presenting formal charges against such person. Arrests can be made either with or without a warrant of arrest (street arrests are usually made without a warrant.). A warrant of arrest may be executed at any time of the day on any day of the week. Courts issue warrants of arrest after an accusatory instrument has been filed. A warrant of arrest issued by a District Court, a New York City Criminal Court or Superior Court may be executed anywhere in the State. A warrant issued by a Town Court, or a Village Court may be executed in the county of issuance or an adjoining county, or anywhere in the state upon written endorsement of a Local Criminal Court of the county in which the arrest is made (Criminal Procedure Law (CPL) of New York State, Article 1200).

Arraignment

The first judicial step in all criminal proceedings is the arraignment. At the arraignment:

- The judge informs the defendant of his constitutional rights.
- The Court presents the charges against the defendant.
- The question of bail is discussed.

From *Internal Auditing Report*: Warren. Gorham & Lamont / RIA Group (Reuters) – Thomson Publications. November 2000 – openlibrary@archive.com.

The Grand Jury

The Grand jury represents the bridge between the Lower Court and the Superior Court. The Grand jury is made up of less than sixteen and no more than twenty-three persons, who are impaneled by a superior court. The functions of a grand jury are to hear and examine evidence concerning offenses, misconduct, nonfeasance, and neglect in public office and to act with respect to such evidence.

Search Warrant (Cpl: Article 690)

A search warrant is a court order directing law enforcement to conduct a search of designated premises, or of a designated vehicle, or of a designated person for the purpose of seizing designated property and to deliver said property to the court that issued the warrant.

Jury Selection (Cpl: Article 270)

In a criminal trial that requires a jury, the first function performed by counsel for the people and counsel for the defense is jury selection. Jurors are average citizens of a community selected from the voting roles in the community for service on a jury. If the trial is in a local court the jury consists of six members and one alternate juror. In Superior Court, County or Supreme Court, the jury consists of twelve members and as many alternates as the court deems advisable. The court permits the prosecutor and defense counsel to ask questions ("voir dire") of the jurors to determine the fitness of each juror.

Jury Challenges (Cpl: Article 270)

In Superior Court, either party to the proceeding is limited to the following peremptory challenges by statute:

- Twenty challenges for regular jurors if the highest crime charged is a class A Felony and two challenges for each alternate juror selected.
- Fifteen challenges for regular jurors if the highest crime charged is a class B or C felony and two challenges for each alternate juror to be selected.
- Ten challenges for the regular jurors in all other instances and two challenges for each alternate juror to be selected.
- A Peremptory Challenge is the right of the defendant and the prosecution in a criminal trial to offer objection to a certain number of jurors without giving any explanation.

Jury Trials

The District Attorney makes the opening statement to the jury, outlining the charges and setting forth the proof he or she will offer to substantiate the charges. The court then inquires as to whether the defense counsel desires to make an opening statement.

The District Attorney has an obligation as well as the burden of proof to prove the allegations and guilt of the defendant in criminal cases.

Determining Guilt or Innocence: Standards of Proof

In a Criminal Case the standard of proof for conviction is beyond a reasonable doubt. In a Civil Case, the standard of proof for conviction is by a preponderance of the evidence.

Glossary of Legal Terms and Definitions

- Accessory After the Fact: A person who, after the commission of a felony, conceals the offender with the intent that the latter may avoid arrest.
- Accessory Before the Fact. A person who aids and abets in the planning of the commission of a crime, even if he or she did not participate in the actual commission of the crime.
- Accomplice. A person who is liable to prosecution for the identical offense charged against a defendant on trial.
- Affidavit: A written statement under oath.
- Attachment. The legal seizure of the property of a defendant before judgment.
- Autopsy. The dissection of a dead human body, by an authorized doctor, to determine the cause of death.
- Bench Warrant. A court order, in which a criminal action is pending, directing a police officer or a uniformed court officer to take custody of the defendant and bring him or her before the court.
- Circumstantial Evidence. Evidence that includes facts, conditions, and events from which an inference may be drawn as to the existence of the fact to be established.
- Corroborating Evidence. Evidence supplementary to that already given and tending to strengthen or confirm it.
- Direct Evidence. Evidence in the form of testimony from a witness who saw, heard, or touched the subject of interrogation.
- Hearsay Evidence. An out of court statement, offered in court for its truth.
- Physical Evidence. Anything that may be found, by investigators, to have a connection with the crime (i.e., an article of clothing worn by the victim).
- Capital Offense. A crime for which a life sentence or the death penalty is prescribed by law.
- Contempt of Court. Behavior disrespectful of the authority of a court, which obstructs the execution of court orders.
- Contract. An agreement to do or not do a certain thing, which is enforceable in court of law.
- Habeas Corpus. A written order commanding the bringing of the body, of a certain person, before a certain court.
- Corpus Delicti. The body of a crime.
- Inquest. An official hearing to determine the cause of death of a human being.
- Deposition. A sworn statement made before an officer qualified to administer oaths, which is to be used as evidence in a court proceeding.
- Estoppel. A legal prohibition that stops a person from making a particular statement or claim because of something he or she has said or done before.
- Fiduciary. A person who on behalf of or for the benefit of another transacts business or handles money or property not the person's own; such relationship implies great confidence and trust.
- Garnishment. The attachment of debtor's wages or salary to satisfy or pay a judgment.
- Plaintiff. A person who brings a civil action against another.

216 ■ *Healthcare Security*

- Subpoena. A writ or order directed to a person and requiring his or her attendance at a particular time and place to testify as a witness.
- Subpoena Duces Tecum. A process by which the court, at the insistence of a party, commands a witness who has in his possession or control some document or paper that is pertinent to the issues of a pending controversy, to produce it at the trial.
- Tort. A wrongful act; wrong, injury; violation of a legal right.
- True Bill. An indictment handed down by a grand jury.

How Have the Terrorist Attacks of 9/11/01 Affected the Corporate Hiring Process?

Anthony Luizzo

Because internal auditors are generally called upon to review the effectiveness of all corporate programs, including security operations, it is extremely important that audit professionals have at least some knowledge about how security program's function. In this article, we look at how corporate hiring programs are changing in the wake of September 11. The anxious atmosphere since the terrorist attacks of September 11, coupled with escalating reports of workplace violence, employee discontent with corporate downsizing, and a sagging national economy, have compelled organizations to reexamine their hiring practices. From all indications, it looks like many companies that failed to perform background checks prior to that dreadful day in early September 2001 are performing some sort of due diligence today. Seasoned security executives know that one standard strategy employed by terrorists is to seek and gain employment with homeland companies that do *not* perform due-diligence checks. Many of these malefactors actively seek maintenance, engineering, security, and janitorial jobs so that they can more easily document security flaws and weaknesses without attracting unnecessary attention to their clandestine exploits.

Companies Report Increased Interest in Background Checks

In the past few months, there have been several reports in the media about increased corporate diligence regarding hiring practices and background checks. For example: An article in the January 2002 issue of *HR Magazine* called "Background Checks in Focus" notes that since the September 11 terrorist attacks on the World Trade Center and the Pentagon, employment-screening companies report that inquiries about their services are way up. An October 3, 2001, article in the *New York Times* Business Section ("Tense Employers Step Up Background Checks") reports that in a 2000 survey, the Society for Human Resource Management in Virginia found that 61 percent of hiring managers polled had conducted employment screenings within the previous year, compared with 44 percent who said in a separate study two years earlier that they had performed screenings regularly.

In a November 26, 2001, article titled "Background Checks: Now Not the Time to Lie," *Career Builder Magazine* reveals that 69 percent of the human resources professionals polled said that their organization performed background checks in the past year. The corollary to this number is that an amazing 31 percent of firms apparently hire with no background checking at all. This is quite an astonishing revelation, especially considering the thriving underground market for doctored credentials.

Further underscoring the continued need for employment reference checks, various government and private-sector studies indicate that as many as 25 percent of resumes contain false or exaggerated information, and approximately 33 percent of job applicants falsify information in employment applications. Looking even deeper into this abyss of deceit, "The Ways and Means of

---

From *Internal Auditing Report* Warren, Gorham & Lamont / RIA Group (Reuters) Thomson Publications. (2):10, April 2002 – openlibrary@archive.com

218 ■ *Healthcare Security*

Screening," a July 1990 article in the magazine *Security Management*, points to 1985 testimony to the U.S. House Select Committee on Aging that revealed that 60 percent of university and college registrars regularly experience attempts to document fictitious degrees and transcripts.

The Art and Science of Employment Screening

Many organizations, including both the Association of Certified Fraud Examiners (in its 1995-1996 surveys entitled *Report to the Nation on Occupational Fraud and Abuse*) and KPMG Peat Marwick (in its 1993 *Fraud Survey Results*) have championed the checking of employee references as an important corporate strategy to minimize the cost of occupational fraud, waste, and abuse in the workplace. In today's understandably jittery environment, background checks should be a top priority on every hiring executive's agenda. Once upon a time, reference checks consisted solely of companies asking a job applicant for the names of three professional references. Many larger corporations performed only a cursory check of an applicant's past-employment profile, while smaller organizations simply used the "gut feeling" approach to hiring. In this less than adequate environment, how can a hiring executive know with some degree of certainty whether the job seeker has a criminal history, or if he or she is hiding some illegal activity?

Which Employees Need to Be Screened?

All employees should be screened before they are welcomed into the corporate family. Sometimes hiring executives believe that because an employee labors in a lower-level position or does not have fiduciary duties, it is not cost-effective to incur the expense associated with the appropriate screenings. However, it should be kept in mind that courts have held companies responsible for harm caused by employees who have performed criminal acts upon others. Employees requiring due-diligence checks include but are not limited to those who work:

- In security positions.
- In janitorial positions.
- In the public eye.
- In an unsupervised environment.
- Closely with others.
- During off-hour shifts.
- In isolated facilities.
- In off-site positions (e.g., sales or delivery persons).

In-House Versus Outsourcing

Many organizations choose to outsource their background checks to reduce liability and cut staffing costs. Oftentimes, human resources departments outsource these tasks because they lack the in-house expertise required to perform the various searches (e.g., civil, criminal, education, or past employment). This is especially true in smaller firms that rarely have a sophisticated security department to assist management in performing the requisite screening and interviewing functions. Larger firms with multiple locations tend to outsource background screening, primarily because some screening firms design tailored activity reports that fit into the client's universe of special needs. These reports often include a statistical synopsis of activity for each corporate location in a graph, chart, or similar format. Loss-prevention managers find these types of reports helpful in their day-to-day oversight roles.

Individual Privacy Concerns

The safeguarding of personal information is an extremely important issue facing lawmakers today. According to an August 2001 report by the U.S. Department of Justice (*Report of the National Task Force on Privacy, Technology, and Criminal Justice Information*), respondents to a 1999 *Wall Street Journal*/NBC News public-opinion survey were asked, "Which one or two issues concern you the most about the next century?" For 29 percent of the respondents, the potential loss of personal privacy topped the list, finishing ahead of concerns about terrorism, over population, war, and global warming. The task force issued fourteen recommendations covering three broad areas: privacy protection, data quality and security, and data integration and amalgamation. These recommendations are the first steps in the development of a new generation of laws and policies governing criminal justice information.

Questions an Audit Professional Should Ask When Reviewing Hiring Programs

There are certain issues that should be addressed when conducting an audit of the human resources function and its hiring policies and procedures.

Some basic, essential questions are:

- Does the firm have a background-screening program?
- Are such screenings outsourced?
- Does the background-screening program comply with all federal, state, and municipal statutes?
- Does the firm perform background checks on *all* employees?
- Is employee information adequately safeguarded?
- Has legal counsel approved the background-screening program?

Will the Public and Private Sectors Cooperate?

Prognosticating about future trends is like trying to walk on quicksand. However, a glimpse of how employees' background information might be handled in the coming decades is provided in a February 6, 2002, article in the *Wall Street Journal*: "Companies Want the FBI to Screen Employees for Suspected Terrorists." The article discusses how a wide range of industry groups—from trucking associations to sporting-event organizers—are trying to gain access to the FBI's closely guarded database of suspected terrorists and criminals, to screen their own employees. Some associations are even lobbying Congress on this very issue. For an example of how federal and private entities have begun to work together to enhance employee screening, one only needs to look at the Super Bowl. The National Football League had the Super Bowl designated a "national

220 ■ *Healthcare Security*

security special event" so that it could have the FBI run the names of concession workers and stadium employees through its database. Because Congress would have to approve giving private entities access to the federal database, industry mavens see a nationwide privatization effort as unlikely. However, it is quite likely that several future events will be classified as "national security special events."

Background Checks: A Diagnostic Tool to Decipher Deception

Anthony Luizzo, Bernard J. Scaglione, Philip Luizzo

Why perform background checks?

Looking back to our recent past, with the tragic incidents of Oklahoma City, TWA Flight 800, Atlanta Olympic Park bombing, World Trade Center tragedy, the Boston Marathon bombing corporate America understands all too well the value of background screening as a protection tool. An October 3, 2001, article in the New York Times Business Section "Tense Employers Step-up Background Checks" recounted that in a 2000 survey, the Society for Human Resource Management found that 61 percent of hiring managers polled had conducted employment screenings within the previous year, compared to 44 percent who said in a separate study two years earlier that they had performed screenings regularly. A November 26, 2001, article in career Builder Magazine revealed that 69 percent of HR professionals polled said that their organization performed background checks in the previous year. The corollary to this number is that an amazing 31 percent of firms apparently hired without ever performing a background check. It seems that hiring professionals have had a change of philosophy according to the Background Investigator Magazine: December 2013 issue revealed that 92 percent of employers run background checks today. Without a doubt, we have come along way since the turn of the 21st century. Notwithstanding, security mavens should continue preaching the protection gospel to business that performing background checks helps capture crime-related instances before and after crime and deceptive behavior rears its ugly face.

The Healthcare Crime Problem

Healthcare institutions are experiencing increases in domestic violence, assaults, theft of hospital property, fraudulent behavior related to Medicaid and Medicare reimbursement, drug, and supply diversion, as well as theft of medical devices. These and other incidents are not isolated to the patient/visitor population but involve hospital employees as well. Beyond physical altercations, newly acquired access to cash, from insurance co-payments are being diverted into employees' pockets. Moreover, easy access to vital patient demographic information, including patient's dates of birth, social security numbers, home addresses, maiden names, and credit/debit card data, are being purloined and illegally used and/or sold in a galaxy of identity theft schemes. One only need look at the recent corporate data breaches (Target Stores, TJ Max, Marshalls, etc.) to comprehend the massive extent of this problem.

Drug related offenses are on the rise as well. In some cases, drugs are being diverted for the personal use of drug dependent staff, and/or drugs and hospital supplies are being diverted to third world countries or sold on E-Bay. It is estimated that approximately 3,000 items are used on a daily schedule in the healthcare field (from aspirins to stethoscopes). In addition, employees have been found diverting used and new medical devices like endoscopes, blood pressure cuffs,

From *Journal of Healthcare Protection Management*. (30):2, pp. 57–65. 2014.

222 ■ *Healthcare Security*

thermometers, IV pumps and even anesthesia machines to unscrupulous fraudsters and selling these items on E-Bay or to third world countries. Healthcare losses associated with these items are catastrophic, costing healthcare providers millions of dollars in lost revenue each year.

According to an October 2011 congressional report <u>"FOREIGN SPIES STEALING U.S. ECONOMIC SECRETS IN CYBERSPACE"</u> published by the National Counterintelligence Executive Office, health care fraud in the U.S. is estimated at $80 billion a year (a conservative estimate we might add). The executive director of the National Health Care Anti-Fraud Association (NHCAA) estimates that health care related identity theft dominates fraud crimes in all industry categories. Delving even deeper into this abyss of criminality, a 2012 Ernst & Young Survey <u>"GROWING BEYOND: A PLACE for INDUSTRY"</u> estimates that nearly <u>90%</u> of organizations nationwide experienced some type of fraud in the last 12 months. The U.S. Chamber of Commerce estimates that employees purloin approximately 400 billion from business annually. Citing these and other dire statistics, fraud examiners and white-collar investigators continue to sound the siren that a full menu of security approaches including background checks must be instituted to keep patients, medical staff, and visitor's safe, while controlling continued financial bleeding.

The ABCs of Background Screening

Many hospital administrators may be puzzled re which screening tools to use to reduce these and other costly crimes. Some have hired consultants that have added levels of security to the supply chain, implemented complicated firewalls to computer networks, and helped hospitals implement policies and procedures that are intended to reduce and/or mitigate these types of events. Notwithstanding, the simplest and most effective method of reducing violence and theft is often overlooked or grossly misunderstood by hospital administrators. According to many protection management experts the best financial bang for the security buck is to institute a comprehensive *"employee background screening program before corporate assets leave the institution"*. According to the Association of Certified Fraud Examiners in its annual reports to the nation on occupational fraud and abuse, <u>checking employee references</u> is one of the most important and effective strategies corporations can employ to minimize the cost of occupational fraud and abuse. KPMG's fraud surveys also conclude that <u>performing extensive reference checks on new employees best prevents fraud</u>.

Screening-Related Legislation

To help the healthcare industry control violence against patients and reduce product diversion; governmental legislation presently requires healthcare facilities to provide background investigations to most employee classifications. Presently, 36 States have some form of background screening legislation affecting healthcare employees. Examples include: the state of Ohio received a $2.1 million-dollar federal grant to authorize health-care companies to be immediately notified if workers have been convicted of a crime that would ban them from employment. The Illinois General Assembly implemented criminal background check legislation affecting health care workers and employees of licensed and certified long-term care facilities that have or may have contact with residents, financial, medical, or personal records. In 2011, the Michigan legislature modified its statute requiring criminal history checks for employees of nursing homes, county medical care facilities, hospices, hospitals that provide swing bed services, homes for the aged, home health agencies, mental health facilities, and adult foster care facilities.

The National Background Check Program (NBCP) part of the Patient Protection and Affordable Care Act and the Health Care and Education Reconciliation Act of 2010 conducted via the Center for Medicare & Medicaid Services (CMS), requires employees who have access to patients or residents of long-term care facilities to undergo a national background check. Legislation is pending in other states, and it should be anticipated that additional legislation will be mandated in the future.

The Background Investigation Program

There are basic program prerequisites associated with performing a healthcare related background check. First and foremost, the healthcare organization should with concurrence of legal counsel promulgate policies and procedures that guide the institution through the screening process. Policies should include: a general statement that outlines the program's philosophy, offers program objectives, outlines participant's rights under the program. *It is strongly suggested that these policies be written in easy-to-understand language for all to understand.* The program should be written in different languages depending on the labor pool and should be posted in plain view for all persons to see and read. Moreover, policies should outline in detail the steps that will be taken during the process including: how information is collected, collection methods, safeguarding guidelines, and who has access to viewing the information? Pursuant to the Fair Credit Reporting Act (FCRA), these policies should also indicate the penalties associated with each type of finding and indicate the person (s) or third-party companies that the candidate can contact in the event of a dispute.

When instituting a background check program, the most important decision to ponder is which population should be screened, and when the check should occur? Traditionally, institutions commence the background check upon acceptance of employment. But to save money some hospitals resort to checking only specific job classifications or categories, sometimes determined by risk. For example, persons working in the Finance Department are usually screened because they have access to large amounts of patient demographic information, cash and checks. Individuals that work with children are checked to see if they have any prior convictions related to child abuse. Security staff is checked because they protect public safety. The decision to check specific job classifications or the entire population may not be made by the hospital; but determined by State law or Union contract. Either way this decision should be made prior to implementing a program and should be outlined in the background screening policy. <u>*It's important to remember that in the court of protection management opinion, experts suggest that all employees should undergo a background check*</u>.

The next decision which again may be pre-determined by law or contract is when to conduct the background check. Most States require the check only be conducted after the person becomes an employee of the institution. So once an offer is accepted for employment many institutions will include background check release forms to be signed when the new employee comes to the facility to be processed for employment. Fingerprint checks include a statewide check for arrests and convictions, and in some cases include a federal background check as well. Unfortunately, State fingerprint checks only provide information in that particular jurisdiction. Employees who reside or previously resided in other States are not checked through a Statewide fingerprint check.

Even a federal check does <u>not</u> always provide relevant data outside of the State check since some States have lax reporting rules, and/or may not send their conviction data to the Federal

224 ■ *Healthcare Security*

government for inclusion in the background check database. The next step in starting a background check program is the decision to either conduct checks in-house or use a third-party firm that specializes in background screening services. Setting up an in-house program can be expensive and data collection may be limited. Using a contracted service oftentimes means more available staff and an extended network of resources to reach outside of the region for additional information. Many hospitals that have the legislative authority to conduct fingerprint checks do so in-house; and rely on a third-party service to retrieve data outside of the scope of the fingerprint check.

The Human Resources Department usually handles the evaluation of background check results. It is important to note that oftentimes, H. R. staff may <u>not always</u> be familiar with the terminology used in the criminology discipline. It is suggested that seasoned security personnel be contacted for assistance in evaluating and deciphering this often-complex data. This is especially appropriate to help decipher lengthy, often complicated case dispositions or third-party dispositions. Some hospitals send background check results directly to the security department for review and consultation.

Once the review is completed, the results are forwarded back to the HR department for action and storage. If the background evaluation disqualifies a perspective employee, then appropriate action should be taken. If the person disputes the accuracy of the report, he/she should be given time to provide an acceptable disposition. If the person is unable to do so or acknowledges the accuracy of the information, employment should be reevaluated.

One Time Search vs. Perpetual Search

Probably the most misunderstood part of the background check process is the continuation of the check during the life of the employee. Many hospitals' feel it is only necessary to do an initial check at the time of hire, and not thereafter. The problem with that philosophy is that an employee can be convicted of a crime at any time during employment and the hospital may never know it. Property crimes occurring within the hospital can go undetected, and violent crimes may not be uncovered and possibly prevented without this vital knowledge. If a hospital is authorized to conduct a State or Federal fingerprint check then most State agencies will offer the option of being notified when a previously screened employee is convicted of a felony. The decision to continually check employees is a difficult one to ponder but may be the eventual difference between a lawsuit from an affected employee or the loss of thousands of dollars in hospital assets.

Primary Source vs. Secondary Source Data

Primary source documentation is data that is retrieved directly from governmental archives. This type of data includes:

- ■ Court criminal, civil and related records
- ■ Diaries, speeches, manuscripts, letters, interviews, news film footage, autobiographies, and official government records.
- ■ Creative Works: Poetry, drama, novels
- ■ A journal article reporting new research or findings

When conducting background investigations or utilizing a third party to obtain background information, primary source documentation is especially important. The use of primary source documentation provides for a more accurate and comprehensive evaluation of background information. Primary source data connotes an investigator/retriever physically goes to the court or government agency and views and retrieves copies of original documentation.

(It is important to note that there are 3,144 counties in the United States where criminal records are achieved.) It is important to recognize there is no interpretation or evaluation involved – just the facts and data. The investigator then uses the primary source information obtained from: social security info, birth dates, birth records, driver license data etc., to establish the infrastructure for his report.

Secondary Source Data

Secondary source retrieving involves interpreting newspaper and other data base sources that may have originally been compiled from primary source data. Oftentimes, these data sources are one or more steps removed from the original documented event. Secondary sources may have pictures, quotes, or graphics of primary sources in them, but are not original information.

This type of data includes but is not limited to:

- Compiled Data Bases Searches
- Website Searches
- Journal/Magazine Article's which Interpret or Review Previous Findings

It is important to understand that secondary source data has its strong points including the depth, breadth and reach of data availability, coupled with the speed and cost of obtaining it. Notwithstanding, secondary source data should only be used in conjunction with primary source data in the decision-making process. The results of using secondary information exclusively can cost a company more than it wishes to spend and could result in a legion of criminal exposures. Case in point, a January 2014 article **U.S. Accuses Security Background Check Firm of Fraud** published in the Wall Street Journal. The U.S. Justice Department adduces that USIS methodically filed flawed Background Investigations and fined the contractor for using *secondary source* information.

Looking Back to the Future

Due in large measure to all the new federal and governmental screening-related legislation, conjoined with the launch of the internet, screening companies have begun offering many additional search options for companies to consider including: i9, E Verify, Sex Offender, Social Media Reviews, Face Book, and MY Space searches, etc. Casting an investigative eye to the future, some more forward-thinking screening firms have begun offering several expanded services including performing annual update searches of existing employees. It is important to note that prior to commencing any new screening initiatives companies should seek legal counsel's guidance and ensure that their existing general release includes these new provisions.

Conclusion

Preventing and reducing crime is not an easy task! Security requisites vary from institution to institution, industry to industry, and position to position.

Proactive security virtuosi instinctually know that there is no single set of preventative protective strategies that guarantee a crime-free workplace. Notwithstanding, businesses would be wise to launch *man-sized* background screening programs to capture fraud and deceptive behavior before it can wreak havoc on the corporate bottom line. Inasmuch as, fraudsters' have a long history of plying their trade, should not necessarily mean that they can easily become a long-term partner in your enterprise! Consider the alternative; not applying proactive diagnostic protective screening strategies will surely make the **FRAUDSTER'S Day!**

A New Approach to Handling Incoming Verifications

Anthony Luizzo, Bill Roy, Philip Luizzo

Few medical center administrators spend time pondering how incoming requests for employment and salary verifications are managed. Considering that this task puts at risk a considerable amount of personal data, encompassing countless employees, it is important that management cast an investigative eye on how this treasure-trove of sensitive data is lied, disseminated, and safeguarded. Often, when a company does _**not**_ have a corporate policy skeletonizing task specifics most likely the task gets completed in a variety of ways; some of which may not be in the firm's best overall interest. The exact number of verifications that are handled by each company is a hard number to pin down. Depending upon the industry and its turnover rate, experience shows that approximately 50-60% of a company's employee base will generate incoming verifications on an annual basis.

Type of Information being Disseminated

When a current or previous employee worked for your institution and moved on to another entity and/or position, the employee's pedigree (wages, position tenure) is requested by a wide variety of external sources including prospective employers, financial institutions, corporate entities, etc. These sources require the information to substantiate claims on job applications, by financial institutions considering whether to grant a loan or issue a credit instrument, or by a company considering extending credit to the employee to purchase an item. Furnishing this information is oftentimes provided gratis but the company at an expense that is not retrievable. Beyond the expense and budgetary considerations associated with disseminating this information, there is also a question of liability if the information is not distributed accurately. The question that companies need to ask is who in your firm is handling these inquiries and whether the information being disseminated is accurate.

A hypothetical Scenario:

Depending on the size of the healthcare system, a variety of departmental entities may be responsible for handling incoming verifications including but not limited to: HR, Payroll, the external support personnel in nursing homes, clinics, etc. Seeing that many incoming verification requests often list supervisory personnel as a contact, it is always possible that absent a corporate policy mandating that corporate only perform these searches, many may end up being completed by coworkers who may have developed a bias against the employee and/or had previous work-related disagreements. Notwithstanding how a hospital or affiliated medical facility disseminates this treasure-trove of information, it is imperative that a standardized process be put in place to ensure that this data is strictly controlled and disseminated to its intended destination in a safe, secure, and non-controversial manner. Some medical facilities may choose to outsource this sensitive function to reduce liability and reduce internal costs entirely.

From *Journal of Healthcare Protection Management*. (32):2, pp: 95–99. 2016-2017.

228 ■ *Healthcare Security*

Aspects of Handling Inbound Verifications

1. <u>Do you really know where your inbound verification calls are going?</u>
   A good rule of thumb here is to get a pad and paper and map out how requests are being handled and how the staff is performing this task. Check to see whether a written policy is available and if it is being adhered to. And ascertain whether verifications are being provided on a local basis by non-HR personnel?
2. <u>Do you really know if the verification information furnished is accurate?</u>
   Once the data is collected, is anyone in management reviewing the information both for content and accuracy before it is disseminated?
3. <u>Are you ensuring that the requesters are legitimate?</u>
   Are incoming requestors called to verify authenticity?
4. <u>Is it your policy to furnish employment and income information via phone or fax?</u>
   If telephonic and/or facsimile adjudication is allowed does the company have a process in place to verify discrepancies? On example might be to have an internal taping capability to backtrack and retrieve information.
5. <u>Is a signed release required?</u>
   Is anyone in the company auditing the process and are releases received for all requests?

Managing Incoming Verifications: In-House vs. Outsourcing

Handling Incoming Requests In-House

If your company manages verifications in house, are you properly vetting all requestors? Do you verify who forwarded the incoming request, and whether they have a permissible purpose for requesting it? Do you want an administrator or lower-level HR person to have full access to the HRIS or payroll system including salaries for executives, etc.? Do you have policies and procedures specifically stipulating that only the facts: applicant's name, dates of employment, positions held is being disseminated? (Often, some companies with more lax policies may not know that personal information and biases are also being disseminated.)

Reviewing your in-house incoming verification process made simple

Questions you might consider asking might include:

- Who is requesting the information?
- Who in-house is responsible for disseminating the information?
- What information are we disseminating?
- How are we providing the information? (Fax, phone, email, snail mail)

These and other inquiries will help to ascertain how your existing program is working and whether changes should be considered.

Outsourcing Verification Requests

Engaging with an outside vendor is an option more and more companies are considering. Historically, only the exceptionally large companies outsourced verifications; while small and mid-sized companies have their HR and payroll staff handle the incoming flow. Today, however, companies of all sizes are looking at outsourcing verifications for several reasons including reducing labor burdens and HR costs, reducing liability, and improving the turn-around time for fulfilling these requests.

Navigating from the in-house to the outsourcing model

Moving from an in-house verification model to an outsourcing model is simpler than you may think. With today's technology either an API or DIRECT file feeds from your payroll provider is all it takes. Moving to the outsource model helps a company to eliminate a costly and often sensitive assignment by engaging a reliable alternative third part entity. This process can be a win-win for all parties concerned. Moreover, any programmatic shift that helps to pad the company's bottom line without sacrificing reliability is a triumph.

Integration made easy

A simple phone call to your payroll provider mentioning that you will be using the services of a third-party verification firm is all it takes. Integrating can be handled via a flat file each payroll period. You should ensure that at minimum, this is sent using SFTP protocols. An alternative and increasing popular method is to build an API integration that allows the fulfilling entity to request only the pertinent data for each request, as opposed to sending a full file each pay period. While either can be safe, there are benefits to utilizing the API where available.

Benefits of outsourcing incoming verifications

Outsourcing with the right company can improve verification turn-around times and accuracy thereby allowing the individual seeking an apartment to close the deal more quickly, the person buying a new or used vehicle to begin using the vehicle sooner than later, and the new home buyer to move into their new abode more promptly. In all cases, HR will be able to use the time saved to tackle more strategic projects and hopefully generate additional revenue for the firm. Outsourcing verifications to a professional firm can improve the overall dissemination policy, reduce labor costs, and diminish liability exposures.

Stretching the Shrinking Healthcare Dollar

Stretching the healthcare dollar especially in today's budget conscious environment is a most important issue. Healthcare executives would be wise to seek strategies to turn cost centers into revenue centers. The trick is discerning where these programmatic efficiencies can be found. Surprisingly, a few third-party verification companies offer attractive incentive programs which return previously lost dollars to the institution. If you plan on outsourcing inbound verifications, it is wise to check around to find the best deal for your institution.

A Final Thought

Shining sunlight on any process helps growth and wellness! These and other strategies help to deepen and strengthen existing policies and procedures by fostering the philosophy that sensitive information is always handled responsibly. Oftentimes, it is this skillful display of resourcefulness by management and staff that helps to ensure that all incoming verifications are handled appropriately. Over and above performing the verification, it is equally important to properly shield and archive this sensitive data from unauthorized access and conning.

Forensics Role in the Investigative Process

Anthony Luizzo and John Gaspar

We have written several articles for PI Magazine speaking to background checks, proactive security programming, drafting security surveys, and the art and science of interviewing and interrogation [1-6]. This article will focus on testing the accuracy or inaccuracy of information gleaned during an interview and/or interrogation. Whether forensic science brings you to the table or not, once the table is set and all interviews have been completed, it's time for substantiating interview assertions. Skilled sleuths instinctively know that testing the accuracy of all assertions is like peeling back the onion on people, places, and things. Their guiding beacon should always be to *never trust and always verify*. Eyewitnesses are sometimes fallible, but science lays out the truth in plain sight. Looking back over the past century criminologists have moved from fingerprint identification to DNA tagging, tire / foot printing, and fabric pattern deciphering to name a few. To quote Sir Winston Churchill: "The future is undistinguishable, but the *PAST* gives us guidance". What is ahead is to understand that the future of science is yet unwritten!

Definition of forensic evidence

Black's Law Dictionary defines forensic evidence as any evidence that either proves or disproves any matter in question.

Evolution of forensics

Man's quest to solve crimes dates to ancient civilizations. Over 2000 years ago a dynasty emperor in ancient China had one of his closest friends killed by someone from within his court. To solve the crime, the emperor called each suspected person to appear before him for questioning. Everyone interviewed denied having anything to do with the murder. The emperor then ordered each suspect to lay their swords in front of them. The emperor then ordered his "royal archers" to stand at the ready with arrows pointed at each suspect. The visual sword inspection revealed that each of the swords were bloodstain free. The emperor then dispatched one of his subjects to the local slaughterhouse to retrieve a band of flies which he later released where the swords laid waiting. The flies sensing the bloodstain made a beeline to the contaminated sword. The subject who owned the sword immediately confessed and pled for his life. Justice was served as the emperor had his archers furnish justice with a flurry of arrows. The Father of the Forensic Sciences was the French criminologist Dr. Edmond Locard in the late 1800's (called the Sherlock Holmes of France). Locard created a handbook of principles and processes to preserve collect and evaluate evidence that supports or refutes witness accounts of a crime [7]. Lockard's exchange principle is still taught in all accredited crime scene universities and is used today at all criminal and civil crime scenes. The exchange principle states: *wherever one steps, whatever one touches, whatever one leaves at the crime scene is evidence.* This evidentiary mother-load includes but is not limited to fingerprints, footprints, hair follicles, clothing fibers, tool markings, paint particles, impression

---

From *PI Magazine*. (20):172, pp. 8–11. November/December 2020.

232 ■ *Healthcare Security*

evidence, trace evidence blood, bodily fluid and/or semen deposits all of which help forensic crime scene investigators solve crime puzzles.

Unlike eyewitnesses, this type of evidence does *not* forget, *never* becomes confused and is always extremely reliable. In criminologist circles this is factual, super reliable and perjure-proof evidence. The only adverse issue with this evidence is human failure to find it, study it, and understand it!

Evidence types

Evidentiary evidence includes:

- Class evidence – tire tracks, footwear), soil samples, paint chips, pry marks, impression evidence
- Individual evidence – fingerprints, DNA, ballistic striations
- Forensic fiduciary evidence – profit/loss estimations, internal control evaluations, ratio analysis studies, errors, and irregularities canvasses, etc.

Class and Individual evidence

It is important to note that individual evidence has a greater value than class evidence in that this type of evidence helps to put a suspect at the scene of the crime; and is usually irrefutable. Both class and individual evidence are helpful in both criminal and non-criminal cases. The Crime Museum located in Washington DC is an excellent educational resource and repository on the forensic sciences. Their library contains a treasure-trove of insightful factual forensic data on *dangerous substances* (lead, radium, etc.), *biological evidence* (hair, blood, DNA analysis), *impression evidence* (ballistics, bite marks, fingerprints, footprints, tire tracks), *trace evidence* (fibers, soil, glass, handwriting analysis) [8].

Fiduciary evidence

Like other professions, investigators are not all specialists. The forensic investigative sleuth is trained to analyze, interpret, and summarize complex financial and business-related matters. Many firms team CPAs and investigators to work on these often-complex white-collar misdeeds. Typically, these financial sleuths are called to investigate crimes such as bribery, blackmail, embezzlement, extortion, and forgery. Further information on how the team approach delves deep into deciphering criminality can be found in two articles coauthored by the undersigned [9-10]. Customarily, these fiduciary investigators undergo hours of specialized training and are appropriately credentialed. One of the largest organizations offering training and certification in this forensic discipline is the Association of Certified Fraud Examiners [11]. Two examples of how these forensic wizards do their magic can be found by simply looking at the following cases:

Tablecloth case

A business owner reported a huge income drop at his restaurant.

The conventional investigative approach almost always involves interviewing restaurant staff and employing surveillance technologies to hopefully capture the fraudster at work. The forensic specialist's approach almost always begins quite differently in that before any standard conventional investigative strategies are initiated, basic accounting sales vs. cash metric comparisons are immediately employed to gauge the extent of the fraudulent activity. This metric application involves ascertaining the number of meals served for a given period and comparing it to the number of tablecloths used during that same period.

Having this data in-hand helps to immediately gauge the extent of the institution's theft problem and gives the forensic investigator a starting point from which to begin his or her investigative magic.

Skimming case

A seafood restaurant owner reported huge cash losses at her restaurant. In this case scenario, the forensic sleuth would begin by applying the "anti-skimming strategy" to help ascertain whether cash receipts were being removed. Technologically, both video and audit strategies need to be instituted to help ascertain the magnitude of these frauds. The internal mechanics of this form of investigative exercise includes checking whether cash sales dropped or spiked, checking whether currency spikes or drops occurred especially while managerial staff were absent, checking whether cash register tapes disclosed irregularities, checking whether surreptitious video (eye in the sky) recordings revealed irregularities, and ascertaining whether certified audits were regularly completed. More artful forensic detectives know that skimming is most common in cash-rich businesses such as restaurants, food stores, candy stores and other similar retail establishments. Oftentimes, these schemes left unchecked will continue for long periods of time. It is important to note that periodical audits by credentialed audit and accounting firms can help catch these fraud schemes early on before necessitating criminal intervention. These simple audit and video approaches help to quickly gauge the magnitude of the fraud problem and stop the financial bleeding before it totally kills the business.

Looking back to the future

The field of forensic science is traveling at warp speed. Since the turn of the 20th century the main forensic tool used by protection advocates was the fingerprint. Today, there is a galaxy of tools in the investigative toolbox to help fight the war on both white and blue-collar crime. The astute forensic detective's job is to make sure that every piece of evidence is collected, catalogued, safeguarded, and forensically evaluated. The key to solving the crime puzzle may very well be a simple hair follicle, tire track, clothing fiber, blood stain or forensic accounting metric!

References

1. Luizzo, A. & Luizzo, P. Handling Incoming Verifications - PI Magazine: March / April 2017 - pp. 14-17
2. Luizzo, A. The Security Survey: an Investigative Tool – PI Magazine: March / April 2018 - pp. 28-30
3. Luizzo, A. The Security Survey: an Investigative Tool: Part II - PI Magazine: September / October 2018 - pp. 22-25
4. Luizzo, A. A Clinical Approach to Crime Detection – PI Magazine: January / February 2019 - pp. 12-14

234 ■ *Healthcare Security*

5. Luizzo, A. & Gaspar, J. Demystifying the Investigative Process - PI Magazine: November / December 2019 - pp. 6-9.
6. Luizzo, A. & Gaspar, J. Decrypting the Interrogation Process - PI Magazine: March / April 2020 - pp. 10-12.
7. Trace Evidence: Principles www.forensicsciencesimplified.org › trace › principles
8. https://www.crimemuseum.org/crime-library/forensic-investigation/
9. Luizzo, A. & Calhoun, C. Team Partners in Fraud Detection – The CPA Journal: October 1002 - pp.32-35.
10. Luizzo, A. & Calhoun, C. Fraud Auditing: A Complete Guide – New York State Society of Certified Public Accountants and The Foundation for Accounting Education: 1992, (Rev) 1995.
11. https://www.acfe.com

Suggested Reading

Illustrated Guide to Crime Scene Investigations CRC Publisher by Nicholas Petraco & Hal Sherman ISBN# 0-8493-2263-4

Definition of Forensic Evidence - https://thelawdictionary.org/forensic-evidence/

Techniques of Crime Scene Investigations CRS Press by Barry Fisher ISBN # 0-8493-1691-X

Definition of Skimming: https://www.accountingtools.com/articles/2018/1/27/skimming

---

*Reprinted with permission: PI Magazine

Chapter 10

Fraud Detection and Prevention

Play It Safe: A Guide to Preventing Shoplifting, Fraud and Employee Theft

Anthony Luizzo

Shoplifting, check and credit card fraud and employee theft plague merchants of all sizes, form the retail giants in Midtown to the corner grocery store. Although these crimes may seem like a fact of business life, they can be dramatically reduced-and sometimes stopped – if you take the right preventive measures. *Play It Safe* is a "hands-on" guide to help you make it harder for shoplifters, forgers, and dishonest employees to steal.

The foundation of any successful theft prevention program is education. You, the storeowner, or manager, must first understand how these criminals think and act – their modus operandi. And then you must teach your employees. Indeed, your employees require not only a firm grasp on how these seemingly "petty crimes" are committed, but they must also understand the detrimental effect they have on the business and their own livelihoods. In the case of dishonest employees, storeowners must be sure that all employees clearly understand what constitutes theft and what the consequences are.

Shoplifting

Recognizing the Shoplifter

Most shoplifters are amateurs. According to the Small Business Administration, half of all shoplifters are minors, many of whom steal for "kicks" or because of peer pressure. These young people often travel through stores in packs, hoping that their numbers will both confuse and intimidate store management. Too often, it does.

From *BROCHURE* Published by the New York City Mayor's Office of Business Services. 1987.

DOI: 10.4324/9781003215851-10

235

236 ■ *Healthcare Security*

Retailers report that most adults who shoplift are women, frequently "average" housewives who would hardly arouse suspicion, and usually first-time offenders. When caught, these women often blame their crime on an uncontrollable – and often unexplainable- impulse.

Then there is the professional shoplifter whose "business" is stealing – the careful criminal who knows all the tricks of his trade. These thieves are harder to detect, but they can be deterred. As in the case of more violent crimes, these criminals look for an "easy mark" and tend to steer clear of stores that have instituted tough theft control programs. Word spreads quickly in the criminal community.

Finally, there is a narcotics addict, the most dangerous of all shoplifters. When dealing with suspected addicts, always call the police for assistance.

Note:

Shoplifting has evolved into a multi-cultural business – featuring gangs from several countries plying their trade in commercial neighborhoods city-wide. Business owners would be wise to contact law enforcement to ascertain crime-related data for their commercial centers.

How People Shoplift

Where there is a will, there is a way, they say. Unfortunately, human ingenuity can be brought to bear on tasks as different as walking on the moon and walking out of your store with expensive merchandise. Over the years, shoplifters have developed a variety of methods – some obvious, some ingenious, all damaging to your business. Here are some of the more common ones to look out for:

Palming – An obvious method. The shoplifter merely carries a stolen item out in the palm of his hand, often while concealing it with another object, such as a newspaper or umbrella.

Bagging – Also obvious. The shoplifter enters the store carrying a bag of some type – a shopping bag, large purse, briefcase, knitting bag, diaper bag, etc. – and leaves with more than he or she entered with.

"Special" Clothing – Some shoplifters wear special clothing to conceal merchandise – outer garments with slits or vents in the pockets, pants and skirts with elastic, expandable waistbands, oversized underwear, blocked hats, unusually baggy ski hats, or clothing with pins or hooks sewn into them to hold merchandise.

The Try-On Method – The shoplifter innocently enters the dressing room to try on several items … and casually leaves with one or more items concealed under his or her own clothing, perhaps thanking the salesperson as he heads for the door.

The Grab and Run Method – Crude but effective. The thief finds an unattended section of the store, usually near a convenient exit, grabs several items and beats a path to the door.

The Team Approach – Shoplifters commonly work in teams, using a variant of the "Hey, look over there" method of swiping. One person creates a disturbance to occupy the clerk's attention while a partner steals your merchandise.

How to Stop Them

Despite all the clever techniques employed by shoplifters, there are ways to shift the odds in your favor. Here are some of the most important:

"Check Your Bag at the Door Please" – It seems an obvious precaution, but many storeowners choose not to check bags either because of the added labor or because they do not want to give the appearance of distrusting the customers. A sign announcing your store's bag-check policy should be prominently displayed at entrances and merchandise areas.

"Only Three Items Per Customer in Fitting Rooms" – Another simple precaution designed to keep customers honest behind the curtain. Simply post an employee at the entrance of the fitting room area to issue numbered tags (correlated to the number of items) to entering customers. The employee's job is to make sure that every customer who enters with three garments also comes out with three garments.

Note:

One of the most effective methods of <u>PREVENTING</u> shoplifting is to install ELECTRONIC ARTICLE SURVEILLANCE TECHNOLOGIES AT INGRESS AND EGRESS POINTS & TO FASTEN ALARM SENSOR TAGES TO INDIVIDUAL ITEMS.

Plan a Smart Store Layout

Store layout is an important component in making the shoplifter's life difficult. The key is to keep sight lines open, so that would-be shoplifters have few hidden spaces in which to work. Here are some tips:

- Keep store windows free from obstructions and keep to a minimum in-store display materials that can obstruct visibility. Instead, suspend these materials from the ceiling whenever possible.
- Expensive clothing items should be displayed away from exits. Either attach hangers to racks by a chain or alternate the position of every other hanger. By alternating hangers, the "grab and run" shoplifter can only grab one item at a time. More important, you will break his rhythm and force him to draw attention to himself.
- Small, high priced items such as jewelry should be kept in locked display cases. And position display counters in a broken, random sequence, rather than one continuous aisle leading to the door. With this design, a fleeing "grab and run" shoplifter will have a more difficult dash for the street.
- Keep large, expensive items away from the flow of exiting traffic. One effective way of maintaining visibility for these products while also safeguarding them is to keep a secured sample in high traffic areas.

Fraud

Bad Checks and Credit Card Fraud

Bad checks and fraudulent use of credit cards can seriously hurt any merchant's business. But there's hope. The first step is to establish a clear policy on check cashing and credit card use at your store and post it conspicuously.

238 ■ *Healthcare Security*

> **Note:**
> 1. The dissemination of counterfeit bills has become a major concern of business owners nation-wide – it is strongly recommended that counterfeit currency scanners be used at all point-of-sale registers
> 2. Suspicious checks should be reported to the U.S. Secret Service @ www.secret service.gov/fieldoffices - checks received by mail should be reported to the U.S. Postal Service @ 1-877-876-2455

Detecting Bad Checks

The key to detecting bad checks is checking identification. Always ask customers to print their address and telephone number on checks and insist on two forms of I.D., including valid driver's license, local bank or charge cards, or major credit cards. Never accept Social Security or library cards. As a final safeguard, require the store manager's approval on all checks.

Always be on guard for the following kinds of checks, which often signal trouble:

- Out-of-state checks
- Blank checks (without customer or bank name printed on them)
- Typewritten checks
- Checks that have a discrepancy between the numerical and written amounts
- Checks with an illegible signature
- Two-party checks
- Monthly government checks
- Checks that do not have at least one perforated edge, and
- Checks written for a larger amount than the purchase

Avoiding Credit Card Fraud

The phony or stolen credit card has become the scourge of business – a thriving illegal industry that runs up billions of dollars in fraudulent charges every year at the public's expense. But you can limit your liability by following some of these precautions:

- Treat all credit card transactions as seriously as you would a sale.
- Always follow the credit card company's instructions to the letter.
- Always get a credit card authorization from the company, regardless of the amount being charged.
- Watch closely for indiscriminate buying. If a shopper is making purchases as if he or she were spending someone else's money, maybe they are. And be especially aware of customers who seem restless, impatient, or nervous.
- Always obtain verification that the card is valid.
- Always compare the customer's signature on the back of the credit card with the signature on the credit card slip.
- Always try to determine if the customer is the card owner, or if they are authorized to use the card, if available, check photograph on the card.
- Always look carefully at the credit card; check the expiration date and be suspicious if the card appears to have been altered in any way.

Fraud Detection and Prevention ■ **239**

- If you are suspicious for any reason, ask to see more identification.
- Always return carbon slips to customers or tear them up immediately. This prevents credit card criminals from obtaining "live" names and numbers to create fraudulent cards.

Employee Theft

When Employees Steal

You pay them a fair wage and treat them well. So why do some employees steal? There are as many reasons for theft as there are incidences. Some employees simply do not consider taking an item or two stealing – they would rather think of it as one of the "perks" of the job. Others point to a spur of the moment impulse, the same reason cited by some shoplifters. Unfortunately, some employees are calculating criminals who have penetrated your organization because it is often easier to steal from the inside.

How Employees Steal

As in the case of shoplifting, dishonest employees have a variety of methods of bleeding your business. Like a shoplifter, they can carry out merchandise in pocketbooks and bags or wear it out as if it were their own – these are the "Carry-Out" and "Wear-Out" methods. Working with confederates, they can either hand out merchandise in the store or have it mailed out or delivered- these are the "Hand-Out" and "Send-Out" methods.

Stealing cash is an even more frightening prospect. Some of the more common techniques in this area include:

- Failing to ring up a sale and pocketing the cash, sometimes leaving a $00.00 or "no-sale" transaction recorded on the register.
- Under-ringing a sale and removing the cash difference.
- "Voiding" a legitimate sale and removing an equal amount from the register, and
- Writing a fraudulent document, usually a refund slip or a substitute register slip, and pocketing the sum written.

Stopping Employee Theft

Employee theft sounds so easy…and it is unless you take steps to make it harder. Here are some general guidelines:

Know Who You are Hiring – Conduct a thorough pre-employment screening and background check on all prospective employees. Take extra precaution when hiring temporary employees during high-volume periods, such as holiday season.

Temporary employees have even less of a stake in your business than full-timers, so theft can be even more tempting. So, avoid assigning them to cash register duties and theft prone departments such as refund/return, shipping, and merchandise marking.

Be Candid with Employees – Don't' Shrink from the task of acknowledging employee theft, or the serious legal consequences. The goal is to prevent crime by making certain that everyone

240 ■ *Healthcare Security*

knows the rules. If possible, have employees sign a document that confirms their knowledge of what constitutes theft in your store.

Create Team Spirit – Theft prevention requires cooperation. Draw employees into your plan – after all, the health of your business directly affects their livelihood.

Here are more specific ways to curbing employee theft:

Stopping the 'Carry-Out' Thief

- Launch a package inspection program to put employees on notice that carrying items home is theft and will not be tolerated.
- Have employees enter and exit through a designated door. Ideally, post a security guard there to inspect packages.
- Require all store employees to abide by the same rules, managers and supervisors included.
- Do not allow employees to carry handbags on the selling floor. If necessary, provide lockers for storage of personal items.
- Do not permit employees to shop before hours, and never allow them to write up, ring up or wrap up their own purchases. Designate one register and one employee to handle employee purchases.
- Require employees to charge all discount purchases on an "in-house" charge account. This will give you the opportunity to detect abuse of employee discount privileges.
- Authorize one employee to remove trash. All cardboard cartons should be crushed, and a supervisor should periodically inspect outgoing waste materials and to be certain that goods are not being smuggled out. If possible, use clear see-through trash bags as an added safeguard.

Stopping the Wear-Out Thief

- Do not allow employees to wear store merchandise on the job. Employees often "forget" to return the items before they leave.
- When possible, keep jewelry and cosmetic showcases locked and off limits to employees from other departments. Only designated employees should have keys to the display cases.

Stopping the Hand-Out Thief

- Always try to maintain a separation of functions between the salesperson, cashier, and the wrapper. This creates a natural system of checks and balances.
- Do not allow merchandise to accumulate around the cash registers. Return items to stock as soon as possible.
- Allow employees to serve relatives and friends, but never allow them to both ring and wrap their purchases. Do not make theft tempting. In addition, teach employees how to say "no" to relatives and friends who ask for extra merchandise or lower prices.

Stopping the Send-Out Thief

- Limit the number of employees who are authorized to handle and wrap garments for shipping.

Fraud Detection and Prevention ■ 241

- Always assign two or more employees to handle outgoing packages. They will police each other.
- When possible, have an independent carrier handle merchandise delivery, rather than employees. If an employee handles this assignment, maintain a receipt book, and inspect it regularly.

Stopping the Cash Thief

- Instruct employees to be certain to close the cash register after each transaction. It sounds obvious, but an open till catches everyone's eye and increases temptation.
- Inquire about all "no sale" transactions to confirm that they were on the level.
- Document all voided transactions (over-rings) in a log, with all entries requiring a supervisor's approval. Include in this log the date, register number, amount and reason for the void, a re-ring transaction number and the signatures of the cashier, customer, and supervisor.
- Conduct register readings only after the cash has been removed, counted, and placed into a locked deposit bag. Reading the register is the manager's job, not the cashiers.
- Clear all cash register transaction numbers at the end of each day. Try to use entire rolls of tape (without discarding portion at the beginning or end), to keep your transaction numbering true and easy to track.
- Select a bank as close to your store as possible and establish a random schedule of deposits, so that deposits are made at different times each day. Juggle the pattern periodically to thwart any theft plots. Also, have your bank retain deposit bag keys.

Specialty Situations

On Hiring Security

High-volume seasons sometimes require hiring additional security personnel or an outside security company. In the interests of keeping the fox out of the chicken coop, so to speak, know who you are hiring in this important area.

Here are some tips:

- Check the reputation of the security firm with your local Chamber of Commerce, your local development corporation, the Better Business Bureau, and local merchant associations.
- Be sure to hire security firms that are fully insured and whose employees are bonded.
- Draft a detailed contract to make sure that the firm is clear on what services will be expected, such as what areas of the store are off-limits, whether uniforms will be required and whether the guards should be armed of unarmed.

A Final Word

As you probably know before reading *Play It Safe*, there are an endless number of ways in which your business can suffer at the hands of criminals. We are all vulnerable, but none of us are helpless, and there are countless ways to stop theft before it hits. The key for you is to get started, even if you institute only some of the methods of prevention outlined here. Do it today, as if your business depended on it, it does.

242 ■ *Healthcare Security*

Note:

ADDITIONAL SECURITY STRATEGIES INCLUDE:

- Retailers should avoid using identifiable passwords and pin numbers
- Loss prevention training should include ID Theft prevention and computer security strategies
- Retailers should be familiar with RETAIL SECURITY WEBSITES THAT OFFER UP-TO-DATE DATA ON CRIME TRENDS AND RELATED CRIME PREVENTION INFORMATION.

A Team Approach to Fraud Prevention

Anthony Luizzo

To identify and deal with the perpetrator of a fraud, the skills of both auditing and criminology professionals are frequently called for. The auditor labors on *how* fraud is perpetrated by analyzing the system in which the fraud was committed. He focuses on the internal controls to determine if there was a breakdown or endeavors to determine how the controls were overridden.

The criminologist (security/loss prevention manager, private investigator, security consultant) labors on *who* committed the fraud by interviewing witnesses and interrogating suspects, and on how fraud avoidance policies and systems were circumvented. He conducts security surveys to isolate and minimize risk and loss exposures. He also formulates protective guardian systems (closed-circuit television, alarms, and access control, etc.) to help maintain a watchful eye over corporate personnel and assets.

In hospital security, rarely do internal audit and security departments work together as team partners in detecting and preventing fraud. This is distressing, since there is a common mission between the two disciplines: each seeks to control criminal misbehavior.

From a disciplinary perspective, auditors/accountants and criminologists are, by the nature of their work, accustomed to looking behind the scenes and challenging things that are, or appear to be, irregular or out of character. Prior to addressing how these disciplines might work together, it is important to take a moment to discuss the magnitude of today's skyrocketing fraud problem and why frauds are committed.

The Breadth of the Fraud Problem

Data from the business sector compute the cost of economic crime in 1990 at a conservative $114 billion. Other independent studies estimate that *one* dollar is lost to external crime vis-à-vis *eight* dollars to internal crime, and that *one* out of *three* employees steals. Consulting firms specializing in forensic accounting/auditing cite that 75% of people who commit white collar crime did so at another company. Moreover, firms specializing in employee screening allege that 17% of screened applicants admit to stealing from previous employers.

Why Frauds are Committed

Experience has shown that many frauds occur because the perpetrator believes that the corporate climate of the company offers the opportunity to commit the crime. Further, it is purported that many criminals believe that apprehension and prosecution in the white-collar crime area is sporadic at best. There is also a perception (often justified) that companies rarely prosecute.

From the criminology point of view, frauds are committed for a variety of reasons some of which include:

- *Settling Alleged Inequities.* Obtaining monies believed due for past raises, bonuses, and/or overtime.

From *Journal of Healthcare Protection Management.* (9):2, pp.76–80. Summer 1993.

244 ■ Healthcare Security

- *Gaining Revenge.* "Getting Even" for a perceived mistreatment.
- *Securing Self-Enrichment.* Acquiring the luxuries to enhance self-image and standard of living.
- *Soliciting Psychological Excitement.* Thirsting to become a modern-day Master Thief.
- *Viewing the Crime as "Victimless."* The company will never miss the funds and/or insurance will offset any loss.
- *Winning Peer Acceptance.* Seeking to belong to the subculture which depends on one another for protection.

Framing a Hospital Fraud Deterrence Program

Inasmuch as both internal audit and security share the responsibility for controlling loss, it makes sense that they should be working together as a team. In fact security's input is rarely a part of the audit review process. The need for synergy between these disciplines is underscored quite eloquently by the Statement on Internal Auditing Standards (SIAS) #3, which speaks to the fact that internal auditors are not expected to have knowledge equivalent to that of a person whose primary responsibility is detecting and investigating fraud. An excellent approach to promulgating such a program is to team members of both disciplines during the periodical inventory inspections and routine audits. As the auditor addresses audit issues such as conducting inventory counts, ascertaining whether the inventory was recorded as received, etc., the security team member could be addressing physical security requirements within inventory storage areas, background screening of employees with fiduciary positions, and reviewing integrity testing policies.

For the purposes of illustration, a team audit of missing inventory might proceed as follows:

How did the loss happen?

The auditor's inquiry might include:
- Was the missing inventory received?
- Was the inventory received at the proper point?
- Was the inventory recorded as received?

Security's inquiry:
- Did security countersign invoices?
- Is physical security adequate?
- Is access control adequate?
- Are inventory control devices (seals, etc.) utilized?

When did the loss occur?

Auditor's inquiry:
- Ascertain when the last inventory count was conducted.
- Review available inventory records.

Security's inquiry:
- Ascertain whether lapses in access control were noted.
- Review CCTV tapes for suspicious activity.
- Review other security technology applications for suspicious activity (alarm logs, pass control journals, etc.)

Who could be responsible for the loss?

Auditor's inquiries:
- Request that the security department screen all employees with fiduciary responsibilities.
- If possible, pinpoint a window of time when the loss might have occurred.

Security's inquiry:
- Interview all individuals who had access to the inventory or records, or who may shed light on the case.
- If available, review the entity's disgruntled employee file.
- Where appropriate, liaison with local law enforcement.
- Query the risk management department for abnormal insurance premium fluctuations.
- Interrogate potential suspects.

An important benefit in this team process is the swiftness in which preventative measures can be put forward. In addition, since both departments are involved from the commencement of the audit process, there is a greater chance that thieves will be apprehended.

Preparing the Final Report

Experience has shown that it makes good sense to have the audit department take the lead in this area by being responsible for preparing the final report. The security segment of the project should be prepared by the security department and included as a part of the audit department's final submission.

Conclusion

Inaugurating a fraud prevention program in the healthcare environment is especially important since it is estimated that some 3,000 items, from aspirins to stethoscopes, are a part of a healthcare provider's inventory. Over and above the vast number of items on display, a great many of the items are of the disposable variety and have either household and/or resale applications. The seeds of success in launching a sound fraud prevention program in any environment lie in the entity's ability to keep its assets free from danger or loss. An excellent method of keeping the door to criminal misbehavior closed is to develop new procedures and systems to strengthen existing security.

Procedures and systems might include:

- Developing cross-training programs between auditing and security management personnel.
- Requiring that security departments have a role in the audit process
- Ensuring that fraud prevention personnel keep current within the profession by attending appropriate training and seminar programs and by attaining industry certification.

Delving Deeper to Decipher Fraud

Anthony Luizzo and George Van Nostrand

Traditionally the corporate fraud problem has been addressed as an accounting exercise. Many security professionals incorrectly assume that periodic audits by both the in-house accounting staff and outside auditors provide a sufficient safeguard against fraud. Audits, however, are performed to determine the degree to which a company complies with standards and practices that have been mandated by the company's management.

An auditor does not necessarily look for fraud or go beyond what is presented in the company books and records. A new breed of professional, the fraud auditor, does! The fraud auditor, sometimes referred to as a forensic accountant, usually has an education in accounting and auditing. He or she then may get a job with some public agency that is engaged in investigations. Although the variations on this scenario are countless, the definition remains the same: the melding of knowledge of both accounting and investigations within one individual is the hallmark of the fraud auditor.

The accountant and the investigator may look at the same problem from two different perspectives. The fraud auditor, however, is trained to look at a problem with two sets of eyes simultaneously.

A forensic accountant is frequently engaged as a consultant after an auditor has noted some irregularity. Most industrial companies are subject to three layers of financial review – internal auditors, auditors employed by a bank or other lending institution, and independent public auditors. If any of these financial reviews uncovers suspicious activity, particularly transactions involving officers of the company, they may decide to call in a fraud auditor. The inquiry of the forensic accountant will differ from that of the previously described audits in that the forensic accountant will be specifically looking for fraud. The fraud auditor typically builds a case by carefully examining records. When something out of the ordinary is noted, he or she delves deeper to find out why it occurred. A recent case provides a good example of how a fraud auditor investigates a fraud problem.

A large metal processing company with manufacturing facilities in three separate eastern states was recently forced into bankruptcy because of reported declining sales and increased expenses. Company management placed the blame on poor economic conditions and specifically on decreased defense spending. This explanation satisfied many of the company's creditors, but a local bank ordered a full accounting review prior to accepting the losses that would have to be sustained in the event of a bankruptcy.

This audit found irregularities in several areas that directly reflected on the company president and controller. Inventory figures on the books did not accurately reflect the raw material or the finished product on hand. Additionally, after directly contacting several customers who had done business with the company, the accounts receivable ledger was found to be overstated.

The creditor's committee insisted that an independent forensic accountant be retained to determine whether fraud had caused the company to fail. During a typical inventory procedure, approximately 25 percent of the raw material and finished product is counted the remainder is estimated or derived from preexisting records. In this case, the forensic accountant conducted a full inventory, including a stand-still count of inventory in transit. The actual inventory was found to be overstated in the last financial statement by approximately $500,000. In addition to the

---

From *Security Management Magazine*: pp. 113-116. September 1994.

incorrect count, the inventory valuation was inflated. Similarly, direct contact with the company's customers determined that the accounts receivable ledger was overstated by more than $1 million.

Based on these findings, interviews with accounting department personnel and management were conducted. The accounting background of the fraud auditor is an essential element when conducting these interviews. In this case, the discussion frequently involved technical accounting terms and questions about why and how certain entries were made in the company books. It was essential that a trained accountant conduct these interviews so that suspects could be pinned down on their responses. These interviews of the president and controller, revealed that false entries were made in the inventory, accounts receivable, and the plant and equipment accounts. All these accounts were overvalued to present an attractive picture of the company's operations. This rosy financial statement enabled the company to continue to borrow money and funds at favorable rates. Additionally, the president and the controller were allowed to continue receiving performance bonuses and to falsely increase the value of their stock. The fraud committed by the president and the controller ultimately resulted in the bankruptcy of the company, causing the loss of more than 300 jobs and a financial loss estimated at $4 million. Criminal charges of bank fraud were filed against the responsible parties. Civil suits are certain to follow.

Teaming. Another method of combating fraud is the team approach. This approach is the team approach. This approach involved the employment of an auditor and an investigator. The auditor is usually charged with the responsibility of analyzing the system in which a fraud was committed. This type of inquiry focuses on whether there may have been a breakdown in the internal control process. The investigator assumes that because a crime has been committed, the controls have, in some manner, been breached. His or her focus concentrates on who committed the fraud. Auditors and investigators employ different techniques in the pursuit of their differing objectives. To determine what controls, if any, have been abrogated the auditor formulates an audit plan designed to test certain transactions or procedures. A detailed examination is made of the frequency and categories of variations from stated or accepted practices. The process involves an examination of pertinent books and records. When significant variations are detected, the auditor determines the extent of these violations and assesses the financial impact on the company. The auditor is also responsible for devising remedial measures that address the breakdown in internal controls.

The investigator may also begin his and her inquiry with an examination of the pertinent records and documents. This examination is, of course, conducted from a different perspective. The focus on who violated procedures, altered records, or did not fulfill his or her responsibilities. This examination is frequently followed by the interrogation of possible witnesses and suspects. The skills required for this kind of activity are clearly inter-personal and call for a different kind of training and background than that of the auditors.

The team concept of fraud auditing can be seen more easily by using an example built around a case study. In this example, a loss has been detected by the security manager in a mid-sized electronics company. The preliminary inquiry, conducted by the security manager, indicated that the loss emanated from the warehouse. Since the manager does not have accounting training and the policy of the company's law firm is to use outside investigators in any possible inquiry that may involve company personnel, the manager decided to employ the team concept in the investigation of this matter.

In determining how the loss occurred, the auditor may ask: Was the inventory in question received? What do the inventory logs reveal? Was the inventory received at the correct point of entry? Was the inventory received and signed for by an authorized person? Was the inventory correctly documented as received and entered into the "inventory on hand" records? What is the extent and dollar value of the loss?

248 ■ *Healthcare Security*

When trying to answer this same question, the investigator may ask: Did a security officer countersign the invoices relating to the incoming inventory? What do the security logs show about unauthorized persons or visitors in the warehouse? Is physical security adequate? Is access control adequate? Are inventory control devices used? Are they appropriate? What is the aftermarket for the missing merchandise? The next question both professionals will ask is when did the loss occur? An auditor seeks to answer that question by examining when the last inventory count was conducted, the results of that check, how much of the inventory was counted, and how much was estimated. He or she then conducts a careful review of inventory records for the past year or beginning when significant staff or procedural changes took place in the warehouse administration.

The investigator, on the other hand, looks for noted lapses in access control. He or she reviews CCTV tapes for any suspicious activity or unknown persons and determines the time and duration of any unusual activity, such as strikes or weather-related work stoppages, in the warehouse. When determining who is responsible for loss, the auditor determines who had legitimate access to the missing inventory, considering shifts, holidays, management changes, and other variations from normal procedures. He or she narrows down the time frame in which the loss occurred and considers the possibility of insurance fraud by discussing insurance fluctuations with the insurance department or risk manager. The investigator investigates which employees may have a drug or gambling problem. Then he or she locates and interviews all employees, including managers, who had access to the missing inventory or to the appropriate inventory records. The investigator studies the company's files regarding disgruntled employees, dismissals, and lay-offs and establishes liaison contacts with the appropriate local or federal law enforcement officials. Once law enforcement becomes involved, the role of both the auditor and investigator becomes one of support. Company management should, of course, be briefed about this development, and full cooperation should be given to the authorities. Both auditors and investigators must maintain their notes and documentary evidence for possible assistance with a prosecution. Whether the case if referred to law enforcement or not, a clear and concise report must be rendered at the end of the inquiry.

The company is entitled to a full and complete final report, but any support material, such as original notes, tapes, or photographs, remain the property of the outside experts. Fraud detection and prevention is clearly within the security manager's purview, and he or she should take every opportunity to attend seminars and training sessions devoted to financial crimes. Security professionals engaged in this ongoing educational process should take note of the role forensic accounting can play in uncovering corporate fraud.

---

*Reprinted with permission: Security Management Magazine

The Fraud Prevention Jackpot

Anthony Luizzo, Frank A. Luizzo, George Van Nostrand, and Phillip Luizzo

A small group of men flew into Las Vegas. Before arriving, they had set up a $100,000 account with a New York City bank, then phoned a large casino on the strip, informing the credit office of their intention to come for a weekend of play and requesting a $60,000 line of credit. After checking with the New York City bank, the casino credit department granted the request and set up complimentary rooms for the potential big spenders.

When the men arrived late on Friday night, they went to the casino and took out a $5,000 marker. This was traded for chips, and they began to participate in the casino games. Over the course of the weekend, the men received a total of $55,000 in markers, trading them for chips. While absent from the gaming tables for dinner or other breaks, they inconspicuously slipped chips to a third party, who cashed them in at the casino's cage without attracting attention. By the end of the weekend, they had taken out $55,000 in credit, pocketed $40,000, and lost $15,000 to gambling, although, because they had surreptitiously cashed in chips, it appeared to the floor persons who monitor "big action" that they had lost much more. When the casino cage sent in the markers to the New York City bank, they found that the account had been dumped and closed on Friday afternoon. The con men were gone, and the casino was left holding worthless IOU's.

Based on several real incidents, this composite example illustrates the challenges facing security managers in today's gambling environment. Security managers must possess the expertise to detect and deter schemes ranging from usurping a stranger's credit line to collecting unauthorized slot jackpots. Fraud is a hidden business expense that can substantially diminish the profitability of any company. In a 1995 study, *A Report to the Nation on Occupational Fraud and Abuse*, the Association of Certified Fraud Examiners estimated that the average organization loses more than $9 a day per employee to fraud.

In a gambling environment, certain procedures are particularly vulnerable. These include the opening and closing of table games, the acceptance of cash from players for chips, the issuance and repayment of markers (credit instruments or a written promise to pay back funds extended for the purpose of casino play), the handling of cards and dice by players and dealers, maintenance of slot machines, and the movement of chips to and from the games and the casino "cage" (the cashier's office on the casino floor where money is changed for chips).

The passing of counterfeit currency can be all too easy in a crowded, active casino. Currency and paperwork placed into the gaming table's bank drop box may not be examined for up to twenty-four hours. In addition, during an eight hour-shift, several dealers will have manned the table, and it is difficult for the casino to establish whether a dealer has given out more chips than he or she collected in cash.

The issuance and payment of markers is another vulnerable activity. Markers are exchanged for chips. As a rule, a floor person, pit boss, host, or games manager is empowered to approve the issuance of thousands of dollars in chips based solely on markers. Many casinos rely heavily on the ability of their key personnel to recognize a given player to whom they will issue a marker. He or she usually knows the player from previous visits or has been introduced by a host who has verified the customer's credit line.

From *Security Management Magazine*, pp 70–75. August 1996.

250 ■ *Healthcare Security*

This system falls short of optimum security by placing too much responsibility on individual employees. For example, a dishonest player connives with a floor person, pit boss, or host, and a dealer. The floor person agrees to record a $1,000 marker using the credit line of a known customer. The player then uses the $1,000 marker to get $3,000 in chips from the dealer, who is also in on the con. The player stays at the table for a few games, then moves to another table to make the transaction look legitimate. Then he chases in the $3,000 of chips, pays off the $1,000 marker, and shares the ill-gotten gains with his partners.

During the day's activity, cash in the form of chips must be moved from the tables to the cage, and from the cage to the tables, depending on the ebb and flow of the games. When a game loses, it must be filled with more chips; when the game wins, the table sends the excess winnings to the cage. The paperwork associated with these fills and credits enables the accounting department to determine whether a table game is winning or losing. Sloppy paperwork, illegible signatures, and erroneous fill or credit amounts may be simply mistakes or attempts to cover up an act of fraud at the tables or in the cage operation.

Handling playing cards and dice in a casino is another critical area of concern. The receiving, storage, issuance, collection, and cancellation of cards and dice must be adequately controlled. When these functions are not strictly monitored, several fraudulent schemes become possible. Two prominent examples are card marking and "cooler" scams.

A" cooler" is a term used for a prearranged group of cards inside a card dispenser, or "shoe", that is introduced into a game of blackjack. In this form of scam, a dealer allows access to a shoe, usually by taking it out of the casino. The perpetrators of the fraud will arrange the cards to ensure that the players win, and the house loses. They take all the places at a single table. On being seated, they create a distraction to mask the shoe switch. The group then bets to maximum limits, often "winning" thousands of dollars in a short period of time. Once the shoe is empty, that evidence of the scam is gone forever.

There are numerous scams and fraudulent schemes associated with slot machine operation, including the payments of jackpots and credits, the filling of machines, and the issuance and collection of player markers. Even with the most aggressive prevention measures, paying out cash for jackpots that never hit or paying out more than was due is still possible. Casinos with computerized slot tracking systems have greater protection against such scams than those without this technology by limiting the authority to override the system. Casinos without such technology must rely totally on the trustworthiness of management personnel.

A final form of fraud – once considered a major form of cheating, but now rarely seen – is the physical altering of dice. A common method would be loading dice or shaving them to avoid the number seven, for example.

Prevention strategies. The 1991 Federal Sentencing Guidelines for Organizations specifies that corporate entities formulate in-house fraud prevention programs managed by high-level corporate executives. Briefly, this statue mandates that organizations bear the primary responsibility for detecting, investigating, and preventing various federal crimes. Further, the statue calls for proactive measures concerning investigations and training to prevent corporate officers, employees, and agents from engaging in fraudulent practices, including virtually all fraud-related violations.

Hiring. One of the best preventive measures is to hire honest employees. To that end, all potential casino employees should be thoroughly screened. Background checks of potential employees should be conducted in all the states and counties in which the individual has resided, including temporary residences and summer homes. Credit checks should be run, and all businesses where the candidate has acted as an executive should be investigated to see whether bankruptcy was declared, or criminal activity transpired during the candidate's time of employment.

Surveillance. Deepening and strengthening CCTV surveillance is the next step in the process of limiting fraud. A surveillance system is designed to safeguard both people and property. To strengthen fraud surveillance, many security managers are opting to divide the surveillance function into two separate operations. The first is standard nongaming surveillance, focusing on property and personal safety. This type of installation includes the monitoring of hotel entrances, the front desk, elevators, hallways, grounds, inventory assets, and back-house operations. The second strategy is gaming surveillance dedicated to keeping a watchful eye over the casino cage, slots, and table games. In today's bigger casinos, the trend is to dedicate one CCTV camera per game to record the action in real time. This enables surveillance to later conduct player and game pace audits – both of which are invaluable to the casino to determine whether the game was "clean" or whether illegal actions and ethically gray activities such as card counting have occurred.

Card counting is not strictly illegal. It is the genuine ability to memorize how many cards of a certain face value remain, for example, in a six-deck show during a game of blackjack. If the counter knows that the majority of the low number cards have been played in the game, he or she knows that the remaining cards in the show are likely to be high value and that the dealer is likely to exceed twenty-one and go "bust" on the hand, making everyone at the table winners. Consequently, he or she will place higher bets and win more. Casinos will usually ask card counters to leave if they can be identified.

The surveillance department's player audits help the casinos determine who is a card counter. Surveillance staff watch the tapes from the dedicated camera on a game, looking for consistent winners who appear to concentrate heavily on the play (most regular players are busy laughing, talking to friends, or ordering drinks). Once a counter has been determined, the pit bosses and floor people can be on the lookout.

In a game pace audit, the surveillance team reviews the videotape to determine how many hands a dealer dealt in n hour, how often the dice were thrown in a craps game, or how many times a roulette wheel was spun. In this case, the surveillance department is helping the casino to ascertain the profitability of its table games – slow dealer movement loses the casino money. The gaming surveillance department must be able to record the counting of currency, the movement of cash and coin from the count room to specific cage windows, the issuance of fills and credits, and the handling of patron activity at the cashier windows. All of these provide a visual record in case of later investigation.

Tracking. Some casinos have successfully implemented electronic tracking of high rollers and their credit lines via computers in the pits and the cage linked to a centralized database. Part of the job of floor people is to introduce themselves to patrons making large wagers and to get a name and other information such as their hotel. The floor person then goes to one of the casino pits and creates a file on the player. The floor person updates the player's file whenever he or she visits that gaming area, making notations on how long the patron played and whether he or she won or lost.

These records are created and maintained primarily to provide the casino with a record of its best players for future marketing purposes. However, this procedure eventually also creates a player profile and allows security to analyze the player's behavior. In the case of consistent high winners, the profile may lead surveillance to discover fraud through a player analysis. The tracking system also allows the casino cage to keep track of the best players' credit lines and prevent credit appropriation by con artists. When a new player applies for a line of credit, the cage personnel enter the personal information, as well as take a video photo and capture a digitized signature that can be compared whenever additional credit is requested.

Another new occurrence is the computerization of markers. Many casinos are now beginning to use hand-held computers – like those used by package delivery services – to issue electronic markers signed for with digital signatures. The computerization of all marker transactions cuts down on lost or incorrectly completed paperwork and lessens the chances of some types of marker fraud.

Cancellations. Gaming procedures stipulate that when dice and carks are removed from table games, they must be stored and later collected for cancellation or destruction. To cancel a deck of cards, a hole is drilled through the deck, or a corner is shaved off the cards. Used dice are stamped or marked in such a way as to make it clear that they are no longer usable. Old cards and dice are usually resold in the casino gift chops.

Dealer rules. The prevention strategy must also address the way dealers influence the game. The gaming industry is regulated by state control commissions that issue the rules under which the dealer works during the game. Casinos train their dealers in procedures that can seem arcane at first examination. For example, dealers must always clap when leaving a table to show they are taking nothing with them; they must always tap their "tokes" – tips received in the form of chips – on the table to notify players that they are not removing the chips from the game illegally. Dealers should never touch chips, cards, or dice without reason.

Dealers who touch chips and then move their hands towards their bodies without first "clearing" – turning their palms up and down to show patrons they are empty handed – or who fumble chips, drop, or spill cards, and lose track of bets, may represent a danger to the house. Security personnel should determine whether they merely need more training or are attempting to create a diversion as a prelude to theft.

Fraud recognition training. The security team should also teach dealers how to recognize and prevent scams. These lessons can be as simple as correctly shuffling cards to prevent card counting. As an example, in many casinos the floor people are not only trained to recognize card counting but also to disrupt it by breaking the concentration of a suspected counter by personal interaction. Floor persons, who are charged with watching the dealers, should receive even greater training in scam recognition, as should the pit bosses, who watch the floor persons, and the managers, who watch the put bosses. The intensity of fraud-recognition training should escalate with each level of increasing responsibility. For example, managers in casinos with specialty games that cater to foreigners should be aware that a table where the dealer and all players speak a foreign language that no floor person understands is ripe for cheating and fraud. Consequently, a floor person should always be present who can understand the language being spoken. Training should be repeated frequently. In casinos, training is often done on the job; however, gambling establishments should also take advantage of industry seminars on cheating offered by private companies, associations, and the state's gaming control board.

Partnership. In certain gaming establishments, both security and surveillance fall under one directorship. However, in many casinos, the security function is split into both a traditional security department and a separate surveillance department. In either case, the head of surveillance should maintain an ongoing liaison with the directors and managers of the casino operations and especially with the accounting/internal audit department. The two should have an independent – but combined – function, sharing the responsibility for managing and securing the casino cage, count rooms, and casino credit operations.

All procedural manuals, employee schedules, and other pertinent information must be shared with appropriate management. Procedures naturally evolve as more efficient methods are found, but if new procedures are not written down and shard, then soon the official procedures will differ drastically from the practiced one. All changes should be shared with everyone in the loop – especially with the surveillance department, which is charged with making sure correct procedures are always followed. Any changes made to employee schedules should be communicated

Fraud Detection and Prevention ▪ 253

to surveillance immediately as part of the fraud-fighting effort. Something as simple as a recurring swap of workdays between floor people could signal an attempt at fraud – for example, the reason may be to allow a floor person to work with a particular dealer and play to perpetrate a scam.

The accounting/internal audit department must check and double check all activity and paperwork daily. Communication between the cage manager and surveillance director must be constant and two-directional to make the most of the information from banks and other organizations that both departments independently receive.

Security managers should be aware that accountants view their responsibility somewhat narrowly in fraud detection. The most recent professional accounting guidelines are nonspecific concerning the responsibility of accountants and auditors in fraud detection and resolution. The *Statement on Accounting Standard* (SAS 53), the most recent pronouncements of the America Institute of Certified Public Accountants, states that the auditors are only responsible for designing the audit to provide "reasonable assurances that errors and irregularities that are material to the financial statements are detected."

Where does this leave a multibillion-dollar casino just defrauded of several hundred thousand dollars? While the independent auditors can say that the loss was not material, management will still have a difficult time explaining such losses to shareholders. Since the external auditors focus primarily on material fraud, management's problem then becomes how to address all frauds in the company. A solution may be a team approach to detecting and preventing fraud. Studies of major corporations have revealed that the surveillance and accounting departments rarely work jointly on an audit or share their findings. To heighten awareness of fraud, abuse, and waste, one approach is to have the loss/crime prevention specialist team with the auditor during internal audits and security surveys. High rollers, for example, are often given complimentary rooms, food, and beverages while at the hotel casino. If the high roller loses while playing, it is usually the casino that pays the player's airfare. Scams have been discovered by loss/crime prevention teams during audits where airfare has been covered although it should not have been. In these cases, the hosts bringing the gambler to the casino to work with travel agents to convert the airfares for their own use or for cash. Player analyses by the surveillance department proved the players were not losers, and the auditing department picked up the internal doctoring of information.

Slots. Procedures must be developed for the safeguarding of slot machine keys and the monitoring of those who enter the machines. Slot machine keys usually fit all of the machines of a certain type – for example, nickel slots – or all machines in a certain casino zone. These keys can fetch high prices if sold. It is important that a strict system be developed, with a log and surveillance tapes, to document when keys were picked up and returned and by whom. If a technician leaves work forgetting to turn in keys, this should ring a major alarm, because that technician may be out having the keys copied for sale. Slot machine keys provide access to the machine's hopper and its bill validator, allowing anyone with a key to potentially walk off with several thousand dollars in cash and coins. More sophisticated cheats use the keys to set up larger jackpots. The criminals case the casino to ascertain the location of CCTV, then return with a group of accomplices who surround the player, pretending to watch, and blocking the view of the camera. He or she then opens the door, pops out the electronics board, and replaces the chou and tells the machine to signal a large jackpot. They then move on, leaving behind a fresh "player" to win the multi-thousand-dollar pot.

To combat this type of high-tech fraud, casinos have begun to seal the electronics chips to the boards and lock the boards so that they can only be removed with a separate key that is more tightly controlled – perhaps only used under security escort. Another helpful tool is the slot tracking system, like the player tracking system, linking all slots in the casino to a central computer tracking the play, machine performance, and win percentages.

Casinos issue their best players a credit card that can be used on the slots. When this occurs, the computer records the transactions. It also records the visits of employees who use a similar card to identify themselves to the machine. Casino security managers can use the information from the tracking system to piece together investigative strategies, formulate fraud-related chronologies, and frame covert and overt patrol and surveillance initiatives. Uniformed officers should patrol slot corridors to discourage snatch and grabs, where one person distracts the player while his associate steals handbags, coins, and other personal items. The officers can also watch for protracted interactions between players and slot attendants.

A casino environment is a money machine, a system in constant motion where opportunities for fraud abound. Fraud prevention is a team effort requiring a series of trained eyes focusing on all aspects of the operation. Fraud prevention can be a casino's biggest house jackpot.

*Reprinted with permission: Security Management Magazine

Safeguarding Assets Against Fraud

George Van Nostrand and Anthony Luizzo

Although detecting fraud is everyone's business, ultimate responsibility rests with the top-level personnel (president, CEO, or corporate counsel) of the company. If there was ever any question concerning who in the company is the responsible party, the 1991 Federal Sentencing Guidelines erased all doubt. The guidelines mandate stiff financial penalties for companies found guilty of a variety of federal offenses. Legal scholars tell us that the guidelines are based on the concept of Respondent Superior: "Let the master answer." In other words, organizations and their officers are responsible for the illegal acts of their employees and agents. This framework places the responsibility for fraud detection and investigation, as well as training and monitoring, squarely on the shoulders of the company.

Maintaining Fraud Controls

During the initial organizational stages of corporate development, procedures are established to determine duties and responsibilities of corporate employees. Too often, however, companies find out only when a problem arises – often accompanied by a financial loss – that their procedures are no longer applicable. Companies should ensure that audit procedures continually re-examine the effectiveness of key company policies.

Recognizing Existing Fraud

If controls fail to prevent fraud, the next step is for the responsible parties of an organization to recognize red flags of fraud. A "red flag" is a significant change in an employee's lifestyle that seems to indicate increased access to money.

When an employer notices that an employee is buying a new luxury car or vacation home or is otherwise spending money far more than his or her salary, the employer should consider the possibility that the employee came by the extra income via fraud.

Other red flags are abrupt changes in personality, personal relationships, or habits. In fact, the variety of red flags visible to management is virtually limitless. Increased spending or changed habits are not certain indicators of the presence of fraud but should alert management that further inquiries are in order. While there are important privacy issues to be considered, recognizing red flags is a company's first line of defense.

Creating Mechanisms for Reporting Fraud

Although the atmosphere for protecting "whistle blowers" has improved, a company should ensure that steps are taken to protect employees from some of the consequences for reporting fraud, especially fraud committed by their superiors.

From *Financial Fraud* Warren Gorham & Lamont/RIA Group (Reuters) Thomson Publications. (1):3, September 1997 – openlibrary@archive.com

256 ■ *Healthcare Security*

The Federal Sentencing Guidelines strongly suggest the adoption of an independent reporting system to ensure the autonomy of persons reporting possible corporate crimes.

Responding to Fraud

If fraud is suspected, management is obligated to initiate inquiry. There are many options available. Contacting the personnel department or the security department may be the logical first step. If the problem involves key employees or becomes complex or widespread, the employment of an outside fraud expert may be necessary. Corporate legal counsel can also be helpful in this area. Some companies have successfully used various combinations of these four disciplines.

Objections to Active Fraud Prevention

George Van Nostrand and Anthony Luizzo

Although the operational budget of the typical startup company is almost certainly limited, the future of the company demands consideration of security and fraud reduction. The problem of fraud detection and resolution is complex and not readily solved by halfhearted efforts. The questions posed here are designed to help managers of businesses, particularly managers of entrepreneurial enterprises, to confront specific security-related issues through their honest examination of these queries.

Q1. *Our company is too small to need a fraud specialist or security department. Why should we spend money on this non-value-added activity?*

A1. Although most Fortune 500 companies have devoted some portion of their working capital to security matters, smaller, entrepreneurial enterprises frequently do not devote significant time, or effort in this area. Ironically, it is precisely this kind of company that should make a definite commitment to security matters.

Most new industrial-sector companies are started because they have developed a new product or process. If this new technology is lost, stolen, or otherwise compromised, the company may have difficulty recovering.

Q2. *Hiring a full-time fraud expert will cost the company salaries, benefits, holidays, retirement funding, and other costs. How can we afford it?*

A2. The most obvious answer to financial impediments to security is to employ outside consultants or experts. This course of action is less expensive than hiring a security manager or developing a loss-prevention department. By shopping around, a company can locate a good consultant who is knowledgeable about its needs. There are many reliable experts who will do an excellent job and fulfill the needs of an entrepreneurial company in a cost-effective manner.

Q3. *I am sure that my employees are honest. Who would commit fraud?*

A3. Before becoming too certain of their employees, managers should ask themselves how much they really know about them. According to the Society for Human Resource Management, 25 percent of all resumes submitted for publicly advertised employment openings contain at least one major fabrication. Responsible management will conduct entry-level investigations of prospective employees. This process will weed out the obviously unfit and indicate to employees that the management of the company takes security issues seriously. Such a pre-employment background investigation provides a baseline profile of employees that may be helpful in the future. Upper management positions should require a more thorough background investigation than staff positions. In addition, studies have shown that the "model employee," because he or she is readily placed in a position of trust, is the person most likely to commit a fraud. Interviews with convicted felons indicate that companies are less likely to conform to the demands of internal controls with employees who are thought to be above suspicion.

From *Financial Fraud* Warren Gorham & Lamont/RIA Group (Reuters) Thomson Publications. (1):4, October 1997 – openlibrary@archive.com

258 ■ *Healthcare Security*

Q4. *My company is insured. Why should I be concerned about fraud?*

A4. Depending upon the insurance carrier and the individual policy, most minor losses will probably be covered and reimbursed. Most business insurance Is written for minor theft problems, however, not major frauds. If a major fraud occurs within the business, the insurance company will likely conduct an independent investigation. The insurance company may deny payment if its investigation finds that the fraud was preventable.

Any detected fraud problem will result in increased premiums at best, or, at worst, a finding of insurability. KPMG Peat Marwick's 1993-1994 fraud surveys found that companies victimized by fraud are more likely to attempt to recover losses through civil litigation than to file an insurance claim.

Q5. *Why not allow law enforcement to deal with fraud problems?*

A5. Because of limited budgets, limited manpower availability, and a lack of training and experience in fraud response, law enforcement may not be able to respond to a given problem. The U.S. Attorney's Office in most districts has established minimum monetary loss levels for the prosecution of different categories of fraud. Although no fraud loss is unimportant, on a practical level, some cases may not receive satisfactory investigative or prosecutorial attention.

Conclusion

Corporate fraud is a $400 billion a year growth industry. Objections notwithstanding, management must take steps to prevent and detect fraud.

Steps in a Fraud Audit

Anthony Luizzo

Oftentimes, accountants and investigators work together as a team on performing stand-alone fraud audit investigations as independent consultants. A simplified version of how these two disciplines often work together is that the accountant performs forensic accounting record reviews, and the investigator conducts background investigations on prospective wrongdoers. Both parties may perform related interviews and/or interrogations, network with law enforcement, and work shoulder-to-shoulder on preparing the final report. The independent consultant should be aware that there are two significant limitations in performing a fraud audit investigation:

1. There are no guarantees that a fraud investigation will find all the fraud
2. There is no guarantee that the fraud investigation will result in successful legal action against the assailant (s)

Fraud consultants should make sure that their clients understand these limitations. Methods of planning a fraud audit include but are not limited to:

1. The Planning Phase
2. The Investigative Phase
3. The Reporting, Packaging and Prosecution Phase

The Planning Phase

This phase involves:

- Meeting with the client and the client's attorney to discuss the objectives of the investigation, ascertain the known facts, and ascertain whether the client will prosecute. The number of known facts varies from engagement to engagement. Sometimes, the client may have a significant amount of evidence and knowledge of the fraud at hand.
- Information might include:
  - o When did the fraud occur?
  - o What assets or accounts were involved?
  - o How was the fraud committed?
  - o Who committed the fraud?
- Considering whether to accept or not accept the engagement? The decision to accept a fraud audit engagement is a matter of professional judgement. Specific factors to consider in making this decision vary based on the objective of the engagement, case facts, investigative requirements, business risks, the ability to provide services, staffing considerations, and possible conflicts of interest.
- Obtaining an engagement letter. It is important to obtain an understanding with the client of the terms of the engagement. Engagement letters often include:
  - o Identification of the client
  - o Description of the scope of the fraudulent behavior

From *Financial Fraud* Warren Gorham & Lamont/RIA Group (Reuters) Thomson Publications. (2):10, April 1999 – openlibrary@archive.com

260 ■ *Healthcare Security*

- o Objectives of the engagement
- o Description of services
- o Listing of specialists to be employed
- o Overview of invoicing arrangements
- ■ Preparing an investigative strategy:
  - o Who will be the client's point person?
  - o Will the engagement be an overt or covert exercise? In some cases, client's request that the investigation be completed covertly, in complete secrecy. Arrangements will be required to have all client documents related to the investigation delivered to the designated work location.
  - o Who will deliver client files? This often involves obtaining applicable documents in the client's possession. In many cases, the client's attorney on behalf of the company or other party engages the fraud investigator. Oftentimes, the client may have a concise figure re assets purloined, transactions or accounts thought to be manipulated, and a list of possible employees, etc., who had the opportunity to commit the fraudulent act.
  - o Where will forensic document review take place?
  - o Drafting a work plan and budget estimate
  - o Soliciting approval of the work plan and budget estimate

The Investigative Phase

This phase involves:

- ■ Assessing fraud exposures
  - o Interviewing employees, witnesses, etc.
  - o Preparing background investigations of potential targets – a background investigation might include:
    - Performing criminal/civil record checks
    - Performing asset checks – release required
    - Performing social security verifications – release required
    - Performing previous employment history checks
    - Performing other checks as required
    - Conducting follow-up interviews with potential targets
    - Interrogating suspects (if required)
    - Evaluating the evidence
    - Safeguarding the evidence

The Reporting, Packaging and Prosecution Phase

This phase includes:

- ■ Discussing preliminary evidentiary evidence with the client
  - o Meeting with law enforcement (if required)
  - o Assisting law enforcement prosecution issues

Fraud Detection and Prevention ■ 261

    o Writing the formal report (verbal or script) – If a formal written report is requested, the report should be signed by the lead principals who worked on the engagement

    o Reviewing the report and with the client

    o Delivering the report to the client- it is suggested that all reports be "hand delivered" to maintain confidentiality

    o Performing follow-up procedures as required – After completion of services, follow-up procedures may be necessary. Services may include conducting exit conferences and other matters normally associated with independent fraud consultants. In addition, many consultants offer their services to help companies draft fraud prevention policies and procedures and help them design proactive "fraud awareness" workshops for audit and security personnel

    o Assisting the client's attorney with court related documents

    o Preparing for court testimony

After an engagement is completed, it is always a good idea to ascertain from legal counsel how to safeguard related review points, workpapers, and other documents.

Investigating Money laundering Schemes

Anthony Luizzo

Audit investigators should become familiar with the various schemes associated with taking illegal money and disguising it as legitimate income.

According to studies conducted by the Association of Certified Fraud Examiners, Fraudsters often devise complex schemes to integrate dirty money into legitimate money. Since these schemes are often complex, law enforcement bloodhounds do not always have the time needed to untangle the mystery. In many instances, the company's internal audit or security department conducts the internal investigation, or an outside forensic investigative firm is contracted.

Fraudsters often use "Straws" (anonymous transients using fictitious names and addresses) to open bank accounts, fictitious DBA's, and other guises to move the money from place to place. Once the money is deposited, it is often transferred by wire to local and/or offshore accounts in such places as South America, Bermuda, and Panama. Opening an offshore account is easy.

Ironically, finding a less then ethical lawyer is the difficult part. Fraudsters know that once the illegally obtained money gets into the commerce marketplace, it become more difficult to distinguish the illegal from the legal.

Fraudsters' hide illegal assets in several ways, including:

- Hoarding the stash in their homes and other safe houses
- Breaking the illegal stash into smaller amounts and temporarily parking the money in cashier's checks and traveler's checks
- Depositing the stash in financial institutions, often opening domestic bank accounts, shell companies, mailbox drops, and wire transferring the proceeds to fictitious parties
- Investing the stash in off-book clandestine deals
- Investing the stash in legitimate securities, annuities and insurance policies often opened in a trusted friend's name or a transient's name
- Purchasing bearer instruments
- Investing in fraudulent loans, gifts and transfers using family affiliations
- Investing in assets such as real estate, businesses, jewelry, and other valuables
- Investing in cash-intensive type businesses and drawing profits
- Investing in small acquisitions of precious metals and shipping purchases to fictitious co-conspirators avoiding paper trails

The most common methods of moving money offshore include:

- Physically transporting the money in small amounts under $10,000, thus avoiding the U.S. Custom's Currency Transaction Report (CTR) (Experience fraudsters know that approximately $140,000 in cash can easily fit into a standard executive briefcase, which is rarely inspected while traveling.)
- Wiring the funds (wire transfer)
- Sending Cashier's Checks
- Investing in foreign brokerage accounts

From *Financial Fraud* Warren Gorham & Lamont/RIA Group (Reuters) Thomson Publications. (2):12, June 1999 – openlibrary@archive.com

Fraud Detection and Prevention ■ 263

- Sending Internet money orders
- Sending "E-Money"

Investigative Approaches

When investigating suspected money laundering activities, the following checklist can be used as a helpful guide:

- Become familiar with the company's record keeping system
- Determine the financial condition of the business
- Locate all company assets
- Locate all company bank accounts
- Identify incoming and outgoing cash flow patterns
- Review domestic and foreign bank accounts for questionable transactions
- Review the travel portfolios or corporate executives
- Review the company's loan records
- Review payment ledgers for suspect disbursements for services
- Identify questionable abnormal transactions
- Conduct a business profile analysis of questionable corporate investments
- Compute the net worth of the company ("Assets − Liabilities = Net Worth")
- Evaluate company expenditure patterns ("Known Expenditures − Known Sources of Income = Funds from Unknown Sources")
- Perform a Bank Deposit Analysis ("Total Deposits − Transfers = Net Deposits + Total Cash Expenditures = Total Receipts From all Known Sources")
- Determine the fraud scheme
- Identify key personnel germane to the inquiry
- Review the personal background history of targets and/or suspects
- Review the activities of possible targets and/or suspects

Auditors and investigators should have sufficient knowledge of how perpetrators hide assets, move money, and the approaches auditors and investigators can utilize to deter money laundering. ■

264 ■ *Healthcare Security*

Fraud Audit Checklist

Anthony Luizzo

The objective of the fraud audit checklist is to determine susceptibility of the organization to fraud related opportunities. Depending on the size of the company, the checklist may be used on firm-wide or departmental bases. The more "No" responses, the greater the propensity of irregularity. It should be noted that no single instrument can guarantee that fraud will be found, however, delving deeper into the areas identified in this checklist will help to guide the investigator to areas where fraud has been known to flourish.

Employee Considerations:

1. Does the company utilize an appropriate employment application?
   ☐ Yes ☐No

2. Does the employment application adhere to Federal and State guidelines?
   ☐ Yes ☐No

3. Are routine background checks performed on all new hires?
   ☐ Yes ☐No

4. Do competent personnel prepare background checks?
   ☐ Yes ☐No

5. Are background checks performed on existing employees with fiduciary responsibilities?
   ☐ Yes ☐No

6. Are detailed background checks performed on employees seeking sensitive positions?
   ☐ Yes ☐No

7. Are release forms signed and maintained as per the "Fair Credit Reporting Act"?
   ☐ Yes ☐No

8. Are conflict of interest statements and ethics statements signed and maintained?
   ☐ Yes ☐No

9. Are internal controls affecting cash handling procedures adequate?
   ☐ Yes ☐No

10. Are changes in employee behavior noted and investigated?
    ☐ Yes ☐No

11. Are exit interviews performed?
    ☐ Yes ☐No

From *Financial Fraud* Warren Gorham & Lamont/RIA Group (Reuters) Thomson Publications. (3):2, August 1999 – openlibrary@archive.com

Fraud Detection and Prevention ■ **265**

Operational and Control Considerations:

12. Are annual audits performed?
    ☐ Yes ☐No

13. Are audits performed by Certified Public Accountants?
    ☐ Yes ☐No

14. Does the firm have an internal audit function?
    ☐ Yes ☐No

15. Does the firm have a security or loss prevention function?
    ☐ Yes ☐No

16. Are audit and security personnel adequately trained in fraud prevention techniques and technologies?
    ☐ Yes ☐No

17. Does the internal audit and security functions work together?
    ☐ Yes ☐No

18. In an independent fraud audit performed periodically.
    ☐ Yes ☐No

19. Does the internal auditor address the issue of fraud in each audit?
    ☐ Yes ☐No

20. Are all internal control breaks examined?
    ☐ Yes ☐No

21. Does the firm have internal mechanisms in-place to report fraudulent behavior?
    ☐ Yes ☐No

22. Are surprise test counts periodically performed on cash and inventory?
    ☐ Yes ☐No

23. Are financial statements adequately analyzed?
    ☐ Yes ☐No

24. Are errors in financial statements promptly addressed?
    ☐ Yes ☐No

25. Are customers and vendors aware that they can contact the audit and/or security department for assistance in following-up on problems?
    ☐ Yes ☐No

The Fraud Equation

Anthony Luizzo

The Fraud Equation: Motivation + Opportunity = Fraud

According to research from the Association of Certified Fraud Examiners, one-third of all employees, managers and executives steal either money or merchandise from their employer, while two-thirds of employees pilfer.

According to the 1994 study "Ethics in America Business: Policies, Programs, and Perceptions," two of the most common types of transgressions observed by employees were "lying on reports or falsifying records" (41%) and "stealing or theft" (35%).

Motivation

Companies pay employees a fair wage and treat them well. So why do some employees steal? There are as many reasons for theft as there are incidences. Some employees simply don't consider taking an item as stealing – they believe it is one of the perks of the job. Others point to a spur of the moment impulse as the reason for committing theft.

Other reasons why people steal include:

- They believe the company will not suffer from the loss.
- They view it as a victimless crime.
- They succumb to peer pressure.
- They experience psychological excitement while committing the act.
- They want to exact revenge for a perceived mistreatment.
- They are looking for financial gain

Opportunity

The company usually has control over this segment of the fraud equation. If a company institutes strong internal controls over cash handling procedures, the opportunity for large cash thefts is reduced. In contrast, a business with weak internal controls might allow large sums of cash to build-up in cash registers, thus tempting both employee and customer theft.

How can Internal Theft by Reduced?

More forward-thinking Loss Prevention and Internal Audit Managers know that locating theft targets susceptible to criminal behavior and instituting theft prevention initiatives to thwart possible criminal activity reduces criminality (See exhibit one).

Strategies to thwart internal theft include:

- Promulgating strong corporate ethic's policies.
- Ensuring that management champion's theft reduction programs.

From *Financial Fraud* Warren Gorham & Lamont/RIA Group (Reuters) Thomson Publications. (2):12, June 1999 – openlibrary@archive.com

- Instituting strong internal hiring policies.
- Performing background checks on all new hires.
- Implementing strong internal controls.
- Establishing a company "hot line" for anonymous tips.
- Establishing reward programs for internal criminal information.

There are numerous ways your business can suffer at the hands of criminals. All businesses are vulnerable; none, however, are helpless. There are many strategies to stop internal thievery. The key is to institute these strategies before theft wreaks havoc on the companies' bottom line.

Exhibit 1: Ten Environment Susceptible to Theft:

1. Accounting	a. Reused Invoices b. Fictitious accounts payable c. Cancellations or reductions in account payable
2. Purchasing	a. Fictitious purchase orders b. Diversion of purchased goods c. Vendor shakedowns
3. Receiving	a. Diversion of goods b. Collusive under-receiving c. Receiving differing quantities d. No countersigning of invoice by security
4. Warehousing	a. Product diversion b. Record tampering
5. Distribution	a. Diversion in less than truck load b. Diversion in will-call pickups c. Invoice cancellation post pickup d. Inflated drayage or freight charges e. Falsified demurrage fees
6. Manufacturing	a. Exaggerated breakage b. Unauthorized quality assurance rejects for diversion
7. Cashier	a. Short counts b. Under-ringing sales and removing the cash difference c. Voiding legitimate sale/removing the cash equivalent d. Falsifying refund slips/pocketing cash equivalents e. Fabricated petty cash vouchers f. Unexplained inability to reconcile or balance receipts
8. Returns	a. Diversion charged to warehouse repairs b. Falsified salvage decorations
9. Travel or Traffic	a. Inflated travel vouchers b. Falsified travel vouchers
10. Scrap or Salvage	a. Substitution of materials b. Under market scrap sales

Ten Questions an Entrepreneur Should Ask About Fraud

Anthony Luizzo

Who is Responsible for Fraud Prevention?

Although everyone is responsible for crime or fraud prevention, top management is ultimately responsible. One of the most important preventative tools a company has in its tool kit is the ability to screen-out criminals before they are hired. Most experts agree that, in the conventional corporate setting, the following departmental entities have a role in the hiring process:

- The Human Resources Department. This department is usually tasked with framing company pre-hiring requirements and ensuring that potential candidates have the skills to perform required job tasks.
- The Security Department. This department is usually tasked with conducting background checks of potential new hires (i.e., criminal history check, social security verification, pre-employment credit history, and previous employment check).
- The Legal Department. This department is usually tasked with promulgating legal directives to ensure compliance with state, municipal, and federal law.

Who is Responsible for Fraud Detection and Resolution?

- The 1991 "Federal Sentencing Guidelines" are specific about who is responsible for fraud detection and resolution. According to the guidelines, corporate officers are responsible for fraud detection, investigation, and resolution.
- The guidelines require that companies adopt and implement a compliance program to prevent violations of federal law by the corporation and its agents.

What types of fraud affect a business?

Fraud is believed to come in all types and sizes; one type *does not* fit all business environments. Some of common varieties include:

- Purloining of cash by employing "fuzzy" accounting principles not taught in academic institutions of learning.
- Diverting inventory to non-company entities.
- Contractor corruption frauds.
- Promulgating fraudulent financial statements.
- Check and credit card frauds.
- Racketeering related frauds.

From *Internal Auditing Report* Warren, Gorham & Lamont/RIA/Group (Reuters) Thomson Publications. February 2001 – openlibrary@archive.com

Why has Fraud Skyrocketed?

There are many factors believed to contribute to a marked increase in the escalation of fraud. Some of these factors include, but are not limited to:

- Corporate downsizing. In many instances, non-revenue producing employees such as security are the first to be laid-off, thus leaving less eyes and ears to watch-over company assets.
- Population shifts. As a result of increased migration post World War II, employers are no longer able to determine the fitness of potential job applicants based on knowledge of the applicant and their community.
- Increased litigation. Many employers are hesitant to provide any information re previous employment, beyond name, rank and serial number.
- Lack of criminal prosecution. Many businesses fail to prosecute criminal offenders, thus leaving the door open for offenders to remain anonymous.
- Lack of background checks. Most businesses use the "gut instinct" approach to hiring new employees, simply perform a cursory check of previous employment and bring the person on board.

Will Insurance Cover All of my Fraud Losses?

Most insurance carriers require that client firms have some security systems and procedures in place before coverage. Notwithstanding, with respect to incidents of fraud, insurance firms usually conduct an independent investigation of the incident, and if they conclude that the fraudulent incident was preventable, they may deny reimbursement. It is also a fact that many companies victimized by fraud are more likely to attempt to recover losses via civil litigation than filing a claim with their insurance carrier. Besides, from a fiscal point of view, any fraud claim will certainly lead to increased corporate insurance premiums.

How can business best gauge criminality?

Diagnosing crime and writing a prescription to cure frail security programs is both an art and a science. Crime control planning specialists use the security survey as the evaluative tool to measure a company's crime risk exposures.

It is often said that what a 'cat scan' is to a physician, the security survey is to a security diagnostician. Taking note of the correlation between having an annual check-up and good health, security experts theorize that executing an annual security survey is one of the most effective methods of evaluating a company's crime risk exposures.

What can Businesses do to Deepen and Strengthen Crime Prevention Initiatives?

The foundation of any theft reduction effort is education. Corporations would be wise to recruit and train all employees to properly fulfill their role as departmental "security advocates."

A security advocate is a department employee who is responsible for ensuring that all incoming visitors and/or strangers are properly challenged (may I help you). Corporate-wide crime prevention initiatives might include:

- Educating employees to identify internal theft red flags.
- Promoting corporate wide crime prevention awareness programs.
- Establishing an employee 'hot line' to confidentially report criminality.
- Establishing employee reward incentive programs for reporting criminal behavior.

Can Law Enforcement Handle Corporate Fraud Problems?

If it were not for budget constraints and manpower considerations, law enforcement would be the best consultative source to handle the internal theft and fraud problem. Experience has shown that because of limited resources and lack of training in certain fraud case scenarios, law enforcement may not be equipped to tackle fraud related problems. Moreover, the United States Attorney's Office in most districts has established a minimum monetary threshold for prosecution of certain kinds of fraudulent activities. It is important to recognize that this does not relegate the case to a lower level of importance, but in a practical sense, cases may not receive the kind of investigative or prosecutorial wherewithal required.

Who Should Handle Corporate Fraud Problems?

Over the past decade, many professional organizations and institutions of higher learning have begun fraud prevention training programs for executive management and internal audit or security department personnel. The sum and substance of these educational initiatives is to cross train accountants and investigators to use numbers and records as clues to delve deeper to uncover fraud. The accountant and the investigator often look at the same fraud problem from two different perspectives, while this new fraud specialist is trained to look at a fraud problem with two sets of eyes simultaneously. In most fraud cases however, knowledgeable accountants and investigators team-up to work on solving sophisticated fraud problems. It is important to note that forensic accounting teams are frequently engaged as consultants after an upper-level manager, auditor or loss prevention executive has noted some irregularity.

What are the Corporate Red Flags of Fraud?

Fraud prevention experts have coined a few activities strongly associated with increased fraudulent behavior. These red flags include, but are not limited to:

- Weak internal controls.
- Inordinate number of internal control breaks.
- Corporate checks returned for insufficient funds.
- Customer complaints.
- High employee turnover.
- Large payments for unspecified services.

- Excessive agent fees or commissions.
- A disparity in periodical analysis ratios (i.e., sales vs. expenses).
- Changes in employee lifestyles (i.e., unexplained wealth or work habits).
- Increased inquiries from creditors or collectors

It is important to note that each of the items listed above could be an indicator of criminality but should not be considered proof positive of a fraud scheme without further investigation.

What is Business Espionage and How Can it be Effectively Controlled?

Anthony Luizzo

Most companies would love to capture the essence of their competitor's successful product lines. In 1986, for example, the Kellogg Company, on the advice of its security consultants, stopped visitors from touring its corporate plant in Battle Creek, Michigan, after European spies were caught posing as tourists. That same year, the Thomas Baking Company accused Entenmanns Baking Company of sponsoring a clandestine operation to ascertain how to duplicate the famous nooks and crannies of its successful English muffin line. In May 2001, two Lucent Technologies scientists were arrested in London for stealing key trade secrets. Apparently, the duo intended to use the secrets to form a data networking enterprise.

Business Espionage

Simply defined, business espionage is the theft of business secrets among competitors. Espionage is often referred to as the illegal or unauthorized gathering of business information. The goal of the industrial thief is to steal company secrets without arousing the suspicions of fellow entrepreneurs. The corporate thief is often a trusted company employee, a professional spy working for a competitor, or another entity that stands to gain a financial advantage from whatever is illegally obtained. Often, company employees see industrial theft as an opportunity to make extra money by stealing company secrets that they have access to and are paid to protect. Finding willing buyers of company secrets is often not difficult.

Who is at Risk?

All businesses with secrets to safeguard are at risk. Whether it is a soft drink company formula or a missile component for a NASA project, any information about company's operations is at risk. To keep company secrets out of a thief's hands, every business must formulate strategies to deepen and strengthen global security.

Who are the Security Gatekeepers?

The first line of defense in any protection strategy is the crime prevention force. To win the industrial espionage war, companies must formulate protective strategies to mitigate or remove risk exposures before they wreak havoc on a company's bottom line. Internal auditors play a crucial role in the process, preparing the periodic audits that measure program compliance and effectiveness.

From *Internal Auditing Report* Warren, Gorham & Lamont/RIA/Group (Reuters) Thomson Publications. June 2001 – openlibrary@archive.com

Strategies to reduce criminality include

- Formulating comprehensive corporate conduct and ethics policies and procedures.
- Advocating confidentiality. The adage "loose lips sink ships" should be every company's espionage prevention motto.
- Performing background checks on all company employees, vendors, and contractors.
- Piecing together security programs (e.g., guards, alarms, and locking systems.) that effectively keep intruders out.
- Using the talents of the security and internal auditing department specialists to investigate allegations of wrongdoing.
- Conducting security surveys and loss prevention audits.
- Designing plans, procedures, and controls to protect assets, operations, and personnel.
- Recruiting the services of countermeasure specialists to check corporate boardrooms and office suits for illegal listening devices (e.g., bugs).

Industrial spies are known to ply their trade from a variety of locations both inside and outside of the company. Often, key employees and their residences are targeted as information sources.

A security check of a key employee's residence should ensure that:

- The perimeter shrubbery is regularly trimmed.
- Residential alarms and surveillance systems are in place.
- Exterior lighting is adequate.
- Residential keys are secured.
- Keys are not left in parked vehicles.
- Vehicles are safely parked in locked garage facilities.
- Exterior doors and windows are constructed of industrial-strength materials.
- Doors and windows are fitted with industrial strength locking devices.
- Lock cylinders are changed when keys are lost, misplaced, or stolen.
- Residential keys are kept separate from car and office keys.
- Personal identification tags are removed from key chains and holders.
- Timers are used to automatically switch on interior lights at appropriate times.
- Safes are in good working order and properly alarmed.
- Alarm codes and safe combinations are periodically changed.

A security checklist of office complexes should ensure that:

- Corporate facilities are properly alarmed.
- Important papers are shredded after they are discarded.
- Conference rooms and offices are periodically swept for illegal listening devices.
- Employee identification programs are in place.
- Critical records and valuables are safeguarded in alarmed safes and locked file cabinets.
- Keys are properly safeguarded.
- Security guards are patrolling office suites and storage facilities.

Conclusion

An effective proactive security program helps to reduce incidents of espionage. One of the best methods of keeping company secrets out of the hands of spies is to make all employees part of the security team.

274 ■ *Healthcare Security*

Auditing for Identity Fraud

Anthony Luizzo

With Identity Theft on the Rise, Internal Auditors Need to Understand the Challenges Their Companies Are Facing

Identity fraud is one of the fastest growing white-collar crimes in the United States. According to a September 3, 2003, survey by the Federal Trade Commission (FTC), 27.3 million Americans have been the victims of identity theft in the past five years, including 9.9 million people in the last year alone. The survey estimated that the financial impact on businesses and financial institutions totaled nearly $48 billion and consumer out-of-pocket expenses totaled $5 billion. Moreover, in the past 12 months, 3.23 million consumers were shocked to learn that several new financial and business accounts had been illegally opened without their knowledge and consent. (See "The Cost of Identity Theft Is High for Businesses" in the October 2003 issue of *Internal Auditing Report* for more on the FTC survey.) Delving even deeper into this abyss of deceit, in 2002, the FTC released its top 10 consumer complaint categories. Identity theft topped the list—accounting for 43 percent of complaints logged in the FTC's Consumer Sentinel database. Considering the disastrous effect these crimes have on business operations, internal auditors should have some knowledge of how these crimes are perpetrated, and how they can be effectively curtailed.

How Do Identity Thieves Obtain and Use Personal Information?

Identity snatchers steal another person's personal identity (e.g., name, address, Social Security number, date of birth, mother's maiden name, or other personal identifiers) to open new credit card accounts, take over existing accounts, obtain loans in the victim's name, purloin funds from the victim's checking account, lease cars and apartments, and apply for utility services. According to security experts, despite the best efforts to manage personal identifying information, skilled larcenists use a variety of both sophisticated and unsophisticated methods to gain access to this treasure trove of data.

Various methods employed by these imposters include

- Purloining wallets, purses, briefcases, computers, etc.
- Stealing residential or business mail.
- Completing false "change of address" forms to divert mail to other locations.
- Dumpster diving "—rummaging through personal or business trash in search of personal identifiers.

From *Internal Auditing Report* Warren, Gorham & Lamont/RIA/Group (Reuters) Thomson Publications. March 2004 – openlibrary@archive.com

- Fraudulently obtaining copies of credit reports discarded by unscrupulous employers, landlords, and service providers.
- Spotting personal information in the home or rummaging through discarded refuse.
- Obtaining personal information via Internet transactions.
- Scamming targets by sending e-mails posing as legitimate companies or government agencies (a practice known as "phishing").
- Pilfering business records of customers, employees, patients, or students.
- Bribing employees who have access to select files.
- Hacking into electronic files.

How Is Illegally Obtained Personal Information Used?

- Identity thieves call credit card companies pretending to be the cardholder and asking to change the mailing address on the account, thus keeping the true cardholder in the dark during the scam.
- They open new credit card accounts using the stolen identification (the legitimate card holder usually finds out about the theft after the delinquent charges appear on their credit report).
- They establish phone and related wireless services using stolen identification.
- They open bank accounts and write bad checks on these accounts.
- They counterfeit checks and debit cards to draw cash.
- They take out loans to purchase cars and other big-ticket items.

Minimizing the Risk of Identity Theft

While all identity thefts cannot be prevented, they can be materially minimized by managing personal information wisely. Companies should always restrict access to personal employee records.

For consumers, the keys to preventing identity theft include

- Regularly ordering copies of credit reports from any one of three credit bureaus: Equifax, Experian, and TransUnion. Credit reports contain information about where a person works and lives, the credit accounts that have been opened in their name, a history on how they pay their bills, and civil litigation histories (bankruptcies, judgments, etc.). Legally, credit bureaus cannot charge more than $9.00 for an individual credit report. By checking credit reports on a regular basis, consumers can catch mistakes and fraudulent activities before they wreak havoc on their personal finances.
- Avoiding using easily recognizable passwords such as family birth dates and addresses. When opening new accounts, in lieu of using a mother's maiden name, consumers should use a password instead. They should always try to avoid giving out Social Security numbers if possible.
- Always safeguarding passwords. This is especially important if the consumer has roommates, employs outside help, or has heavy traffic in their home or workplace.

276 ◾ *Healthcare Security*

- Avoiding giving out personal information over the phone, through the mail, or via the Internet, unless the original contact was self-initiated, or the person is known with whom he or she is dealing. Oftentimes, identity thieves pose as bank representatives, Internet service providers, and municipal agency employees to get people to reveal identifying information. It is important for consumers to remember that they do not have to give a business a Social Security number just because the company asks for it. One should ascertain why the company needs it and how they are going to safeguard it before providing this information.
- Always trying to deposit mail in official post office collection boxes or at the local post office.
- Always shred all personally identifying trash.
- Always using compactor services in lieu of conventional Dumpster storage containers.
- Always pay attention to billing cycles and follow up with creditors if bills are tardy.
- Being wary of promotional scams that request personal information.
- Always update computer virus protection software. Computer viruses can introduce program functions that can command the system to send out sensitive files or other stored confidential data.
- Never download unknown files or activate unknown hyperlinks.
- Always use firewall programs, especially if one uses a high-speed Internet connection like cable or DSL services. A firewall capability helps to stop illegal hacking.
- Making sure that the browser has the most up-to-date encryption capabilities.
- Prior to disposing of an outdated computer, delete all personal information. Simply deleting files using the keyboard and mouse commands is not enough; the files must be removed from the hard drive to prevent retrieval.
- Taking advantage of "opt out" programs that limit the information that is shared with third parties or is used for promotional purposes.

What to Do if You Are Victimized

If you suspect that your personal information has been stolen or misused, the FTC suggests that you take these steps:

1. Contact any one of the three major credit-reporting agencies to place a fraud alert on your credit report. This helps to prevent an identity hijacker from opening additional accounts in your name. Upon confirmation of the fraud alert, the other two credit bureaus will automatically be notified to place fraud alerts on your credit report and send you a copy of your credit report free of charge. Remember to scrutinize your report carefully. Look for inquiries you did not initiate, accounts you did not open, and unexplained debts you did not incur.
2. Close any accounts that have been tampered with or opened fraudulently. If you are asked to settle fraudulent charges or debts, immediately initiate a fraud dispute resolution process with the creditor.
3. File a report with your local law enforcement agency and remember to keep a copy of the complaint report and complaint number to validate your claims to creditors.
4. File a complaint with the FTC.

Auditing the Security Process

Questions an internal auditor should ask when auditing for identity theft prevention include:

- Does the firm have a formal, written identity theft program?
- Are employees aware of the program?
- Are personal confidential files securely maintained?
- Is access to confidential files strictly regulated?
- Are computer systems properly protected?
- Are the internal controls over confidential identifying information adequate?
- Are background checks of employees routinely conducted?
- Are effective security strategies employed to safeguard identifying information?
- Are identity theft prevention bulletins disseminated to employees?
- Are theft incidents logged?
- Are theft complaints routinely reported to local police and the FTC?
- Are perpetrators of identity theft prosecuted?

Looking to the Future

Effectively resolving identity theft problems is often a time-consuming and frustrating task. It is well worth the time and trouble, however, because identity theft ruins reputations, destroys credit ratings, and depletes bank accounts. The good news is that there are federal, state, and local resources to assist consumers. The Fair Credit Reporting Act (FCRA) establishes procedures for correcting mistakes on credit report records. Under the FCRA, both the credit bureau and the organization that furnishes information (the information provider), such as a bank or credit card company, are responsible for correcting inaccurate or incomplete information in a report. The Identity Theft and Assumption Deterrence Act of 1998 made identity theft a federal crime. Many states have enacted local ordinances as well. To obtain state-by-state information, contact your state attorney general's office or local consumer protection agency.

278 ■ *Healthcare Security*

Aspects of Fraud Prevention: Where Loyalty Dies, Fraud Grows

Anthony Luizzo

The one trillion-dollar question facing the mercantile community in these financially challenging times is how best to detect and reduce fraud waste and abuse. Some more seasoned fraud prevention executives attribute the rise in workplace fraud to the loss of management and employee loyalty. There was a time in America when a person could get a job; and if they played by the rules and did their job they would be rewarded with long-term employment and retirement. In today's commercial environment, greed and fraud are the rule and not the exception. Chief executives are more interested in "golden parachutes" than corporate ethics.

Tragedy as a Catalyst for Change

In the court of investigative reality, prior to that dreadful day in early September 2001, few American firms performed extensive pre-employment screening. According to a November 26, 2001, article in Career Builder Magazine titled **"Background Checks: Now Not the Time To Lie"** – 69 percent of human resources professionals polled said that their organizations perform background checks.

Why is Fraud Committed?

From both the audit and investigative perspectives, experience has demonstrated that a great number of fraud exposures occur because perpetrators are given the opportunity to ply their trade. Moreover, many less loyal employees believe that they are smarter than the oversight mechanisms employed in the workplace and that they will ultimately get away with the crime. Typical of this philosophy is the employee who embezzles from his employer and perceives and rationalizes the theft in a variety of fashions including but not limited to:

- ☐ **Offsetting Alleged Inequities**. Obtaining monies believed due for inadequate raises, bonuses, and/or overtime
- ☐ **Obtaining Revenge**. "Getting even for a perceived mistreatment
- ☐ **Gaining Self-Enrichment**. Acquiring the luxuries to enhance self-image and standard of living
- ☐ **Thrusting for Psychological Excitement**. Viewing himself or herself as a modem day "Robin Hood" or master thief
- ☐ **Securing Peer Acceptance**. Desiring to become a part of the sub-culture who depend on each other and protect one another
- ☐ **Modern Day Greed**. Rationalizing that if the corporate bad guys can employ accounting principles not taught in schools and get bailed out for their judgment lapses – who will fault the little guy for his transgressions in these financially challenging times
- ☐ **Simply Being Stupid**. With the economy being what it is, anything is possible especially when it comes to living the American Dream

From *The Journal of Healthcare Protection Management*. (25): 1. 2009.

Who is Responsible for Fraud Prevention?

In protection management circles, often criminologists and accountants are tasked with this awesome responsibility. To better understand how this team works, it is necessary to grasp the basic functions of each group involved. The accountant focuses on ***how*** the fraud was committed via analyzing the fiscal system in which the fraud occurred, and the security professional focuses on ***who*** committed the transgression via applying standard investigative approaches. Together they form the fulcrum upon which good fraud deterrence is built.

The Fraud Prevention Team in Action

For purposes of illustration, assume that a director of internal audit identified an inventory shortage, which cannot be accounted for in the maintenance department's storage facility. Therefore, the security department is contacted and asked to participate in the investigative exercise. The investigation might proceed as follows:

Accounting Department Investigative Approaches

How did the loss occur?
- ☐ Was the missing inventory received?
- ☐ Was the inventory received at the proper point?
- ☐ Were the items countersigned by anyone – hopefully by security operatives?
- ☐ Was the inventory recorded as received?

When did the loss occur?
- ☐ When was the last physical inventory conducted?
- ☐ Can a window of time be pinpointed when the crime possibly occurred?

Who could be responsible?
- ☐ Do sign-in documents note any irregularities?
- ☐ Has the risk management department been queried regarding abnormal fluctuations in insurance premium spikes?

Security Department Investigative Approaches

- ☐ Are all employees background checked?
- ☐ Are special integrity tests given to employees that have fiduciary responsibilities?
- ☐ Are Surveillance technologies in place (CCTV, alarms, EAS systems, etc.?
- ☐ Are readouts available for review?
- ☐ Are outside vendors restricted from sensitive areas?
- ☐ Are ID cards utilized?
- ☐ Do key control policies exist and are they adequate?
- ☐ Have all individuals with access to inventory records been interviewed?
- ☐ Are restrictions in place re access control?

☐ Does the company maintain a "disgruntled" employee file?
☐ Has law enforcement been notified?

It is amazing that in many corporate entities security and audit operatives rarely work shoulder-to-shoulder on fraud cases. In fact, the two departments rarely if ever share their investigative findings.

Controlling Fraud Via Background Screening

Volumes have been written about how to hire the right person for a given job. Human resources executives have developed a wide spectrum of interview techniques to determine if an applicant can do a given job. Conversely, only a few programs are available to appropriately assess trustworthiness. More often that not applying integrity-related evaluation techniques is an art and not a science and corporate executives would be wise to hire a professional with the appropriate loss prevention expertise to perform this task.

Looking Deeper into the Abyss of Deceit

Many articles have been written speaking to the need for due diligence in the hiring process. One such article comes to mind that appeared in the Hartford Courant in June 2003 by John Jurgenson *"There are often many deceivers in our midst".* In his excellent expose, Mr. Jurgenson while speaking on fraud indicators cautions that:

☐ 80 percent of all resumes are misleading
☐ 20 percent of education assertions are bogus
☐ 40 percent of salary declarations are inflated
☐ 27 percent of all resumes contain sham references

The Relationship between Corporate Downsizing and Fraud

No one knows if there is a link between fraud and downsizing. Downsizing has been a central element of business since the 1980s. Many economists view downsizing as a necessary correction in the inevitable ups and downs of the normal business cycle. Many security executives see a definite correlation between employee theft and downsizing, especially when they hear news reports of how CEOs are leaving the firm with oversized severance packages. A great many more forward-thinking security executives privately say that corporate business has broken the social contract it once had between it and its employees. From the turn of the 20th century to the 1980s, there existed an unwritten and unspoken contract between workers and management. That contract said that if a worker gave a good day's labor and did not violate any major rules of the firm, long lasting employment while not guaranteed, was assured. That contract worked well for both the employer and employee. The stable work force was as much of a benefit to the company as secure job tenure was to the worker. In today's corporate environment, company loyalty has long died, many employees feel that they work day-to-day and do not have a stake or role in the company's overall health and stability.

Ironically, the areas where cutbacks often occur are in positions like security and accounting that may not *directly* contribute to the corporate bottom line but are responsible for keeping assets safe from potential predators. When security and oversight positions are downsized – the company is more vulnerable to the risk of fraud and thievery.

Steps in a fraud audit

It is imperative that fraud consultants advise their clients of the following: There are two significant limitations in performing a fraud audit:

1. There are no guarantees that a fraud investigation will find all the fraud
2. There is no guarantee that the fraud investigation will result in successful legal action against the assailant

Methods of performing a fraud audit include

- ☐ **The Planning phase** – Meeting with the client to discuss framing the parameters of the audit. The consultant needs to obtain an engagement letter authorizing the audit, and the letter should spell out exactly what is to be included and excluded in the investigative oversight. Moreover, the consultant needs to ascertain whether the audit is to be conducted openly or surreptitiously
- ☐ **The Investigative phase** – Physical assessment of fraud risk exposures. At times, clients wish to have the investigation conducted in total secrecy – in these cases, all the case work is done after hours and investigative approaches are conducted without personal contact with potential targets associated with the investigation
- ☐ **The Reporting, packaging, and prosecution phase** – Discussion of evidentiary findings, meeting with law enforcement, drafting the final report, and personally HAND delivering the final report to the client.

A final thought, after the engagement is completed, it is always an excellent idea to meet with the client's legal counsel to ascertain whether any confidentiality requirements apply to the exercise at hand.

Conclusion

The seeds of success in formulating a fraud audit investigation lie in the entity's ability to keep its assets free from danger or loss. Captains of industry would be wise to have a fraud audit survey performed on an annual schedule by a seasoned fraud prevention expert. A list of seasoned fraud examiners can be found via contacting the Association of Certified Fraud Examiners @ www.acfe. com. The Association is a 50,000-member organization that was established in 1988. They are responsible for certifying fraud examiners and maintaining educational requirements.

Aspects of Controlling Fraud in Healthcare Facilities: Taking the Threat Seriously

Anthony Luizzo and Bernard J. Scaglione

Magnitude of the Fraud Problem

In recent years, an increasing number of healthcare-related virtual and physical frauds have been paraded in the press involving a number of fraudulent practices including but not limited to theft of personal data, diversion and misrepresentation of medical billing, theft of medical supplies, and purchasing of counterfeit products.

It is estimated that over 3000 items are used in hospitals daily. Keeping internal theft to a minimum is a monumental and often arduous task for all concerned. Financial losses due to healthcare fraud are estimated to range from $70 billion to $236 billion annually. According to industry sources, in 2008 Americans spent $2.34 trillion on healthcare services and the Federal Bureau of Investigation estimates that between 3-10% was lost to healthcare fraud. The U.S. Department of Justice (DOJ) Healthcare Fraud & Abuse Control Program's Annual Report for FY/ 2010 purports that the federal government won or negotiated approximately $2.5 billion in healthcare judgments and settlements and DOJ statistics reveal a sharp increase in investigative activity in the healthcare fraud field. In 2010 alone, DOJ opened 1,116 new criminal healthcare fraud investigations involving 2,095 potential defendants.

To further underscore the healthcare fraud problem an August 20, 2011, article in USA Today by Kelly Kennedy "Feds Go After Health Fraud" reports a dramatic increase in the number of hospital fraud prosecutions compared to 2010. The article specifically refers to several highly publicized Medicaid/Medicare billing prosecutions that cost taxpayers well over 225 million dollars. Beyond healthcare, many other mercantile sectors are also enduring increased numbers of commercial frauds. According to Association of Certified Fraud Examiner's (ACFE) 2010 Report to the Nation of Occupational Fraud & Abuse estimates that a typical organization loses 5% of its annual revenue to fraud with a medium loss of $160,000, of which nearly a quarter of the frauds reported involved losses of at least $1 million. Applied as a percentage of the 2009 gross world product; fraud losses totaled more than $2.9 trillion.

Types of Healthcare Frauds

ID Theft In healthcare some fraud occurs either from identity theft or provider deception. Identity fraud or ID Theft is quite simple to explain; hospital staff as part of the registration and/or billing process illegally gathers, use and/or sell patients' personal identification and credit documentation to unscrupulous miscreants. These persons then take the personal identifying information and create new accounts to purchase consumer goods etc.

Provider Deception Provider deception is more complicated, however, and oftentimes occurs in a wide variety of circumstances. One of the most common forms of thievery is Billing Manipulation. It involves the billing for treatment of patients who never were treated.

From *Journal of Healthcare Protection Management.* (28):1, pp. 21–27. 2012.

Other fraud-related offshoots include duplicate billing from different insurance carriers for the same medical procedures, incorrect reporting of diagnoses or procedures to maximize payments, billing non-covered services as covered items or eligible provider billing services.

Subscriber Fraud Subscriber fraud involves enrolling someone for coverage on his or her insurance contract, altering amounts charged on claim forms and prescription scripts, claim fabrications, and furnishing false application documentation.

Non-Subscriber Fraud Non-subscriber fraud includes using purloined ID cards for medical services, providing false employer group and/or group membership data, and changing subscriber addresses to intercept subscriber payments.

Other Common and Not-So-Common Healthcare Frauds Healthcare frauds also includes frauds committed by providers in the workers' compensation system, such as doctors, rehabilitation counselors, or chiropractors. This form of fraudulent behavior occurs when a healthcare provider knowingly and intentionally submits a material misrepresentation re medical treatment to the insurance carrier for payment. Other healthcare frauds that are not so common include: falsification of expense records, stealing funds from petty cash, suspense, and commercial accounts, falsifying invoices, fictitious invoicing, theft of materials, payroll fraud, accounting misstatements, inappropriate journal vouchers, fraudulent expense claims, exaggerated employment credentials, vendor forgery, tax frauds, not reporting revenue or illegally avoiding taxes, kickbacks, and bribery.

Demographics of Healthcare Fraud

In the court of security opinion, industry studies have shown that smaller organizations are disproportionately victimized by fraud since they often lack sophisticated technologies that only larger entities can afford. According to the ACFE 2010 study, approximately 80% of fraud is committed in one of six departments: accounting, operations, sales, executive management, customer service and purchasing departments.

Conducting a Security Audit

The study also indicated that fraud was most likely to be detected via anonymous "Tip" as compared to any other means. From the protection perspective, surprise security-related audits were deemed to be extremely effective in detecting fraud. One of the most important functions of healthcare security is to champion the proactive security model and conduct security audits of critical departmental functions on a periodical basis. A security audit should provide four basic protection tenets:

1. Asset Protection
2. Information safeguarding
3. Operational efficiency
4. Programming adherence

A critical component to launching a security audit initiative is finding the right professionals for the job. Operatives should be highly trained and experienced, they should be capable of diagnosing crime and fraud exposures, and they should be skilled in drafting after-action reports on both a periodical and annual schedule.

Fraud Reduction Strategies

First and foremost a fraud-related risk assessment should include an extensive review of all prior incidents and include information of existing audits previously performed by both internal and external professionals. Let us not forget that auditing departments also perform audit reviews, as such it is important that their work product be included in the security auditors report.

Hospital-Specific Fraud Prone Areas

Obviously, all areas of a healthcare facility should be inspected when conducting a security audit. Nevertheless, if the audit is focusing on loss prevention rather than general protection requisites, the following departmental operations should include and not be limited to:

- Dietary
- General Stores
- Pharmacy
- Facilities Management
- Purchasing
- Contract Compliance
- Human Resources (Background Screening)
- Clinics
- Information Technology

If the general focus of the security audit is on general protection, it should include and not be limited to:

- Security Systems (CCTV, Locking, EAS, Detecting Systems, Etc.)
- Parking Security
- Visitor Access
- Patient Information Systems
- Employee Information Systems
- In-house Voucher Systems
- Safes
- General Patrol Management
- Executive Protection

The Need for Auditors and In-House Security to Work Together

The ACFE 2010 report lists auditing as one of the most underutilized tools used to thwart fraud. The study specifically recommends that surprise audits be regularly performed by skilled professionals and that tight inventory controls be implemented. One of the major problems encountered in almost all institutions from healthcare to telecommunications is that AUDITORS AND IN-HOUSE SECURITY RARELY IF EVER WORK SHOULDER-TO-SHOULDER ON AUDITS, NOR DO THEY SHARE THEUR WORK PRODUCT. It is strongly recommended that these two departments work more closely so that fraud and other deceptive practices are uncovered before they have an opportunity to wreak havoc on the firm's assets and bottom line.

Perform Adequate Background Screening

Another tool often neglected in the war on fraud is performing adequate background screening. All individuals who work for the healthcare facility should be adequately checked. Beyond employees, contractors, and other part-time staff everyone should undergo screening.

Exception Modeling

Data modeling and data mining techniques should also be utilized. Also known as exception modeling, auditors look for abnormal patterns of behavior within the working structure of the day-to-day operations of any single group of users to possibly ascertain the first glimpse of a fraudulent affiliation. The concept of exception reporting is not new. It is the basis for many types of statistical analyzes. It is a bell-shaped curve in statistical analysis and suggests looking at those patterns of behavior that have strayed from conformity or the majority viewpoint. Much of the information in this new and exciting area can be found in computer log-on data on software from desktops and procurement systems, payroll records, client records, collectively together producing a clear picture of behaviors. The goal to reducing fraud is in the collection of behaviors that can determine patterns of unusual and abnormal odd couple affiliations.

General Protection Strategies: Assigning Security Advocates

With respect to in-house management, routine inspections should be completed by department executives for their specific areas of responsibility. As an example, senior executives might want to make unannounced spot inspections as part of their regular departmental rounds, "security advocates" should be assigned in each department to oversee safety and security within their geographical areas of responsibility, and security administrators might wish to inaugurate crime prevention workshops and seminars for all in-house employees and contractors. Some larger corporations hire a Corporate Security Officer (CSO) to coordinate the activities of procurement, auditing, and financial services, legal and risk management. Whether the coordination of efforts is through a single CSO or with a unified effort of several departments working together, in a planned, coordinated approach to fighting fraud is an extremely effective strategy.

Future Fraud Fighting Tools

The National Healthcare Anti-Fraud Association in a white paper published in 2010 entitled "Combating Healthcare Fraud in a Post-Reform World: Seven Guiding Principles for Policymakers" offer the following seven strategies:

1. The sharing of anti-fraud information between private insurers and government programs be encouraged

2. Data consolidation and real-time analysis must be at the forefront of healthcare fraud fighting efforts
3. Pre-payment reviews and audits be increased and strengthen
4. Public and Private health plans should be allowed to protect their enrollees by barring or expelling providers suspected of perpetrating healthcare fraud
5. Healthcare providers caught participating in fraudulent practices be sanctioned by their respective licensing authorities
6. Further strengthening healthcare identifier numbers
7. Further investment in innovative healthcare fraud prevention efforts

A Final Thought

The problem of fraud within healthcare environs is quite broad, encapsulating many differing aspects. The reduction of fraud within healthcare is possible and attainable. All institutions are vulnerable, but none are helpless. There are countless ways to stop fraud cold; it requires a concerted effort by all. The key is to get started, even if it means instituting some of the methods of prevention outlined. Do it today, as if your institution depended on it. It does!

Chapter 11

Interview and Interrogation

Interview vs. Interrogation

Anthony Luizzo

Generic Definition of an Investigation

An investigation is the medium through which facts necessary for successful criminal prosecution or civil litigation are discovered, gathered, preserved, and subsequently prepared as evidence in anticipation of a legal proceeding.

Interview versus Interrogation

An interview is a conversation with the subject or interviewee. Usually, the interviewee is ready, willing, and able to tell what he or she knows. An interrogation probes and draws out information from an unwilling subject by asking precise, trenchant questions. Interview and interrogation objectives often include but are not limited to:

- Extracting truthful information
- Ascertaining case facts
- Developing details of possible criminality
- Ascertaining the identity of suspects, accomplices, or conspirators
- Obtaining corroborating testimony
- Recovering purloined goods
- Obtaining written statements
- Developing new leads

From *Financial Fraud* Warren Gorham & Lamont / RIA Group (Reuters) Thomson Publications. December 1999 – openlibrary@archive.com.

DOI: 10.4324/9781003215851-11

287

288 ■ *Healthcare Security*

Twenty Tips When Conducting an Interview:

1. Determine information needs before beginning the interview
2. Pre-plan interview questions
3. Schedule interviews at the time of day when you have the most personal energy
4. Select an interview location free from distractions
5. Allow sufficient time for the interview
6. Maintain control of the flow of the interview
7. Establish a rapport with the interviewee
8. If interpreters are required, ensure that all communication takes place between the interviewer and interviewee – not between the interpreter and the interviewee
9. Accept the emotions of the interviewee without criticism
10. Put the interviewee at ease
11. Show a personal interest in the interviewee
12. Keep interviews conversational
13. Listen carefully to verbal dialog
14. Note any non-verbal signals
15. Refrain from interrupting the interviewee
16. Structure questions so that they can be easily understood
17. Do not take extensive, distracting notes during the interview
18. Use shorthand when taking notes
19. Leave the door open for follow-up interviews
20. Upon completion of an interview, try to obtain a written statement of facts from the interviewee

Interview Note Taking Tips:

✓ Always try to employ the subject's vernacular
✓ Always focus on the interviewee
✓ Do not attempt to record all information verbatim
✓ Important statements should be recorded word-for-word
✓ Avoid becoming distracted by your note taking
✓ Always preserve interview notes for future legal use

Glossary of Investigative Shorthand

Investigators employ a variety of shorthand abbreviations while recording information. The following is a list of abbreviations often used by investigative operatives:

Q&A: Question and Answer
RQ: Repeat Question
RA: Repeat Answer
IR: Interviewer
IE: Interviewee
IW: Interview

POB: Place of Birth
DOB: Date of Birth
NA: Not Applicable
ID: Identification
CM: Crime Method
ICB: Internal Control Break

DMV: Motor vehicles Info
PDI: Police Department Info
AKA: Aliases
MPH: Miles Per Hour

SSF: Security System Failure
AF: Audit Failure
SF: Security Failure
BSR: Background Search Required

Conclusion

Over the years, successful investigators develop a sixth sense, instinctively recognizing clues; the secret is to leave no stone unturned. The ability to observe and recognize clues is more of an art than a science, but this sixth sense can be easily developed once the investigator learns to be properly prepared for interviews and interrogations.

Demystifying the Investigative Process

Anthony Luizzo and John Gaspar

Generic Definition of an Interview

Over the years, investigators have come up with several generic definitions for the investigative exercise. Our definition: An investigation is the medium through which facts are discovered, gathered, preserved, and prepared as evidence for legal proceedings.

The Difference Between an Interview and an Interrogation?

An interview is a leisurely conversation with a person of interest, which can rise to a fact-finding excursion where warranted. An interrogation is a probing conversation with normally unwilling or unknowing subjects to extract secretive information. The primary objective of the interrogation is to obtain incriminating evidence and ultimately get to the truth of what happened.

A Window Into the Investigative Process

One of the tenets of the investigative process is to gather as much pertinent information as possible during the interview. Oftentimes, the interview is analogous to a written play, and the interviewer and interviewee are the lead actors. The interplay between both is like a well-rehearsed symphony, wherein the interviewer tries to marry the apparently connected to the unconnected and the interviewee tries to either answer the questions forthrightly or attempts to dance around the truth. The investigative process follows the universal academic learning model: "Assess the facts, criticize assertions and integrate conclusions." From the business perspective, private investigators often call this exercise "connecting the dots" or "peeling the onion." As the layers of the onion are pulled back, the onion begins to reveal its true nature. Whether performing a law enforcement or business-related interview/interrogation, it is most important to always come to the interview or interrogation prepared. Being prepared includes but is not limited to:

- Using control-type questioning—a control question is an incident related query intended to elicit a psychological response
- Observing kinetics
- Establishing rapport
- Controlling the flow of the interview
- Allowing uninterrupted dialogue
- Keeping an open mind
- Following the facts wherever they may lead

From *PI Magazine*. (19):166, pp. 6–9. November/December 2019.

Investigative experts instinctively know that active listening is the fulcrum upon which effective interviews are constructed. Often the interviewee is ready and able to tell what he or she knows, and interviewers should always allow him or her to tell their story uninterrupted.

At times, interviewees are not interested in cooperating. In these instances, the interviewer needs to wear two hats and try to conduct both the interview and interrogation in one session.

This takes tremendous skill and should only be performed by seasoned sleuths. The interrogation, on the other hand, is a formal session designed to elicit a confession of guilt and involves probing and extracting information from an unwilling subject by asking trenchant questions. The objective is to seek evidence and an admission of responsibility or guilt. The interviewer needs to leave the impression that the incident at hand has already been solved and that the interviewee is somehow involved.

Interview Types

Initial Interview: Identifies the circumstances surrounding the incident, lists possible witnesses/suspects, catalogs physical evidence, and classifies the incident as a crime, civil event or as an informational report.

Canvass Interview: Usually completed as a follow-up to the initial interview and involves canvassing of neighborhoods, searching out witnesses, and following all possible leads. Oftentimes these canvasses are door to-door inquires of residences, business establishments, bus stops, delivery carriers (Federal Express, USPS, Parcel Post, etc.) and transportation companies (Uber, taxi cabs, car services, buses). In many instances, the canvasser is searching for evidentiary materials, including video camera footage, eye or ear witnesses, or any related information that can shine further light on the incident under scrutiny.

Victim Interview: Often involves searching for the who, when, why, how and where of the incident.

Witness Interview: The objective of these interviews is to obtain eyewitness information from a wide variety of locations (stores, apartment complexes, shopping malls, etc.) captured during the initial interview, leading to sketch characterizations and other evidence-related exhibits.

Suspect Custodial Interview: The questioning of a person regarding their involvement or suspected involvement in a criminal offense or offenses. As a matter of course, suspect interviews are performed by law enforcement officers as part of their regular criminal justice process.

Non-Custodial Interview: These interviews are usually performed by private security personnel and are fact-finding exercises. In this type of interview, it's important that the interviewer establishes rapport with the interviewee and ensures that the interviewee is comfortable and relaxed.

National VS. International Investigative Considerations

In a June 1995 article by the undersigned, "Investigating in a New Environment" in Security Management Magazine, discusses the unique differences associated with performing investigations in foreign lands. It's important to recognize that performing investigations and conducting interviews and interrogations abroad can be perilous. Because many corporations have multi-national footprints, the way interviews and interrogations are performed internationally should be carefully researched. First and foremost, it is imperative that investigative professionals entering

292 ■ *Healthcare Security*

these markets understand that they pose a markedly different, and sometimes dangerous, cultural, and legal landscape.

Many issues that are taken for granted in domestic investigative interviewing and interrogating exercises must be addressed in the context of the host country's political, legal, and cultural climate. One of the most important issues that needs to be researched before interviewing and/or interrogating anyone is to seek legal counsel and check out the host country's legal system thoroughly. Every country has its own legal system, which affects all aspects of the criminal and civil justice process, including security and investigations. These systems vary greatly from country to country. Permissible investigative approaches in Mexico may be prohibited in France, for example. Protections that are taken for granted in the United States pertaining to search and seizure, self-incrimination, Miranda Warnings, interview taping, etc., most likely are quite different than our justice system requirements. The major exceptions to this rule are the United Kingdom and India.

The U.S. legal system is an outgrowth of the English common law system, and many of the principles of the American justice system apply there. Beyond the legal system, it is equally important that the investigative specialist become extremely familiar with the host country's culture and language. It is also important that the investigative professional read as much about the host country as possible before endeavoring to jump in and perform any due diligence excursions.

The Homework Phase: Aspects of Preparing for the Interview or Interrogation

The key to ensuring success is being prepared. A successful interview and/or interrogation begins and ends with getting all your ducks in a row before beginning the exercise. Before contacting a witness or the subject of an investigation, whenever possible, review police and civilian reports and CSI reports, as well as comprehensive background, social media searches and computer-assisted dispatch (CAD) reports on the subject and location. If possible, talk directly to the responding officers and/or interested parties to obtain detailed accounts of the incident. Finally, it is most important that the interviewer determine whether one-party or two-party consent is required for electronically taping potential proceedings. This is especially important if electronic taping will be part of the investigative envelope.

Preparing for the Interview

- Pre-plan interview questions
- Put the interviewee at ease—develop a rapport
- Structure interview questions so that they are easily understood
- Show a personal interest in the interviewee
- Always keep interviews conversational
- Listen carefully to verbal and non-verbal dialog
- Refrain from interrupting the interviewee
- Determine information requirements before beginning the interview
- Schedule interviews at the time of the day when you have the most personal energy
- Select an interview location that is free from distractions
- Always allow ample time to conduct the interview

Interview and Interrogation ■ **293**

- Always maintain control of the interview flow
- Try to establish rapport with the interviewee
- Always accept emotive responses without criticism
- Refrain from taking extensive notes during the interview – shorthand helps
- Refrain from interrupting the interviewee
- Always leave the door open to follow-up interviews
- Obtain a written statement of facts at the conclusion of the interview
- When using interpreters, make sure that all communication takes place between the interviewer and interviewee, not between the interpreter and the interviewee

Note Taking Tips

- Refrain from trying to write verbatim responses—audio- or videotaping should be practiced whenever possible (in many states you need to get all parties consent to the being recorded)
- Avoid becoming distracted by your notetaking
- Always preserve interview notes for future use

Shorthand Notetaking Suggestions

- Q&A: question and answer
- RQ: repeat question
- RA: repeat answer
- IE: interviewee
- IR: interviewer
- IW: interview
- MVI: motor vehicle information
- PI: police information
- AKA: aliases
- MPH: miles per hour
- POB: place of birth
- DOB: date of birth
- NA: not applicable
- ID: identification
- CM: crime method
- ICB: internal control break (fraud and audit term)
- SSF: security system failure
- AF: audit failure (fraud and audit term)
- SF: security failure
- BSR: background search required

Interview Methods

- Good Guy – Bad Guy: One interviewer attacks the interviewee while the other defends
- Role Reversal: The interviewer reverses roles with the interviewee, e.g., "If you were looking into this matter, what would you do?"

Interview Techniques

- Pregnant Pause: Asking a question … pausing—this often-uncomfortable silence creates the opportunity for the interviewee to continue conversing
- Trade-Off Technique: Offering a promise of helping the interviewee by suggesting that their assistance will be taken into consideration later, if necessary
- Breaking Down the Story Technique: The gradual process of obtaining the truth by pointing out inconsistencies in the facts, thus hopefully getting the interviewee to make broader remarks and possible admissions
- Graceful Exit Technique: Allowing the interviewee to furnish excuses for their behavior by offering a sympathetic ear, thus keeping the door ajar for future interactions

Deceptive Behavior Traits: Types of Liars

- Panic Liar: Rarely wishes to face the consequences of his or her confession
- Occupational Liar: Has lied for years—it's a way of passage
- Tournament Liar: Loves the challenge lying brings
- Ethnological Liar: Taught over the years to never squeal on another
- Sadistic Liar: Will never give the interviewer the satisfaction
- Psychopathic Liar: No conscience whatsoever

Helpful Investigative Hints

More astute interviewers never fail to take special notice of clothing, jewelry, tattoos, accents, and other personal identifiers. To the perceptive sleuth, a college ring identifies schools attended; sports jackets, elbow patches and button-down shirts signify possible academician affiliation; bow ties often signify non-conformist characteristics; lapel pins showcase organization and association affiliation; the list goes on and on. It really pays to observe!

Performing Due Diligence: Testing Information Accuracy

Once the interview and/or interrogation is completed, it is time for fact-testing. Each assertion offered during the interview and/or interrogation must be truth-tested. Witnesses must be located and interviewed, background checks and related due diligence performed, tips and leads verified, etc.

Conclusion

In the court of protection wisdom, conducting interviews and interrogations is truly both an art and a science. The art involves setting the proper environment and stage for the interview, whilst the science embodies using your observation and intuitive abilities to capture the ever-elusive truth. Interviewers spend countless hours probing, examining, researching, listening, observing, and pondering before they tear a page from their "RX" pad and begin preparing their final report.

References

Lyman: publisher Pearson 6th edition ibsn# 3-978-0-13- 506057-5 https://pressbooks.bccampus.ca/criminalinvestigation/chapter/chapter-9-interviewing- questioning and-interrogation/

Luizzo, A. Van Nostrand G.: "Investigating in a New Environment" – Security Management Magazine – June 1995.

Luizzo, A. "Interview Vs. Interrogation": Financial Fraud Report – Warren Gorham & Lamont / RIA Group Reuters -- Thomson Publications – December 1999.

Luizzo, A., Calhoun, C., "Fraud Auditing: A Complete Guide": The Foundation for Accounting Education / New York State Society of Certified Public Accountants – 1992, Rev. 1995.

---

*Reprinted with permission: PI Magazine

Decrypting the Interrogation Process

Anthony Luizzo and John Gaspar

Definition of Interrogation

An interrogation is analogous to essentially peeling back an onion layer by layer on people's lives, places and/or things. Seasoned sleuths systematically probe and draw out information from willing and/or unwilling individuals by asking precise and trenchant questions to test the validity of information. An interrogation is quite different from an interview in that the interviewee is often directly or indirectly connected to the incident under review. Further information on interviewing can be found in a November/December 2019 article by the undersigned: "Demystifying the Investigative Process" – PI Magazine. Prior to performing an interrogation, investigative sleuths normally spend countless hours following leads and testing theories before walking into the interrogation room armed with a strong cross-examination strategy.

Special Virtues That All Good Interrogators Possess

Good interrogators are taught to always remain composed, never interrupt and/or disrupt the ebb and flow of the interrogation, listen twice as much as talk, never be afraid to leave the land of the familiar for the land of the unfamiliar, and always shine a bright light on inconsistencies. These and other attributes help to make a solid soldier in the war on criminality.

Difference between Law Enforcement and Private Security Interrogation?

Law enforcement interrogators must follow strict legislative requirements, including Mirandizing interviewees when setting out to perform an official interrogation, whereas private interrogators have fewer legislative restraints placed upon them. According to the *Encyclopedia Britannica:* interrogation, in criminal law involves questioning by police to obtain evidence. Private investigators also have the power to interrogate suspects but lack the power to compel testimony or detain witnesses and are not required to Mirandize suspects. Consequently, private investigators can be more creative in their efforts to legally extract truthful information from unwilling witnesses and suspects during interrogations.

Differences do exist, however, in the way an interrogation is conducted. Police normally have the benefit of extensive resources far beyond what their private counterparts have, such as access to criminal reports, subpoena process, crime labs, video footage, etc. Moreover, they can take their investigation to another jurisdiction(s), including state and federal task forces, and share information. Private security interrogations do not enjoy the enormous resources that their counterparts have at their disposal. The big difference between conducting a police interrogation versus a private security interrogation is that security interrogators do NOT have to advise the persons of interest of their constitutional rights – an exception may be if the interrogation is being performed on behalf and/or promoted by the law enforcement.

From *PI Magazine*. (19):168, pp. 10–12. March/April 2020.

What are the Objectives of an Interrogation?

Plain and simple, the objective of an investigation is to gather and test the validity of information. The investigator(s) working the case need to:

1. Learn the facts and develop the evidence
2. Extract truthful information from reluctant, evasive, lying or hostile witnesses
3. Decipher the plan or conspiracy
4. Identity possible suspects, accomplices, or conspirators
5. Obtain corroborating testimony, supportive evidence and admissions of guilt or confession
6. Recover purloined fruits of the criminal enterprise
7. Establish guilt or innocence of the suspect(s) being interrogated
8. Obtain written, audio statements, admissions, or confessions
9. Ascertain related evidence, such as hideouts, weapons, gang affiliations
10. Locate and catalog all case-related evidence

The ABCs of Selecting Interrogators

Selecting the right person to perform an interrogation begins and ends with EDUCATION, PERSONALITY, AND TEMPERAMENT. Specifically, the person must be inquisitive, possess an excellent moral compass, embrace truthfulness, retain excellent interpersonal skills, and enjoy laboring in criminological career surroundings. All interrogators should have the ability to:

- Pay attention to detail
- Conduct independent research
- Examine physical evidence
- Decipher human motive responses
- Solve problems
- Listen intently

Further guidance can be found in an excellent criminal justice degree school guide: "How to become a criminal investigator" https:www.criminaljusticedegreeschools.com/criminal-justice-careers/criminal-investigator/

Preparing the Pre-Interrogation Checklist

Prior to an interrogation, it is critical that interrogators prepare a needs assessment checklist to ensure that the interrogative exercise goes off without a hitch. One of the most important attributes that an interrogator needs to bring with him or her into the interrogation room is patience. Other considerations include:

- Framing an appropriate game plan
- Selecting the right interrogation site
- Arranging room furniture, lighting, water glasses, ashtray
- Allowing ample time for the interrogation

298 ■ *Healthcare Security*

- Devising an appropriate questioning strategy
- Outfitting the room for audiovisual serviceability
- Ensuring that notetaking does not interrupt the ebb and flow of the interrogation

Arranging the Interrogation Room for Optimum Effect

The physical layout of an interrogation room should be designed to maximize a suspect's discomfort and their overall sense of powerlessness from the moment he or she steps into the room. The room should have video/audio capability and related signage announcing that the session will be recorded.

The room should be a small soundproof chamber with limited seating and bare walls, and the interviewee should never be physically seated near light fixtures or thermostats. Additional information on interrogation logistics can be found in an excellent book *Criminal Interrogation and Confessions* by F. Inbau, et al: Abe Books – 1967.

How is an Interrogation Performed?

In general, an interrogation takes place in a formal interview room and is often tape-recorded. It is important to note that a video recording is always preferred over a non-video session. For the most part, the seating should be comfortable, and the chairs positioned for a face-to-face confrontation. It is important that the interrogator not stand over the interviewee so as not to make him or her feel intimidated. The interviewee should be offered a cold beverage and/or food and advised of where the restroom is located. Prior to beginning the interrogation, an interrogation schematic needs to be prepared. Interrogation schematics often include the who, what, when, and where of the incident under review. It is said that "doing one's homework helps to ensure success of any and all undertakings." Further information on interrogation and process can be found in an excellent book by Rod Gehl and Darryl Plecas, "Introduction to Criminal Investigation: Process, Practices and Thinking" – Justice Institute of British Columbia Press: August 1, 2017.

Utilizing Interpreters

It is always a good idea to have a certified non-partial bilingual interrogator available to perform the interrogation. If an interpreter is required, however, it's important to make sure that all communication is between the interrogator and the interpreter, and not between the interviewee and the interpreter.

What is Social Media Harvesting?

Social media harvesting is a way to collect data unobtrusively and automatically from social media platforms, such as Facebook and the like, by employing simple programing tools to extract relevant messages from these platforms for various research purposes. Data harvesting, as its agricultural name suggests, is like gathering crops because it involves collection and storage for future reward. Data can be harvested in different ways, ranging from simple copy-and-pasting to more complicated programming strategies. Media mining is the process of obtaining data from social media sites and the internet. There are many social media research companies available to investigators. The prices of these services range from $5 to $500.00.

What is a Forensic Interrogation?

A great many private investigative firms are called on by major corporations to perform financial investigations. Company X believes they have a financial loss problem. Oftentimes, these specialized investigations require specialized audit-related investigative expertise that not all private investigators and accounting professionals offer. Over the past forty years, however private investigators and accounting professionals began working and training together to perform these specialized forensic investigative assignments. Looking back at the evolution of forensic auditing and investigations, it was not until the savings and loan crisis of the 1980s and 1990s hit businesses smack in the pocket that forensic audit investigation made its official debut.

In response to the hue and cry from business to do something, professional organizations specializing in fraud examination began making their debut. Ons such organization, the Association of Certified Fraud Examiners, began cross training security and accounting professional to find fraud forensically. Further information on how investigators and accountants often work together on a financial investigation can be found it an article co-authorized by the undersigned, "Team Partners in Fraud Detection" (October 1992) The CPA Journal. The article crystalizes how these new team fraud fighters go about conducting a forensic audit investigation. It is important to note that, as of today, forensic accounting professionals' number in the tens of thousands.

What Role do Background Checks Play in an Interrogation?

As a matter of course, once the interrogation is completed, it's time to commence verifying the information gleaned from the interrogation. Beyond reaching out to verify persons, places and locations, etc., the tool often used to assist interrogators is ascertaining information accuracy about individuals in the background check, According to an excellent article featured in Good Hire – https://www.goodhire.com/blog/complete-guide-to-background-checks "The Complete Guide to Background Checks," a background check, simply put, is a process a person or company uses to verify that a person is who they claim to be. The purpose of a background check is to furnish helpful information about a person's history. Additional information on performing due diligence and background checks can be found in an article written by the undersigned, "Background Checks: A Diagnostic Tool to Decipher Deception": (2014) Journal of Healthcare Protection Management – Vol. 30., No. 2, pp 57-65.

Conclusion

Conducting an interrogation is a five-phase undertaking.

1. Phase one – selecting the right interrogator
2. Phase two – selecting the right interrogation facility
3. Phase three – selecting the right interrogative game plan
4. Phase four – selecting the right question/notetaking strategy
5. Phase five – selecting the right interpreter arrangements

References

Luizzo, A. & Gaspar J. "Demystifying the Investigative Process" *PI Magazine – November/December 2019* pp. 6-9.

"How to become a criminal investigator" https://www.criminaljusticedegreeschools.com/criminal-justice-careers/criminal-investiagtor/

Inbau, F. et el: "Criminal Interrogation and Confessions" Abe Books – 1967.

Gehl, R. & Plecas, D. "Introduction to Criminal Investigation: Process, Practices, and Thinking" *Justice Institute of British Columbia Press* – August 01, 2017.

Luizzo, A & Calhoun C. "Team Partners in Fraud Detection" *CPA Journal* – October 1992.

Good Hire: The Complete Guide to Background Checks" https://www.goodhire.com/blogcomplete-guide-to-background-checks

Luizzo, A., et al: "Background Checks: A Diagnostic Tool to Deciphering Deception" *Journal of Healthcare Protection Management – Vol. 30, No. 2. Pp. 57-65 – 2014.*

---

*Reprinted with permission: PI Magazine

The Art of Non-Target Interviewing

Anthony Luizzo and John Gaspar

In two recent PI Magazine articles authored by the undersigned on interviewing and interrogations we focused on how to interview and/or interrogate individuals who have some connection to specific incidents under scrutiny [1] [2]. This article will focus on interviewing individuals such as neighbors, bystanders, business owners who at first blush appear to have no apparent connection to the incident; but may knowingly or unknowingly advance the evolution of the investigative exercise. Performing this type of investigative exercises could be a simple walk in the park and leisurely chat with a neighbor, but it could also be a perilous encounter with a potential accomplice and/or a close relative or close friend of the target. The key to conducting these types of interviews begins and ends with doing your Homework. To properly set the table, skilled interviewers need to draft a pre interview checklist, locate interview targets, initiate contact-tracing, formulate an interview blueprint, and perform non-intrusive background screening.

Pre-interview checklist

It is said that prior planning prevents poor performance. The first step begins with preparing a needs assessment list to ascertain what will be needed to move forward. A sample checklist might include:

- Developing an interviewee profile folder. Profile folders often includes, interviewee photos, relationship to the target (friend, relative, other), marital status, employment information
- Checking whether outside law enforcement or private security assistance is needed if the interviewee resides in another jurisdiction?
- Ascertaining whether the interviewee is retired or employed?
- Deciphering whether the interviewee will be a hostile or non-hostile engagement

Locating interview targets

It is important to note that much of the initial target information is normally unearthed during the initial target interview. As the interviewer questions the target, names, places, and locations are uncovered which becomes the roadmap to follow in identifying future interviewees.

Contact tracing

This process begins with good gum shoe detective work. Contact tracing is in many ways analogous to what is normally done when tracing a pandemic flu patient. Contact tracing helps to identify other individuals who should be included in the interviewer's contact list. Contact tracing works best when broad-based tracing methods are used. In essence, contact tracing is like a genetic family history search. A hypothetical real-life contact tracing episode can be likened to an infected

From *PI Magazine*. (20):171, pp. 10–11. September/October 2020.

302 ■ *Healthcare Security*

COVID-19 patient coming into close contact with 10 others. The seasoned investigative sleuth's mission is to expeditiously locate all 10 contacts.

Interview blueprint

Interviewing family, neighbors, work associates, casual acquaintances, and others requires a differing interview strategy. The key to ensuring success is to do your homework before sitting down with an interviewee. Each of the above have one thing in common, they know the target in some way shape or form. Knowing that, it's imperative that the interviewer prepare an effective question design strategy that extracts information without impugning the target. A hypothetical example might be when the interviewer believes the target of the inquiry committed a crime, it's imperative that this sensitive information is not revealed during the interview. Seasoned interview sleuths instinctively know that questioning witnesses is fraught with peril and tread wisely in this explosive minefield.

Nonintrusive background screening

Background checks come in a wide variety of models and sizes depending on who is being checked and for what reason. With respect to interviewing neighbors and business owners oftentimes a non-intrusive screen is sufficient. This type of screen may include, informally speaking to neighborhood store owners, neighbors, employers, reaching out to local police beat officers, and conducting surveillance shadowing activities. From an investigative technological perspective seasoned sleuths often employ web-based sources to get emails, phone numbers and physical address. As a matter of preference, many sleuths use video chat (DUO, FACTIME, GOOGLE, ZOOM) and/or audio calling methods. Other options include emails and US mail. Oftentimes, a video chat allows the interviewer to develop a rapport with the interviewee, whilst also offering a visual window to assess verbal and nonverbal mannerisms.

Questioning strategies

A seasoned sleuth knows how to do his or her homework before setting out to interview family members, business owners, bystanders, and others. There is no single questioning strategy that snuggly fits all types of interviews. As a practical matter, non-target interviewing is quite different than target interviewing in that the focus of the exercise is to gather as much peripheral information as possible from individuals who are not remotely associated with the case under consideration. With this in mind, we offer the following tips.

Questioning family members

Interview questions might include:

- When was the last time you spoke to the target?
- Do you know why you are being questioned? – oftentimes family members have inside knowledge of the incident under scrutiny

Questioning business owners

Interview questions might include:

- Do you know this person – have a photo of the target if possible?
- Do you know why you are being questioned?
- Do you feel uncomfortable being questioned?
- Do you recall whether the target has ever come into your establishment?
- Do you recall whether you ever had a conversation with the target?
- Is there anything you would like to tell us about the target?
- When was the last time you spoke with the target?

Questioning bystanders

Interview questions might include:

- We are seeking information about this specific occurrence
- Do you know this person – show a photo if available?
- Do you recall seeing and/or speaking to the target?
- Is there anything you would like to tell us about the target?
- Do you feel uncomfortable being questioned?
- When was the last time you saw the target?

Questioning law enforcement

Prior to questioning law enforcement personnel, it's important that the interviewer perform a cursory check of municipal and state legal statutes to ascertain permissibility. Assuming that it is permissible, interviewers must refrain from ever asking interviewees to violate ethical or legal obligations. A short-list of statutes that apply herein includes state and municipal sunshine laws, and the Freedom of Information Act (https://www.foia.gov/). Sundry public records that interviewers may need from law enforcement to buttress their case might include:

- Incident reports
- Investigative follow ups
- C.A.D. reports
- Crime scene reports including photos and diagrams
- Body and auto cam footage
- Charging affidavits

- Do you feel comfortable being questioned?
- Is there any reason why we should not be talking?

Program management and oversight

In the court of protection wisdom, many security executives instinctively know that optimum programmatic oversight is often akin to a well-run assembly line. If the security chain breaks somewhere – it can quickly unravel everywhere. A proficient method of ensuring that a program is running effectively is to periodically inspect it. The tool often used my many administrators to get this job done is the After-Action Report (AAR). AAR assessments normally embody an oversight and monitoring schedule, a technological and procedural step test plan, and a long-range compliance calendar. In competent hands, these reports help security managers keep a watchful eye over their institution's protection programming. Further information on AARs can be found in an article written by the undersigned [3].

A final word

The information herein is intended to furnish a roadmap for professional interviewers to follow when preparing their non-target interview game plan. Skilled sleuths instinctively know that interviewing family members, bystanders and others is often a delicate walk through the tulips. The art of conducting these types of interviews lies in the interviewer's ability to set the proper stage for the interview, whilst the science embodies using the interviewer's intuitive skills to properly capture every morsel of fact. Looking back at police history: as the notorious TV police show "Dragnet" so eloquently recounted: *we are only seeking the facts and only the facts.*

References

Luizzo, A & Gaspar J. "Demystifying the Investigative Process" PI Magazine – November / December 2019 pp.6-9.

Luizzo, A & Gaspar J. "Decrypting the Interrogation Process" *PI* Magazine – March / April 2010 pp. 10-12.

Luizzo, A. *"What are After-Action Reports"* Internal Auditing Report – WGL / RIA Group: Reuters: Thomson Publications June 2002.

---

*Reprinted with permission: PI Magazine

Effective Interview Techniques

Anthony Luizzo

What is the Object of an Interview?

The object of conducting an interview is to collect accurate information through a systematic and structured format. One of the most important skills an interviewer should possess is being able to recognize truths and untruths. Research suggests that people are surprisingly bad at detecting lies. According to an excellent article by Kendra Cherry, research indicates that 96% of people admit to lying at least sometimes (Cherry, 2018). Cherry's article also notes that a laboratory study found that only 54% of participants were able to detect lying accurately. The article goes on to mention that even trained investigators can be remarkably poor at deciphering untruths. Obviously, deception is big business, and deciphering it is *vital*!

The Interview Defined

In essence, an interview is a conversation carried out in a question-and-answer format. Seasoned investigators consider the investigative exercise to be the meat and potatoes of their profession and often describe it as the artery through which facts are discovered, gathered, preserved, and prepared as evidence for legal or contractual purposes.

How do Interviews and Interrogations Differ?

From a purely investigative perspective, an interview is a *leisurely* conversation between two individuals (an interviewer and interviewee). An interrogation is a probing conversation with an unwilling subject. The interview is typically a *less formal, less accusatory* chat intended mainly to elicit information, whereas an interrogation is a much *more formal* conversation, designed to elicit secret information or a confession. Interrogation involves probing and extracting information from an unwilling subject by asking trenchant questions meant to yield evidence and an admission of responsibility or guilt. Regardless of who is conducting the interview or interrogation (private security, healthcare agencies, law enforcement, or others), the goal of the art and science of the exercise is the same for all: to obtain information and get to the truth.

For simplicity, in the text that follows, my advice for "interviewing" refers to both interviews and interrogations, unless I state otherwise.

An Investigative Snapshot

One of the tenets of the investigative process is to gather as much pertinent information as possible during the interview. Often, watching an interview is like watching a well-acted movie script in

---

From *Journal of Healthcare Protection Management.* (35):2, pp. 110–117. 2019.

306 ■ *Healthcare Security*

which the interviewer and interviewee are the lead performers. An investigator assesses facts, criticizes declarations, and integrates conclusions. From a business perspective security operatives call this peeling the onion. It is most important that interviewers use control-type questions while plying their trade. (Such questions are designed to arouse a subject's concern about their past truthfulness.) "The Control Question: A Technique for Effective Introduction," an article by Stanley Abrams, is an excellent resource on control questioning (Abrams, 2009).

Further, when preparing for an interview, always have an open mind, so that you can follow the facts presented easily, without being misled by preconceptions. Be objective, listen intently, be well prepared, employ sound observation skills, and observe body language and related mannerisms. Never forget that the first stage on any interview is developing rapport. A successful interview depends on the interviewee as much as the interviewer. How comfortable you make the subject may determine the success of your fact-finding exercise. *Often, the interviewee is ready and able to tell what they know, and the interviewer should always allow them ample time to tell their story uninterrupted.* If the interviewee in an initially informal question-and-answer discussion is not willing to cooperate, then it's time to consider moving from a friendly interview to a more formal interrogation.

Interview Types

There are two main types:

- **Standard.** The interviewee usually consents to the process, and the question-and-answer process is *overt*.
- **Undercover**. Usually, these types of interviews are conducted under the guise of fact-finding with an interviewee (possible target) to obtain as much information as possible.

Interview Tips

Here are some actions you should always take in interviews. These tips, and those in the note-taking section below, are meant specifically for standard interviews; some may not apply to certain interrogations of suspects.

- Put the interviewee at ease.
- Structure interview questions so that they are easily understood.
- Keep interviews conversational.
- Listen carefully.
- Pre-plan interview questions.
- Try to schedule interviews at times at times when you feel the most energetic.
- Select interview locations that offer a distraction-free environment.
- Allow ample time to conduct the interview.
- Maintain control of the interview flow.
- Establish rapport with the interviewee.
- Accept emotional responses without criticism.
- Refrain for taking extensive notes during the interview – shorthand helps.
- Refrain from interrupting the interviewee.

Leave the door open to follow-up interviews.
- Try to obtain a written statement from the interviewee describing the sum and substance of the interview.
- REMEMBER: When using interpreters, make sure that all communication takes place between the interviewer and interviewee – not between the interpreter and the interviewee.

Note-Taking Tips

- Know what information must be learned
- Refrain from trying to write verbatim responses.
- Avoid becoming distracted by extensive note taking.
- Always preserve interview notes for future use.

Shorthand Abbreviations

Whether to use shorthand is purely an individual choice. More experienced investigative professionals devise and use their own list of abbreviations. Some examples include but are not limited to:

- DOB: date of birth
- POB: place of birth
- RQ: repeat question
- RA: repeat answer
- IE: interviewee
- IR: interviewer
- IW: interview
- MVI: motor vehicle information
- LEI: law enforcement information
- AKA: alias, or also known as
- MPH: miles per hour
- NA: not applicable
- ID: identification
- CM: crime method
- ICB: internal control break (a fraud and audit term)
- SSF: security system failure
- AF: audit failure
- SF: security failure
- BSR: background search required

Interview Methods and Techniques

- **Good Guy-Bad Guy.** On interviewer verbally attacks the interviewee, and the other defends him or her.
- **Role Reversal**. The interviewer reverses roles with the interviewee – asking, for instance, "If you were looking into this matter, what would you do?"

308 ■ *Healthcare Security*

- **Pregnant Pause**. The questioner stays silent so that interviewee feels compelled to continue talking.
- **Trade-Off**. The interviewer promises to assist the interviewee in some way in exchange for his or her assistance.
- **Breaking Down the Story**. The interviewer continually challenges the interviewee by pointing out inconsistencies.
- **Graceful Exit**. The questioner offers a sympathetic ear to excuses raised, thus keeping the door open for future cooperation.

Verbal Clues to Truthful and Untruthful Statements

Distinguishing true from false statements is an inexact science, but these rules of thumb can help:

- **Truthful** subjects tend to be direct when answering questions
- **Untruthful** subjects tend to be somewhat circumspect with their answers.
- **Truthful** subjects tend to answer questions quickly.
- **Untruthful** subjects tend to take their time in responding while sometimes using delaying tactics, such as asking, "Who me?" or "Why would I do that?"
- **Truthful** subjects tend to not repeat answers.
- **Untruthful** subjects often repeat questions as a ruse to gain time to formulate answers and often repeat answers verbatim or repeatedly asks the interviewer to reiterate previously asked questions.
- **Truthful** subjects tend to use complete sentences.
- **Untruthful** subjects often use fragmented or incomplete sentences.
- **Truthful** subjects usually don't take an accusation lightly.
- **Untruthful** subjects sometimes try to be polite when addressing the accusation and might use flattering terms, such as "Sir" or "Madam."
- **Truthful** subjects tend to be vehement in their denials.
- **Untruthful** subjects tend to recite oaths when confronted, such as: "I swear to God, I did not do that," or "I swear on my father's grave."
- **Truthful** subjects tend to respond to questions forthrightly and with clarity.
- **Untruthful** subjects sometime mumble or talk softly and are evasive.
- **Truthful** subjects usually have little problem denying an allegation in specific terms, as in, "I did not steal the money."
- **Untruthful** subjects tend to have trouble denying an allegation forthrightly; their responses usually skirt the issue at hand and are less specific, as in, "I did not take it."

Verbal Red Flags Linked to Deception

- Consistently offering dim or hazy responses (being vague).
- Consistently repeating questions before answering them.
- Consistently offering fragmented answers and sparse details in response to queries.
- Consistently overthinking answers.

Nonverbal Clues to Deception

Certain behaviors may suggest deception. These include:

- Not looking directly at the interviewer when answering a question, or answering with an emblem expression, such as a thumbs-up gesture, a circled finger, a broad wink, or a shrug of the shoulders (often to indicate ignorance of the event under scrutiny).
- Engaging in "manipulators," such as touching oneself, grooming hair constantly, wringing hands, or picking at imaginary lint.
  - o Irregular breathing patterns.
  - o Excessive perspiration.
  - o Frequent swallowing.
  - o Muscles tightening around the eyebrows.

Do not Forget the Obvious

Investigators can gather a bushelful of information about a subject by simply paying attention to the obvious clues staring at them.

The trick is knowing where to look:

- The location or décor of a person's office indicates status; portraits adorning the walls indicate family connections and whether the person is an adventurer or outdoorsy and the like.
- A lapel pin indicated association affiliation
- The type of jacket worn can reveal whether a person is an academician or conservative in philosophy.
- Suspenders may indicate a staunch, established professional, or possibly a young millennial.
- A bow tie may signal a non-conformist or a person of the liberal persuasion.

Clues abound. All one must do is seek them!

Performing due Diligence

Once the interview is completed, it's time to test the accuracy of the information. Each assertion offered during the interview must be truth-tested. Witnesses must be located and interviewed; background checks and related due diligence must be performed; and tips and leads must be verified.

Conclusion

Many, many articles have been written offering suggestions for deciphering dishonesty. In practice, one of the subtler methods of achieving this elusive goal might be to listen to and follow your innate INSTINCTS. Closely observing gestures during Q & A sessions helps the seasoned sleuth to frame investigative conclusions. In law enforcement and private security parlance, this is often called "reading the target." This is a special gift that law enforcement, private investigators, and hospital security operatives develop over years of interacting with humanity. As such, these sleuths become quite proficient at quickly recognizing deceit, impostures, flimflams, fraudsters, terrorists, hoaxes, phonies, swindlers, liars, and the like. Having these perceptive professionals on board is truly a divine asset!

References

Abrams, S. (2009). The control question: A technique for effective introduction. *Polygraph* 38 (1), 13-14. https://www.polygraph.org/assets/docs/APA-Journal.Articles/2009/the_control_question_-_a_technique_for_effective_introduction.pdf [originally published in 1976 in Polygraph, 5(4).]

Cherry, K. (2018, August 25). How to recognize the signs that someone is lying. Verywell Mind. https://www.verywellmind.com/how-to-tell-if-someone-is-lying-2795917

Destro, R., Fein, R. A., Otis, P., Wahlquist, J., Coulam, R., Borum, R., ... Rowe, M. P. (2006). *Educing Information: Interrogation Science and Art, Foundations for the Future.* Washington, D.C.: National Defense Intelligence College. https://apps.dtic.mil/dtic/tr/fulltext/u2/a476636.pdf

Interview. Wikipedia. https://en.wikipedia.org/wiki/Interview

Luizzo, A. (December 1999). *Interview vs. Interrogation: Financial Fraud Report.* Warren Gorham & Lamony. RIA Group (Reuters) Thomson Publications.

Luizzo, A., & Calhoun C. (1992, Revised 1995) *Fraud Auditing: A Complete Guide.* Foundation for Accounting Education/New York State Society of Certified Public Accountants.

Nguyen, S. (2012, September 30; updated December 2017). Good liars: Their characteristics and why they are so hard to detect. Workplace Psychology: https://workplacepsychology.net/2012/09/

Chapter 12

VIP Protection

Aspects of Hospital Security: Protecting the VIP

Anthony Luizzo, Bernard J. Scaglione, Michael Walsh

What transpires when a VIP (very important person) in admitted to your hospital? To many the VIP conjures up the image of a bodyguard with sunglasses and earpieces ushering in a celebrity past flashing cameras and throng of onlookers straining to catch a look. In healthcare, the designation "VIP" usually signifies a patient with greater concern for privacy, confidentiality, and security, oftentimes due to their extremely high public profile. They may be celebrity entertainers, super star athletes, politicians, foreign leaders, or royalty. Their needs usually translate to a heightened level of service and privacy. As compared to other protection venues, VIP protection in hospitals is quite different and more challenging regardless of whether the VIP is a patient or visitor. From a protection perspective access must be adequately controlled not only in the general areas of the patient's room, but in and around the entire facility on a 24x7 schedule.

Devising a VIP Protection Plan

Regardless of whether the VIP is a politician, movie star, athlete, etc., protection requires the use of resources that are <u>not</u> generally available in all hospital departments. Hospitals that handle high profile VIP's have some incredibly unique challenges which need to be considered when planning for a VIP visit. Developing a protection plan includes devising policies and procedures to adequately screen & control all aspects of the VIP's visit including:

- Incoming visitors, publicists, bodyguards, and other VIPs.
- Dietary needs and special furniture, linen, and bedding requirements
- Deliveries of incoming flowers, gifts, etc.
- Hospital staffs' quest for autographs.
- General VIP traffic

The VIP security plan should be tailored to meet the special needs of the VIP. While the goal is to mitigate VIP risk, this must be accomplished without interrupting the ebb and flow of the

---

From *Journal of Healthcare Protection Management*. (27):1, pp. 43–48. 2011.

DOI: 10.4324/9781003215851-12

312 ■ *Healthcare Security*

hospital's orderly operation. *A successful visit could be measured by the fact that most people in the facility had no idea that a high-profile personality was on campus at all.* Reaching that goal requires planning which starts and ends with an adequate risk assessment survey.

The Risk Assessment Survey

It is important to individually assess each, and every VIP's needs each time they visit. Each VIP has his or her own unique set of security concerns which can change from visit to visit. So, whether it is a long stay or just a doctor visit, each time a VIP comes onto the property a "pre-event assessment" should be completed prior to the VIPs visit. The assessment is completed for two reasons. First, it is done to determine the level of risk they pose to the hospital. Second, the risk assessment is completed to determine the level of security necessary for the VIP.

More forward-thinking security executives suggest that the VIP risk assessment program be framed in four (4) phases:

Phase 1. Formulating the Pre-Event Assessment:

Things to consider when formulating this needs assessment include but is not limited to:

- The type of VIP being protected?
- The VIP's family considerations
- Public popularity
- Media popularity
- Personal security associated with the VIP
- Medical treatment being provided
- Length of hospital stay
- Protection and dissemination of medical information
- Special needs

Framing the Protection Risk Grid

Developing a VIP risk profile often involves:

- Establishing whether there are threats against the VIP?
- Ascertaining VIP protection availability (private guard or government agents)?
- Formulating access control policy (will there be fixed posts, escorts to procedures/diagnostic visits, etc.)

Devising Transportation Security Prerequisites

Piecing together a transportation security plan often includes:

- Ascertaining which method of transportation (private delivery service or official escort) will be used during the VIP visit?
- Establishing vehicle types to be used during the VIP visit (lights, sirens, and markings)?

Once the pre-assessment phase is completed a clear picture begins to emerge. With these reference points in place, a meeting should be held with representatives from other hospital departments to discuss the visit and draw lines of responsibility. Coordination at this time can reduce the chance of mistakes later.

Phase 2. Physical Survey: Advance or Walk-Through Survey

There are two key contact persons that are most important during the VIP's visit, the medical staff and the VIP's main contact. The key medical person is usually the physician caring for the patient of the physician's office staff. The VIP's contact person, a manager, or their publicist. In some cases, the security contact is law enforcement (i.e., secret service, State, or local police). Oftentimes, the contact person(s) will be able to provide you with all the information that you will need. It is a good idea to also consider meeting personally with the VIP to ascertain if their needs differ from their representative's assertions. Once the risk level is determined, a physical survey needs to be conducted of all the areas that the VIP, his or her family, colleagues, and friends will visit. This survey also referred to as an "Advance" or "Walk Through" examines the points of entry, elevator/escalator facilities, treatment/diagnostic rooms, admission in-take areas property storage rooms, in-patient room(s), as well as routes of travel between these areas.

When evaluating travel routes and pit-stop points, the trained security operative should be casting an investigative eye on:

- Which hospital staff will be required to service the VIP patient?
- Which designated alternate routes are to be used?
- Will in-house staff be made aware that a VIP will be visiting their work area?
- What are the primary and secondary entry points?
- What is the impact on other patients or visitors?
- Will the VIP have their own security, or do they want hospital security?
- How will persons coming to see the VIP be screened? (This includes hospital staff as well as visitors and family members.)
- Who will approve the visitor's list?
- Who is the designated contact person for the VIP during their stay?
- What is the contact information in the event after hours contact is required?

In addition to the security walk-through, a tour should be conducted with both the key hospital staff involved with the patient's care and the VIP's security staff together. It is best to conduct one walk-through with <u>all</u> the parties present so that there are no inconsistencies in the implementation of the security plan. Notwithstanding, if that is not feasible, each group can tour separately. The tour should be completed so that all aspects of the security plan are understood by all parties, and to give everyone an opportunity to offer modifications. Some VIP's will ask to have their security staff conduct an advance visit. This is a highly recommended practice that allows both parties to explore expectations and realities. When a visiting dignitary receives Secret Service or diplomatic security protection, an agent will always call to schedule an advance visit. This is a great opportunity to discuss issues of mutual concern, explain the security plan and adjust it if necessary.

Once the risk assessment is completed and the designated areas surveyed key elements of the program can be put in-place and responsibilities assigned. A meeting with all concerned hospital staff may need to be held and VIP representation may also be appropriate in certain circumstances.

314 ■ *Healthcare Security*

Phase 3. Developing the Security Services Needs Assessment

The next step is determining which security services are necessary and acceptable to protect the VIP. The following list of questions will be helpful in making that determination.

- Who will supply security services? (the - VIP or the hospital security staff)
- Will the VIP be restricted to their room?
- Will there be visitor restrictions?
- Does the VIP use outside security?
- What services does the outside security agency provide?
- Does outside security need to be supplemented by Hospital Security?
- Will hospital security relieve outside security for meals and breaks?
- Is hospital security required to work shoulder-to-shoulder with contract security to assist in screening in-house hospital personnel?
- Will hospital staff have access restrictions?
- Is there food, flower and/or gift restrictions?
- Will nursing or other services need VIP access?
- Does hospital security need to be present with the VIP to distinguish between hospital staff and the Media?
- Should stairwells and isolated areas like waiting rooms be patrolled on a regular basis to look for Media?
- Will the Media try to get a photo via helicopter or from adjacent buildings?
- Will the Media try to get a visitor or other patient on the unit to take a photo of the VIP?
- Will an alias be used for the VIP during his or her stay?
- How will their medical information be protected?
- Who will have access to the VIP's medical records?

Phase 4. Framing the Contingency Plan

A contingency plan consists of emergency procedures for the VIP when entering, exiting or while housed in the hospital. The plan should include several options for escape routes, alternate routes of travel in and out of the hospital, and to and from specialty areas like x-ray or operating rooms. These visits can be fluid and the team may have to adapt to changes in risk level exposures during the stay. The keyword here is "anticipation." As rare as it may be, the facility itself may experience standard emergency situations including fire alarms, infant abduction drills, and rules governing MRI and CAT scan radiological areas; each of these should also be addressed for the safety and comfort of the VIP.

Concluding Comments

First and foremost, pre and post preparation is critical to ensure that every possible contingency is considered. A VIP protection plan is the basis for a coordinated team approach for the care and safety of high-profile patients. In the court of security opinion, the most effective method of controlling crime exposure is to diagnose it before it occurs. Hospital staff, VIP's, their employees as well as government and private security personnel may all share the same goals. Hospital administration may not always consider the security of a VIP an important part of the VIP's stay. Still and all, consider the alternative, poor security can result in loss of life, compromised medical records and photos of the catastrophe on the evening news networks – not to mention the loss of future business.

316 ■ *Healthcare Security*

Aspects of Hospital Security: Protecting the VIP – Part II

Anthony Luizzo and Bernard J. Scaglione

Introduction

The potential for an adverse event due to a VIP visit is a real hospital security concern which has increased significantly since we authored our first article in 2011: "Aspects of Hospital Security: Protecting the VIP" - Vol.27, No.1. The article offered a compendia of security initiatives for security administrators to follow when protecting high profile personage during their hospital sojourns. The article addressed several important issues that hospital security executives should consider when piecing together a VIP security protection plan. It furnished a roadmap to follow when a VIP is admitted to a hospital for both short and long stays. It spoke to aspects of how to prepare the risk assessment survey, how to formulate a pre-event assessment tool, how to frame the protection risk grid, how to adequately handle transportation security-related prerequisites, and how to conduct a walk-through assessment.

Who is a VIP?

To many a VIP (especially important person) conjures up the image of a bodyguard with glasses and earpieces ushering a celebrity amid flashing cameras and throngs of observers straining to catch a quick glimpse and/or take a selfie. In healthcare however, the designation "VIP" signifies a patient with a greater need for healthcare service, privacy, confidentiality and security. Many of these VIPs are entertainers, super star athletes, politicians, foreign leaders, royalty, or simply patients with a unique healthcare need. Notwithstanding, VIP protection in hospitals is a thousand percent more challenging than in other venues because their exposure to scrutiny is more than simply a fleeting second in the limelight – it could be for days and or weeks.

Preparing for a VIP Visit

Preparing for a VIP visit requires the development and implementation of a pre-determined plan. Assessing the risk to the patient, visitor or the hospital and implementing a plan that will mitigate those risks. While the goal is to mitigate risk, VIP medical treatment must proceed without interrupting the ebb and flow of the hospital's orderly operation. This is often, not an easy task since curiosity oftentimes causes diversion and diversion causes delay and delay challenges the integrity of the orderly ebb and flow of the institution's care-giving protocol. From a protection specific perspective, a successful VIP health care visit should be measured by the simple reality that most staff within the institution had no prior clue that a high-profile patient is within the hospitals' inner environs. This is often not an easy task, but viable.

From *Journal of Healthcare Protection Management.* (34):2, pp. 46–52. 2018.

The VIP Security Plan

Every security plan has its own unique set of security challenges which can change from visit to visit.

Whether it is an in-patient stay, a quick doctor visit, or simply a visit to a patient, every time a VIP comes onto the property the level of risk to the hospital needs to be assessed. Developing a protection plan requires devising policies and procedures that adequately control all aspects of the VIP's visit. This includes from the very beginning of the visit to its conclusion. Other than patient-specific protection concerns, the plan must address visitor's protection, oversight of flower and gift deliveries, staff access to the VIP, medical record integrity, media control, dietary needs, electronic and telephonic communications protocol, and the formulation of a customized "unforeseeable incident security plan" that addresses adequately handling all unforeseen occurrences. A physical needs assessment must be conducted of all the areas that the VIP, his family, colleagues, and friends will possibly visit. The assessment should include all possible anticipated routes to treatment /diagnostic rooms, and other areas within or outside the hospital that the VIP might visit during their stay. The key contact persons that need to be interviewed for this process include VIP contact personnel, medical staff, hospital security executives, law enforcement {i.e., Secret Service, State, or local police). Oftentimes, the VIPs contact person will provide all the information needed concerning the VIPs itinerary and related pedigree, personal needs, and potential visitors. Once these initial meetings are effectively adjudicated, it is time to meet with hospital department representatives to discuss the ebb and flow of the visit and draw distinct lines of responsibility. Most important, early coordination can reduce the chance of mistakes later. This process should include a tour with both key hospital staff and the VIP's representative.

Updates in the VIP Process

Since we wrote our first VIP article in 2011, security, safety and terrorism concerns have heightened. Explosive/emotive issues that have measurably contributed to raising the temperature involve: the refugee crisis, Korean disarmament talks, and today's overall political atmosphere. These and other issues, help to make the task of adequately protecting the VIP more difficult. For additional information on hospital terrorism prevention, see a recent article in this Journal written by the undersigned: "Aspects of Combating Terrorist Activities in Healthcare" Vol. 34, No.1. The article offers several terrorism prevention strategies to help security administrators keep their institutions safe, secure, and terrorism-free.

Threats to Consider

It is most important that threats from stalkers, political fanatics, and from highly emotive, patients, visitors, employees, and mentally ill fanatics need to be included in the VIP planning process. These and other issues strongly suggest that a more detailed VIP plan is needed beyond what was previously considered in our first article. We believe that in addition to the approaches previously outlined in our first article, it is important that intensive investigative screens are conducted of the VIP's family, visitors, colleagues, and associates so that all possible impending threats to the institution are anticipated and contemplated. Virtually, everyone including stalkers read newspapers and/or listen to news reports about where VIPs are being treated. One possible strategy to

318 ■ *Healthcare Security*

counteract these raising threats is for hospitals to consider using aliases when admitting VIPs into their institutions.

Political Concerns

One of the most effective methods of ascertaining a VIPs threat level is to contact the appropriate federal/ state and local agencies for assistance and additional guidance. These agencies include: The U.S. Department of Homeland Security, The U.S. Department of State, The U.S. Department of Justice. This will help ascertain whether the VIP has adverse political ideals, or comes from a politically active country, or other relevant information germane to the threat level your institution is likely to face. The more research you obtain prior to accepting a VIP will undoubtedly help to avoid an embarrassing situation from occurring. Lastly, it's important to remember that healthcare staffs who have displayed strong political views and/or opinions should be excluded from treating, visiting or interacting with VIPs.

Protection Requisites

During the VIP visit continued patrols of public areas entrances, stairwells and other areas surrounding the VIPs whereabouts should be continually monitored to ensure there is no one loitering or gathering in and around the quarantined area. In addition, strong consideration should also focus on whether potential demonstrations from outside groups are anticipated. Many hospitals <u>do not</u> consider the potential for internal threats from employees, vendors or volunteers when developing a VIP plan. Oftentimes, staff will volunteer to take care of a VIP as a rouse to voice their opinion or obtain an autograph. They may attempt to view medical records or ask questions about diagnosis or treatment for their own knowledge or to sell to the Media. Careful evaluation of staff used to treat a VIP should be conducted to ensure that the VIP is not subjected to this inappropriate behavior. Moreover, consideration should be given to determining the potential for an attack due to their visit. Often when discussing terrorist attacks, we assume persons from a foreign country with strong political views are the most likely culprit. However, in the evaluation of terrorist activity, local or US based terrorist groups should be considered as well. Information pertaining to the political or personal opinions of the VIP should be reviewed to ensure that their public views are not extreme or influential enough to create the possibility of a fanatical group using a hospital stay as an opportunity to promote violence.

Contingency Planning

Because of the potential for an adverse event, a solid contingency plan should be created and reviewed with the medical team and the VIPs contact person before the VIP arrives. The contingency plan should include several optional escape or evacuation routes, alternate routes of travel in and out of the hospital, to and from the VIP's room and to and from specialty areas like x-ray or operating rooms. These routes should be checked continuously to ensure the environment has not changed and evacuation is still possible. As rare as it may be, the facility itself may experience emergency situations including fire, an infant abduction, chemical spill, natural disaster, or service outages; each of these should also be addressed as well.

Aspects of Framing the Contingency Plan

A contingency plan is in many ways like preparing a security survey. The security survey is analogous to a medical CT scan (Computed Tomography) which is an important device used by medical experts to diagnose and treat illness. Similarly, security executives use the security survey to diagnose and proscribe remedies for frail security programs.

In essence "what is CT scan is to a physician, the security survey is to a security diagnostician. In professional hands, the security survey profiles deficiencies, risks, and hazardous conditions, and offers corrective /creative approaches to correct these shortcomings.

ABCs of Structuring the Survey

A great way to understand how a security survey is structured is to frame the discussion using medical terminology:

- Physicians examine patients – security surveyors examine facilities
- Physicians diagnose ailments – security surveyors diagnose frail security policies and procedures
- Physicians write prescriptions – security surveyors offer corrective solutions to heighten and deepen facility protection availability

The process of drafting the VIP security needs assessment begins with putting pen to paper and drawing a sketch of the area under consideration, beginning with diagrams of the VIPs room, the nursing station, emergency ingress and egress portals, escape routes, surveillance / locking systems, patient room locking systems, and other security-related issues affecting the security and safety of the VIP. The next step begins with asking the institution's engineering department to prepare a diagram of treatment facilities that the VIP will most likely use during his or her stay. These include but may not be limited to radiology, MRI, CT scan rooms, etc. It is important that security save these drawings after the VIP leaves the hospital for future utilization. Oftentimes, more forward-thinking security administrators prepare an after-action report for their superiors suggesting that these same facilities be used to house new VIPs in the future. Additional information on drafting and structuring security surveys can be found in a recent article written by the undersigned "The Security Survey: An Investigative Tool" PI Magazine March/April 2017.

Closing Comments

A VIP protection plan is a coordinated team approach for the care and safety of high-profile patients. In the court of security opinion, the most effective method of controlling crime related exposures is to diagnose it before it occurs. Hospital staff, VIP's, their employees as well as government and private security personnel may all share the same goals but have different implementation schematics. Hospital administration may not always consider the security of a VIP an important part of the VIP's stay. Still and all, consider the alternative, poor security can result in loss of life, compromised medical records and photos of the catastrophe on the evening news networks - not to mention the loss of future business.

320 ■ *Healthcare Security*

References: Suggested Readings

Kowalczyk, Liz: "Was Patient with Apparent Ties to Royalty Worth Breaking Hospital Protocols"? - The Boston Globe – April 03, 2016.

Guzman, Jorge, MD, et el: "Caring for VIPs: Nine Principles" - Cleveland Clinic Journal of Medicine – February 2011.

Herrersley-Gray, Robin: "Protecting VIP Patient Privacy" – Campus Safety Magazine – 2011—https:// www. campussafetymagazine.com

Index

21st century healthcare security, 14, 150
21st century hospital security, 7
    access controls and ED isolation, 9–10
    from elder to holistic care, 8
    federal funding to, 10
    handling new security-related technology, 9
    impact of new diseases, 7
    increase in violence and, 8–9
    investigating financial criminality, 10
    planning for, 139
    survey, 87
    training programs to handle hazardous bacterial
        incidents, 7–8
    training security officers, 9
    unauthorized access to medical records, 8
80-20 rule, 101–102

A

access control security, 82, 182
access control solutions
    basic principles, 168
    determining and implementing, 168
    developing and implementing, 169
accessory
    after the fact, 215
    before the fact, 215
accomplice, 215, 253, 287, 297, 301
active fraud prevention, 257–258
affidavit, 215, 303
Affordable Care Act (ACA), xv, 223
After-Action Report (AAR), 283, 304, 319
after-incident security survey, 82
aggregated shipments, 187
amateur shoplifter, 35
Anthrax, 48, 56
arraignment, 213
arrest, warrant of, 213
Association of Certified Fraud Examiner (ACFE), 12,
        218, 222, 232, 249, 262, 266, 281–282, 299
attachment, 215
audit, definition of, 203
audit/compliance program, issues of
    after-action follow-up, 204

    program compliance, 202–203
    program deviation, 202
    program failure, 202
    program functionality, 201–202
    training and competency testing, 203–204
auditing access control procedures
    access control survey, 192
    analytical exposition, 193
    cost/benefit analysis, 193
    proactive companies access control, 192
    procedural access control approaches, 194
    questions to ask, 194
    risk exposures, cross-examination, 192–193
    security through environmental design, 192
auditing crime analysis programs, 185
    analysis targeting, 185
    analytical factors, 185
    auditor's questions, 186
    communication of information, 186
    framing, 186
auditing hospital security, 182
    auditor's questions, 183–184
    best results, 184
    increased oversight, 201
    issues of an audit/compliance program, 201–203
    manual, 182–183
    security executive piece, 182
auditing loss prevention programs
    controls, 197
    internal auditor role, 195
    internal theft problem, 195
    reducing internal thievery, 196
    restitution, 196
    reviewing company's internal theft
        program, 197
    security surveys, 196
    why do people steal, 195–196
auditing proactive security programs, 175
    consultants, 176
    managing the initiative, 175–176
    night has a thousand eyes, 176
    training, 176
auditing shipping or receiving operations, 189–190
    cargo theft prevention management, 191

321

322 ■ Index

investigation and prosecution of cargo thefts, 190–191

platform security logs, 190

auditing warehouse and loading dock security, 187, 188–189

autopsy, 215

B

Baby Boomers, 8, 11, 13
Bacillus Anthracis, 48
bagging, 36, 236
bandwidth, 162, 164, 166–167
bench warrant, 215
bill of lading, 187
blocking chocks, 187
breaking down the story, 294, 308
Broken Windows theory, 102
bulk freight, 187
Bureau of Labor Statistics (BLS), 123
business espionage
    businesses at risk, 272
    control of, 272
    defined, 272
    meaning of, 272
    security gatekeepers, 272
    strategies to reduce, 273
    theft of business secrets among competitors, 272

C

cables, 163–164
canvass interview, 291
capital offense, 215
cargo, 187
cargo thefts
    investigation and prosecution of, 190–191
    prevention management, 191
category program cable (CAT), 163
CAT scan, 76, 79, 92, 111, 198, 208, 269, 314
Census of Fatal Occupational Injuries (CFOI), 123
Center for Medicare & Medicaid Services (CMS), 223
Certified Fraud Examiner (CFE), 176
Certified Protection Professional (CPP), 176
Certified Security Trainer (CST), 176
checking bags at the door, 237
circumstantial evidence, 215
claimant, 188
clearing house, 188
closed-circuit television (CCTV), 2, 5, 9, 70, 80, 121, 193, 243
coaxial cable, 163
community crime control planner (CCCP), 67–68, 103, 105, 205
concealed loss, 188
consignee, 187, 188
consignor, 188

construction/modernization security, 183
contact tracing, 301–302
contempt of court, 215
contract, 215
corporate hiring process, impact of 9/11 terrorist attacks on
    art and science of employment screening, 218
    background checks, 217–218
    cooperation between public and private sectors, 219–220
    individual privacy concerns, 219
    in-house *versus* outsourcing, 218–219
    need for screening employees, 218
    review of hiring programs, 219
corpus delicti, 215
corroborating evidence, 215
crime and violence avoidance
    bolstering security presence and perception, 132–133
    crime prevention through environmental design strategies, 133
    deepening and strengthening protection education initiatives, 134
    effective background screening program, 134
    enhancing access control strategies, 132
    problem, 131
    security perception, 133
    security's response to emergencies, 134
    solutions and strategies for Workplace Violence, 131–132
Crime Impact Statement (CIS), 68, 97
crime mapping, 104, 112, 116, 122, 138, 148, 207
crime pattern, 5, 101–102, 104, 120, 186
Crime Prevention through Environmental Design (CPTED), 90, 95, 102, 125, 132, 133, 169
crime risk management, 67–68, 79, 88, 108, 112, 115–116, 122
Criminal Procedure Law (CPL), 213
Currency Transaction Report (CTR), 262
customer service initiatives
    attitude to present, 173–174
    customer service right, 171–172
    for healthcare security, 173
    model to follow, 173
cyanide, 49, 56–57

D

database security, 183
data networking enterprise, 272
deciphering deception
    background checks, 221
    background investigation program, 223–224
    background screening, 222
    healthcare crime problem, 221–222
    looking back to the future, 225
    one time search *vs.* perpetual search, 224
    primary source *vs.* secondary source data, 224–225

screening-related legislation, 222–223
secondary source data, 225
deciphering fraud, delving deeper to, 246–248
demonstrating value, developing metrics to, 150–151
Department of Health and Human Services (HHS), 4
deposition, 116, 215
designer shoplifting clothing, 36
digital devices, installation of, 167
digital security technology, 161
digital video components, assessment of, 166
direct evidence, 215
disaster management training, 3, *see also* hospital
security, since 9/11 terrorist attack
disaster preparedness
art and science of training for disaster, 47–48
assessing risks associated with emergent
response, 59
biological agents, 48, 56
changing terrorist threats and tactics, 53
controlling persons and vehicles, 61
decontamination equipment types, 55–56
decontamination/treatment process, 52
directing vehicles, visitors, patients and staff, 51
effective WMD training, 53–54
emergency department lockdown, 52
emergency preparedness readiness
checklist, 64–66
exposure source characteristics, 56
facility lockdown, 54–55
formulating a security response program, 60
full facility lockdown, 51
handling vehicle, visitor, patient, and
media issues, 54
hazardous chemical agents, 49, 56–57
hospital lockdown, 61–62
identifying exposure characteristics, 48
lockdown procedures, 50
mitigation phase, 60
notification of incident, 51
partial facility lockdown, 51
perils of weapons of mass exposure, 53, 59
personal protection devices, 55
personal protection equipment, 50
preparedness phase, 60–61
radiological exposure, 49–50, 57
recognizing virus symptoms, 48
recovery phase, 62–63
removing personal protective equipment, 50
response phase, 61
testing the plan, 63
wearing and using PPEs, 55
dispatcher, 188, 190
dock, 188
dock pass, 188
drones, use of, 20
drug addict shoplifter, 35
dynamic crime risks, 120–121

E

Ebola, 48, 56
effective interview techniques, 305, 309
Emergency Nurses Association, 11
emergency preparedness readiness checklist, 59,
64–66
employee awareness security, 183
employee security, 182
employee theft
'carry-out' thief, 240
cash thief, 241
employees steal, 239
final word, 241
hand-out thief, 240
hiring security, 241
send-out thief, 240–241
stopping, 239–240
wear-out thief, 240
Entenmanns Baking Company, 272
Environmental School of Criminology
art and science of proactive security, 199
auditing security programs questions, 199–200
experienced security professional, 198
origins of proactive security, 198–199
securing the future, 200
estoppel, 215
expert, definition of, 116

F

Federal Emergency Management Agency (FEMA), 59
"Feds Go After Health Fraud" report (2011), 282
fiber optic cable, 163
fiduciary, 14, 144, 146, 201, 215, 218, 232, 244–245
financial value
and program effectiveness of healthcare
security, 150
of security services, 144, 151
of using metrics, 105, 139
firearms, 16, 18–19, 33, 131
fire inspection report, 38–39
fire prevention management, security's role in, 38
fitting room, three item limit in, 237
force policy, use of, 16, 17, 19
forensic accounting and the criminal justice process
arraignment, 213
determining guilt or innocence, 215
grand jury, 214
internal auditors and accountants, 213
jury challenges (Cpl: article 270), 214
jury selection (Cpl: article 270), 214
jury trials, 214
search warrant (Cpl: article 690), 214
warrant of arrest, 213
forensic interrogation, 299
forensics, role in investigative process

324 ■ *Index*

back to the future, 233
class and individual evidence, 232
evidence types, 232
evolution of, 231–232
fiduciary evidence, 232
forensic evidence, 231
skimming case, 233
tablecloth case, 232–233
forklift, 188, 190
frames per second, 166–167
fraud
  audit, 259–260, 264–265
  avoiding credit card fraud, 238–239
  bad checks and credit card fraud, 237
  deciphering of, 246–248
  detecting bad checks, 238
  equation, 266
  reporting, packaging and prosecution phase,
      260–261
  safeguard against, 246
fraud, questions entrepreneurs ask about
  business best gauge criminality, 269
  corporate red flags, 270–271
  fraud prevention and resolution, 268
  fraud skyrocketed, 269
  handle corporate fraud problems, 270
  insurance cover, 269
  law enforcement handle corporate fraud
      problems, 270
  strengthen crime prevention initiatives, 269–270
fraud, safeguarding assets against
  creating mechanisms for reporting fraud, 255–256
  maintaining fraud controls, 255
  recognizing existing fraud, 255
  responding to fraud, 256
fraud prevention, 243
  accounting department investigative
      approaches, 279
  breadth of the fraud problem, 243
  controlling fraud via background screening, 280
  corporate downsizing and fraud relationship,
      280–281
  final report, 245
  fraud committed, 278
  frauds are committed, 243–244
  hospital fraud deterrence program, 244–245
  jackpot, 249–254
  looking deeper into the abyss of deceit, 280
  performing a fraud audit, 281
  responsible for, 279
  security department investigative approaches,
      279–280
  steps in fraud audit, 281
  team in action, 279
  tragedy as a catalyst, 278
free on board (F.O.B.), 188
freight seal, 188

G

garnishment, 215
geographical analysis, 185
good guy-bad guy, 307
grab and run method, 36, 236
graceful exit, 294, 308
grand jury, 214, 216
*Guidelines for Preventing Workplace Violence for Health
    Care and Social Service Workers*, 4, 123, 125,
    128, 131, 135

H

habeas corpus, 32, 215
"hand-off" communication protocol, 45
Health and Human Services (HHS), 4, 8, 31
Health Care and Education Reconciliation
    Act (2010), 223
Healthcare Facilities (HCF), 14, 18, 47, 59, 62, 125–127,
    132–133, 173, 222, 284–285
healthcare facilities, controlling fraud in
  assigning security advocates, 285
  auditors and in-house security, 284–285
  conducting a security audit, 283
  demographics of healthcare fraud, 283
  exception modeling, 285
  fraud problem, 282
  fraud reduction strategies, 284
  future fraud fighting tools, 285–286
  hospital-specific fraud prone areas, 284
  not-so-common fraud, 283
  performing adequate background screening, 285
  types of healthcare frauds, 282–283
healthcare security metrics
  clinical length of stay/discharge rate, 142
  development of, 141–142
  interventions, 143–144
  near misses, 143
  other metrics, 144
  square footage, 142
  staff configuration, 144
  workload/calls for service, 143
Health Insurance Portability and Accountability Act of
    1996 (HIPAA), 8, 12
hearsay evidence, 215
hi-low, *see* forklift
hospital command center (HCC), 62
Hospital Consumer Assessment of Healthcare Providers
    and Systems (HCAHPS) survey, 173
hospital security, since 9/11 terrorist attack
  in the 21st century, 7
  access control advances, 12–13
  arming hospital security operatives, 19
  aspects of, 4
  budgetary issues, 12
  catastrophic occurrences, response to, 2–3

challenges in next few decades, 14
changes affect hospital security, 9
changes since 9/11 attack, 1
changing face of, 11–15, 16–21
cost/benefit considerations, 20
dealing with identified threats, 2
disaster management training, 3
disaster preparedness *vs.* terrorism prevention, 12
disease prevention, 13
elder to holistic care, 8
evaluating security compliance, 3
feel of tomorrow's hospitals, 10
financing medical services, 14
force policy, 19
handle hazardous bacterial incidents, 7–8
house surveillance with public surveillance systems, 16
impact of new diseases, 7
increase in violence, 8–9
investigating financial criminality, 10
investigative advances, 13
legislative initiatives, 4
magnetometers, 18
measuring quality assurance, 5–6
metrics to validate expenditures, 20–21
monitoring counterfeit medical devices, 13
new security-related technology, 9
partial federal funding, 10
post 9/11, 2
prior to 9/11, 1
proactive security initiative, 5
program evaluation, 5
robotics and drones, 20
safeguarding medical records, 12
safeguarding medical supplies and equipment, 13
security budget issues and emerging technology, 5
stringent access controls and ED isolation, 9–10
technological enhancement considerations, 17–18
terrorism *vs.* mother nature, 13–14
training security officers' role, 9
treating disease, 11
unauthorized access to medical records, 8
hot spots, 50, 99, 102, 112, 207
"Hot Spotting" tool kit, 115–116

I

identity fraud, auditing for
    challenges faced by internal auditors, 274
    future of, 277
    identity thieves, 274
    illegally obtained personal information, 275
    methods employed by imposters, 274–275
    minimizing the risk of identity theft, 275
    for preventing identity theft, 275–276
    security process, 277
    steps if you are victimized, 276

ID theft, in healthcare, 282
incoming verifications, handling
    handling inbound verifications, 228
    hypothetical scenario, 227
    information being disseminated, 227
    in-house incoming verification process, 228
    in-house to the outsourcing model, navigating, 229
    integration made easy, 229
    managing incoming verifications, 228
    outsourcing incoming verifications benefits, 229
    outsourcing verification requests, 229
    shrinking healthcare dollar, 229–230
industrial thief, goal of, 272
initial interview, 291
inquest, 215
internal auditors, 120, 178, 184, 187, 191, 198, 217, 244, 246, 274, 277
    auditing of crime prevention programs, 175
    auditing of security department, 122
    as corporate watchdogs, 200
    familiarity with all aspects of the investigative process, 178
    on risks associated with internal theft, 195
    role of, 272
    Security Operation's Manual, 182
    white-collar investigations, 213
International Association for Healthcare Security and Safety (IAHSS), 20, 88, 139, 141
interpreters, utilizing, 180, 293, 298, 307
interrogation, 178–179, 297
    background checks, 299
    crime prevention programs, 176
    definition of, 296
    forensic, 299
    interrogation 101, 176–177
interrogation process, decrypting
    interrogation performed, 298
    interrogation room for optimum effect, 298
    law enforcement and private security interrogation, 296
    pre-interrogation checklist, 297–298
    selecting interrogators, 297
    social media harvesting, 298–299
    special virtues, 296
    utilizing interpreters, 298
interview
    defined, 290, 305
    vs. interrogation, 178, 287, 305
    locations, 179
    methods and techniques, 307–308
    note taking tips, 288
    objectives of, 178, 305
    standard, 306
    successful, 179
    techniques, 294
    tips, 288, 306–307
    types, 179, 306

326 ■ *Index*

undercover, 306
interviewers, qualifications of, 179
investigative process
  deceptive behavior traits, 294
  definition of, 287
  helpful investigative hints, 294
  interview and an interrogation, 290
  interview techniques, 293, 294
  interview types, 291
  national *vs.* international investigative, 291–292
  performing due diligence, 294
  preparing for the interview, 292
  window into, 290–291
investigative snapshot, 305–306
investigative tips, helpful, 180
IP cameras, 161, 164–165, 166
IP recorders, 161, 165

J

Joint Commission on Accreditation of Healthcare
  Organizations (JCAHO), 7
Joint Photographic Experts Group (JPEG), 166
Journal of Healthcare Protection Management, 11, 299
jury, 214

K

Kellogg Company, 272

L

latitude of rejection, 26
Law Enforcement Assistance Administration (LEAA),
  41, 88, 97, 111, 137, 198
legal systems, 32, 292
line driver, 188
local area network (LAN), 162
lockdown
  emergency department, 52
  facility, 54–55
  full facility, 51
  hospital, 61–62
  partial facility, 51
  procedures in mass casualty incident, 50
lossless compression, 166
Lucent Technologies, 272

M

magnetic stripe readers, 75
magnetometers, 2, 16, 17, 18
management information systems (MIS), 26–28
Medicaid, 11–12, 14, 221, 223, 282
medical supply security, 183
Medicare, 11–12, 14, 173, 221, 223, 282
metric considerations, 153

metrics, in security and safety programming, 146
  community security survey, 148
  community wide assessments, 148
  metric related jargon, 148–149
  modifying the standard security survey, 146–147
  value of, 147–148
money laundering schemes, investigation of, 262–263
multi-client /commercial strip security survey, 80
  access control security survey, 80
  community-wide security survey, 80–81
multi-client/community-wide security surveys, 82, 99
multiple source verification, 44–45
Mustard Gas, 49, 57

N

National Background Check Program (NBCP), 223
National Crime Prevention Institute (NCPI), 88, 94–95,
  97, 111–112, 137, 198, 199
National Institute of Law Enforcement & Criminal
  Justice (NILE), 97
National Organization of Downsized Employees
  (NODE), 25
National Patient Safety Goals, 14, 45
*National Strategy for the Physical Protection of Critical
  Infrastructures and Key Assets, The*, 1
Near Miss, concept of, 143
networks, 161–162
  new or existing, 164
  protocols, 162
  redundancy and reliability, 164
Newsweek, 24–25
New York Times survey, 25, 217
non-custodial interview, 291
non-subscriber fraud, 283
non-target interviewing, art of
  contact tracing, 301–302
  interview blueprint, 302
  locating interview targets, 301
  nonintrusive background screening, 302
  pre-interview checklist, 301
  program management and oversight, 304
  questioning business owners, 303
  questioning bystanders, 303
  questioning family members, 302–303
  questioning law enforcement, 303
  questioning strategies, 302
"no prior notice" regulatory audit, 209
  creating departmental standards, 211
  document availability, 209
  establishing metrics, 212
  implementing a dashboard, 212
  physical security systems, 210
  policy and procedure compliance, 210
  program implementation, 211
  safeguarding training records, 210
  training compliance, 211

O

Obama Care, 11, 12
Occupational Safety and Health Administration
        (OSHA), 4, 7, 123, 125, 131, 159
Office of Homeland Security (OHS), 1–2, 79, 91, 111

P

packing list, 188
pallet, 188, 190
palming, 36, 236
pandemic flu, 11, 49–50, 52, 301
patients' bill of rights (1996), 4
patient security, 182
pediatric security, 183
perception of security, 126–127, 133, 152–153
periodical security assessments, 183
Personal Protective Equipment (PPE), 50
        level C protection, 50
        level D protection, 50
        wearing and using, 55
physical evidence, 178, 215, 291, 297
physical security applications
        CCTV studies, 155
        development and implementation, 169
        engineering findings, 155
        enhance CCTV effectiveness, 156–157
        environmental findings, 155
        general findings, 156
        medical findings, 156
        monitor size, staffing issues and supervision, 157
        operations center, 157
        procedure and policy findings, 156
        psychological findings, 156
        security camera, man behind, 155
        staffing considerations, 157
        supervision, 158
        training considerations, 157–158
plaintiff, 215
planned interviews, 179
practical crime prevention
        applying protection strategies for, 121
        auditing the security department, 122
        capturing and evaluating crime risk data, 120
        crime detection, 103
        crime prevention expert role, 115
        crime prevention operatives responsibilities, 112
        crime risk exposure via altering traffic control
                patterns, 113
        crime risk mapping and risk exposure, 120
        crime risks, 120–121
        defined, 115
        differing job titles, 115
        expert's role in crime prevention, 116
        external consultants, 109, 117
        financial value of using metrics, 105

healthcare, 101
hospital security, 107
ID control to prevent workplace violence, 123–124
in-house operatives, 117
locating crime prevention experts, 118
looking toward the future, 105, 119
loss prevention program, 107–108
managing crime risk, 122
measuring cost considerations, 122
metrics in security planning, 105
mitigating crime risk exposure, 113, 114
predictive models for, 101–102
proactive crime control planning, 103
proactive security initiative, 113
proactive security program, 103–104
program evaluation, 109, 117
programmatic evaluation, 104
protection methodologies, 121
reactive *vs.* proactive crime control models, 117
responsibilities of crime prevention staff, 108–109
robotics role, 105
sample proactive security curricula, 104
securing the future, 114
security weaknesses and solutions, 121
selecting in-house or external experts, 117
selecting qualified experts, 110
selecting the right consultant, 118–119
selection criteria, 108
training prerequisites, 118
training requirements, 108
pregnant pause, 294, 308
pre-interview checklist, 179, 301
primary source verification, 44
proactive security, 111–112, 137
        21st century security planning, 139
        agenda, 138
        art and science of, 112, 199
        evaluating security initiatives, 140
        future, 140
        low-cost security initiatives, 138–139
        origins of, 111–112, 137–138, 198–199
        proactive crime control program, 112
        programming, art and science of, 111
        tasks and responsibilities, 104
professional shoplifter, 35, 236
program effectiveness with metrics
        calculating costs, 151–152
        determining, 151
property security, 183, 207
provider deception, 282–283
proximity readers, 74–75
pure crime risks, 120–121

R

radiation poisoning, 49, 57
"Red Flag" legislation, 12

328 ■ *Index*

restitution, 12, 28, 196
ricin, 48, 56
rig, 188
robotics
    role of, 20
    in security/safety planning, 153
role reversal, 293, 307
Router, 163

S

Sarin Gas, 49, 57
SARS, 7, 11
school shootings, 53
search warrant, 214
security
    dollar, dilemma, 5, 29, 30, 42, 89, 103, 105, 137, 140, 49
    gatekeepers, 272
    library, 42
    strategies, additional, 242
security auditing
    asset protection, 206
    defined, 206
    differing job titles, 205
    importance of, 205
    information management, 206
    lexicon, 207–208
    operational efficiency, 206
    program, 206
    programming adherence, 206
    review and oversight, 208
    tasks and responsibilities of, 206
    tips for auditors while writing, 208
    types, 206–207
security management
    amateur shoplifter, 35
    art and science of proactive security
        programming, 41
    aspects of program evaluation, 43
    audience targeting, 42–43
    authenticating an identity, 44–45
    culture, 32–33
    delivering the security message, 41
    dependability of an ID program, 44
    diversity, 41
    documentary evidence, 34
    downsizing and fraud, 23–24
    downsizing of, 24–25
    downsizing of security programs, 29
    drug addict shoplifter, 35
    establish ID standards, 45–46
    establishing a security library, 42
    firearms, 33
    fire inspection report, 38–39
    fire prevention, 38
    four sample-targeted inspections areas, 39
    getting started, 40
    'good' downsizing, 28

hidden cost of downsizing, 23
investigating in a new environment, 31
legal systems, 32
local officials, 34
moving toward fraud, 25–26
outsourcing newsletter preparation services, 42
periodic inspections, 39
personalizing your security newsletter, 42
professional shoplifter, 35
security networking, 40
security workshops and special programs, 43
shoplifter profiles, 35
shoplifters ply their trade, 35–36
store layout plans, 36–37
strategies to consider, 29–30
stretching the security dollar, 29
subcontractors, 33
targeted inspection areas, 39
today's economic climate, 29
travel planning, 31–32
who stays, who goes, 26–28
security survey
    access control security survey, 72, 98
    analytical exposition, 73
    applying control approaches, 74
    architectural security and access control, 74
    aspects of, 79
    availability of resources, 72
    birth of a new breed of, 96
    closing statement, 78
    community and/or neighborhood security
        assessment, 99
    community crime control plan, 67–68
    community wide security survey, 85–86
    completely restricting access, 73
    control and monitoring of access, 73
    cost-benefit analysis, 72
    cross-examination of risk exposures, 72
    defined, 97
    developing the survey, 76–77
    diagnosing and prioritizing crime risks, 100
    diagnosis, 83
    enhancing security, 76
    evaluating the assessment, 94
    evolution of, 88, 92, 97
    examination, 83
    framing the survey, 68–71, 77, 94
    function, 82
    implementation plan, 78
    implementation schedule, 84
    innovation drives change, 96
    levels of access control, 73
    looking behind the survey, 91
    looking to the future, 89, 94
    looking to the past, 88
    many faces of, 96
    metrics usage, 89
    multi-client /commercial strip security survey, 80–81

multi-client security assessment, 98
new 21st century, 87
organizing, 83
partially restricting access, 73
performing, 99
preparing community wide assessments, 85
prescription, 84
procedural application, 74
professional evaluation, 77
rationale, 88
reason for revisiting, 87
reviewing the facility survey, 72
revising, 91
science behind, 97–98
security executive, 79
selectively controlling and monitoring of access, 73
single client security assessment, 98
standard, 92
survey specifics, 92–93
technological application, 74–75
terrorism prevention survey, 93–94
types of, 79–80, 82
"Sentinal Event Alert," 123
September 11, 2001 attack, hospital security, 1, 2
shell hardening, 159–160
shielded twisted pair, 163
shoplifting
checking bags at the door, 36
fraud and employee theft prevention, 235
methods of, 36, 236–237
plan a smart store layout, 36
prominently posting anti-shoplifting signage, 36
recognizing the shoplifter, 235–236
smart store layout, 237
strategies to thwart, 36
shrink wrap, 188
single client security survey, 68, 82, 98, 99
single-client survey, 67, 68, 79–80, 99
skimming case, 233
sleeper, 188
smallpox, 48, 56
social media harvesting, 298–299
"Sonic Ring" network, 164
"special" clothing, 236
spontaneous field interviews, 179
staff configuration, 144
Statement on Accounting Standard (SAS 53), 253
subpoena duces tecum, 216
subscriber fraud, 283
suspect custodial interview, 291
switches, 162–163, 164

T

tablecloth case, 232–233
tare weight, 188
target hardening, 9, 41, 60, 67, 80, 87–88, 92, 98, 99,
121, 132, 207

team approach
to fraud prevention, 243, 247, 253
by shoplifters, 36, 235
VIP protection plan, 314, 319
terrorism, 41, 91, 103, 111, 131, 200–201, 208,
219, 317
9/11 attacks, 137
anti-terrorism technologies, 115
crime risk exposures, 146
vs. disaster preparedness, 12
firearms-related, 131, 136
vs. mother nature, 13–14
prevention survey, 93–94
school shootings, 53
threat of, 1
war on, 53
Thomas Baking Company, 272
tort, 216
trade barriers, 31
trade-off, 294, 308
trailer, 188, 190
true bill, 216
truthful and untruthful statements, verbal clues to, 308
try-on method, 36, 236
twisted pair cable, 163

U

United States (U.S.)
Department of Health and Human Services (HHS),
4, 8, 31
Department of Justice (DOJ), 97, 219, 282, 318
Department of State (USDS), 31, 318
Universal Protocol, 45–46
unshielded twisted pair (UTP), 163

V

Variola Virus, 48, 56
verbal red flags, 308
video compression, 166
VIP, meaning of, 316
VIP protection, 311
contingency planning, 314, 318
developing the security services, 314
devising transportation security prerequisites,
312–313
formulating the pre-event assessment, 312
framing the contingency plan, 319
framing the protection risk grid, 312
plan, 311–312
political concerns, 318
preparing for VIP visit, 316
protection requisites, 318
risk assessment survey, 312
structuring the survey, 319
threats to consider, 317–318
updates in VIP process, 317

330 ■ *Index*

VIP security plan, 317
walk-through survey, 313

W

warrant of arrest, 213
waybill, 188
white-collar investigations, 213
wide area network (WAN), 162
Wiegand Readers, 75
witness interview, 291
workplace violence, 135
   and active shooter resources, 135
   mitigation, 135
   preparedness, 135–136
   recovery, 136
   response, 136

workplace violence prevention, 125
   access control, 125–126
   active shooter resources, 128
   education, 127–128
   handling victims, 129
   mitigation, 128
   preparedness, 129
   recovery activities, 130
   response, 129
   security perception, 126–127
   security presence, 126
   security response, 127
   surveillance capacity, 127

Y

yard, 188